Tell us what y
about Shojo Be

Our survey is now available online. Go to:

shojobeat.com/mangasurvey

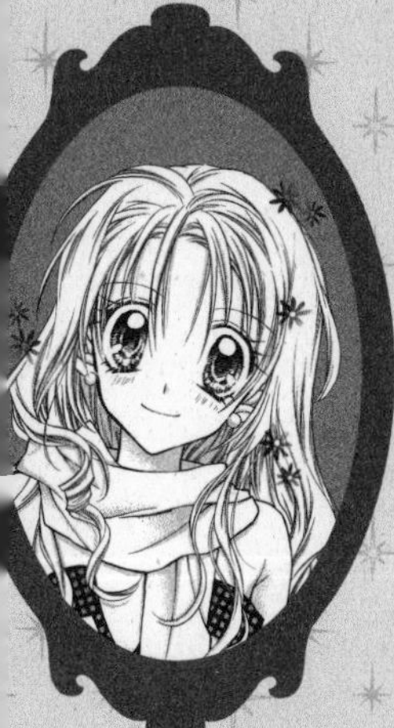

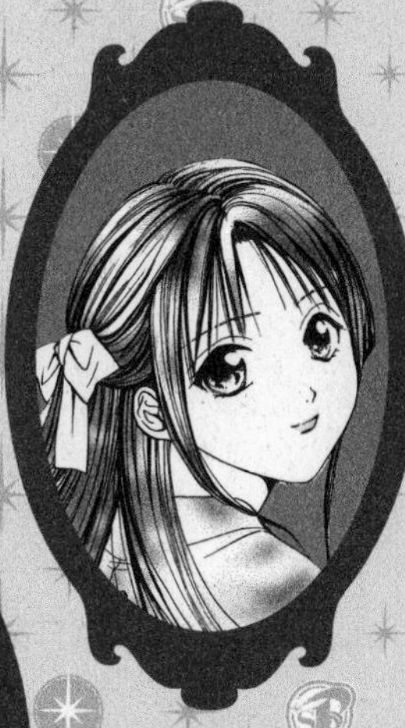

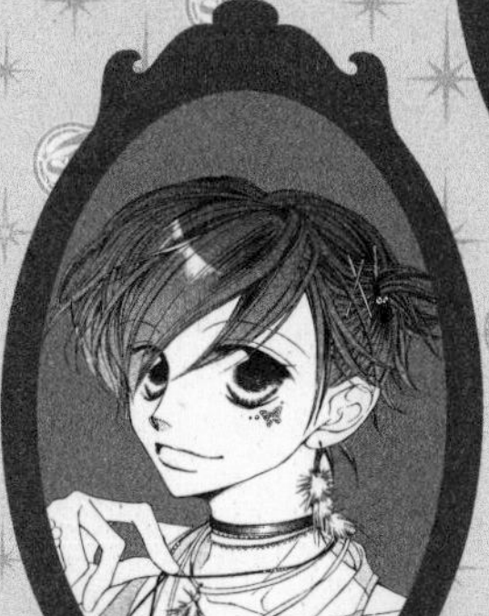

Help us make our product offerings better!

VIZ media

Shojo Beat MANGA from the HEART

THE REAL DRAMA BEGINS IN...

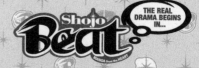

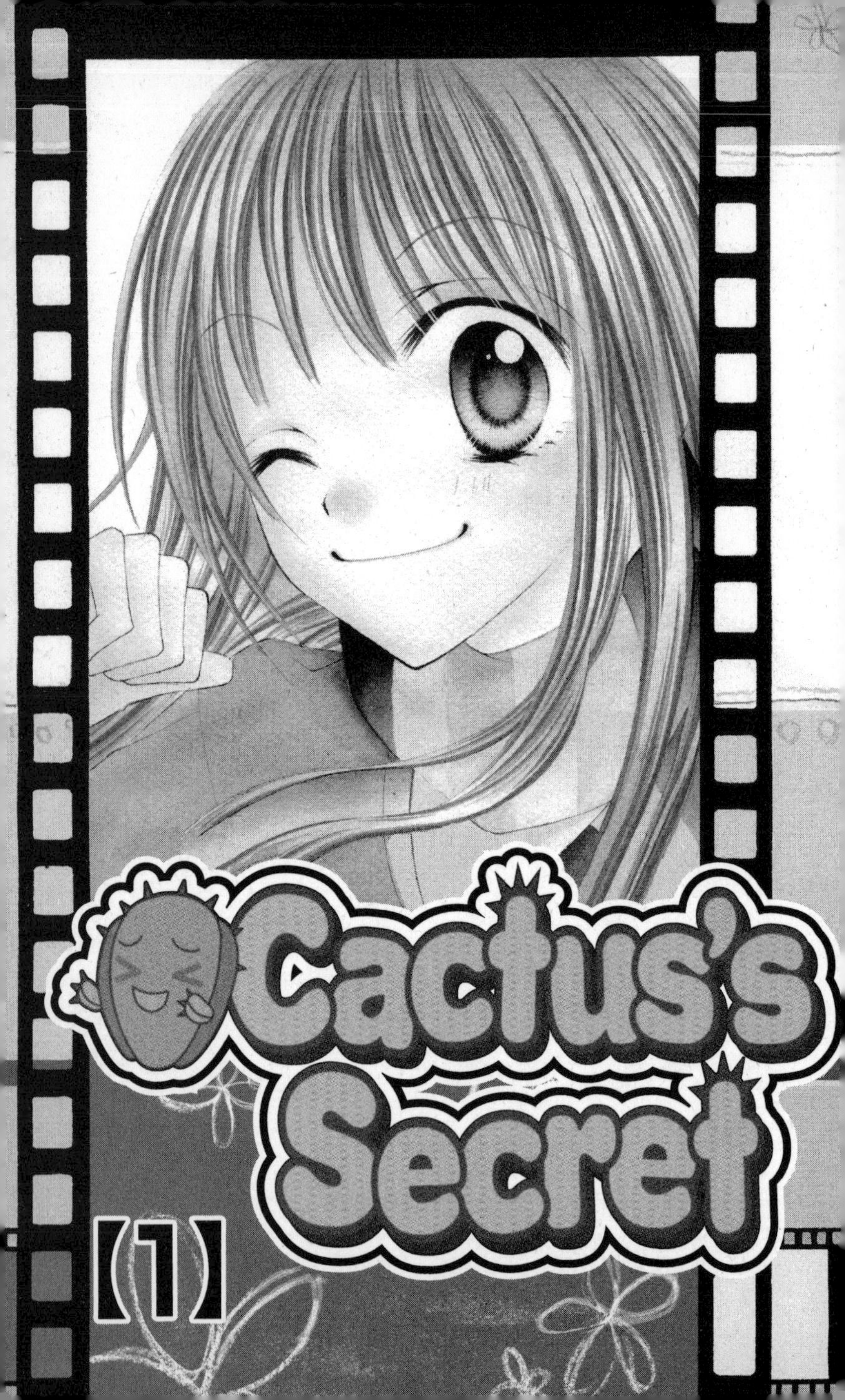
Cactus's Secret
[1]

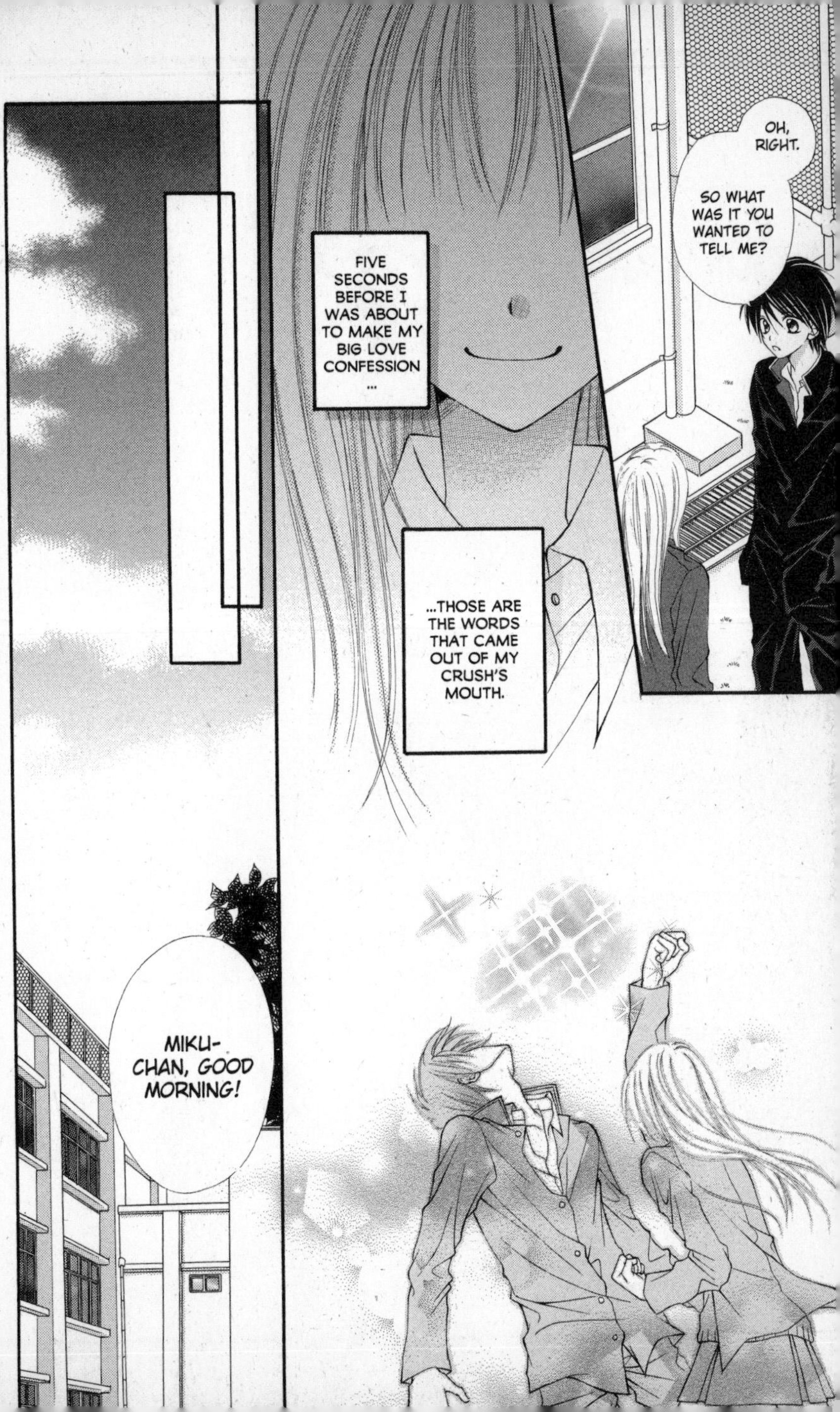
OH, RIGHT.
SO WHAT WAS IT YOU WANTED TO TELL ME?
FIVE SECONDS BEFORE I WAS ABOUT TO MAKE MY BIG LOVE CONFESSION ...
...THOSE ARE THE WORDS THAT CAME OUT OF MY CRUSH'S MOUTH.
MIKU-CHAN, GOOD MORNING!

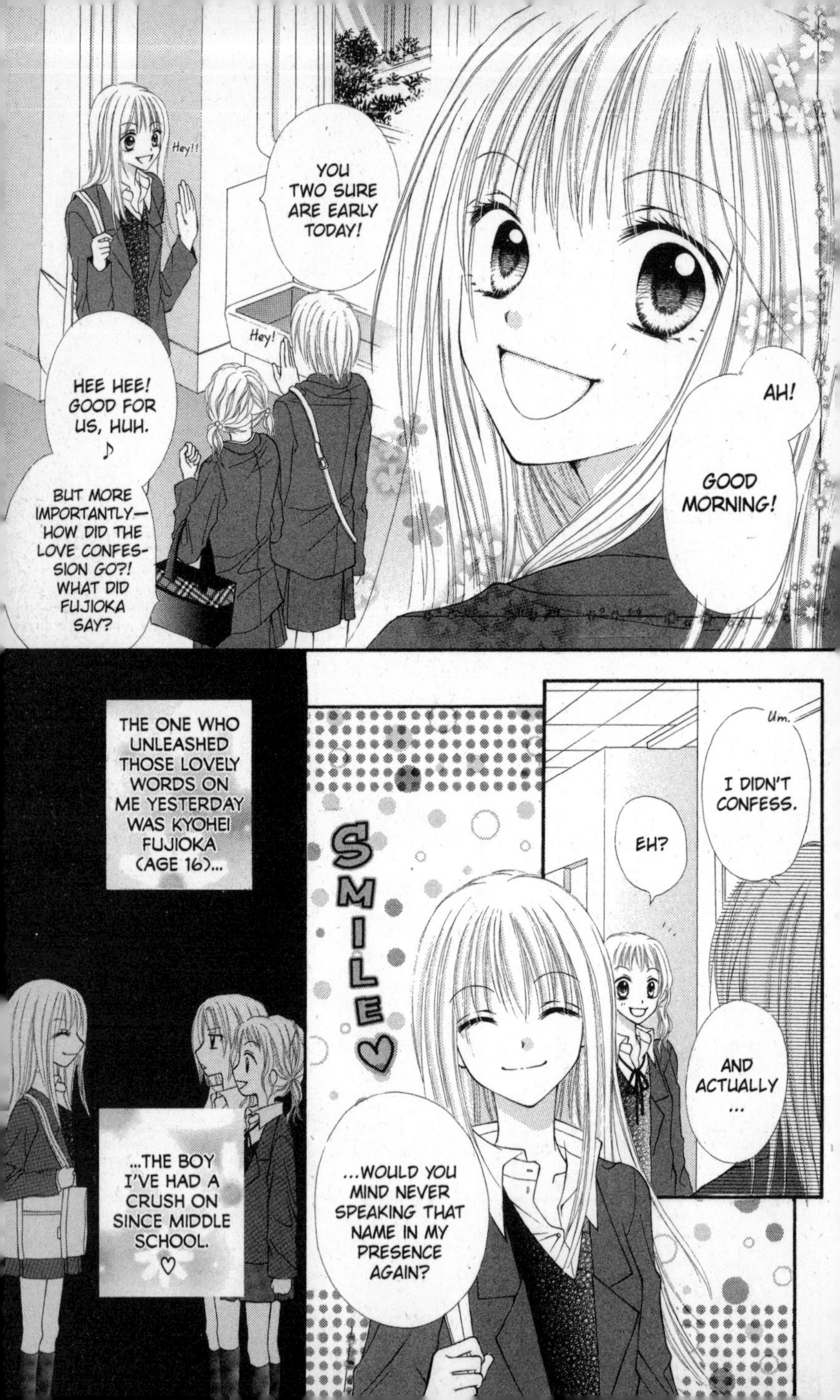
AH!
GOOD MORNING!
YOU TWO SURE ARE EARLY TODAY!
Hey!!
Hey!
HEE HEE! GOOD FOR US, HUH. ♪
BUT MORE IMPORTANTLY—HOW DID THE LOVE CONFESSION GO?! WHAT DID FUJIOKA SAY?
Um.
I DIDN'T CONFESS.
EH?
AND ACTUALLY...
SMILE♥
...WOULD YOU MIND NEVER SPEAKING THAT NAME IN MY PRESENCE AGAIN?
THE ONE WHO UNLEASHED THOSE LOVELY WORDS ON ME YESTERDAY WAS KYOHEI FUJIOKA (AGE 16)...
...THE BOY I'VE HAD A CRUSH ON SINCE MIDDLE SCHOOL. ♡

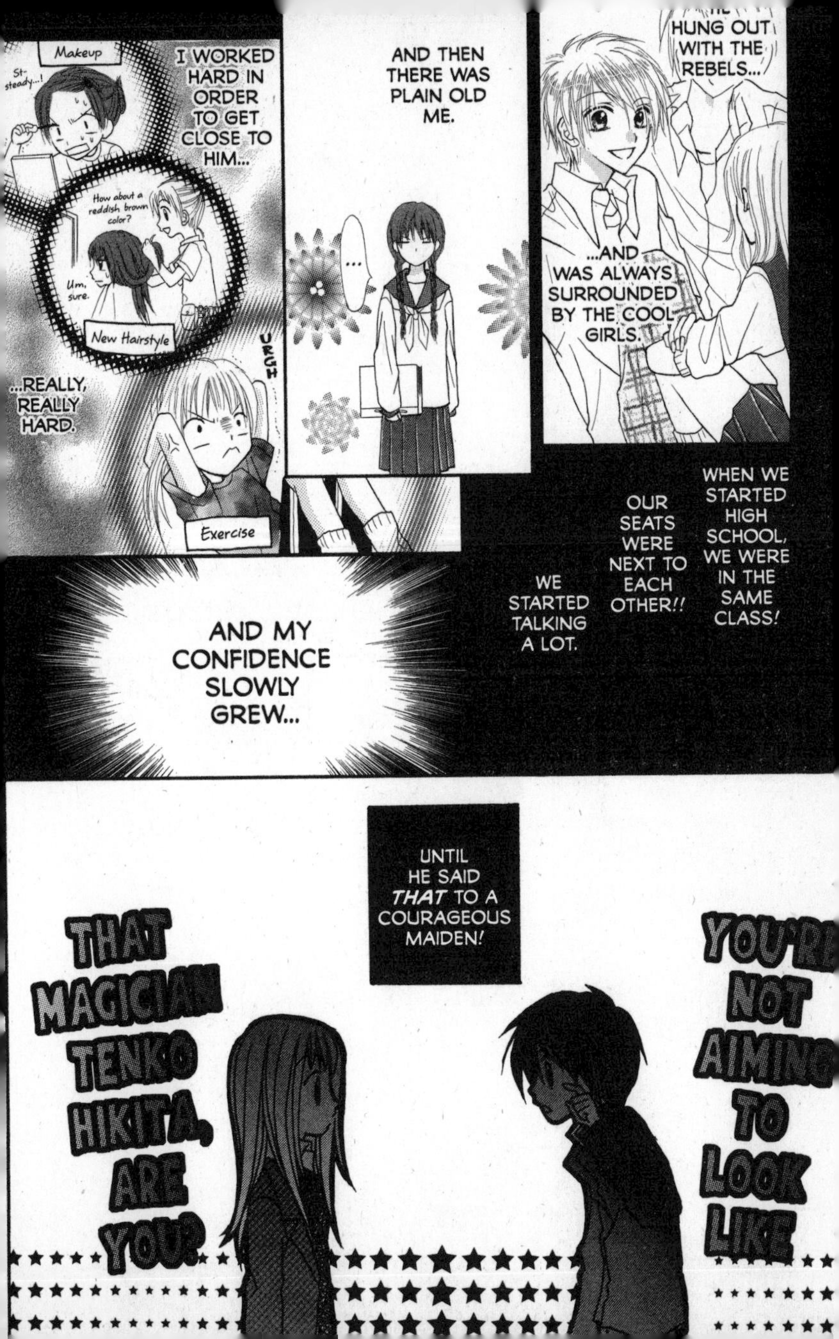
HUNG OUT WITH THE REBELS...
...AND WAS ALWAYS SURROUNDED BY THE COOL GIRLS.
AND THEN THERE WAS PLAIN OLD ME.
...
I WORKED HARD IN ORDER TO GET CLOSE TO HIM...
Makeup
St-steady...!
How about a reddish brown color?
Um, sure.
New Hairstyle
URGH
...REALLY, REALLY HARD.
Exercise
WHEN WE STARTED HIGH SCHOOL, WE WERE IN THE SAME CLASS!
OUR SEATS WERE NEXT TO EACH OTHER!!
WE STARTED TALKING A LOT.
AND MY CONFIDENCE SLOWLY GREW...
YOU'R NOT AIMING TO LOOK LIKE
UNTIL HE SAID *THAT* TO A COURAGEOUS MAIDEN!
THAT MAGICIAN TENKO HIKITA, ARE YOU?

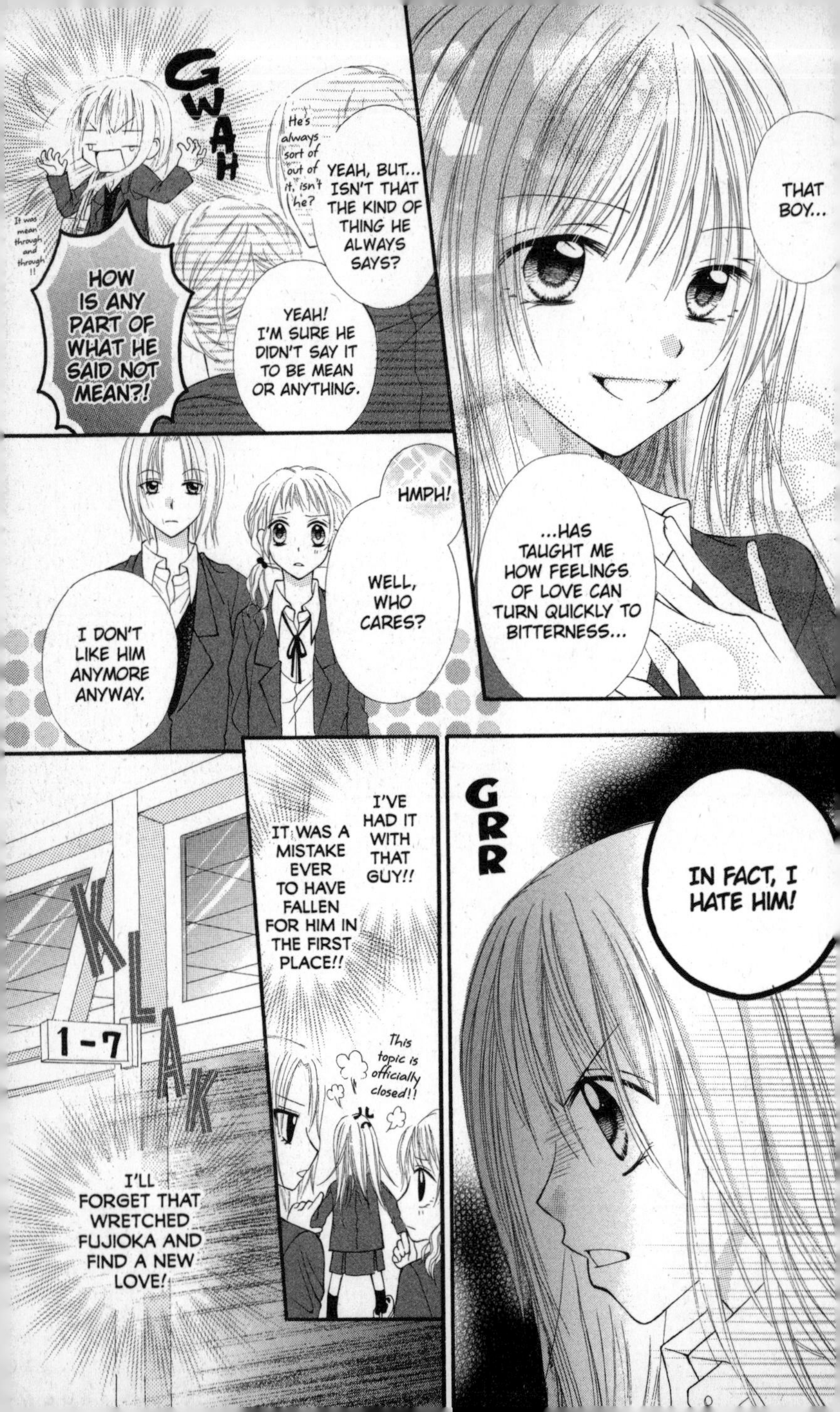
THAT BOY...
...HAS TAUGHT ME HOW FEELINGS OF LOVE CAN TURN QUICKLY TO BITTERNESS...
He's always sort of out of it, isn't he?
YEAH, BUT... ISN'T THAT THE KIND OF THING HE ALWAYS SAYS?
GWAH
YEAH! I'M SURE HE DIDN'T SAY IT TO BE MEAN OR ANYTHING.
It was mean through and through!!
HOW IS ANY PART OF WHAT HE SAID NOT MEAN?!
HMPH!
WELL, WHO CARES?
I DON'T LIKE HIM ANYMORE ANYWAY.
GRR
IN FACT, I HATE HIM!
I'VE HAD IT WITH THAT GUY!!
IT WAS A MISTAKE EVER TO HAVE FALLEN FOR HIM IN THE FIRST PLACE!!
This topic is officially closed!!
KLAK
1-7
I'LL FORGET THAT WRETCHED FUJIOKA AND FIND A NEW LOVE!

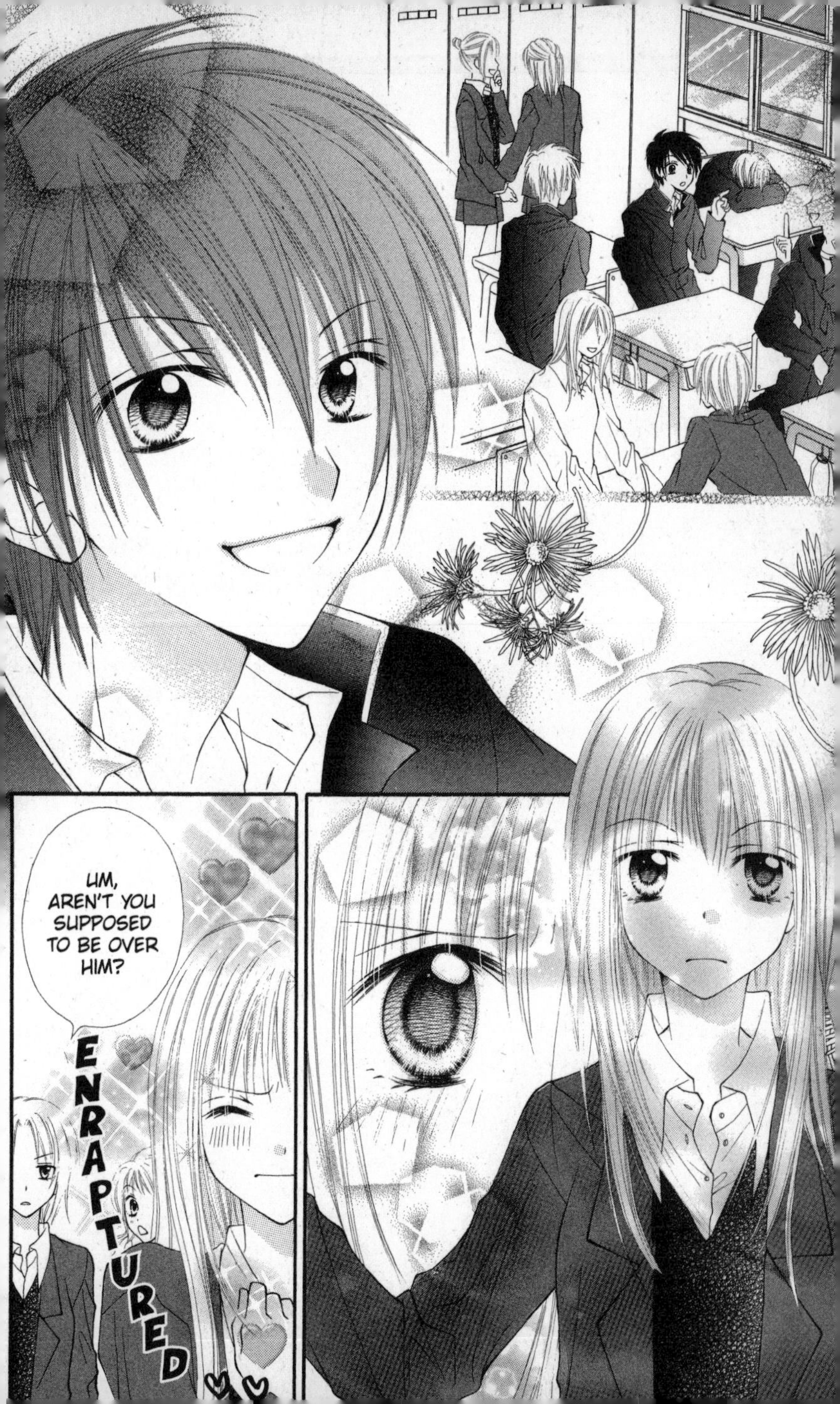
UM, AREN'T YOU SUPPOSED TO BE OVER HIM?
ENRAPTURED

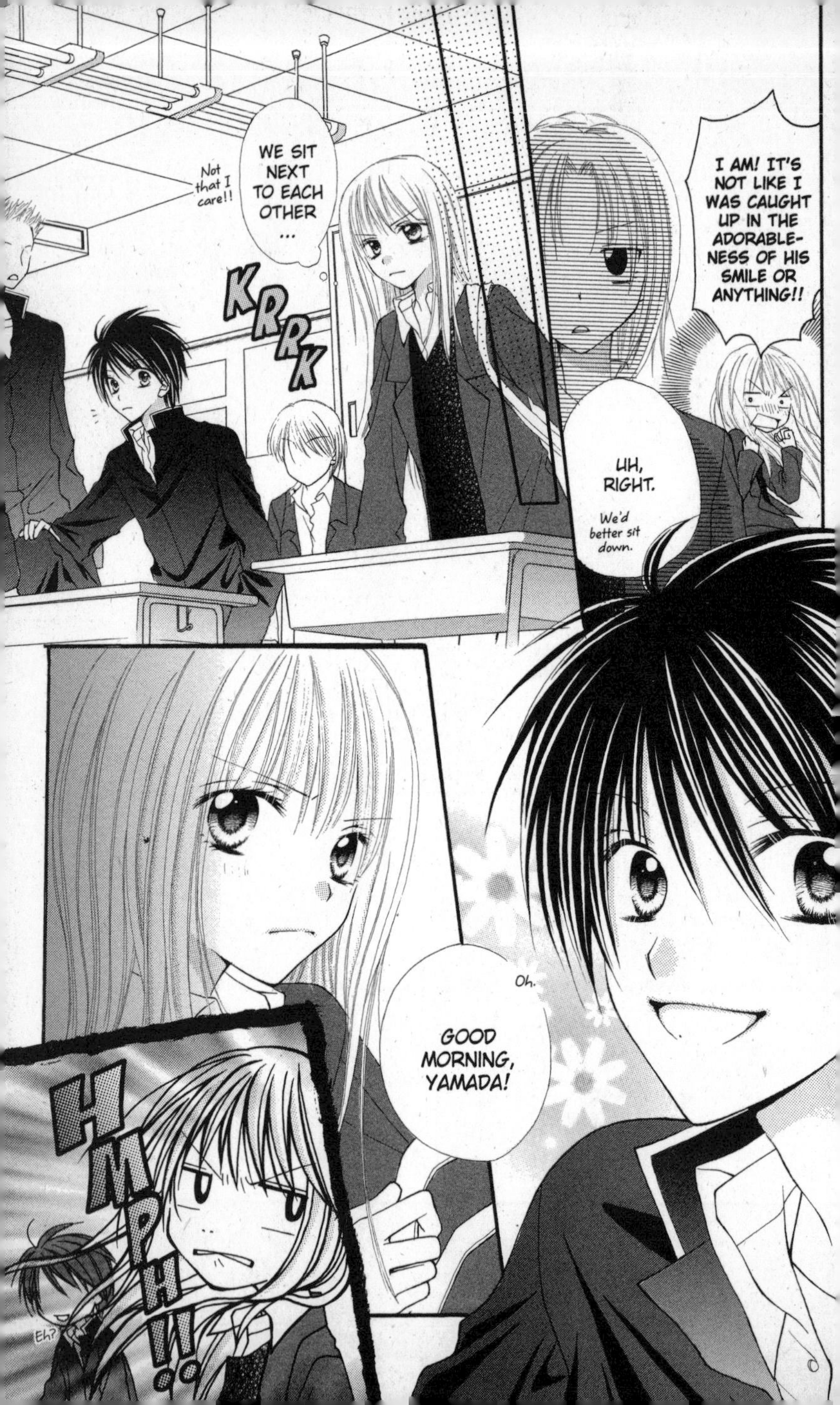
I AM! IT'S NOT LIKE I WAS CAUGHT UP IN THE ADORABLENESS OF HIS SMILE OR ANYTHING!!
UH, RIGHT.
We'd better sit down.
WE SIT NEXT TO EACH OTHER ...
Not that I care!!
KRRK
Oh.
GOOD MORNING, YAMADA!
HMPH!!
Eh?

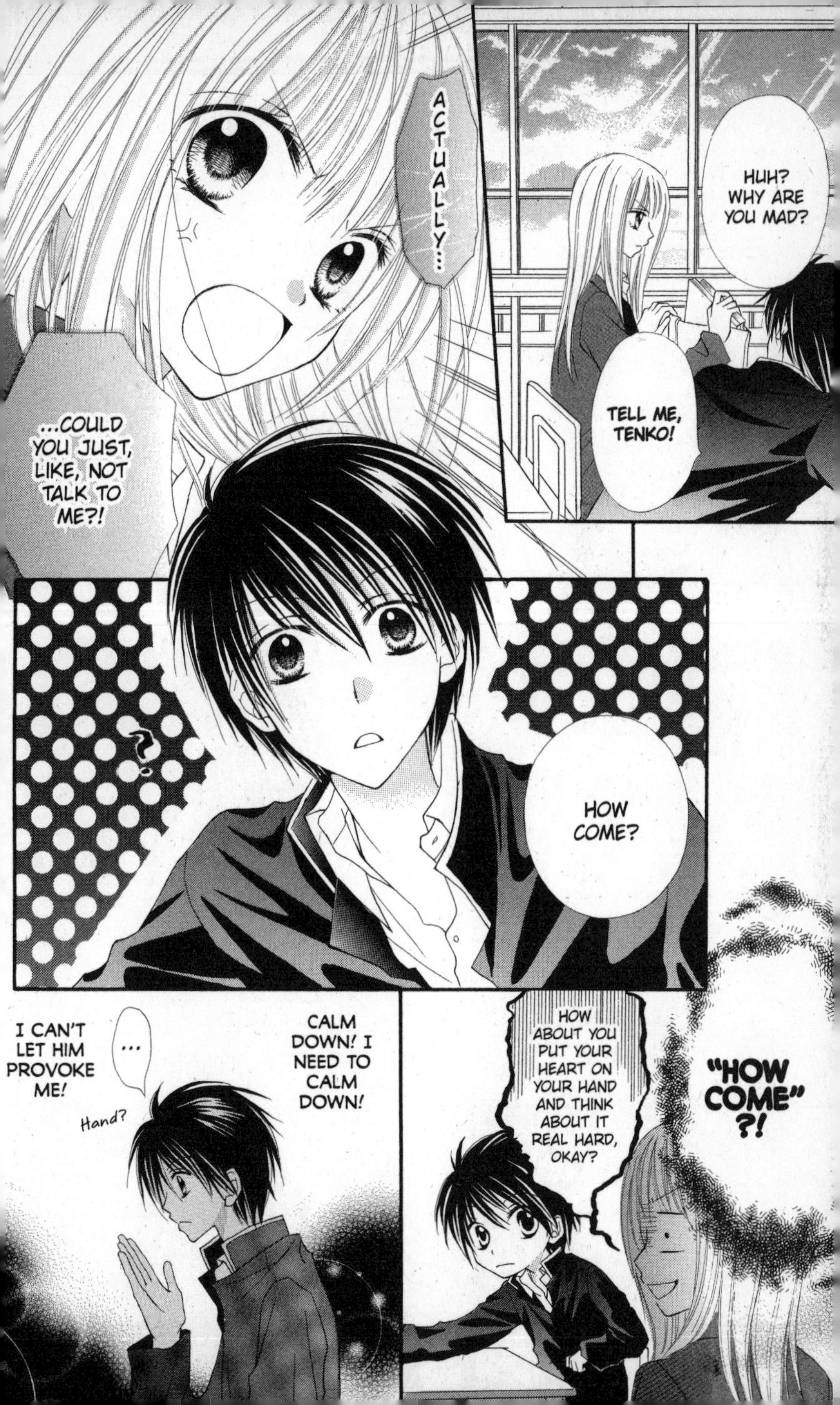
HUH? WHY ARE YOU MAD?
TELL ME, TENKO!
ACTUALLY...
...COULD YOU JUST, LIKE, NOT TALK TO ME?!
?
HOW COME?
"HOW COME"?!
HOW ABOUT YOU PUT YOUR HEART ON YOUR HAND AND THINK ABOUT IT REAL HARD, OKAY?
CALM DOWN! I NEED TO CALM DOWN!
...
I CAN'T LET HIM PROVOKE ME!
Hand?

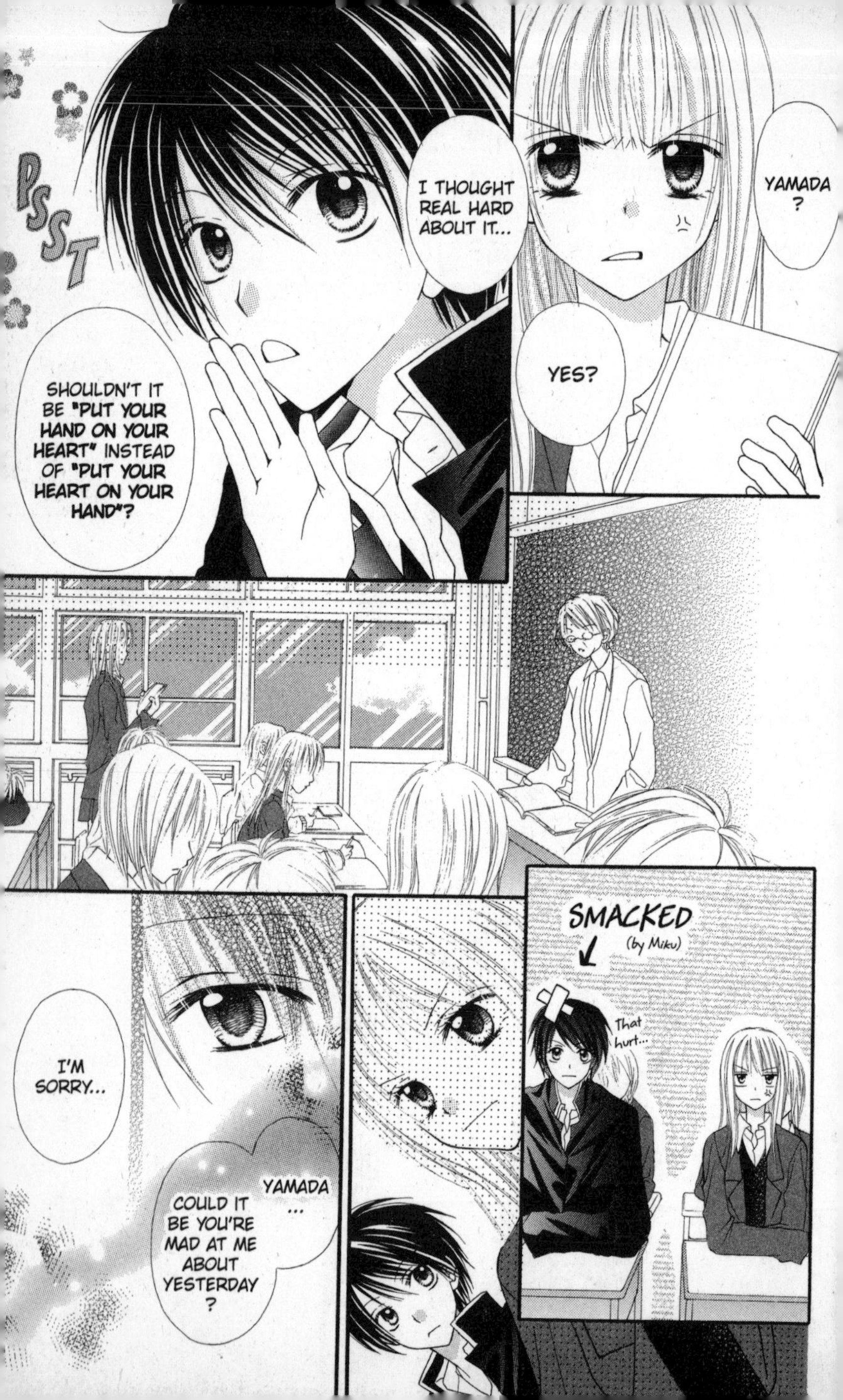
YAMADA?
YES?
I THOUGHT REAL HARD ABOUT IT...
PSST
SHOULDN'T IT BE "PUT YOUR HAND ON YOUR HEART" INSTEAD OF "PUT YOUR HEART ON YOUR HAND"?
SMACKED
(by Miku)
That hurt...
YAMADA...
COULD IT BE YOU'RE MAD AT ME ABOUT YESTERDAY?
I'M SORRY...

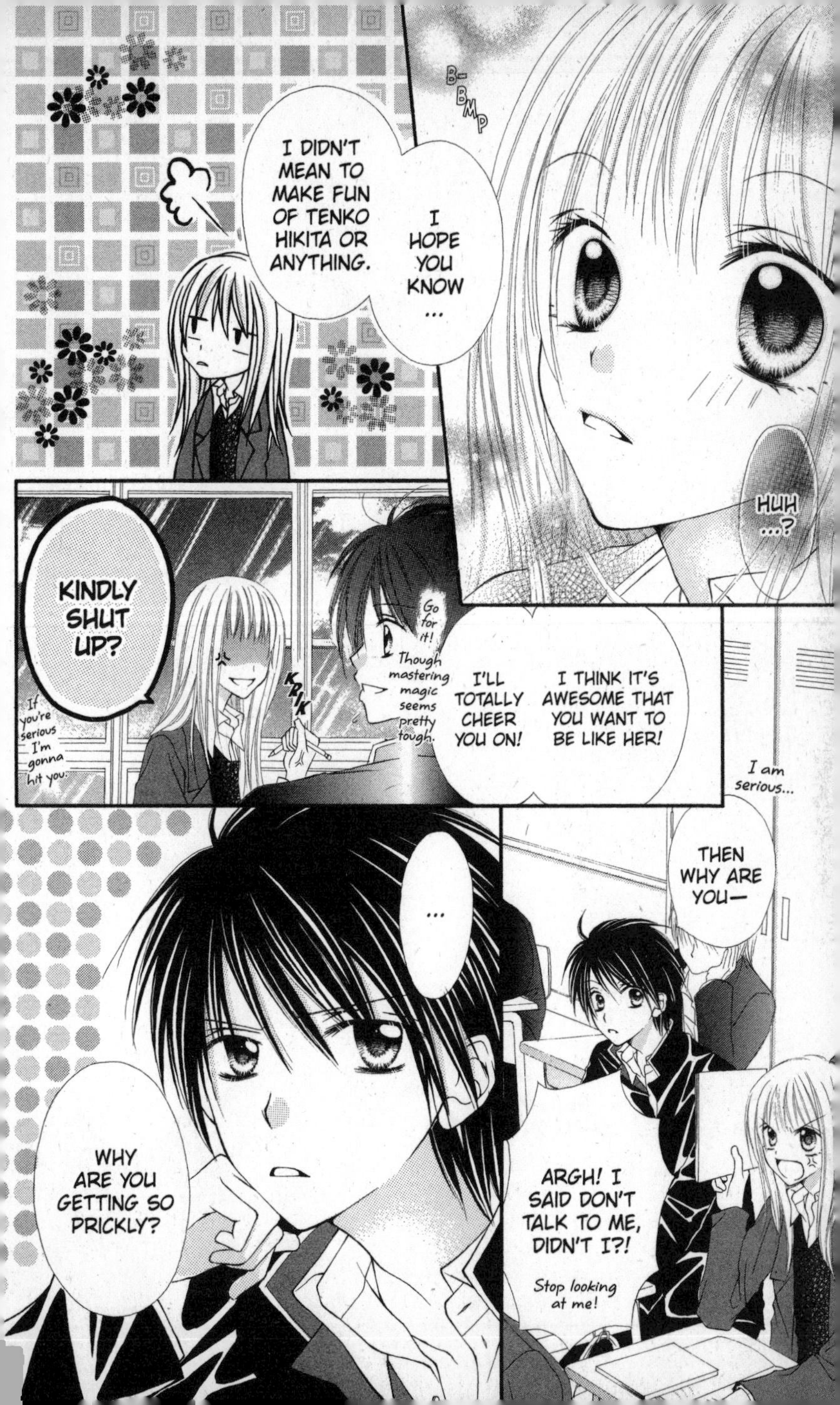
B-BMP
HUH ...?
I DIDN'T MEAN TO MAKE FUN OF TENKO HIKITA OR ANYTHING.
I HOPE YOU KNOW ...
I THINK IT'S AWESOME THAT YOU WANT TO BE LIKE HER!
I'LL TOTALLY CHEER YOU ON!
Go for it! Though mastering magic seems pretty tough.
KRIK
KINDLY SHUT UP?
If you're serious I'm gonna hit you.
I am serious...
THEN WHY ARE YOU—
ARGH! I SAID DON'T TALK TO ME, DIDN'T I?!
Stop looking at me!
...
WHY ARE YOU GETTING SO PRICKLY?

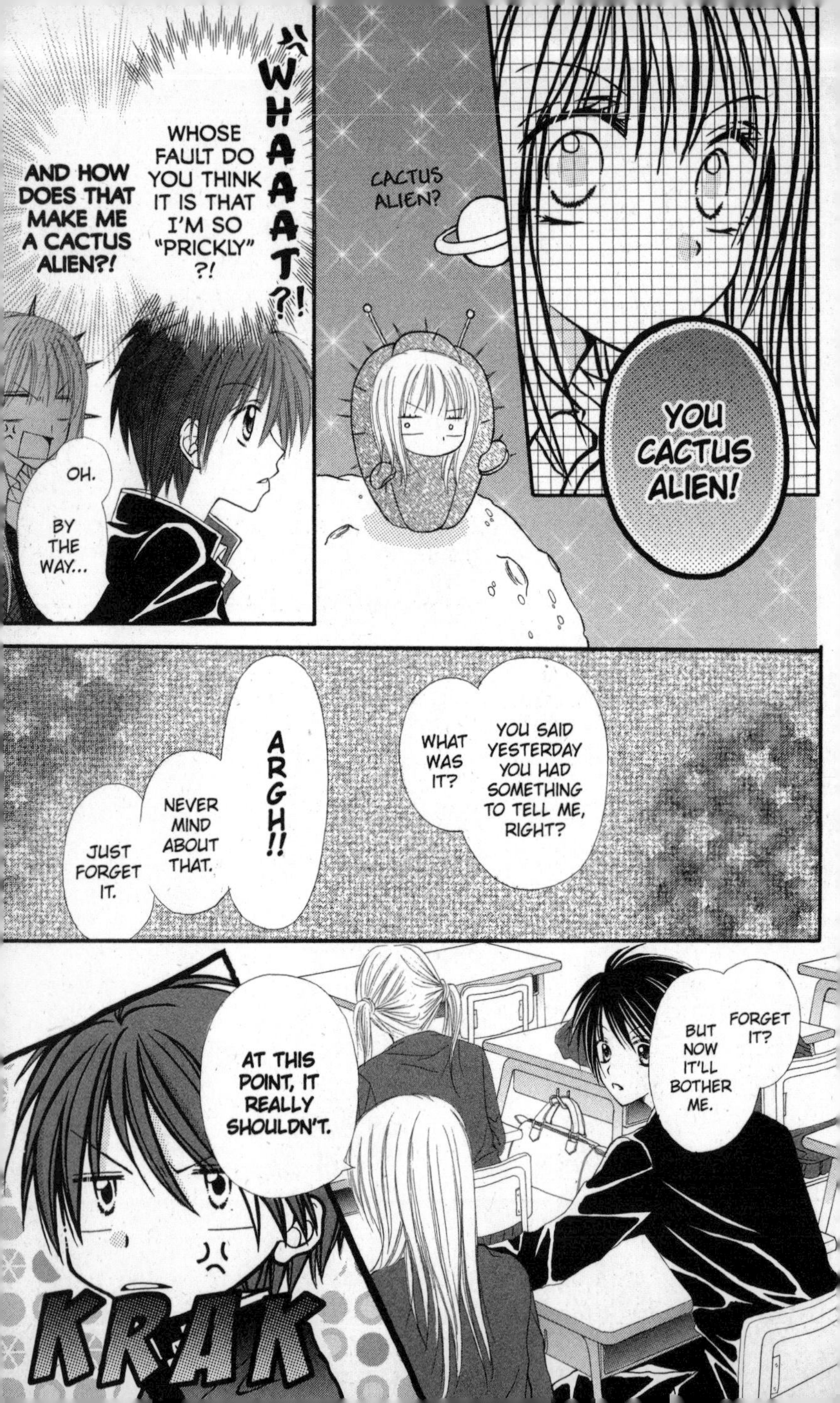
YOU CACTUS ALIEN!
CACTUS ALIEN?
WHAAAT?!
WHOSE FAULT DO YOU THINK IT IS THAT I'M SO "PRICKLY"?!
AND HOW DOES THAT MAKE ME A CACTUS ALIEN?!
OH.
BY THE WAY...
YOU SAID YESTERDAY YOU HAD SOMETHING TO TELL ME, RIGHT?
WHAT WAS IT?
ARGH!!
NEVER MIND ABOUT THAT.
JUST FORGET IT.
FORGET IT?
BUT NOW IT'LL BOTHER ME.
AT THIS POINT, IT REALLY SHOULDN'T.
KRAK

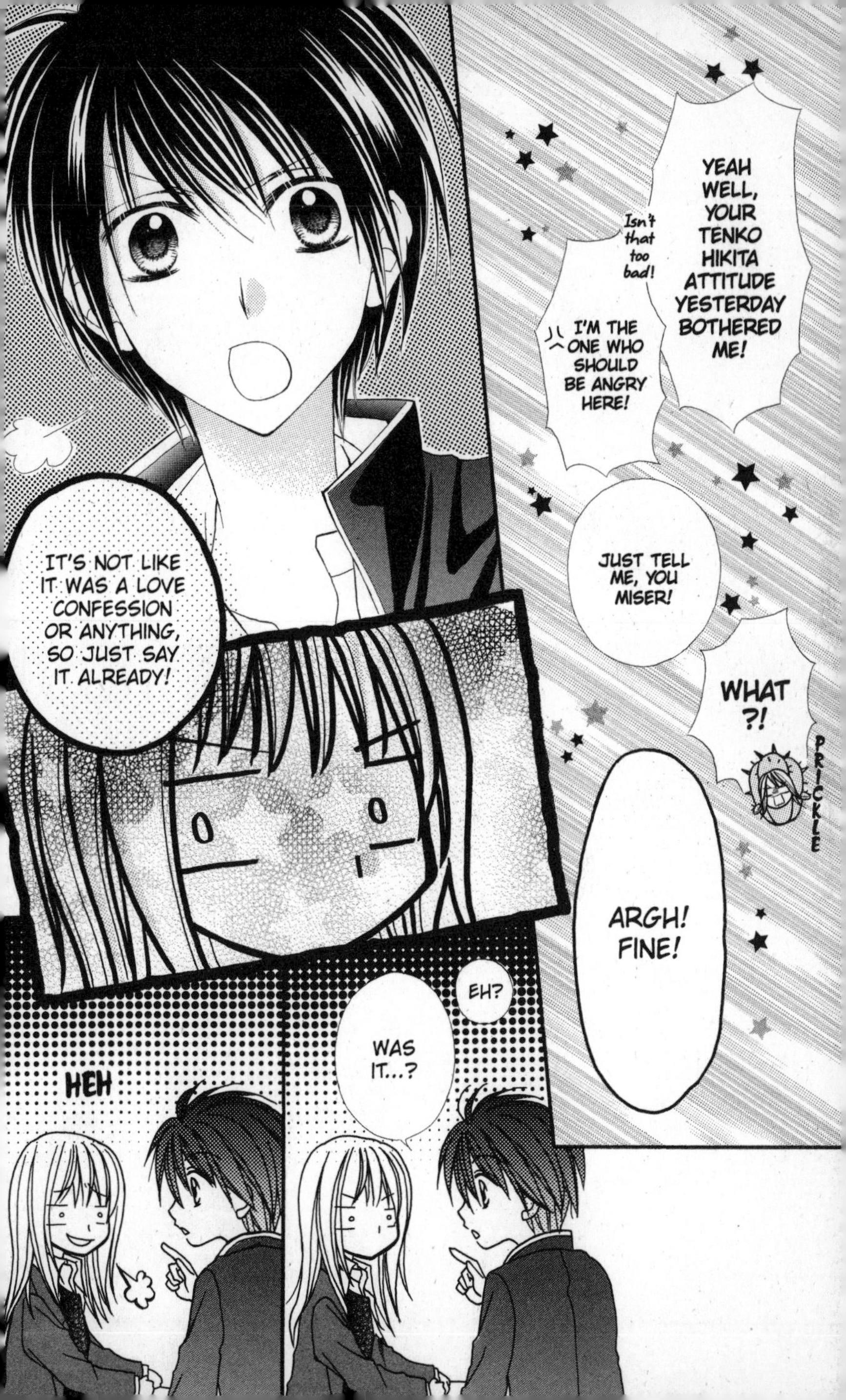
YEAH WELL, YOUR TENKO HIKITA ATTITUDE YESTERDAY BOTHERED ME!
Isn't that too bad!
I'M THE ONE WHO SHOULD BE ANGRY HERE!
JUST TELL ME, YOU MISER!
WHAT?!
PRICKLE
ARGH! FINE!
IT'S NOT LIKE IT WAS A LOVE CONFESSION OR ANYTHING, SO JUST SAY IT ALREADY!
EH?
WAS IT...?
HEH

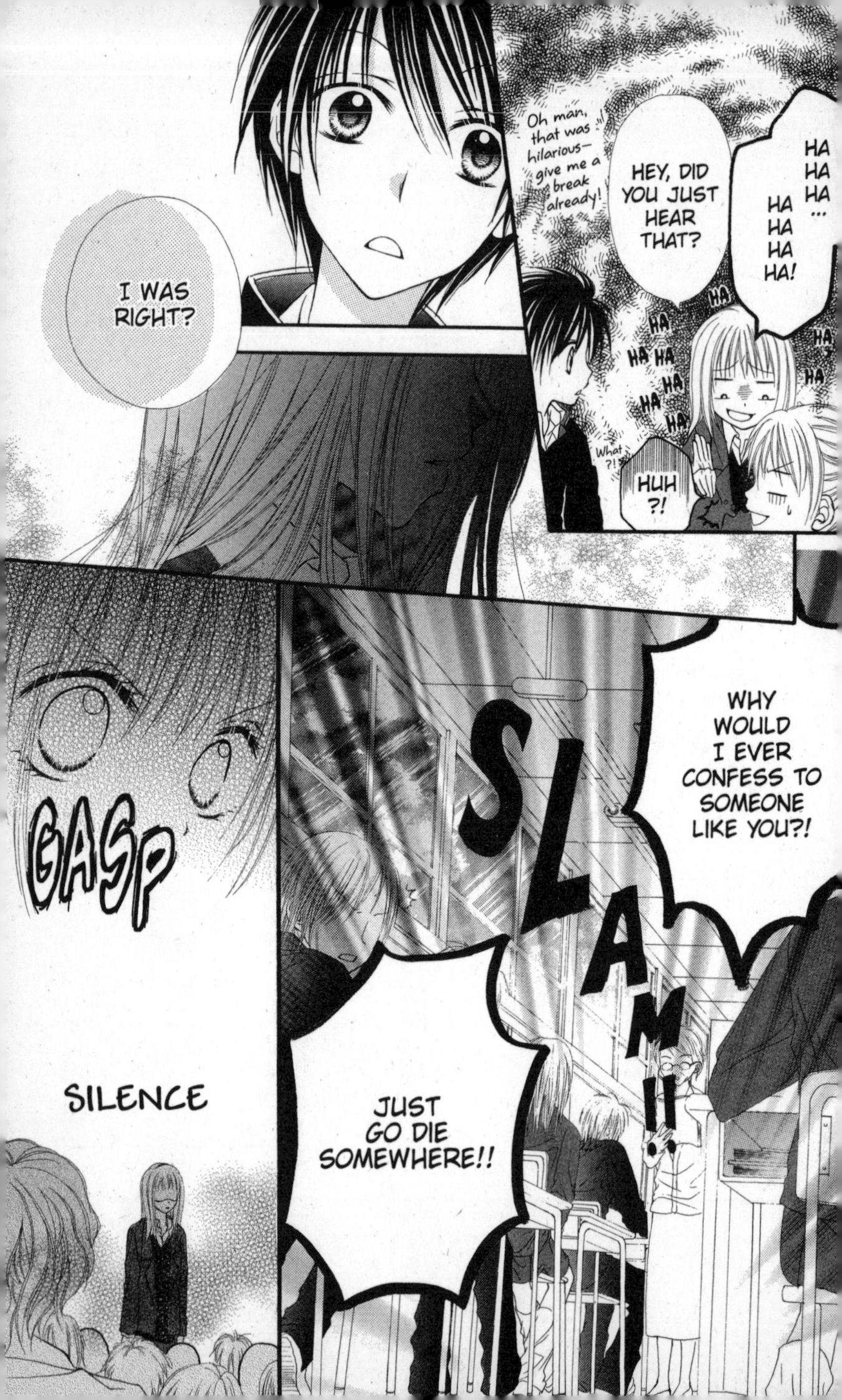
HA HA HA...
HA HA HA HA!
HEY, DID YOU JUST HEAR THAT?
Oh man, that was hilarious—give me a break already!
HA HA
HA HA HA HA HA HA HA HA
HUH ?!
What ?!
I WAS RIGHT?
WHY WOULD I EVER CONFESS TO SOMEONE LIKE YOU?!
SLAM!!
JUST GO DIE SOMEWHERE!!
GASP
SILENCE

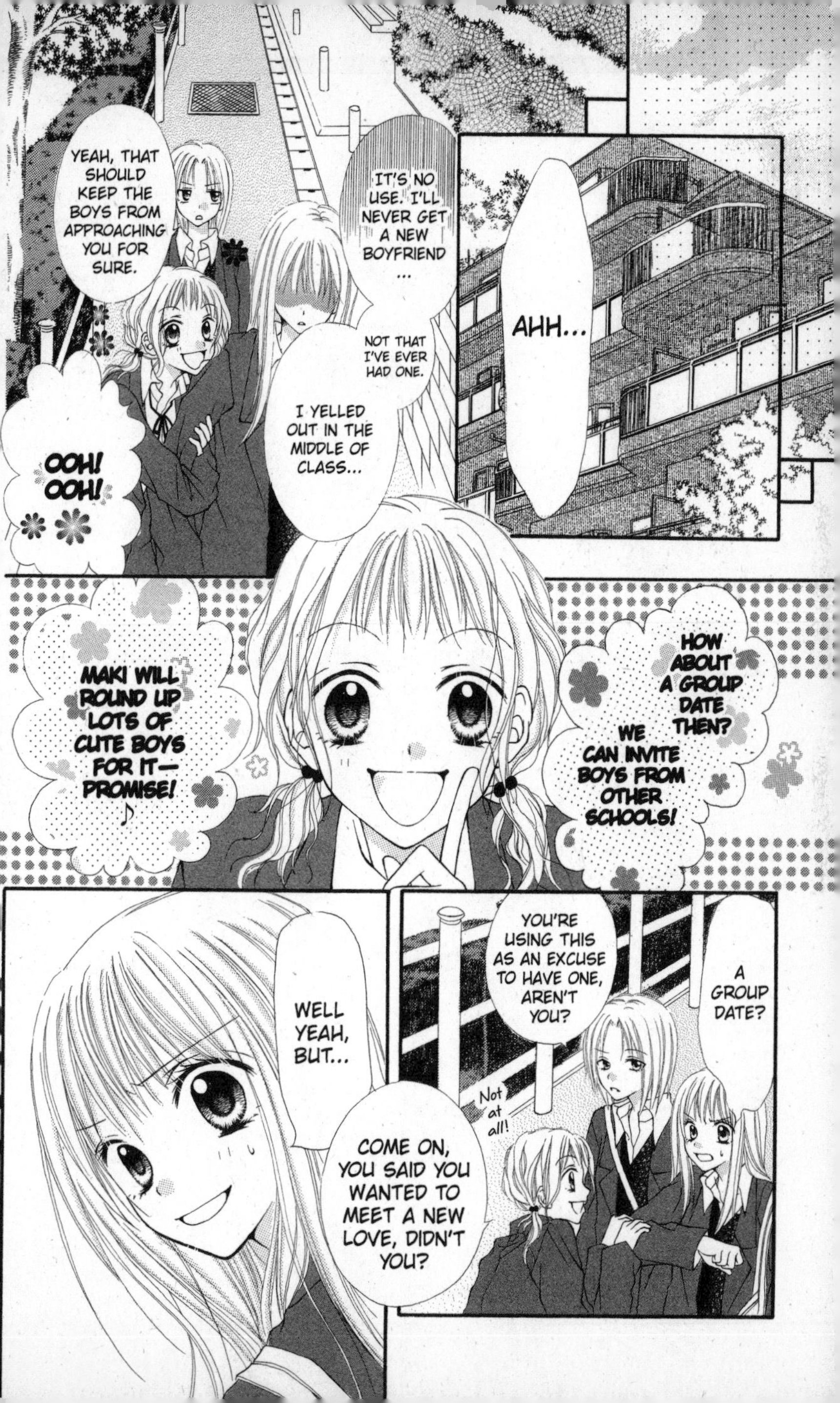
AHH...
IT'S NO USE. I'LL NEVER GET A NEW BOYFRIEND ...
NOT THAT I'VE EVER HAD ONE.
I YELLED OUT IN THE MIDDLE OF CLASS...
YEAH, THAT SHOULD KEEP THE BOYS FROM APPROACHING YOU FOR SURE.
OOH! OOH!
HOW ABOUT A GROUP DATE THEN?
WE CAN INVITE BOYS FROM OTHER SCHOOLS!
MAKI WILL ROUND UP LOTS OF CUTE BOYS FOR IT— PROMISE! ♪
A GROUP DATE?
YOU'RE USING THIS AS AN EXCUSE TO HAVE ONE, AREN'T YOU?
Not at all!
WELL YEAH, BUT...
COME ON, YOU SAID YOU WANTED TO MEET A NEW LOVE, DIDN'T YOU?

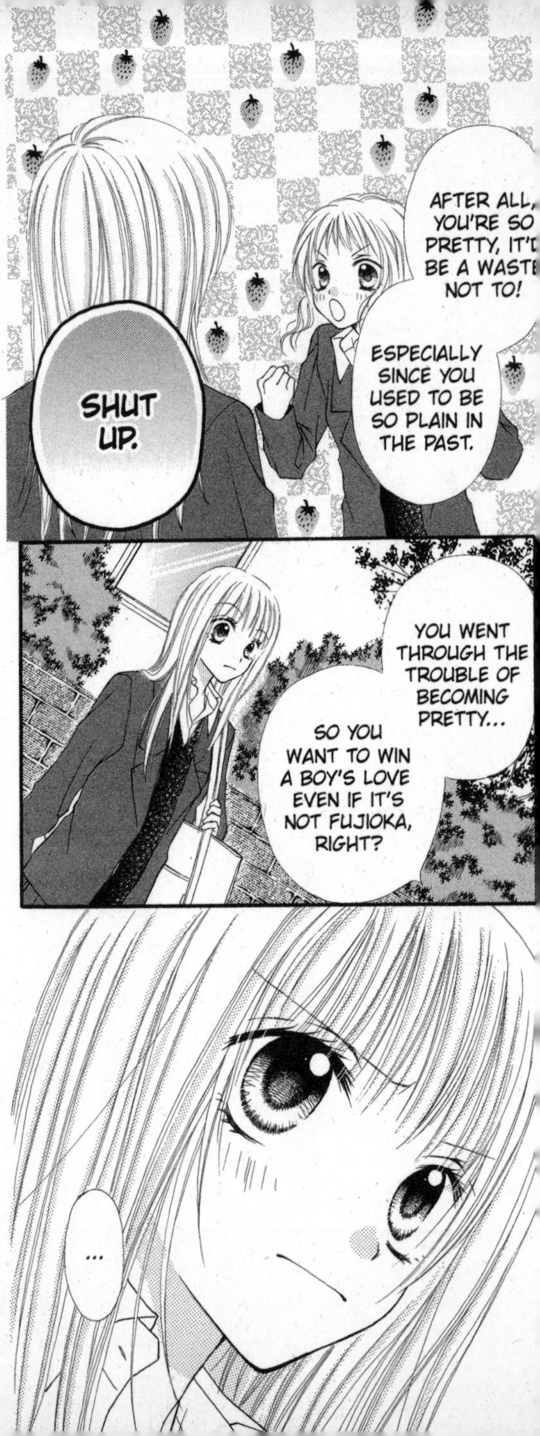
AFTER ALL, YOU'RE SO PRETTY, IT'D BE A WASTE NOT TO!
ESPECIALLY SINCE YOU USED TO BE SO PLAIN IN THE PAST.
SHUT UP.
YOU WENT THROUGH THE TROUBLE OF BECOMING PRETTY...
SO YOU WANT TO WIN A BOY'S LOVE EVEN IF IT'S NOT FUJIOKA, RIGHT?
...

1

Er...

THIS IS CACTUS'S SECRET VOLUME 1.

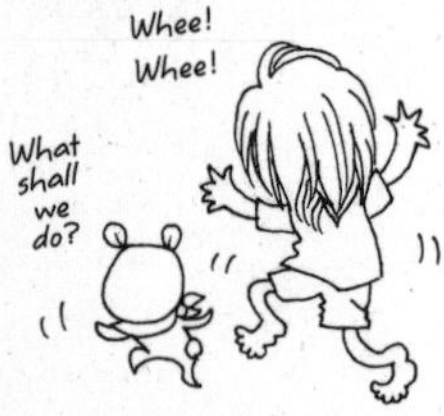
Whee! Whee!
What shall we do?

Hello and greetings. I'm Nana Haruta. I thank you very, very much for buying my fourth published volume of manga, *Cactus's Secret* volume 1. Whee! Whee! And here I thought volume 1 wasn't going to get published. (laugh) Man, I got lucky!! ☆

For various reasons, I'm really happy to see volume 1 out. I really hope you'll enjoy it.

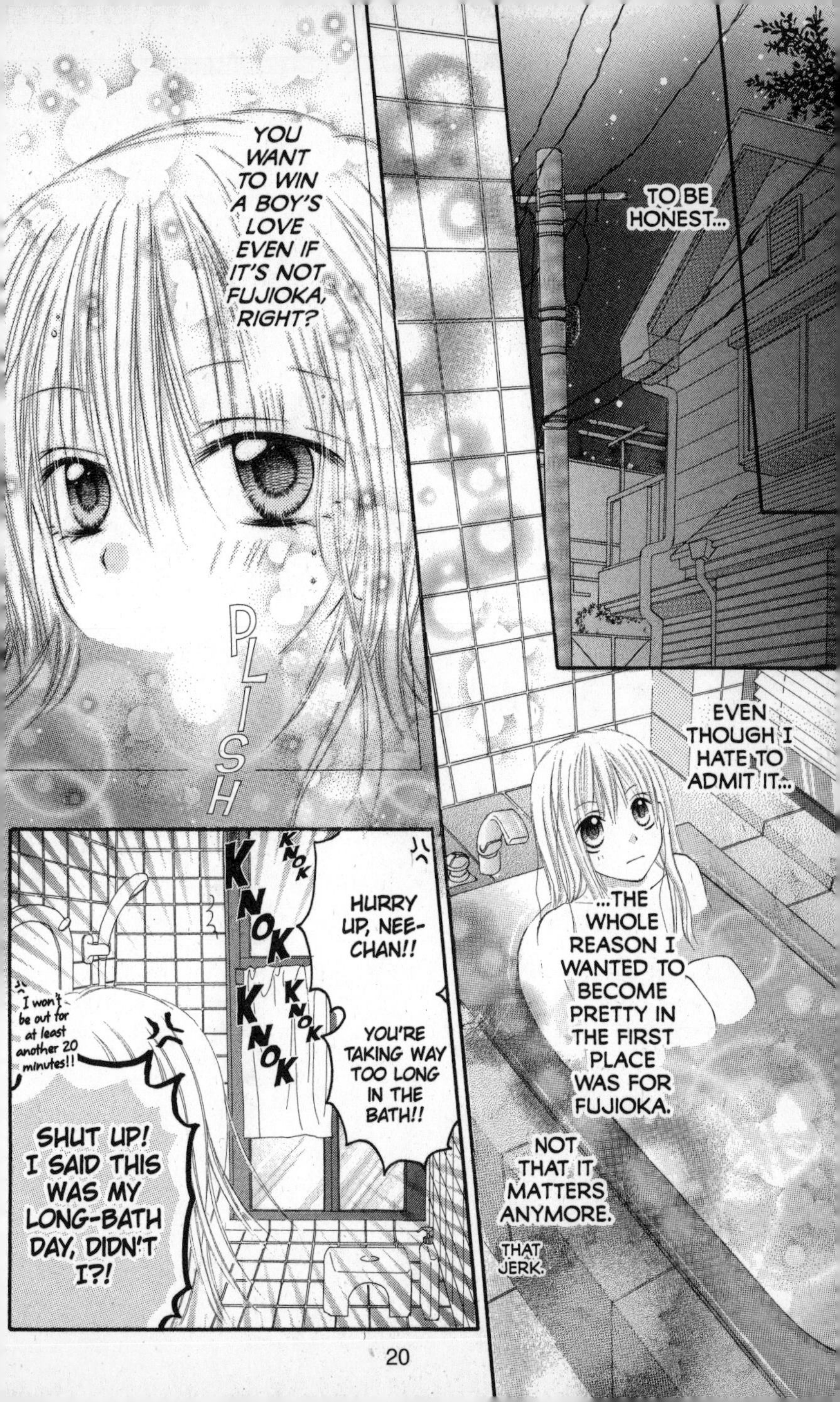
TO BE HONEST...
EVEN THOUGH I HATE TO ADMIT IT...
...THE WHOLE REASON I WANTED TO BECOME PRETTY IN THE FIRST PLACE WAS FOR FUJIOKA.
NOT THAT IT MATTERS ANYMORE.
THAT JERK.
YOU WANT TO WIN A BOY'S LOVE EVEN IF IT'S NOT FUJIOKA, RIGHT?
PLISH
KNOK KNOK
KNOK KNOK
HURRY UP, NEE-CHAN!!
YOU'RE TAKING WAY TOO LONG IN THE BATH!!
SHUT UP! I SAID THIS WAS MY LONG-BATH DAY, DIDN'T I?!
I won't be out for at least another 20 minutes!!

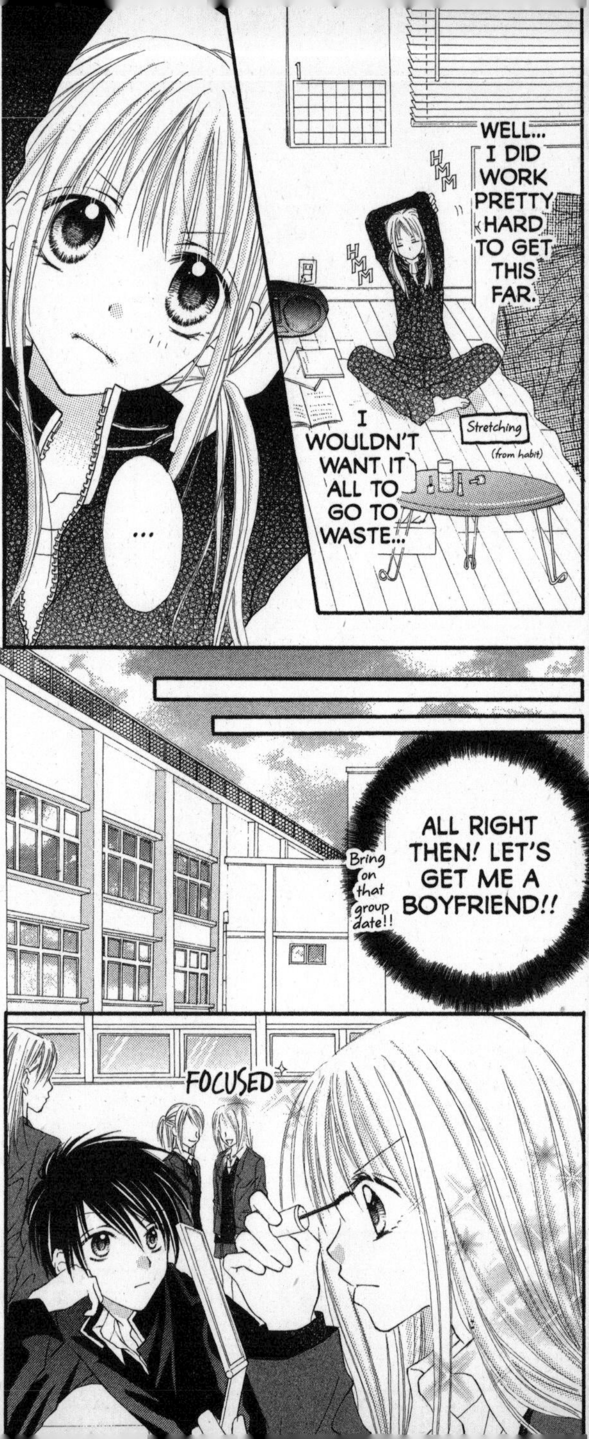
WELL... I DID WORK PRETTY HARD TO GET THIS FAR.
HMM HMM
Stretching (from habit)
I WOULDN'T WANT IT ALL TO GO TO WASTE...
...
ALL RIGHT THEN! LET'S GET ME A BOYFRIEND!!
Bring on that group date!!
FOCUSED

2

Lately my schedule has been so packed I've only been able to draw my manga thanks to the help of many, many people. Several of my angelic assistants have even kindly offered some comments on my work!!

Page 180:
Yumeno Mizuki-sama

Page 181:
Marina Umezawa-sama

Page 182:
Mika Shinano-sama

Now there's the matter of figuring out what to put in for bonus pages... Well, for now, I'll just fill up all the sidebars and then think about the bonus section, I guess. Then again, since I've never even written these mangaka columns before, I fear for the bonus section...!!

Anyway, I guess I'll tell you about how I've been lately and answer some questions from readers too.

I'll do my best!

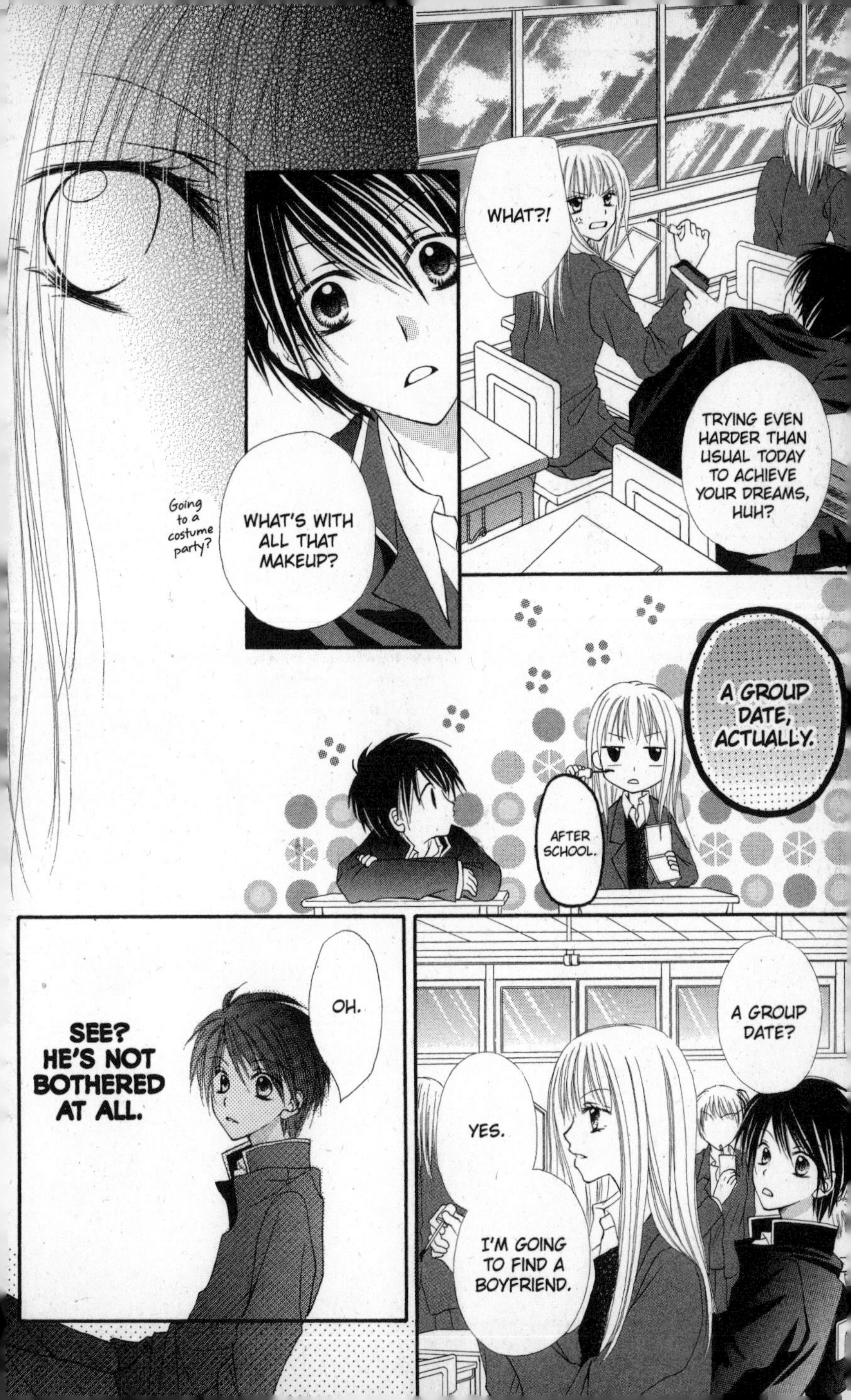
TRYING EVEN HARDER THAN USUAL TODAY TO ACHIEVE YOUR DREAMS, HUH?
WHAT?!
WHAT'S WITH ALL THAT MAKEUP?
Going to a costume party?
A GROUP DATE, ACTUALLY.
AFTER SCHOOL.
A GROUP DATE?
YES.
I'M GOING TO FIND A BOYFRIEND.
OH.
SEE? HE'S NOT BOTHERED AT ALL.

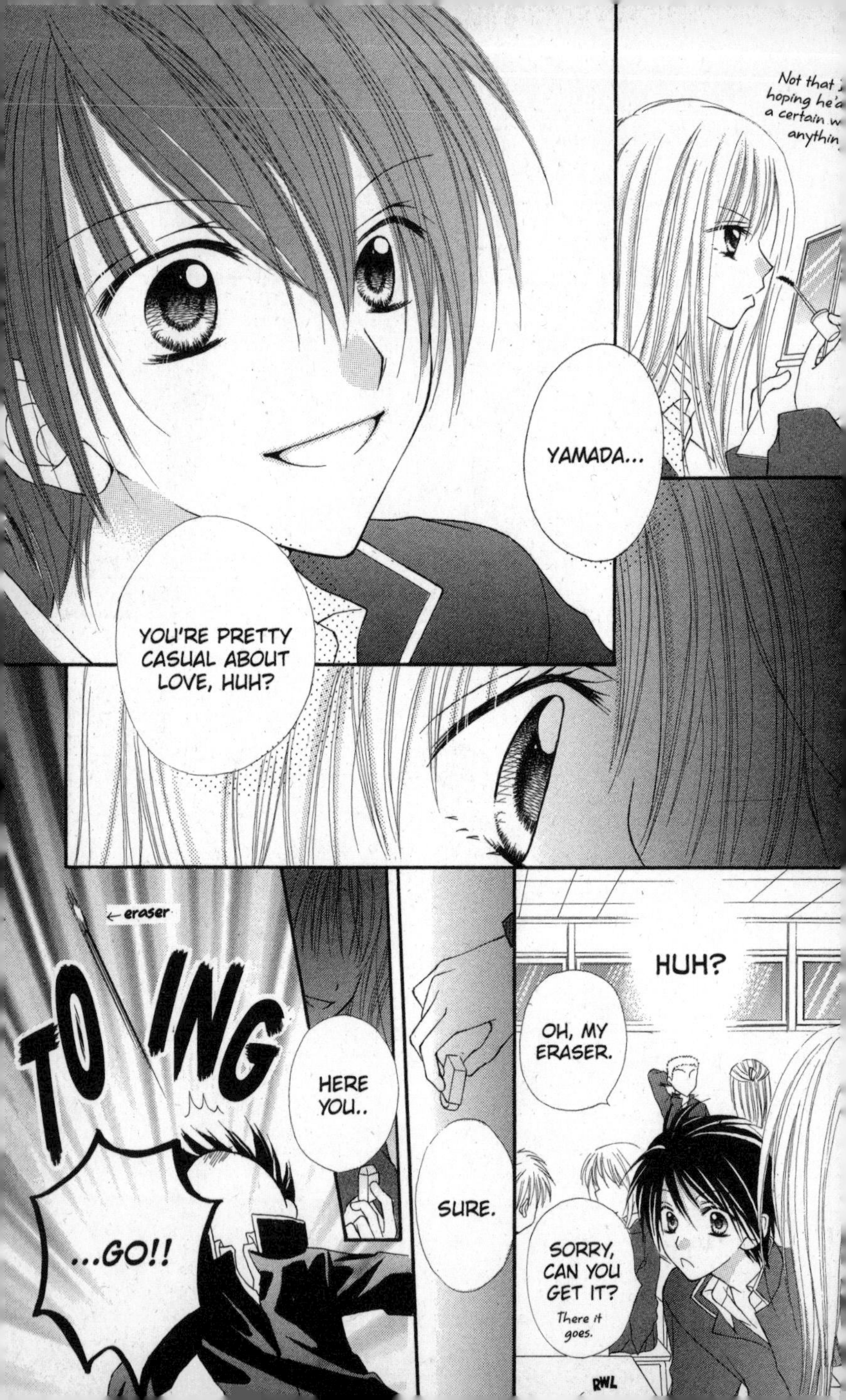
Not that
hoping he'
a certain
anythin
YAMADA...
YOU'RE PRETTY CASUAL ABOUT LOVE, HUH?
HUH?
OH, MY ERASER.
SORRY, CAN YOU GET IT?
There it goes.
RWL
SURE.
←eraser
HERE YOU..
TOING
...GO!!

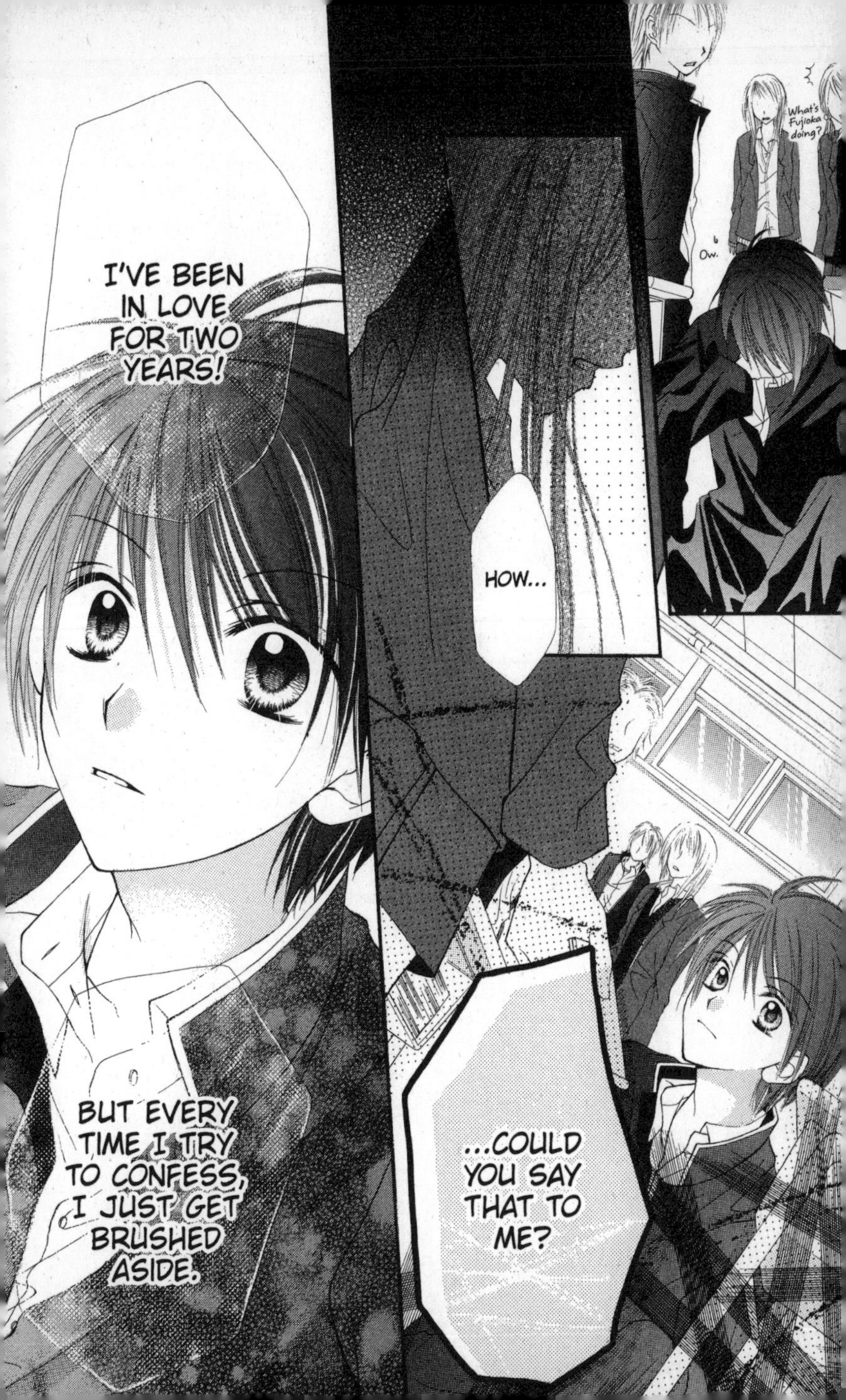
What's Fujioka doing?
Ow.
HOW...
...COULD YOU SAY THAT TO ME?
I'VE BEEN IN LOVE FOR TWO YEARS!
BUT EVERY TIME I TRY TO CONFESS, I JUST GET BRUSHED ASIDE.

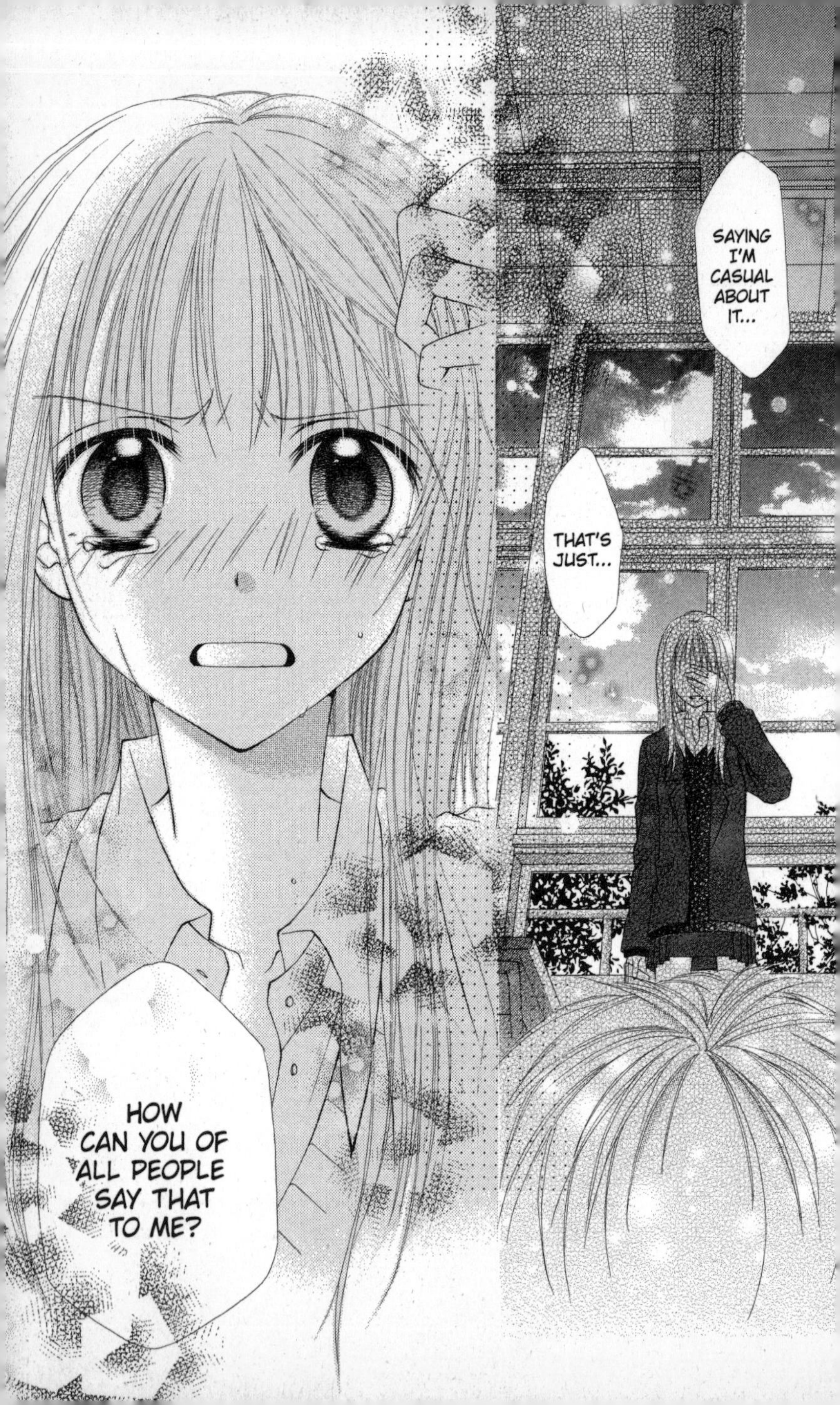
SAYING I'M CASUAL ABOUT IT...
THAT'S JUST...
HOW CAN YOU OF ALL PEOPLE SAY THAT TO ME?

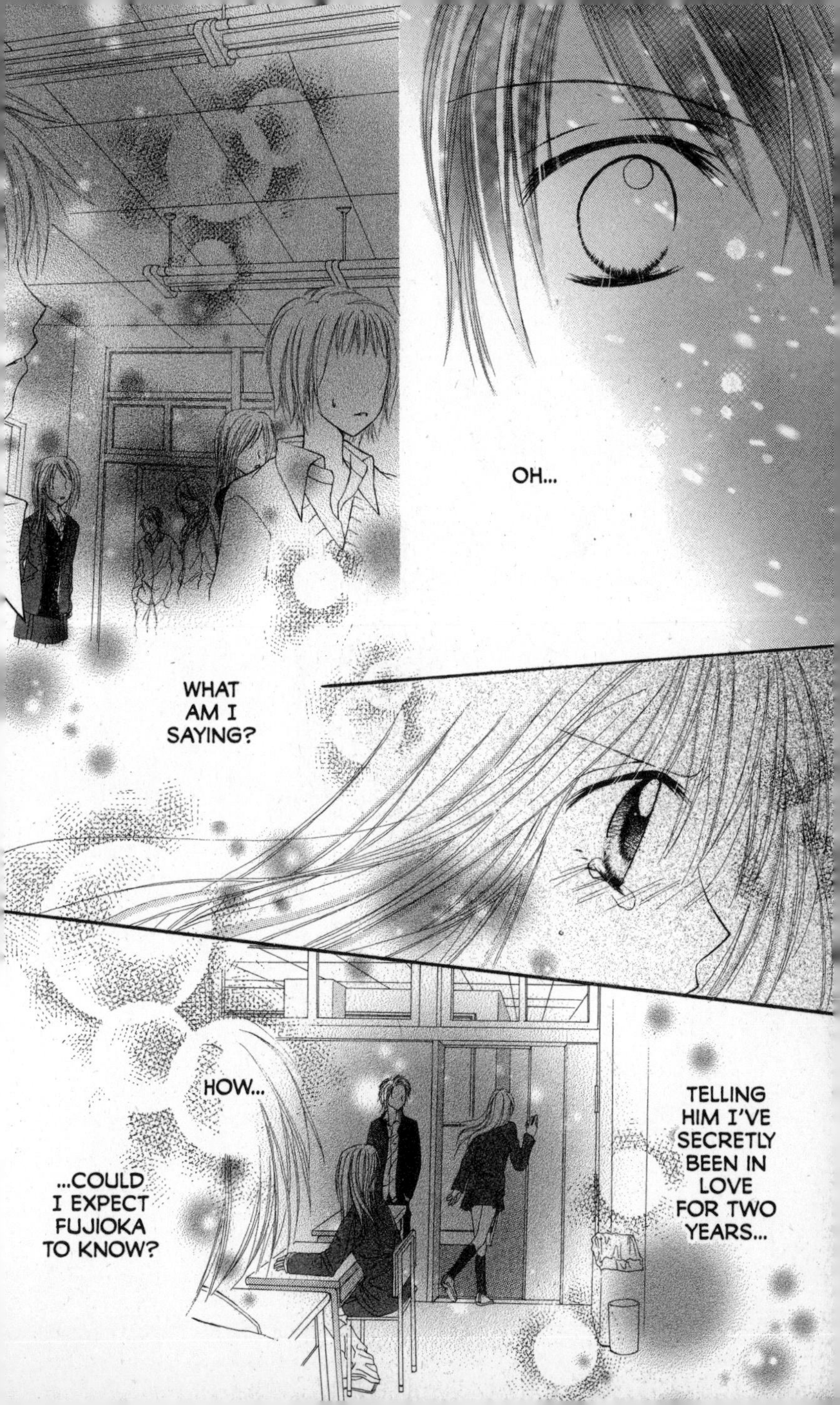
OH...
WHAT AM I SAYING?
TELLING HIM I'VE SECRETLY BEEN IN LOVE FOR TWO YEARS...
HOW...
...COULD I EXPECT FUJIOKA TO KNOW?

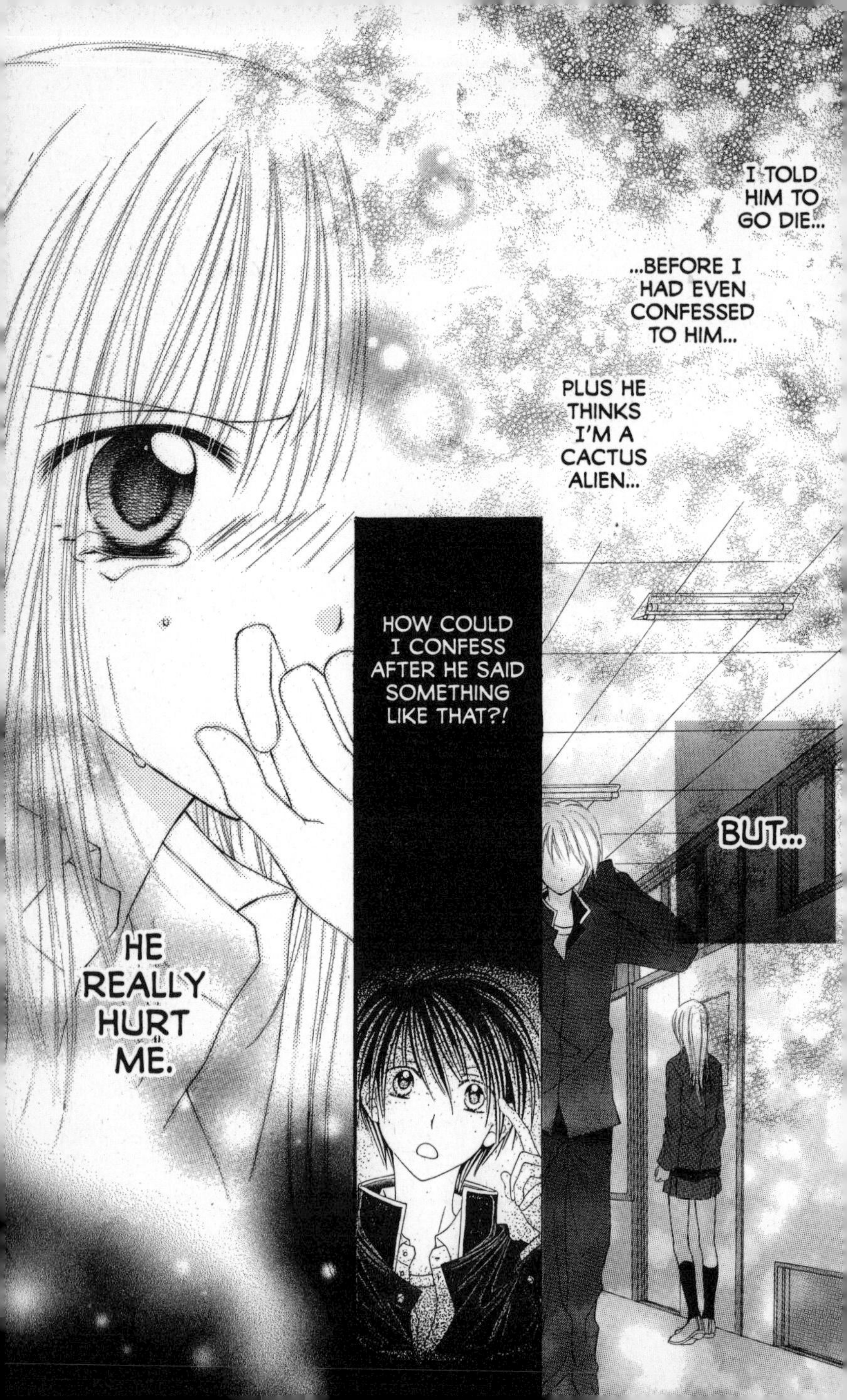
I TOLD HIM TO GO DIE...
...BEFORE I HAD EVEN CONFESSED TO HIM...
PLUS HE THINKS I'M A CACTUS ALIEN...
HOW COULD I CONFESS AFTER HE SAID SOMETHING LIKE THAT?!
BUT...
HE REALLY HURT ME.

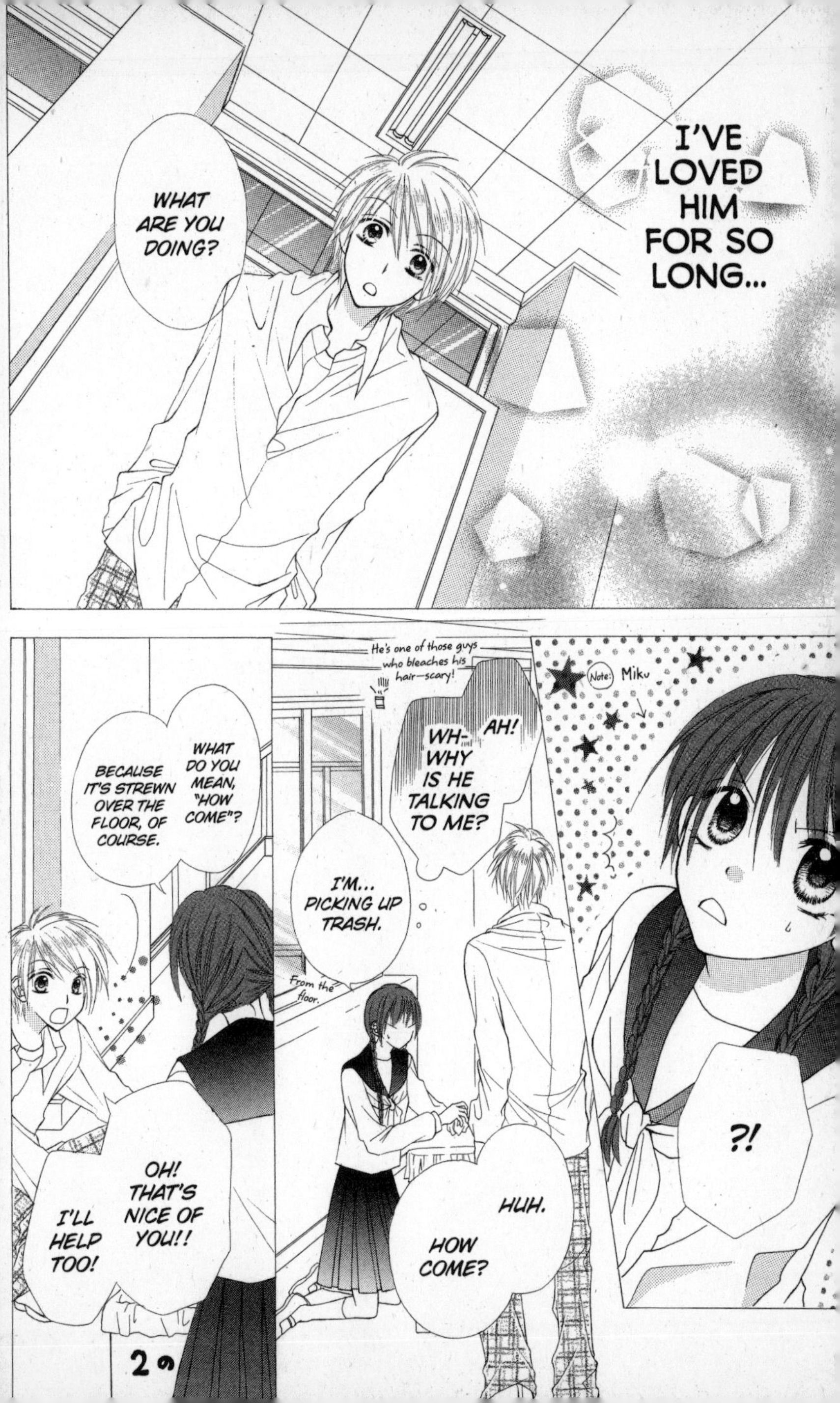

I'VE LOVED HIM FOR SO LONG...
WHAT ARE YOU DOING?
Note: Miku
?!
He's one of those guys who bleaches his hair—scary!
AH!
WH- WHY IS HE TALKING TO ME?
I'M... PICKING UP TRASH.
From the floor.
HUH.
HOW COME?
WHAT DO YOU MEAN, "HOW COME"?
BECAUSE IT'S STREWN OVER THE FLOOR, OF COURSE.
OH! THAT'S NICE OF YOU!!
I'LL HELP TOO!

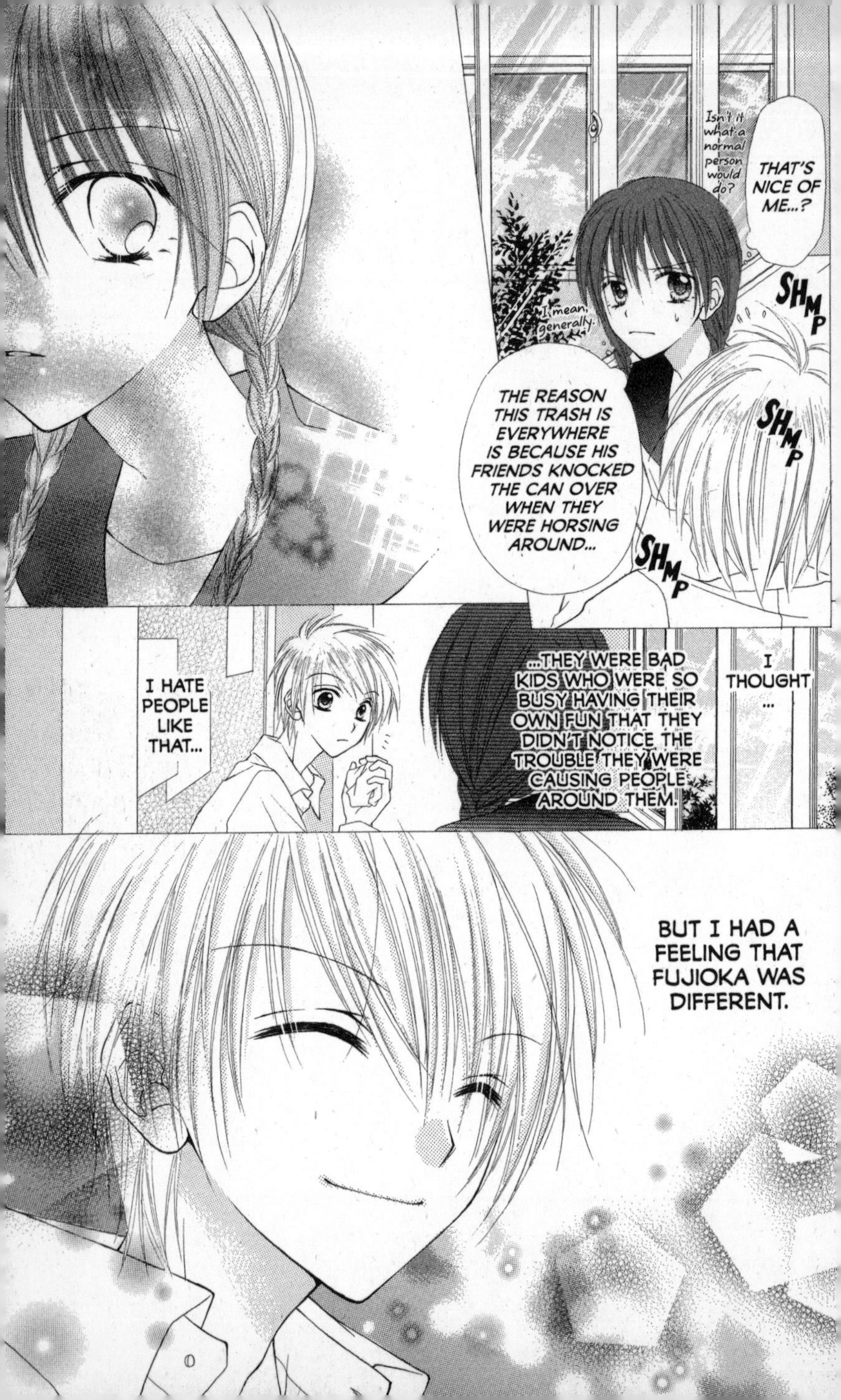
THAT'S NICE OF ME...?
Isn't it what a normal person would do?
SHMP
I mean, generally.
SHMP
THE REASON THIS TRASH IS EVERYWHERE IS BECAUSE HIS FRIENDS KNOCKED THE CAN OVER WHEN THEY WERE HORSING AROUND...
SHMP
I THOUGHT...
...THEY WERE BAD KIDS WHO WERE SO BUSY HAVING THEIR OWN FUN THAT THEY DIDN'T NOTICE THE TROUBLE THEY WERE CAUSING PEOPLE AROUND THEM.
I HATE PEOPLE LIKE THAT...
BUT I HAD A FEELING THAT FUJIOKA WAS DIFFERENT.

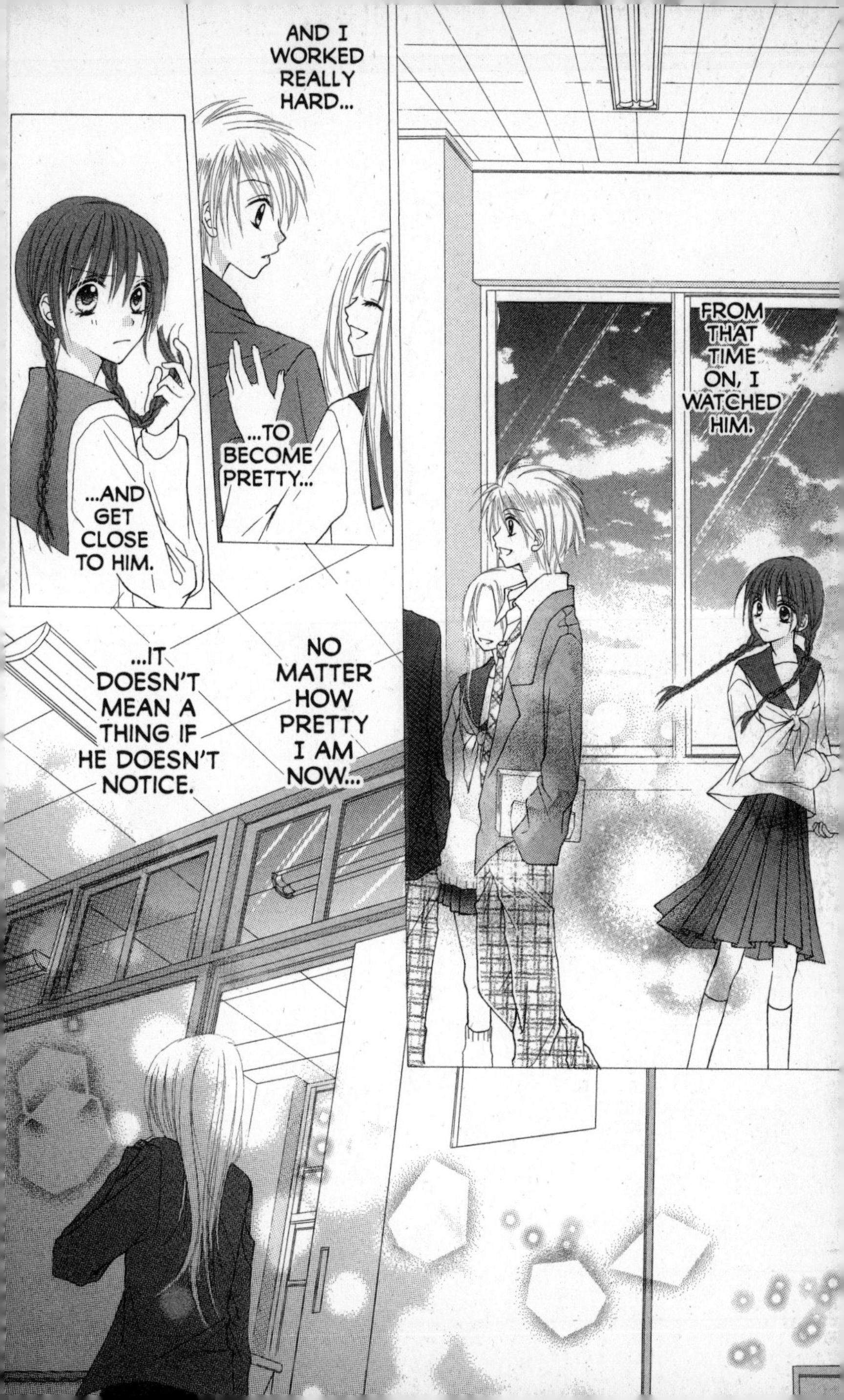
FROM THAT TIME ON, I WATCHED HIM.
AND I WORKED REALLY HARD...
...TO BECOME PRETTY...
...AND GET CLOSE TO HIM.
NO MATTER HOW PRETTY I AM NOW...
...IT DOESN'T MEAN A THING IF HE DOESN'T NOTICE.

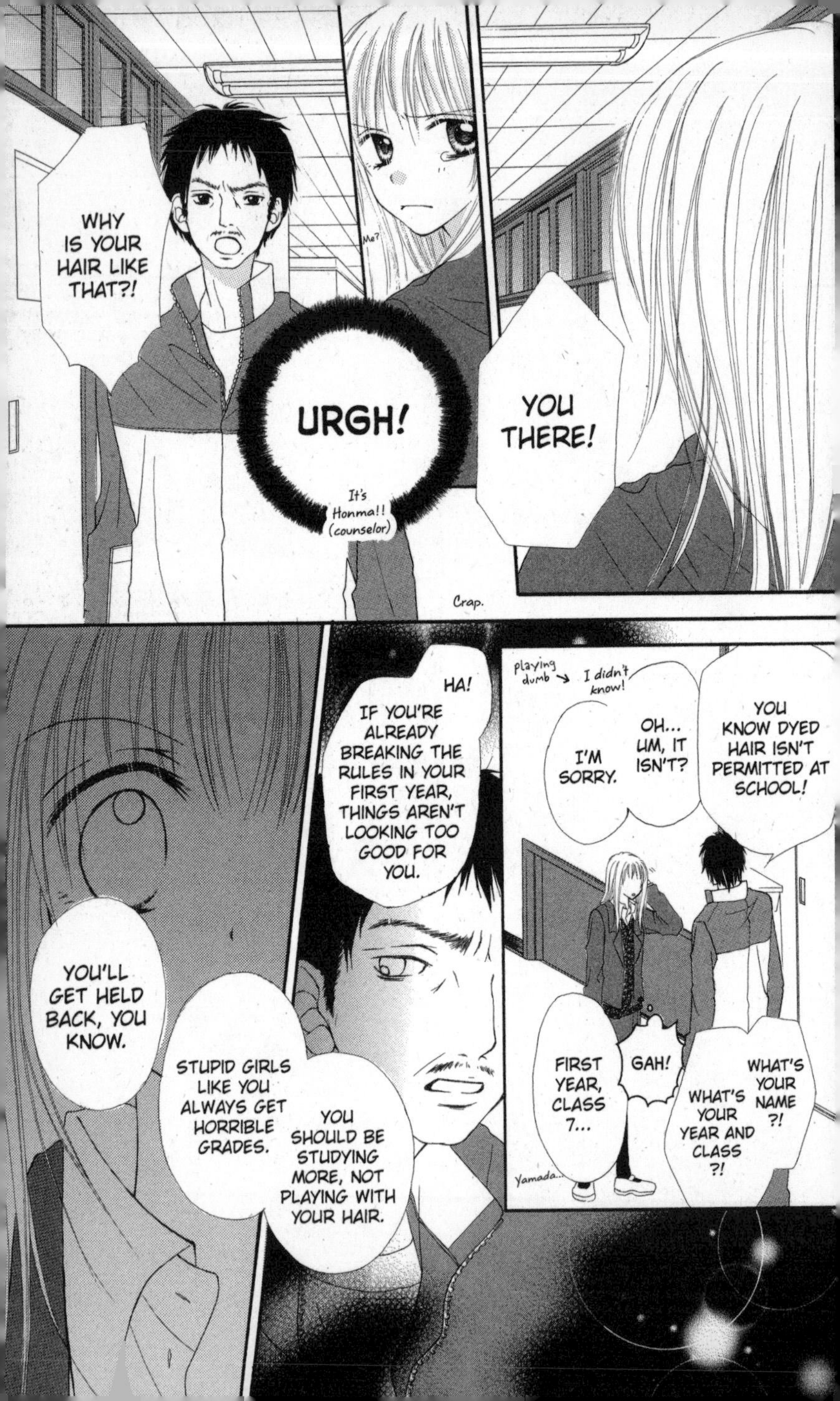
YOU THERE!
Me?
URGH!
It's Honma!! (counselor)
WHY IS YOUR HAIR LIKE THAT?!
Crap.
YOU KNOW DYED HAIR ISN'T PERMITTED AT SCHOOL!
playing dumb → I didn't know!
OH... UM, IT ISN'T?
I'M SORRY.
WHAT'S YOUR NAME?!
WHAT'S YOUR YEAR AND CLASS?!
GAH!
FIRST YEAR, CLASS 7...
Yamada...
HA!
IF YOU'RE ALREADY BREAKING THE RULES IN YOUR FIRST YEAR, THINGS AREN'T LOOKING TOO GOOD FOR YOU.
YOU'LL GET HELD BACK, YOU KNOW.
STUPID GIRLS LIKE YOU ALWAYS GET HORRIBLE GRADES.
YOU SHOULD BE STUDYING MORE, NOT PLAYING WITH YOUR HAIR.

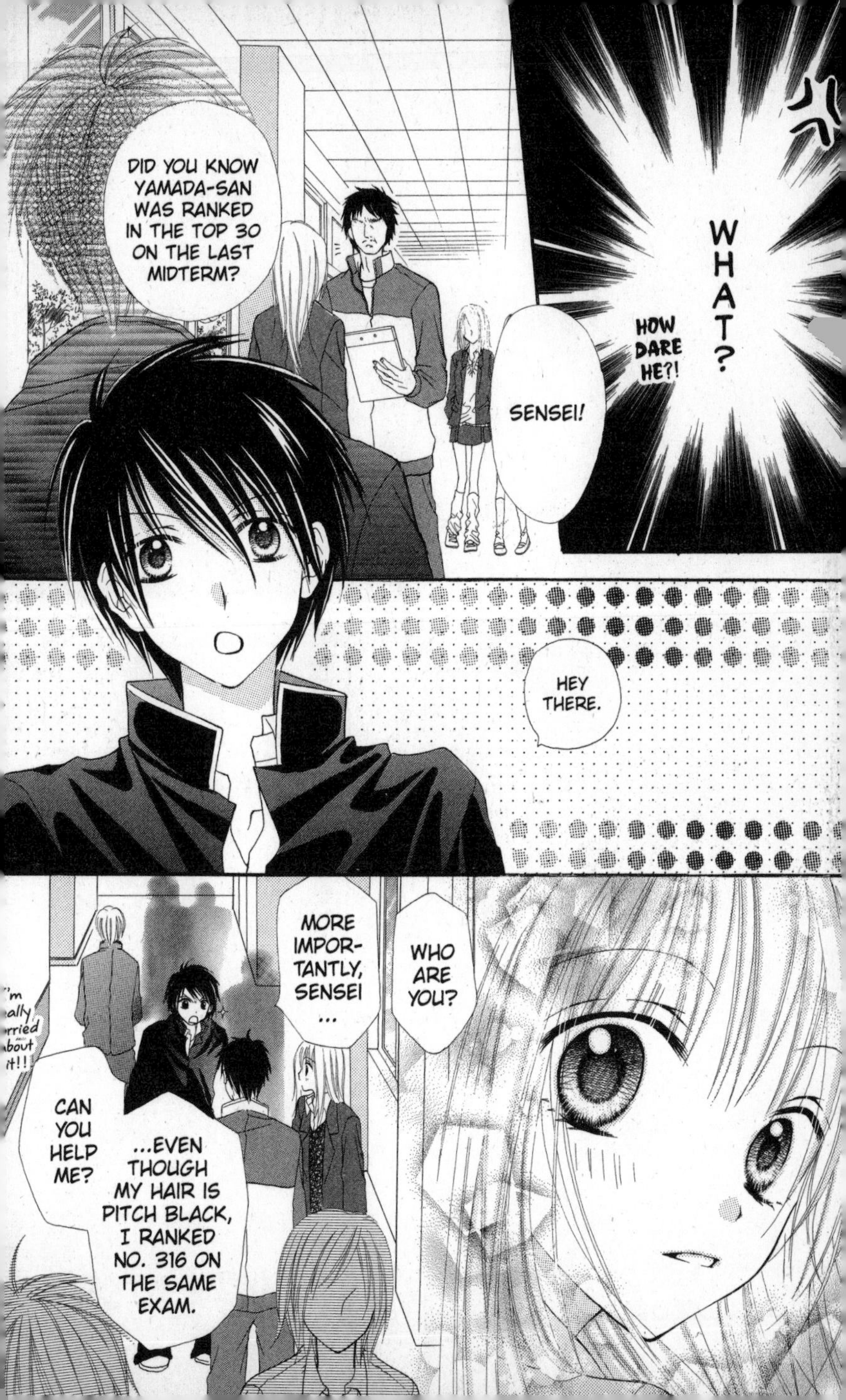
WHAT?
HOW DARE HE?!
DID YOU KNOW YAMADA-SAN WAS RANKED IN THE TOP 30 ON THE LAST MIDTERM?
SENSEI!
HEY THERE.
WHO ARE YOU?
MORE IMPOR-TANTLY, SENSEI...
...EVEN THOUGH MY HAIR IS PITCH BLACK, I RANKED NO. 316 ON THE SAME EXAM.
CAN YOU HELP ME?

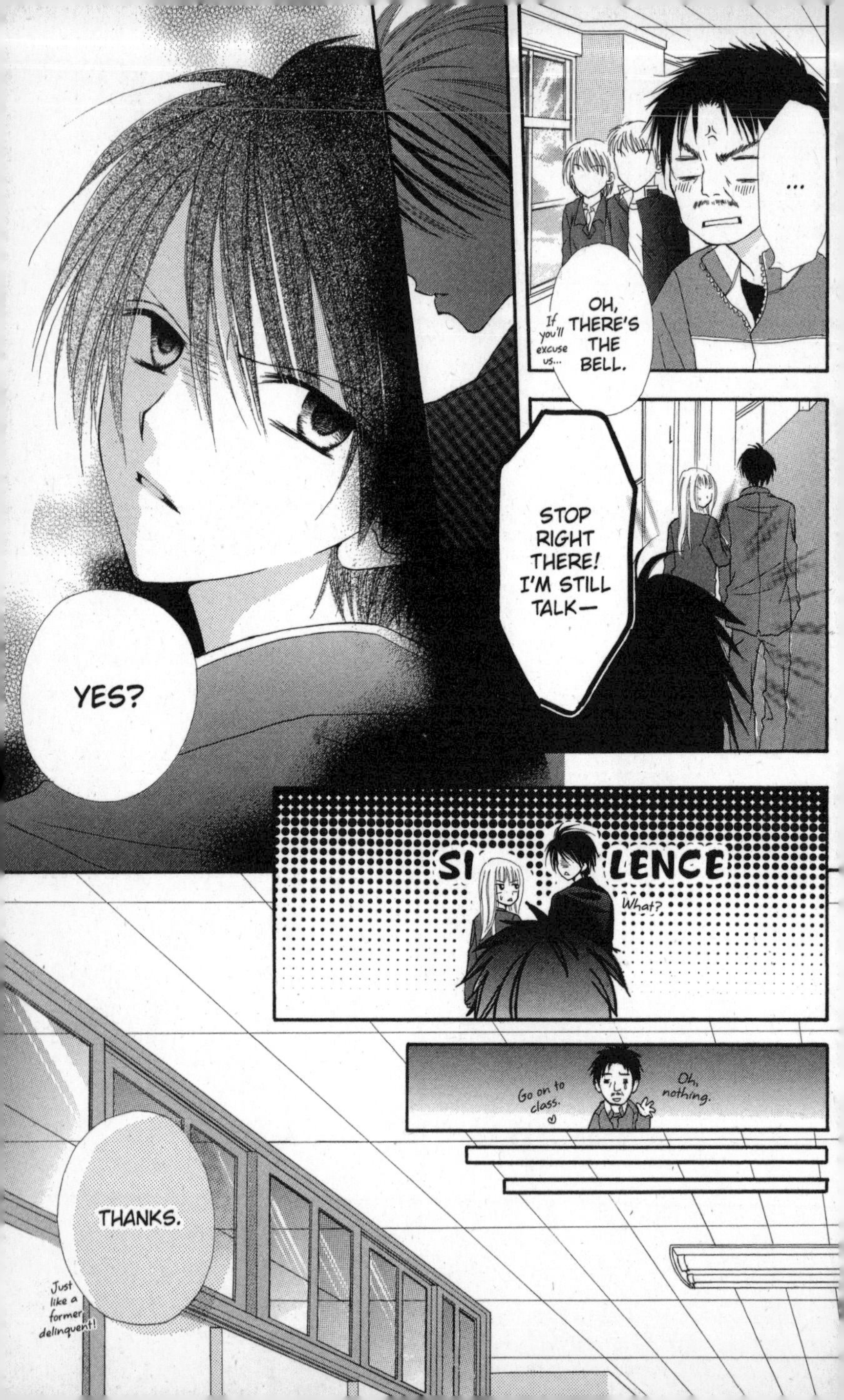
...
OH, THERE'S THE BELL.
If you'll excuse us...
STOP RIGHT THERE! I'M STILL TALK—
YES?
SILENCE
What?
Oh, nothing.
Go on to class.
THANKS.
Just like a former delinquent!

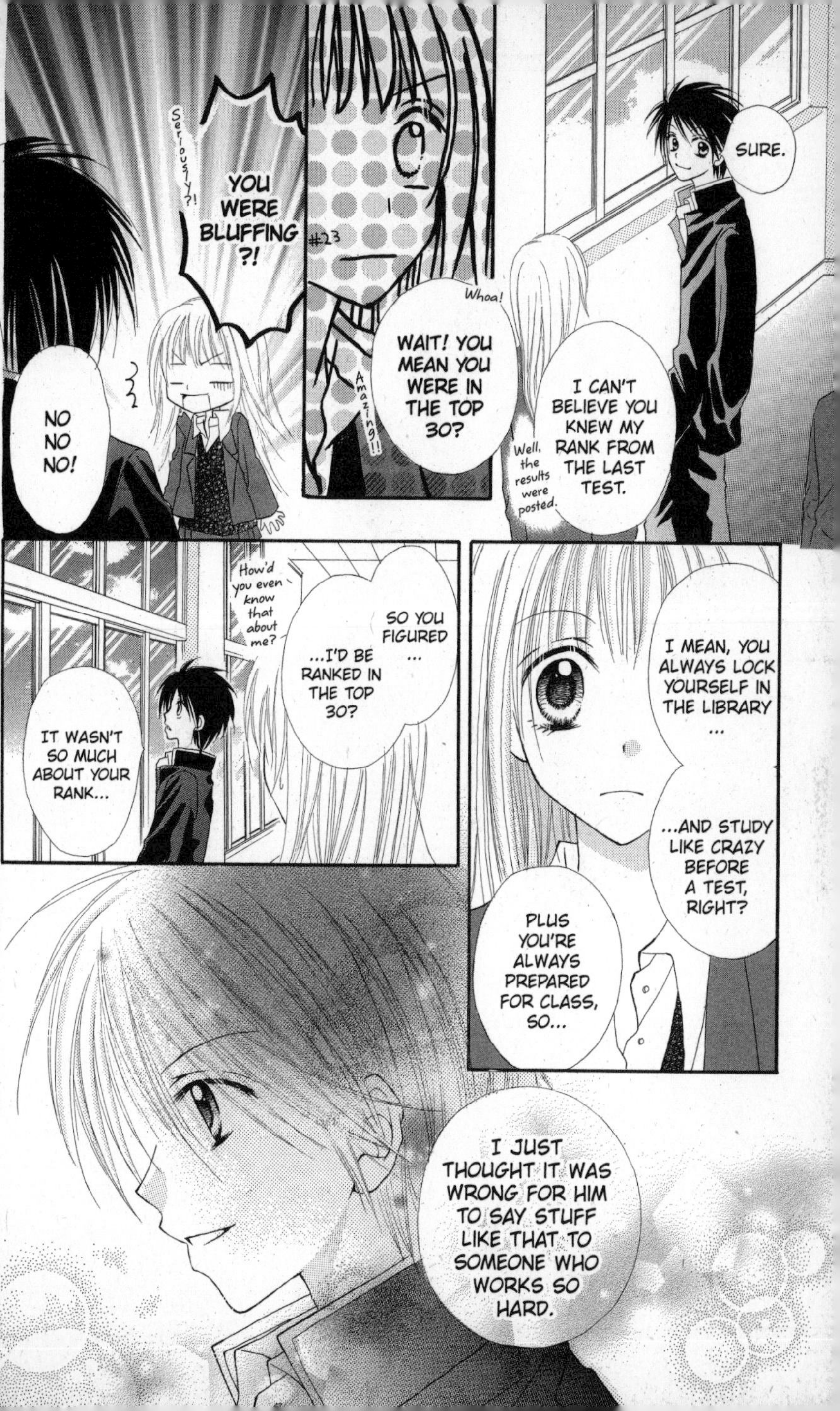
SURE.
I CAN'T BELIEVE YOU KNEW MY RANK FROM THE LAST TEST.
Well, the results were posted.
Whoa!
WAIT! YOU MEAN YOU WERE IN THE TOP 30?
Amazing!!
#23
YOU WERE BLUFFING?!
Seriously?!
NO NO NO!
I MEAN, YOU ALWAYS LOCK YOURSELF IN THE LIBRARY...
...AND STUDY LIKE CRAZY BEFORE A TEST, RIGHT?
PLUS YOU'RE ALWAYS PREPARED FOR CLASS, SO...
SO YOU FIGURED...
...I'D BE RANKED IN THE TOP 30?
How'd you even know that about me?
IT WASN'T SO MUCH ABOUT YOUR RANK...
I JUST THOUGHT IT WAS WRONG FOR HIM TO SAY STUFF LIKE THAT TO SOMEONE WHO WORKS SO HARD.

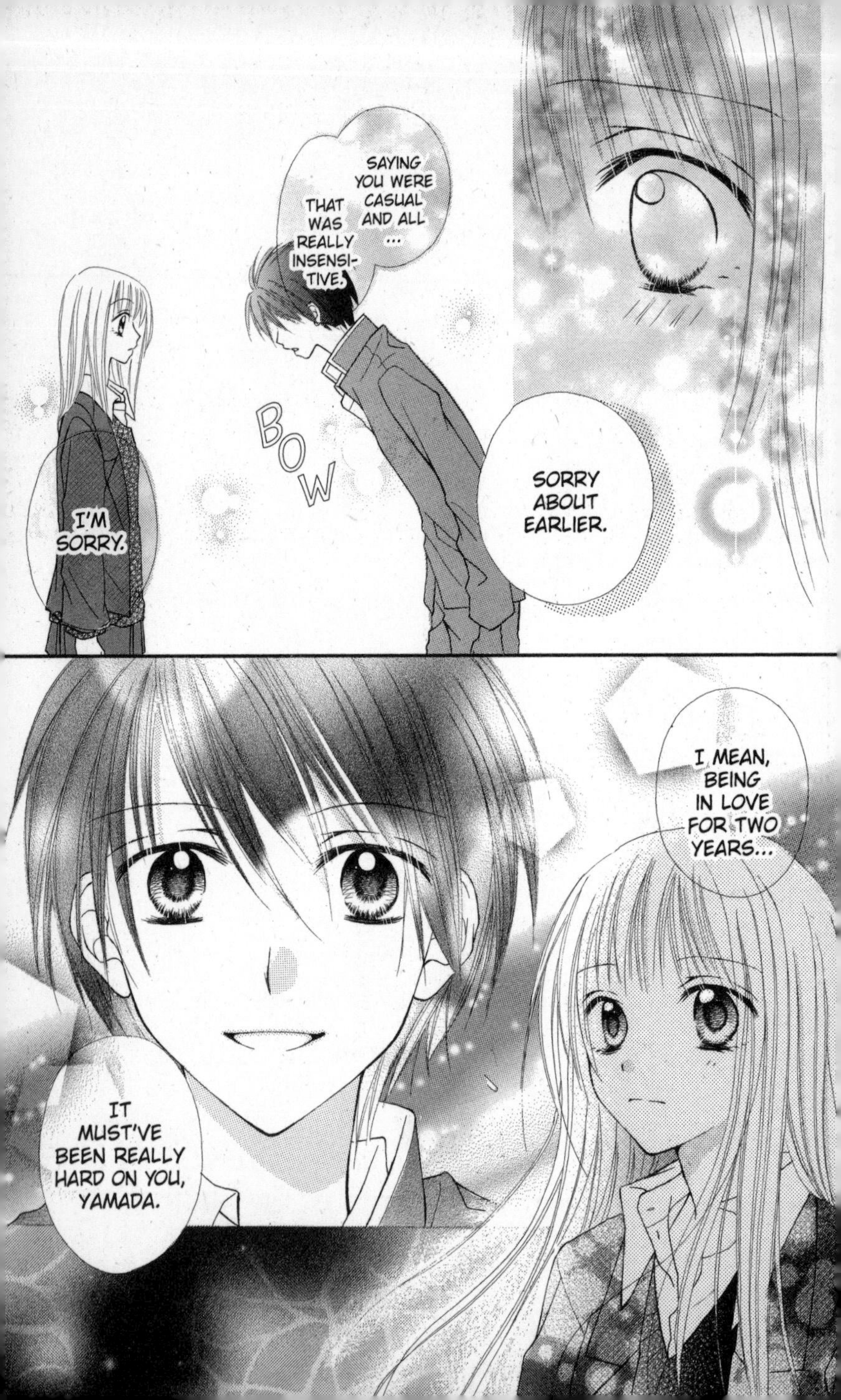
SORRY ABOUT EARLIER.
BOW
SAYING YOU WERE CASUAL AND ALL ... THAT WAS REALLY INSENSI-TIVE.
I'M SORRY.
I MEAN, BEING IN LOVE FOR TWO YEARS...
IT MUST'VE BEEN REALLY HARD ON YOU, YAMADA.

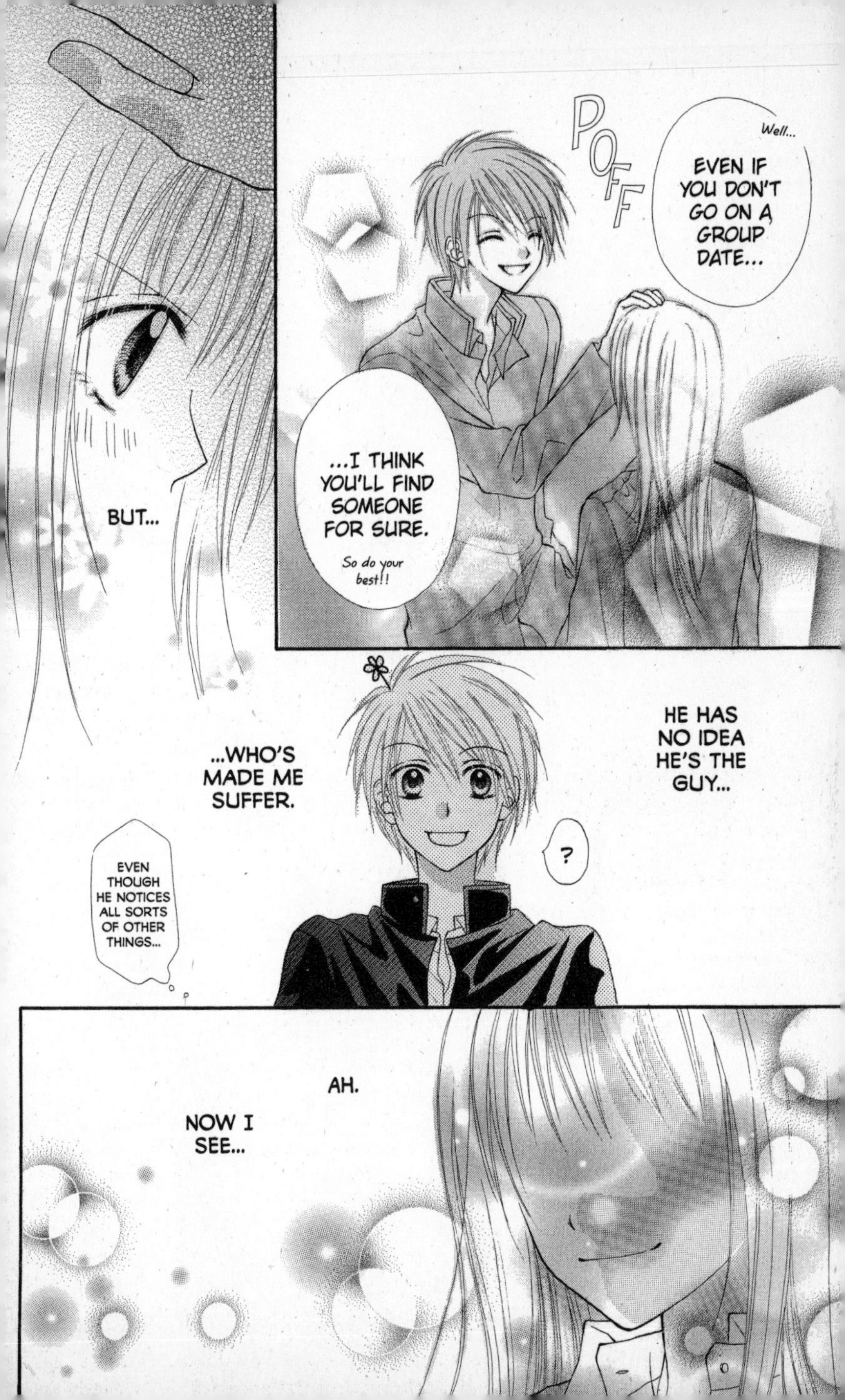
POFF
Well...
EVEN IF YOU DON'T GO ON A GROUP DATE...
...I THINK YOU'LL FIND SOMEONE FOR SURE.
So do your best!!
HE HAS NO IDEA HE'S THE GUY...
?
...WHO'S MADE ME SUFFER.
EVEN THOUGH HE NOTICES ALL SORTS OF OTHER THINGS...
BUT...
AH.
NOW I SEE...

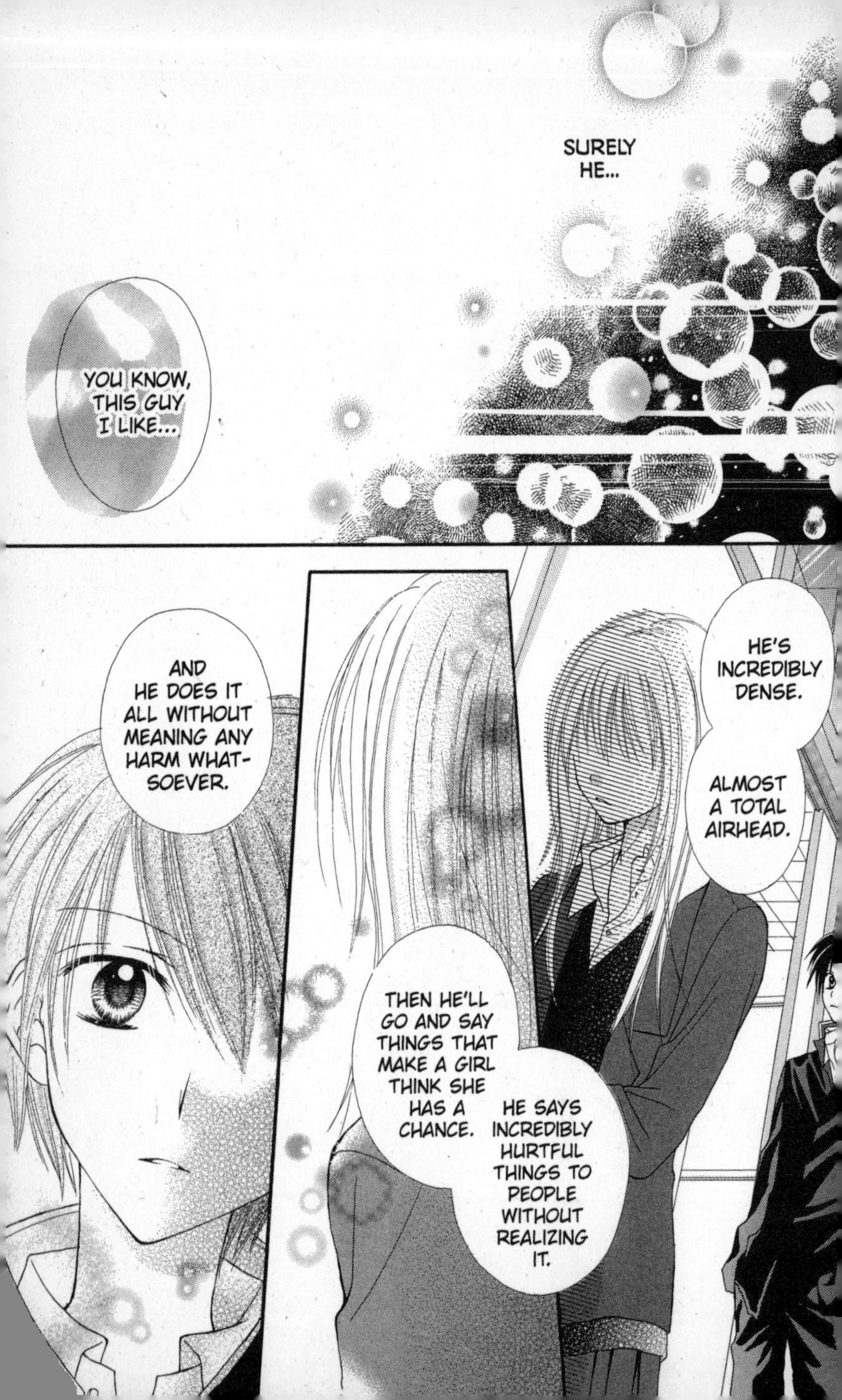
SURELY HE...
YOU KNOW, THIS GUY I LIKE...
HE'S INCREDIBLY DENSE.
ALMOST A TOTAL AIRHEAD.
HE SAYS INCREDIBLY HURTFUL THINGS TO PEOPLE WITHOUT REALIZING IT.
THEN HE'LL GO AND SAY THINGS THAT MAKE A GIRL THINK SHE HAS A CHANCE.
AND HE DOES IT ALL WITHOUT MEANING ANY HARM WHAT-SOEVER.

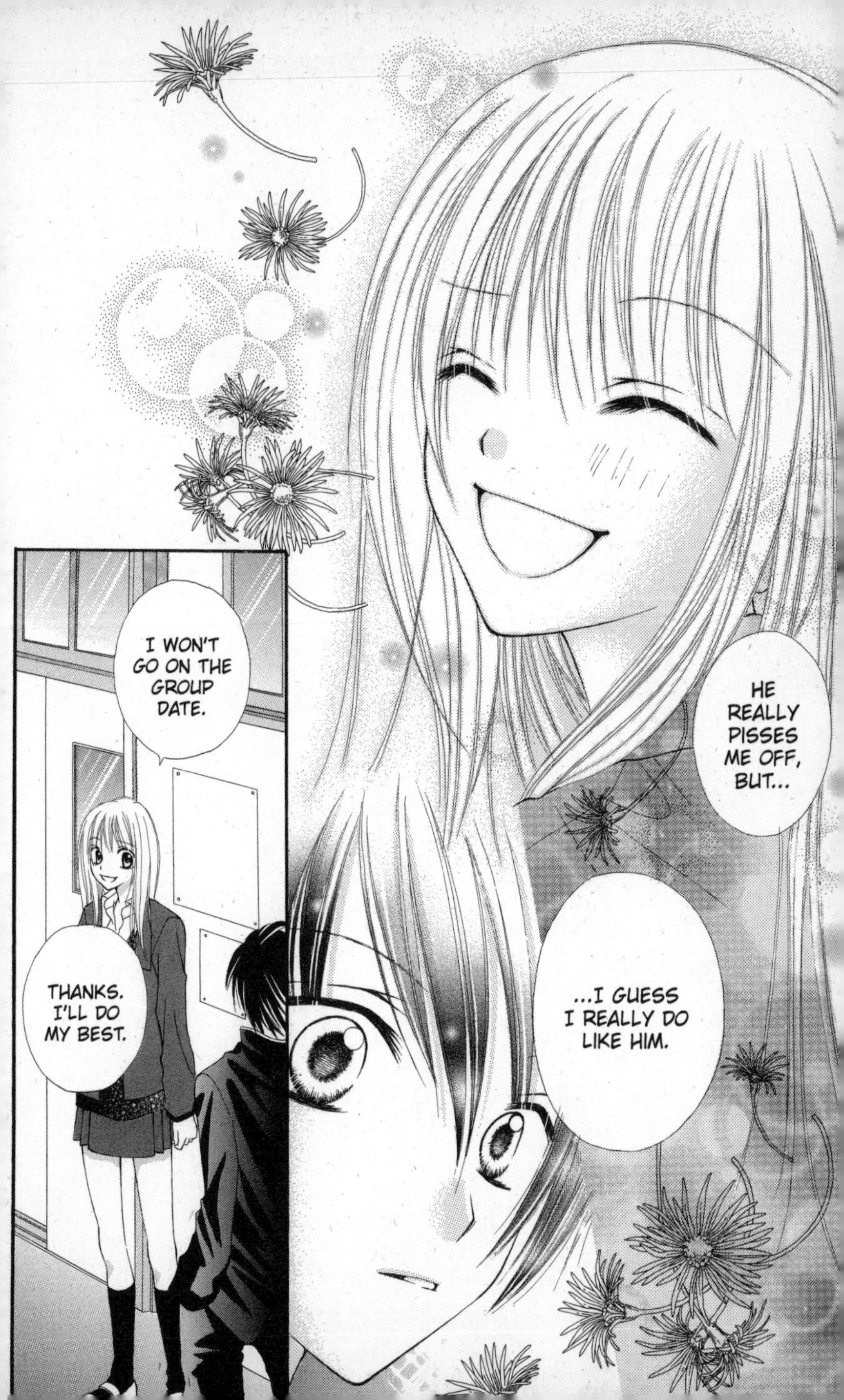
HE REALLY PISSES ME OFF, BUT...
...I GUESS I REALLY DO LIKE HIM.
I WON'T GO ON THE GROUP DATE.
THANKS. I'LL DO MY BEST.

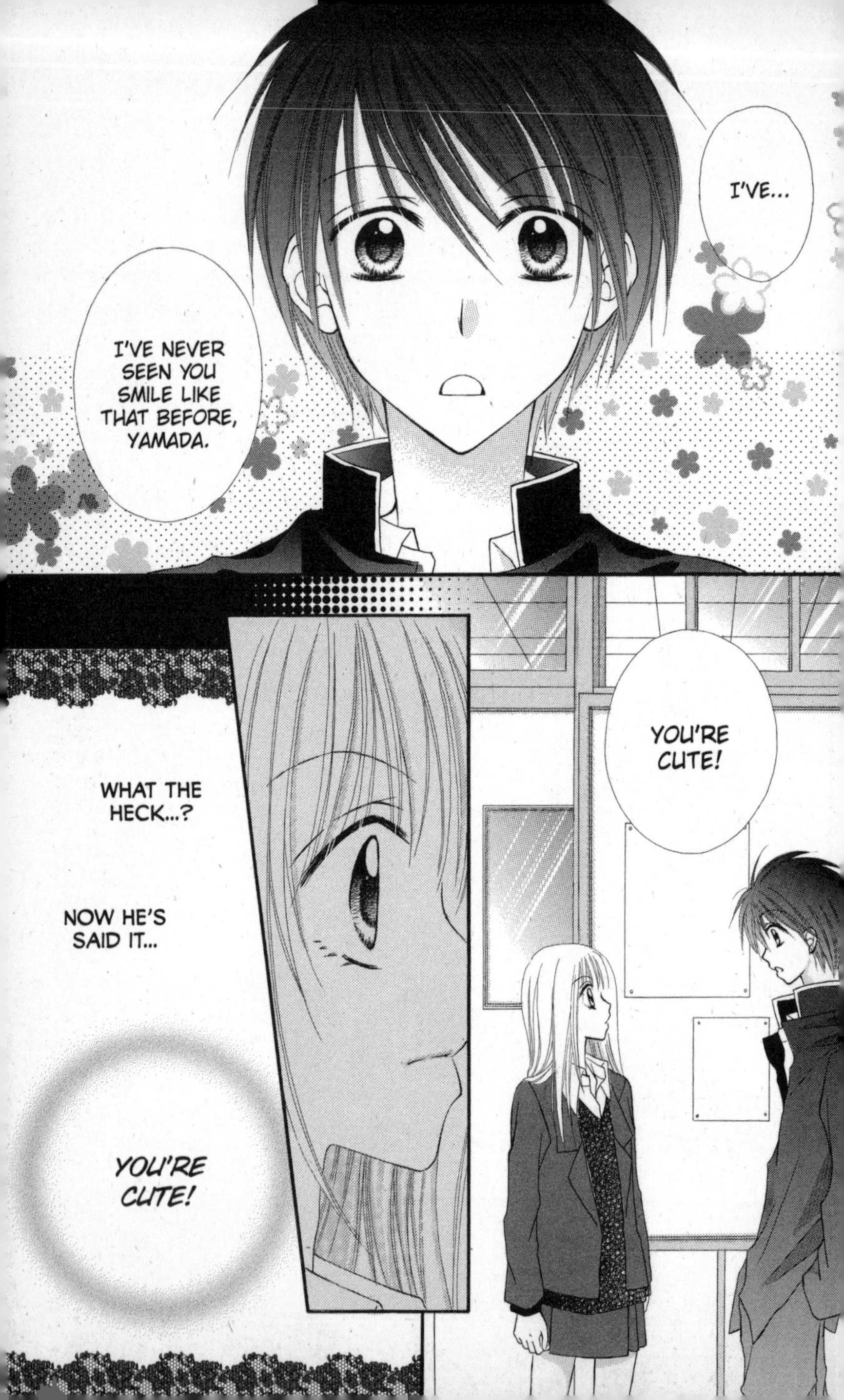
I'VE...
I'VE NEVER SEEN YOU SMILE LIKE THAT BEFORE, YAMADA.
YOU'RE CUTE!
WHAT THE HECK...?
NOW HE'S SAID IT...
YOU'RE CUTE!

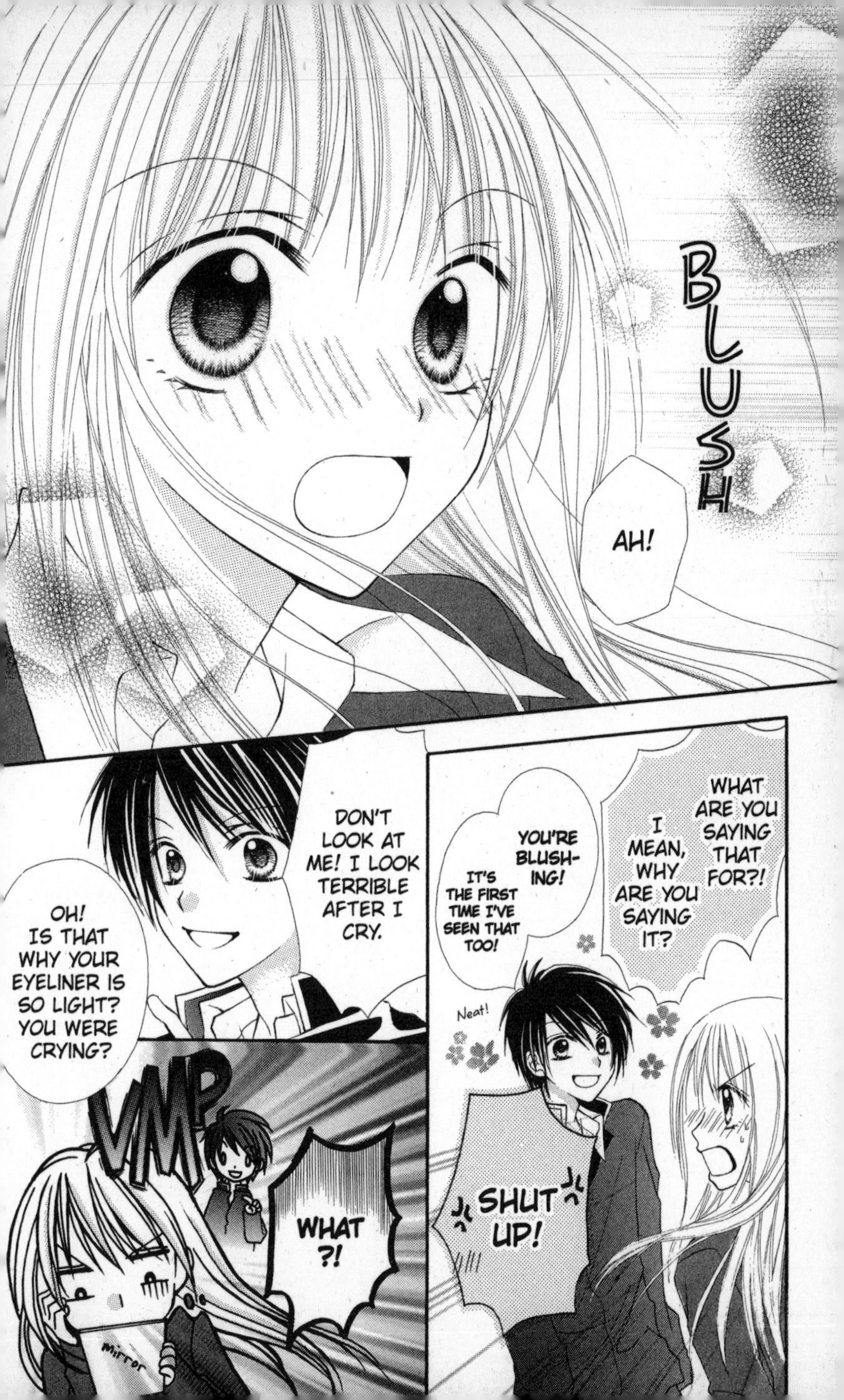
BLUSH
AH!
WHAT ARE YOU SAYING THAT FOR?!
I MEAN, WHY ARE YOU SAYING IT?
YOU'RE BLUSH-ING!
IT'S THE FIRST TIME I'VE SEEN THAT TOO!
Neat!
SHUT UP!
DON'T LOOK AT ME! I LOOK TERRIBLE AFTER I CRY.
OH! IS THAT WHY YOUR EYELINER IS SO LIGHT? YOU WERE CRYING?
VMP
WHAT ?!
mirror

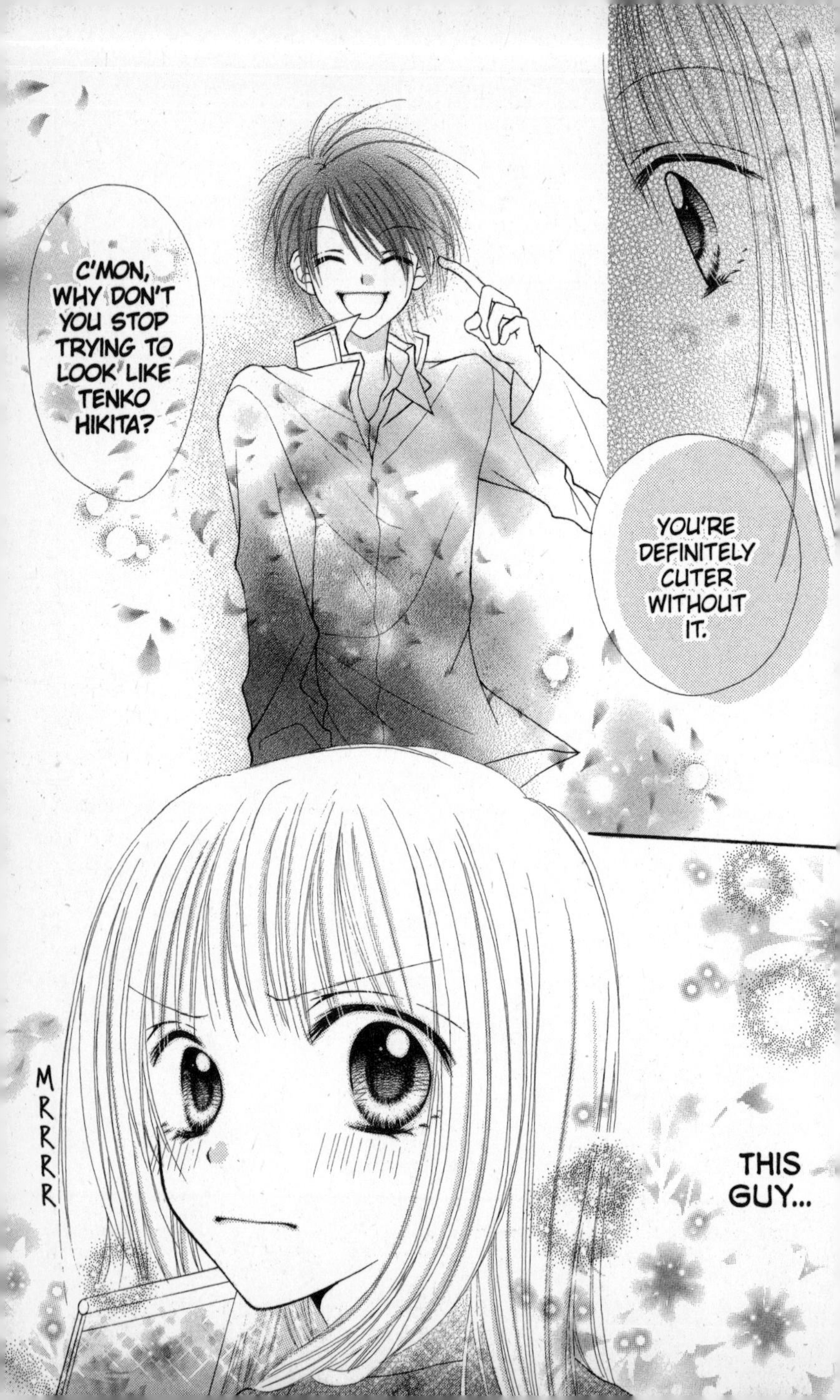
C'MON, WHY DON'T YOU STOP TRYING TO LOOK LIKE TENKO HIKITA?
YOU'RE DEFINITELY CUTER WITHOUT IT.
THIS GUY...
MRRRR

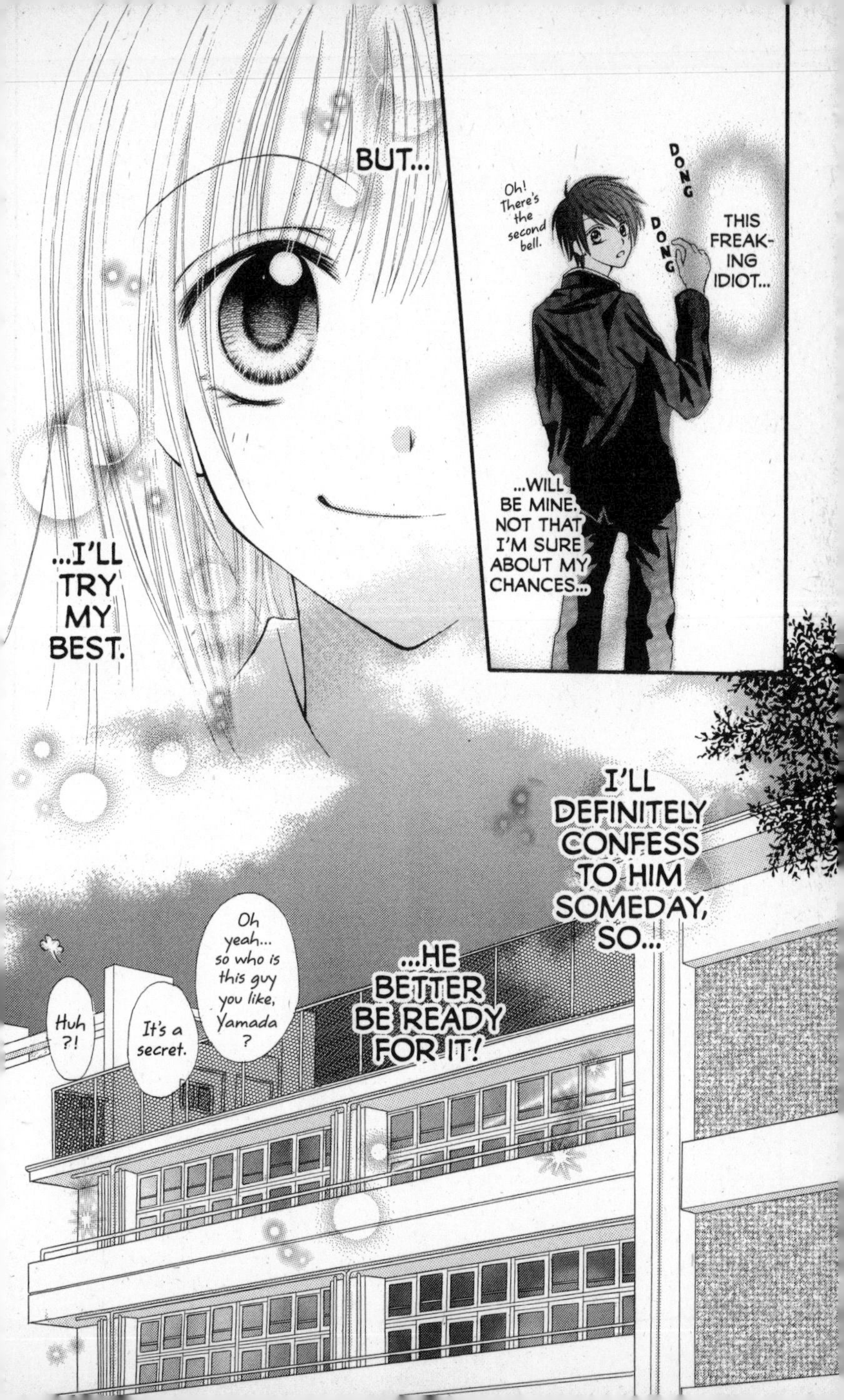

Oh! There's the second bell.
DONG
DONG
THIS FREAKING IDIOT...
...WILL BE MINE. NOT THAT I'M SURE ABOUT MY CHANCES...
BUT...
...I'LL TRY MY BEST.
I'LL DEFINITELY CONFESS TO HIM SOMEDAY, SO...
...HE BETTER BE READY FOR IT!
Oh yeah... so who is this guy you like, Yamada?
It's a secret.
Huh?!

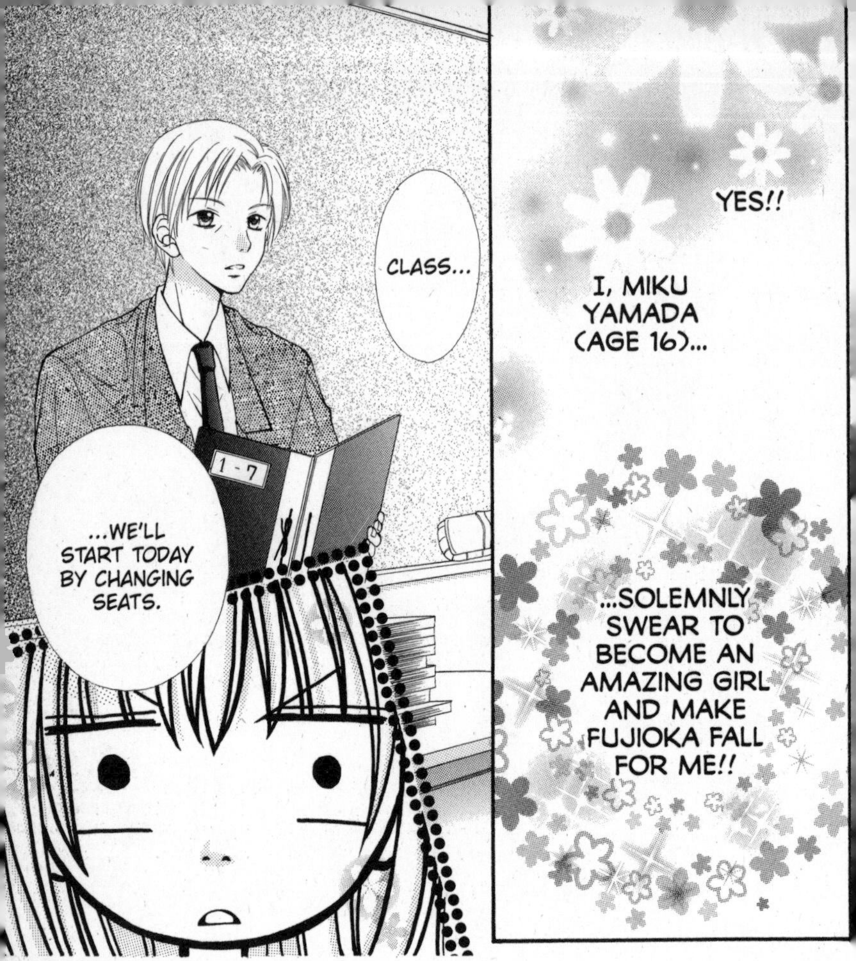
YES!!
I, MIKU YAMADA (AGE 16)...
...SOLEMNLY SWEAR TO BECOME AN AMAZING GIRL AND MAKE FUJIOKA FALL FOR ME!!
CLASS...
...WE'LL START TODAY BY CHANGING SEATS.
1-7

SMALL TALK ①

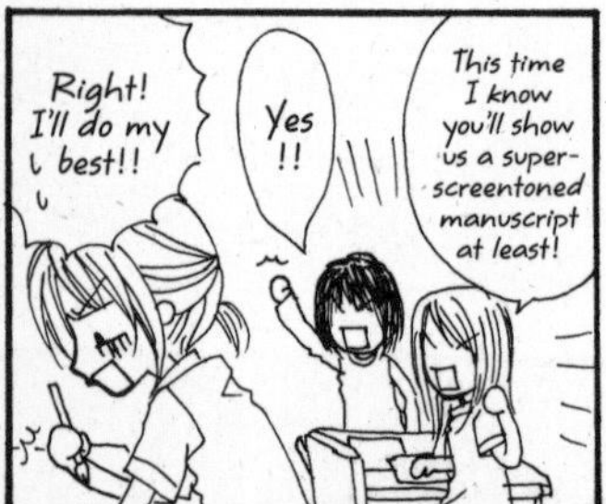
This time I know you'll show us a super-screentoned manuscript at least!
Yes !!
Right! I'll do my best!!

← During production of chapters 1-3, this was heard often.

Like all serialized mangaka, I only get around two weeks or ten days to draw each chapter of *Cactus*. It's my first tim drawing at this kind of pace, so I had a really hard time getting used to it in the beginning. As a result I ended up publishing really sparsely screentoned manuscripts each month... Ouch...

The serialization schedule so far has everything done far in advance—about a month before, actually. Even then, when I think of how I'd already finished chapter 2 by the time chapter 1 was published, it seems incredible to me! (laugh)

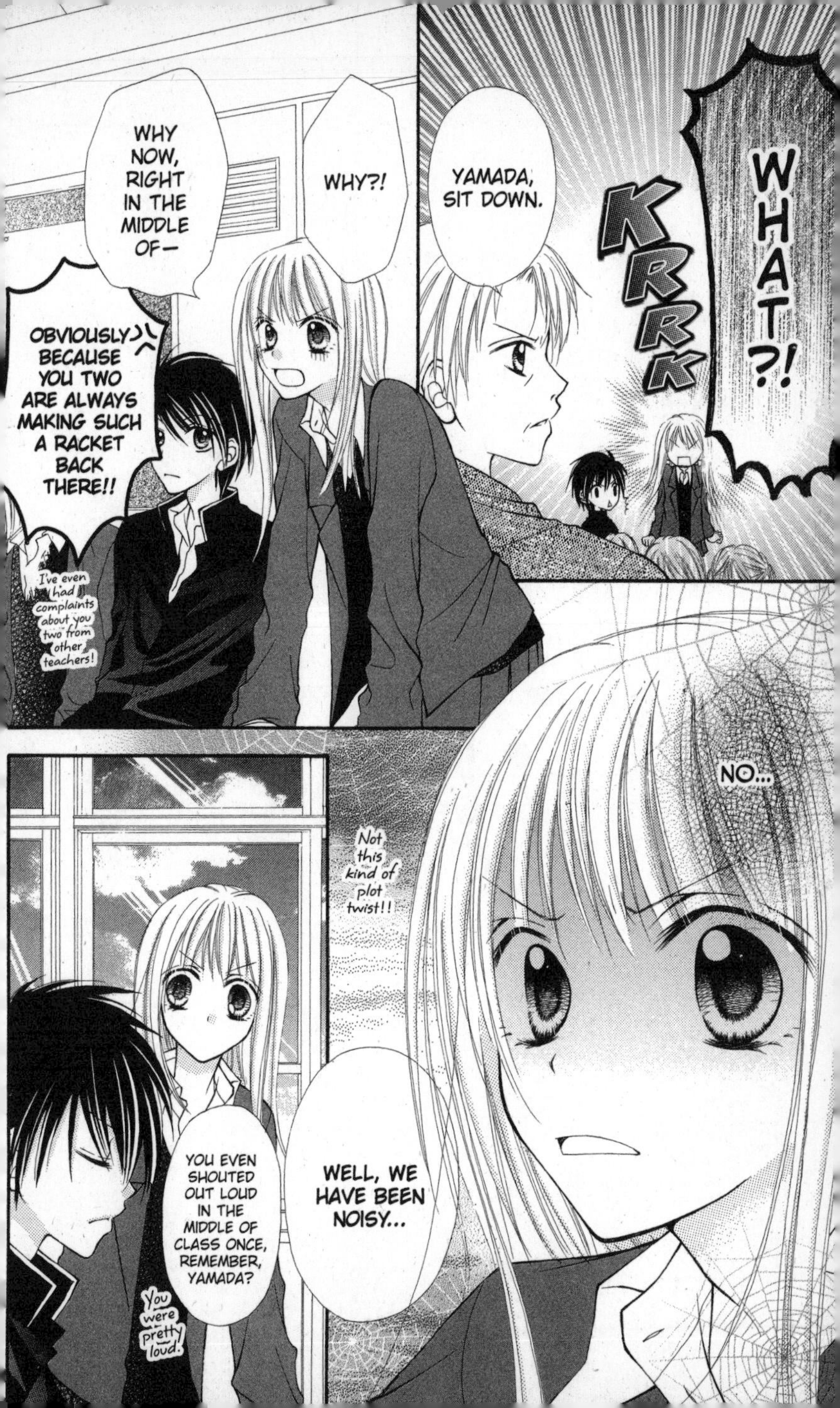

WHAT?!
KRRK
YAMADA, SIT DOWN.
WHY?!
WHY NOW, RIGHT IN THE MIDDLE OF—
OBVIOUSLY BECAUSE YOU TWO ARE ALWAYS MAKING SUCH A RACKET BACK THERE!!
I've even had complaints about you two from other teachers!
NO...
Not this kind of plot twist!!
WELL, WE HAVE BEEN NOISY...
YOU EVEN SHOUTED OUT LOUD IN THE MIDDLE OF CLASS ONCE, REMEMBER, YAMADA?
You were pretty loud!

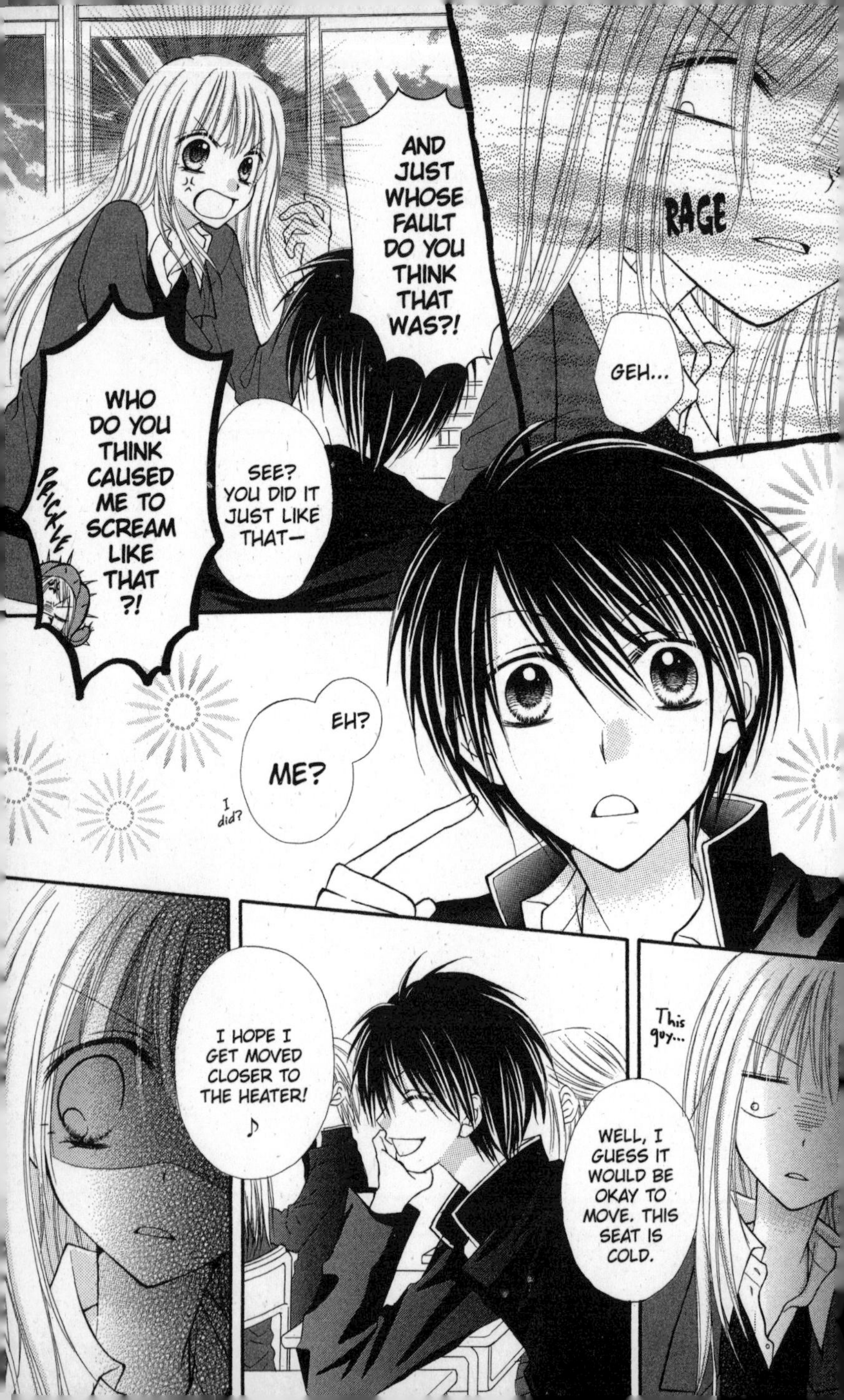
RAGE
AND JUST WHOSE FAULT DO YOU THINK THAT WAS?!
GEH...
SEE? YOU DID IT JUST LIKE THAT—
WHO DO YOU THINK CAUSED ME TO SCREAM LIKE THAT ?!
PRICKLE
EH?
ME?
I did?
This guy...
WELL, I GUESS IT WOULD BE OKAY TO MOVE. THIS SEAT IS COLD.
I HOPE I GET MOVED CLOSER TO THE HEATER! ♪

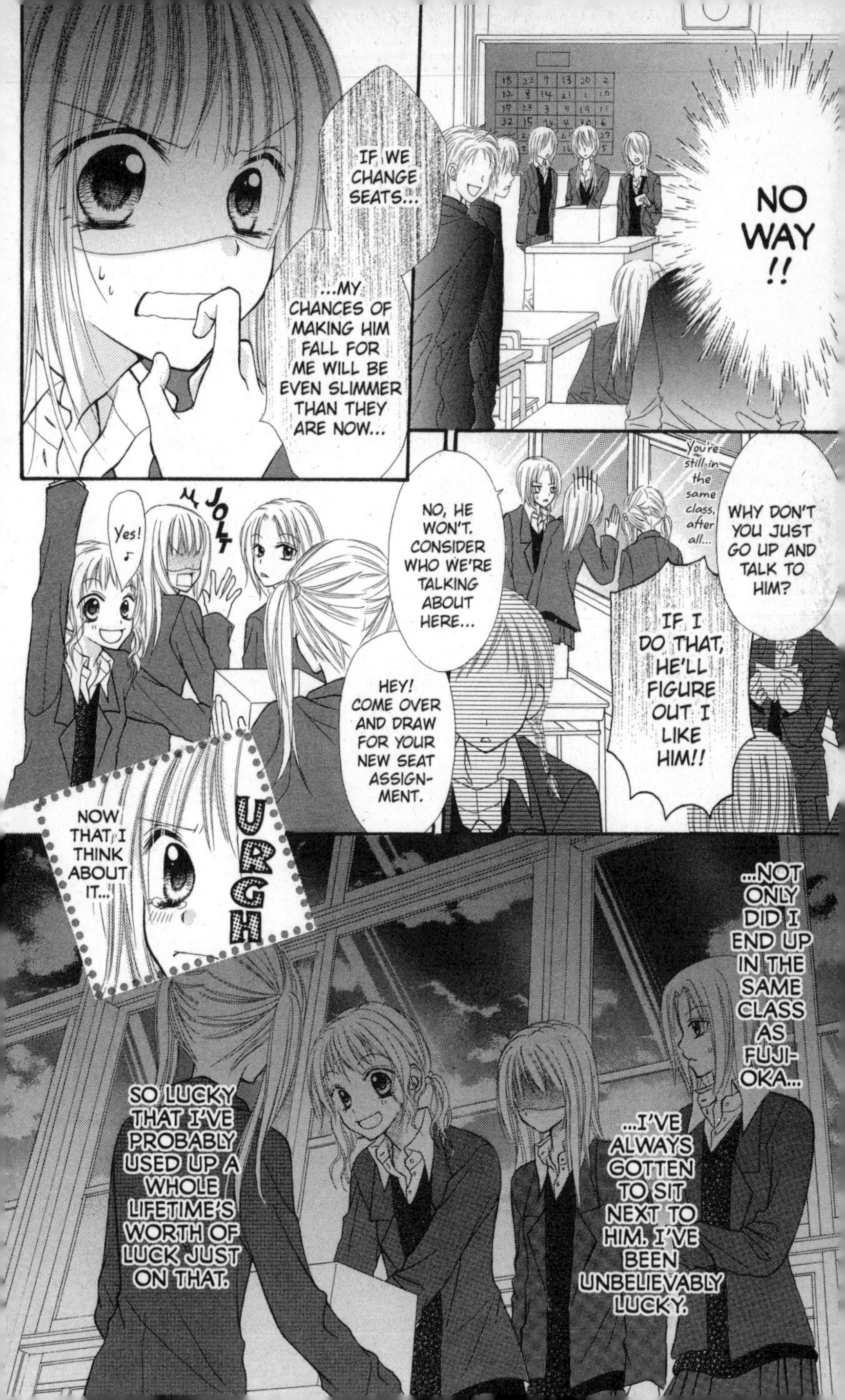
NO WAY!!
IF WE CHANGE SEATS...
...MY CHANCES OF MAKING HIM FALL FOR ME WILL BE EVEN SLIMMER THAN THEY ARE NOW...
WHY DON'T YOU JUST GO UP AND TALK TO HIM?
You're still in the same class, after all...
IF I DO THAT, HE'LL FIGURE OUT I LIKE HIM!!
NO, HE WON'T. CONSIDER WHO WE'RE TALKING ABOUT HERE...
HEY! COME OVER AND DRAW FOR YOUR NEW SEAT ASSIGNMENT.
JOLT
Yes! ♪
URGH
NOW THAT I THINK ABOUT IT...
...NOT ONLY DID I END UP IN THE SAME CLASS AS FUJI-OKA...
...I'VE ALWAYS GOTTEN TO SIT NEXT TO HIM. I'VE BEEN UNBELIEVABLY LUCKY.
SO LUCKY THAT I'VE PROBABLY USED UP A WHOLE LIFETIME'S WORTH OF LUCK JUST ON THAT.

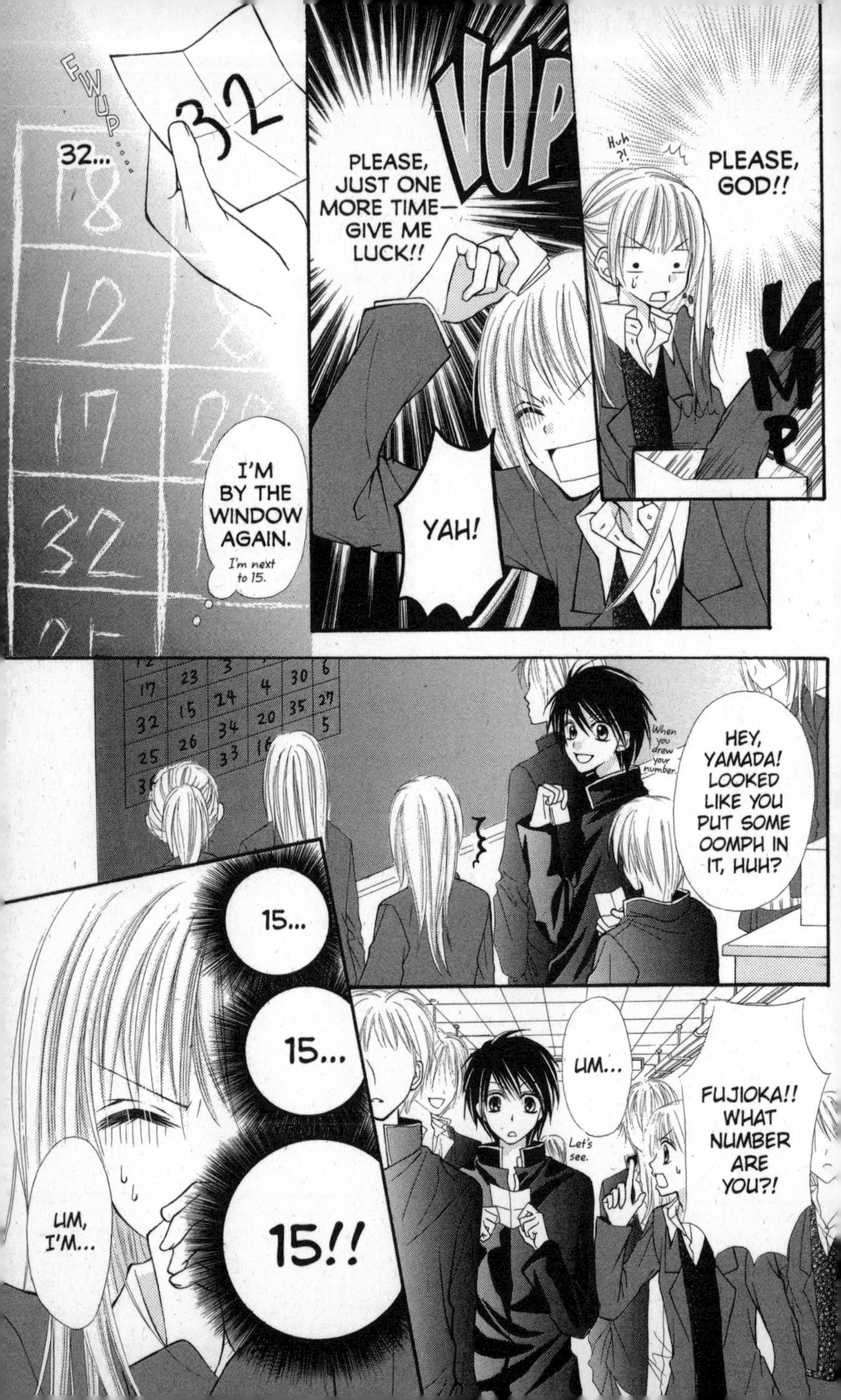

Huh ?!
PLEASE, GOD!!
UMP
VUP
PLEASE, JUST ONE MORE TIME—GIVE ME LUCK!!
YAH!
FWUP
32
32...
I'M BY THE WINDOW AGAIN.
I'm next to 15.
HEY, YAMADA! LOOKED LIKE YOU PUT SOME OOMPH IN IT, HUH?
When you drew your number.
FUJIOKA!! WHAT NUMBER ARE YOU?!
UM...
Let's see.
15...
15...
15!!
UM, I'M...

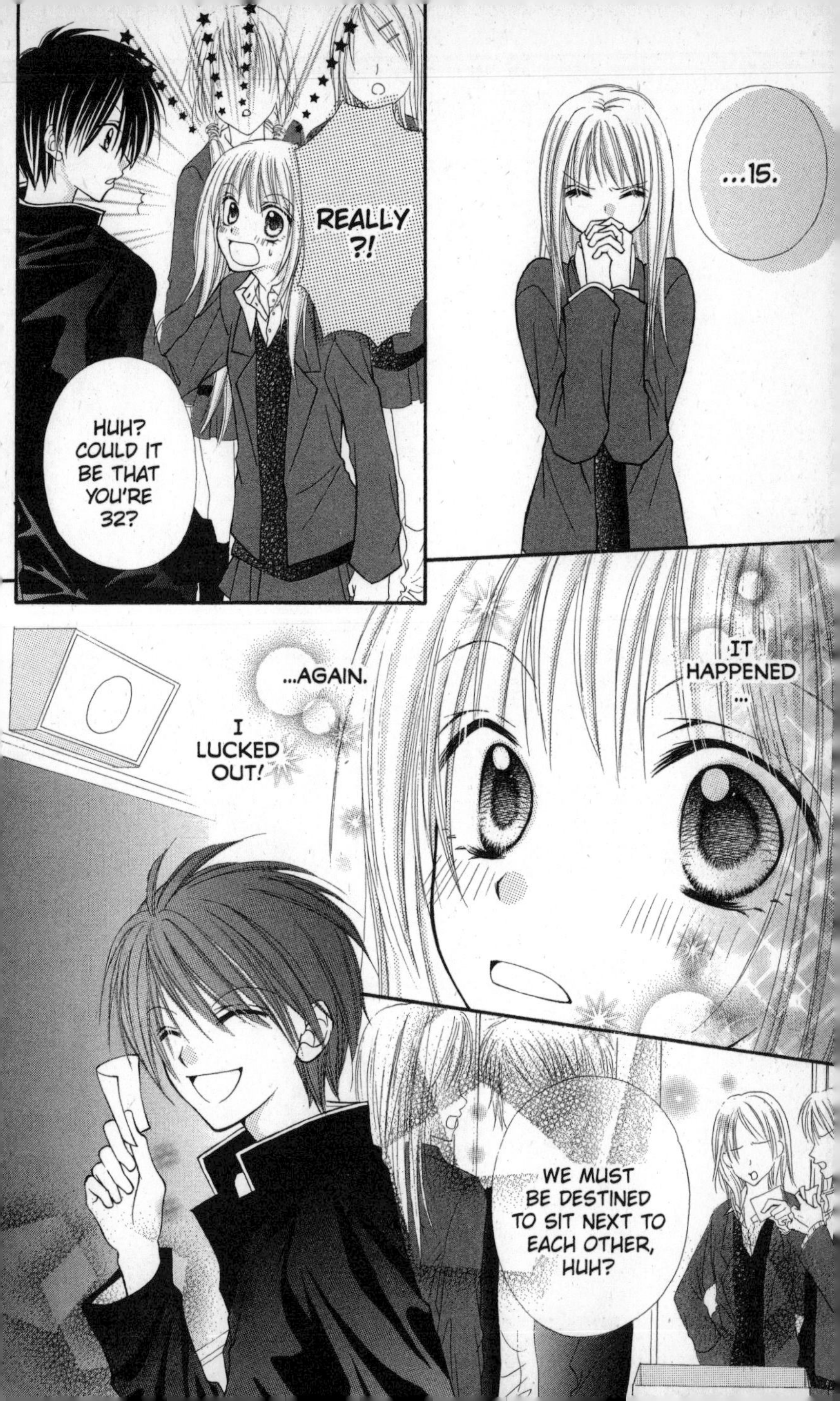
...15.
REALLY?!
HUH? COULD IT BE THAT YOU'RE 32?
IT HAPPENED...
...AGAIN.
I LUCKED OUT!
WE MUST BE DESTINED TO SIT NEXT TO EACH OTHER, HUH?

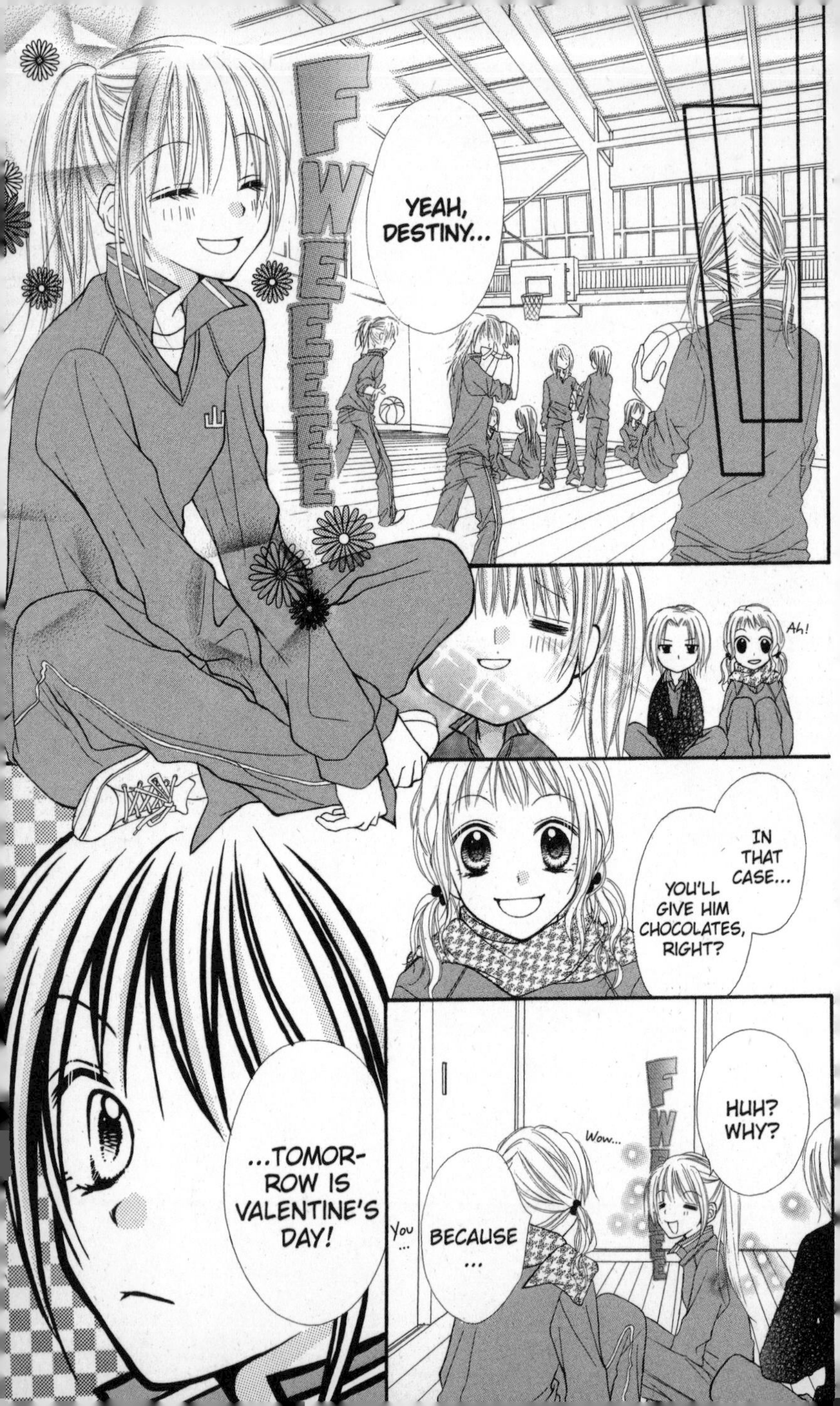
FWEEEEE
YEAH, DESTINY...
Ah!
IN THAT CASE...
YOU'LL GIVE HIM CHOCOLATES, RIGHT?
HUH? WHY?
FWEEE
Wow...
BECAUSE ...
You ...
...TOMOR-ROW IS VALENTINE'S DAY!

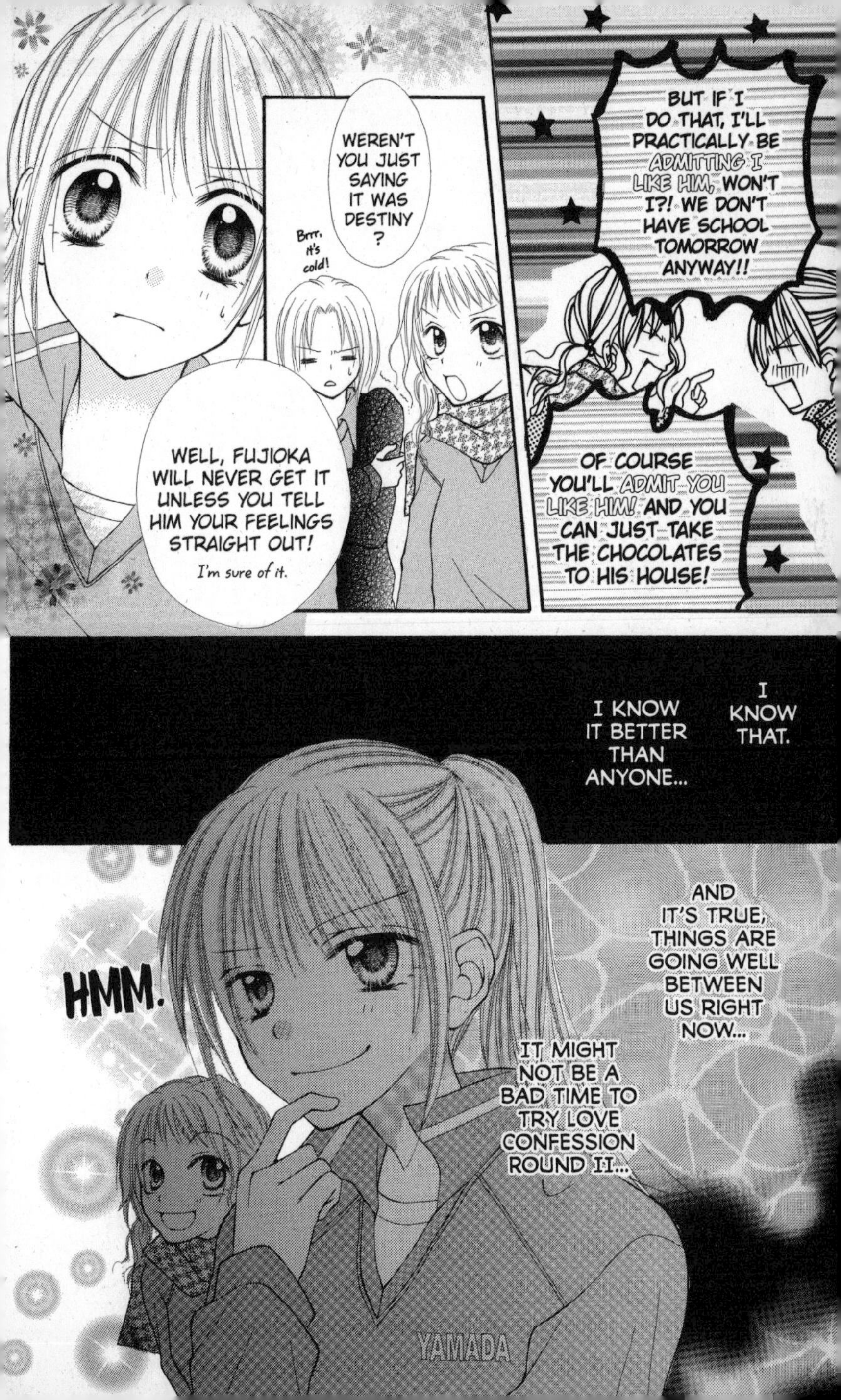
BUT IF I DO THAT, I'LL PRACTICALLY BE ADMITTING I LIKE HIM, WON'T I?! WE DON'T HAVE SCHOOL TOMORROW ANYWAY!!
OF COURSE YOU'LL ADMIT YOU LIKE HIM! AND YOU CAN JUST TAKE THE CHOCOLATES TO HIS HOUSE!
WEREN'T YOU JUST SAYING IT WAS DESTINY?
Brrr, it's cold!
WELL, FUJIOKA WILL NEVER GET IT UNLESS YOU TELL HIM YOUR FEELINGS STRAIGHT OUT!
I'm sure of it.
I KNOW THAT.
I KNOW IT BETTER THAN ANYONE...
AND IT'S TRUE, THINGS ARE GOING WELL BETWEEN US RIGHT NOW...
IT MIGHT NOT BE A BAD TIME TO TRY LOVE CONFESSION ROUND II...
HMM.
YAMADA

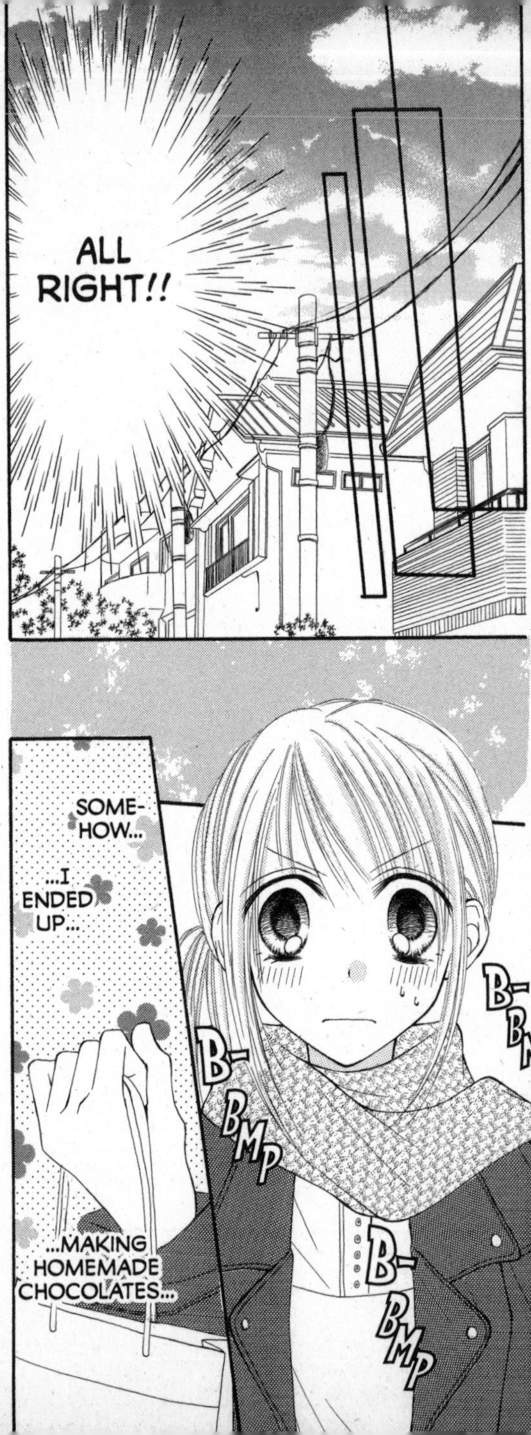
ALL RIGHT!!
B-BMP
SOME-HOW...
...I ENDED UP...
B-BMP
B-BMP
...MAKING HOMEMADE CHOCOLATES...

3

It seems a lot of people have written in requesting my bio. Here it is!

↓

- Nana Haruta (Real name. Okay, kidding—it's a pen name.)
- Birthday: June 30 (Same as Sailor **on!)
- Blood Type: O ("Sociable." I'm not.)
- Height: 157 cm (Give or take.)
- Born in Niigata Prefecture. (Where awful pop music resides.)
- I'm the younger of two sisters. (We're three years apart.)
- I love Disney to the extreme. (But I am not too fond of the way the characters are drawn overseas.)
- I truly hate bugs. (Their very existence repulses me.)

I also love "Ojarumaru!" It really comforts me, and it's so darn cute! ♥ Also, I really hate horror and ghost movies. They're so scary!! Seriously, just don't show them to me.

I'm often asked what my favorite bands are, but I don't really have any, to be honest. ♪ There are artists I like, but none to the degree that I could call myself a fan. That said, in July I'm going to a w-inds concert with my friend Marinakko Umezawa! I'm so looking forward to it! In the w-inds DVD Marinakko showed me, the band looked so incredibly cool...! I immediately jumped on the phone and got us tickets to their next concert. I'm glad we got tickets!!

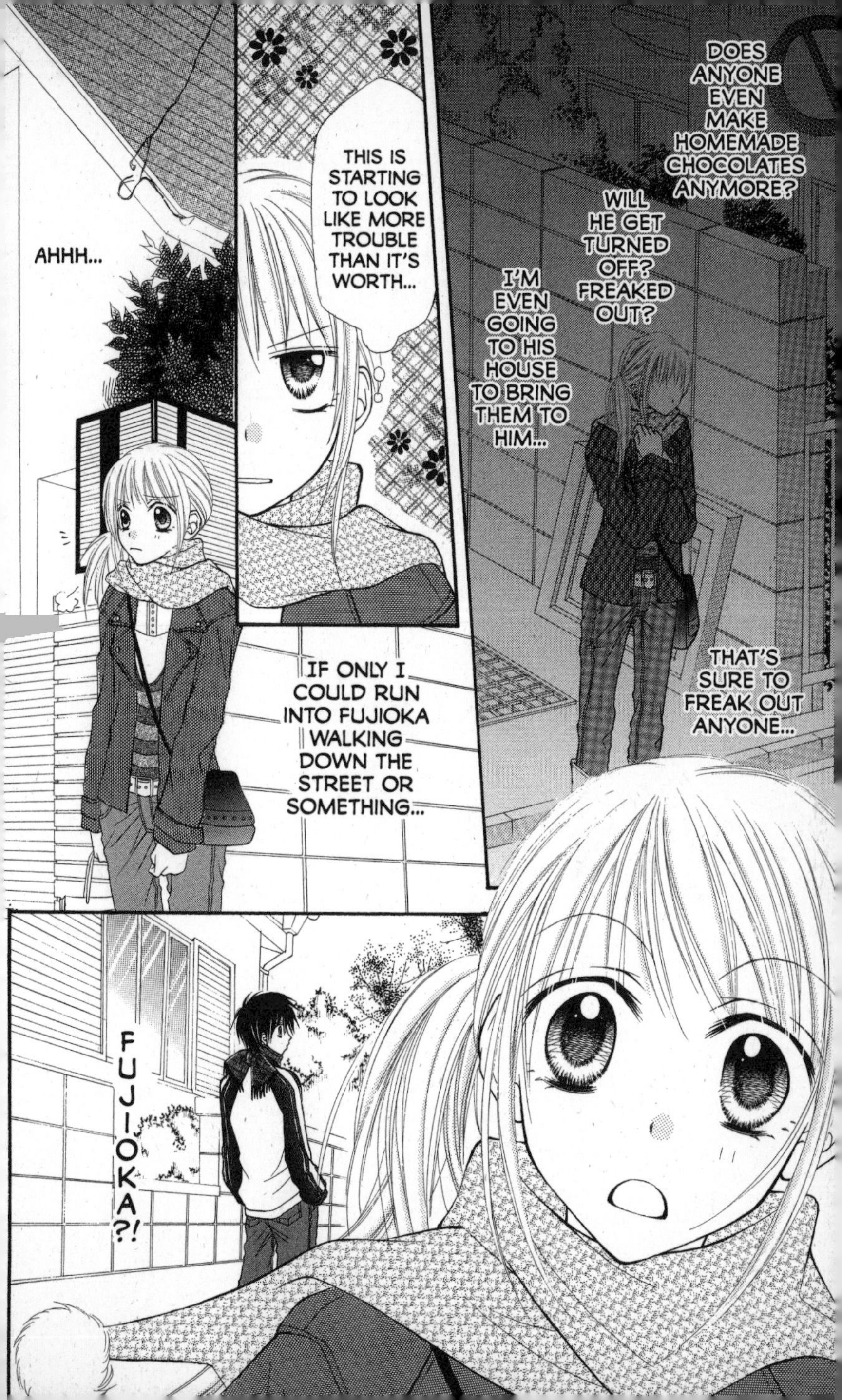
DOES ANYONE EVEN MAKE HOMEMADE CHOCOLATES ANYMORE?
WILL HE GET TURNED OFF? FREAKED OUT?
I'M EVEN GOING TO HIS HOUSE TO BRING THEM TO HIM...
THAT'S SURE TO FREAK OUT ANYONE...
THIS IS STARTING TO LOOK LIKE MORE TROUBLE THAN IT'S WORTH...
AHHH...
IF ONLY I COULD RUN INTO FUJIOKA WALKING DOWN THE STREET OR SOMETHING...
FUJIOKA?!

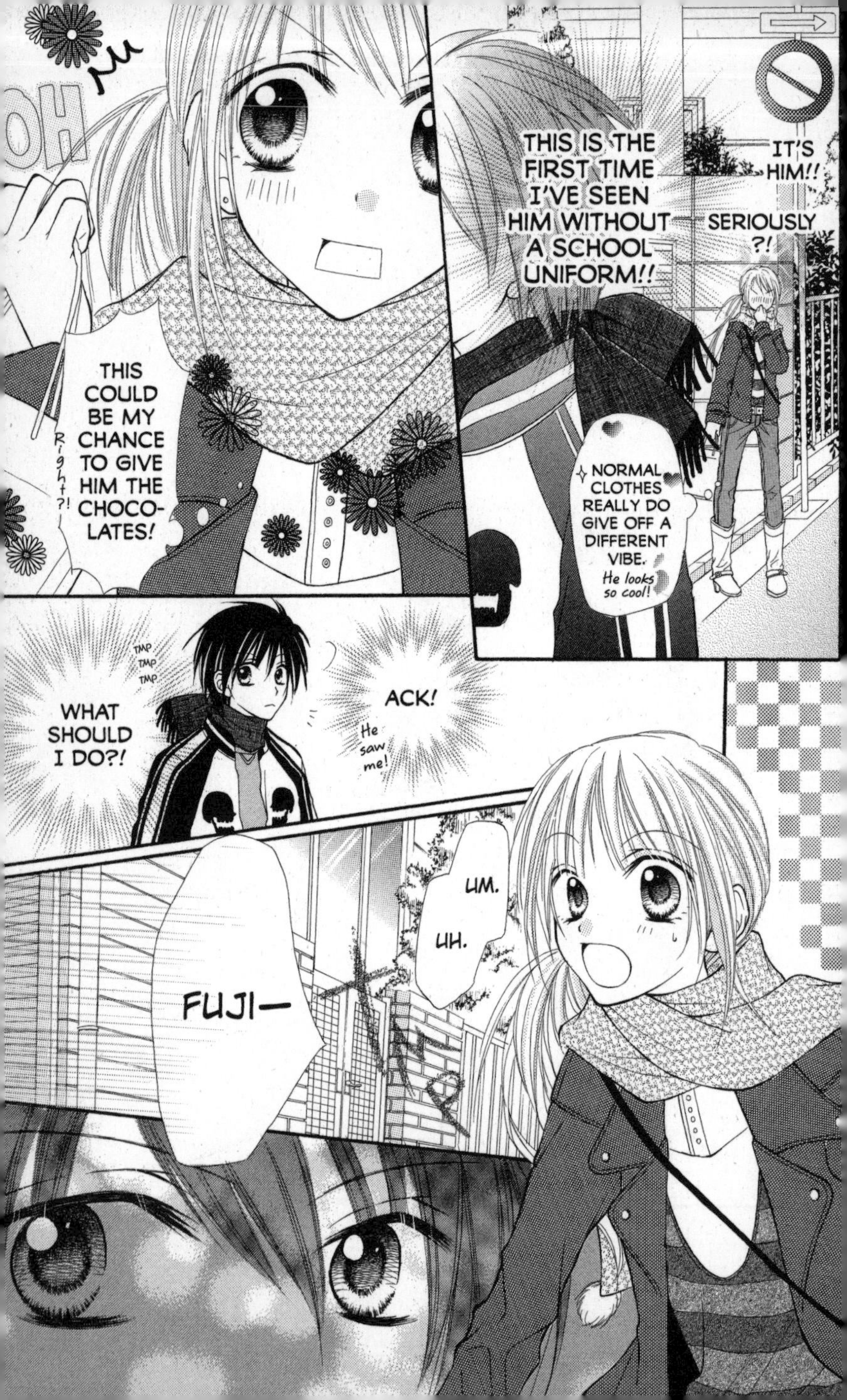
IT'S HIM!!
SERIOUSLY?!
THIS IS THE FIRST TIME I'VE SEEN HIM WITHOUT A SCHOOL UNIFORM!!
NORMAL CLOTHES REALLY DO GIVE OFF A DIFFERENT VIBE.
He looks so cool!
OH
THIS COULD BE MY CHANCE TO GIVE HIM THE CHOCO-LATES!
Right?!
ACK!
He saw me!
TMP TMP TMP
WHAT SHOULD I DO?!
UM.
UH.
FUJI—

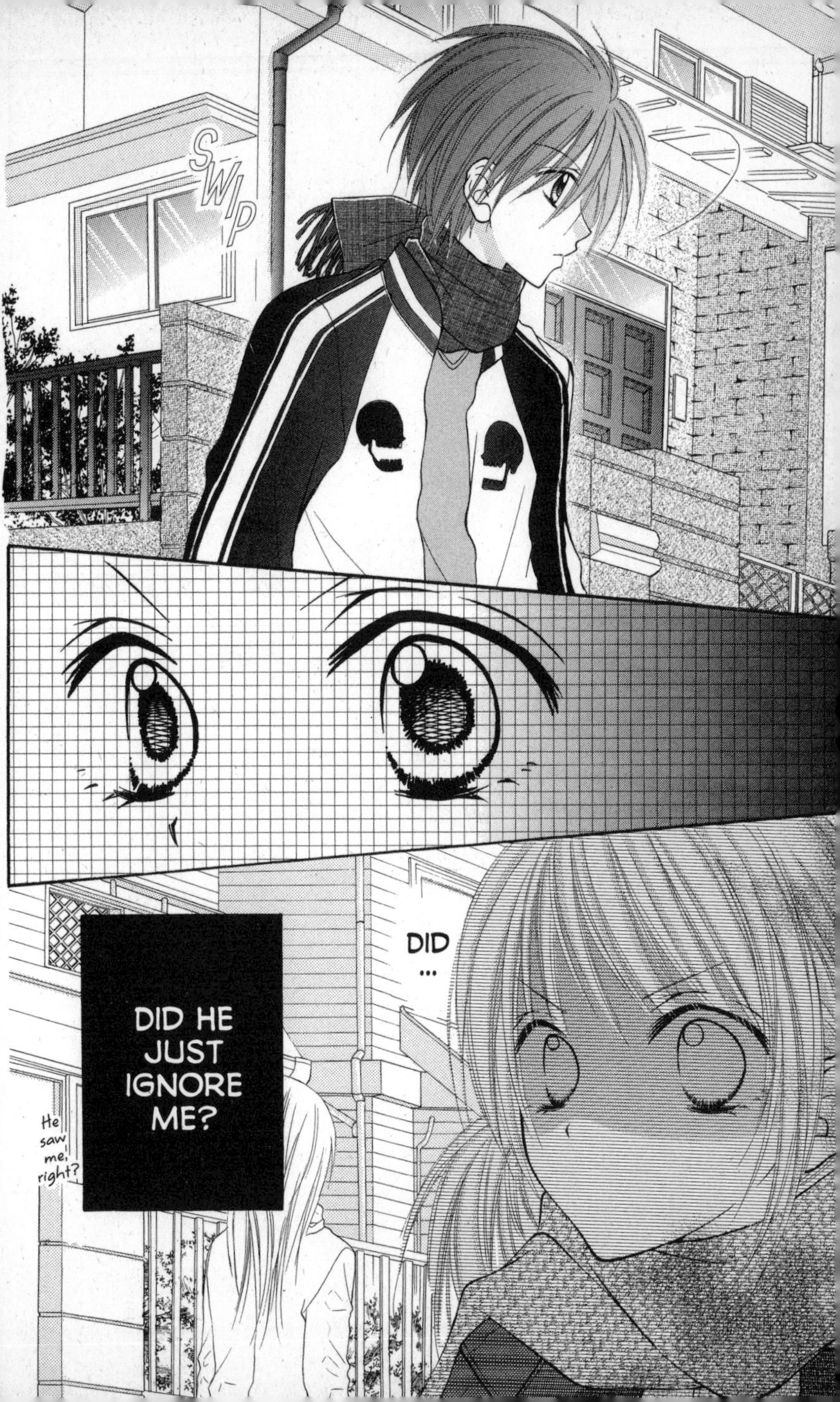
SWIP
DID...
DID HE JUST IGNORE ME?
He saw me, right?

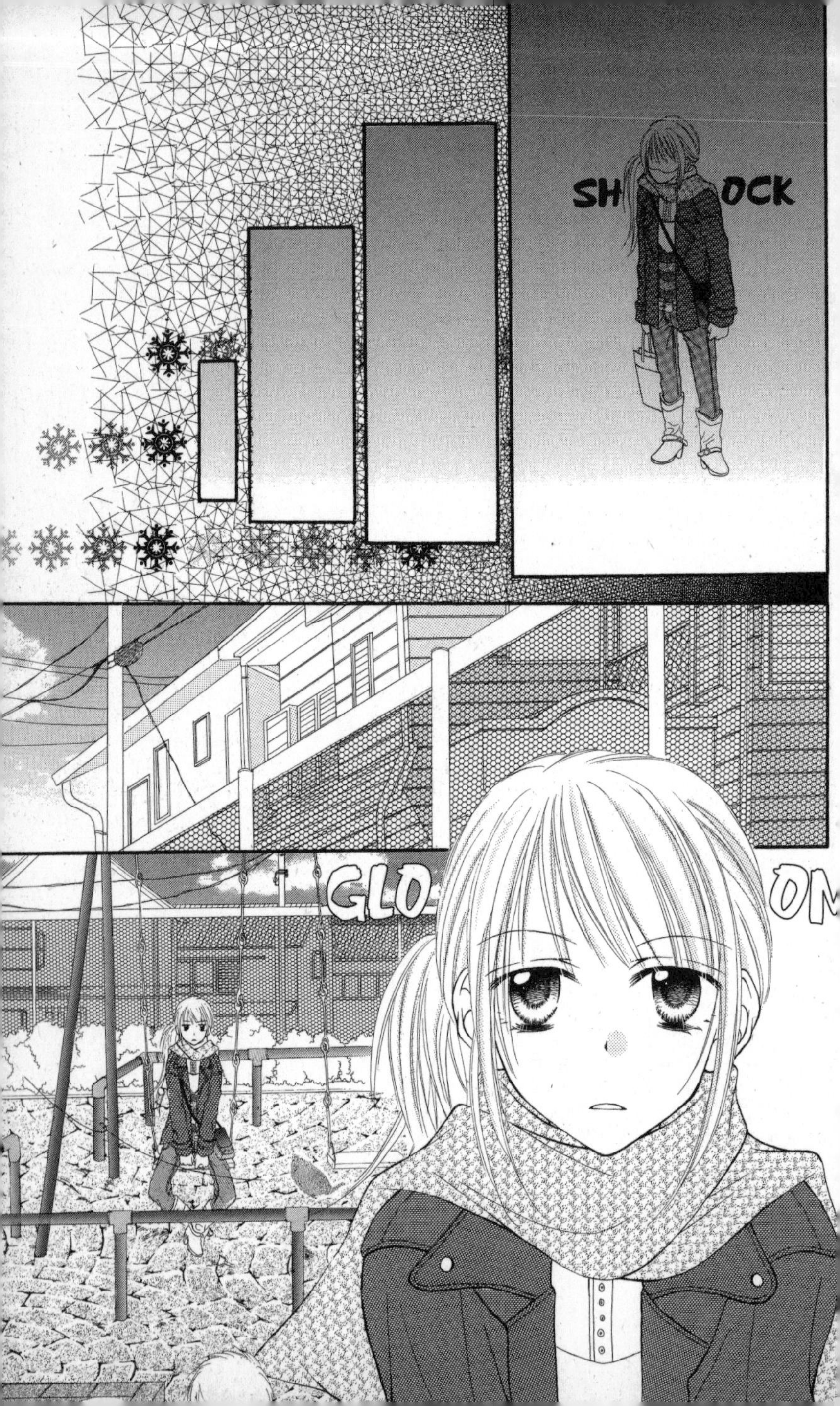
SHOCK
GLOOM

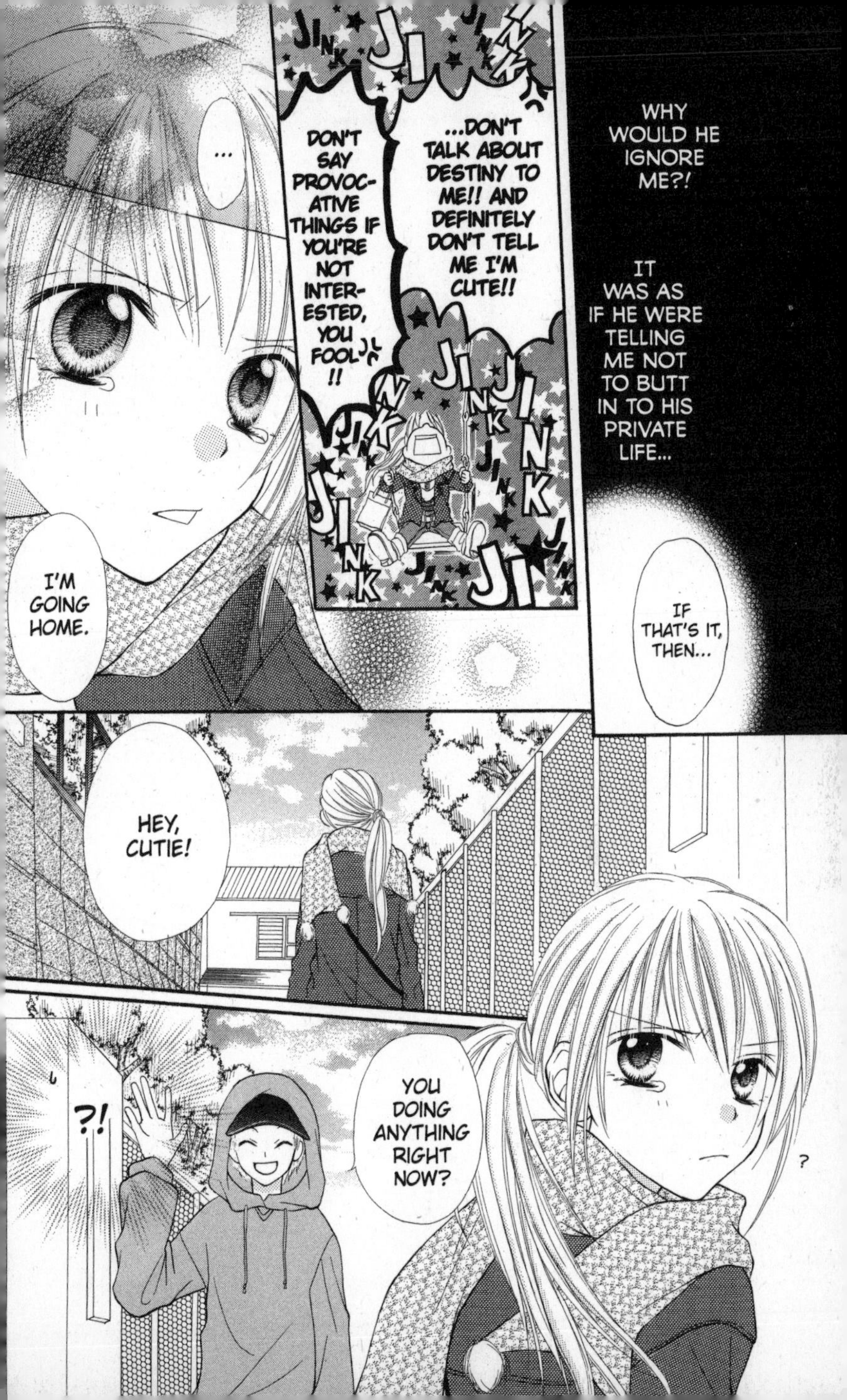
WHY WOULD HE IGNORE ME?!
IT WAS AS IF HE WERE TELLING ME NOT TO BUTT IN TO HIS PRIVATE LIFE...
IF THAT'S IT, THEN...
JINK JI JINK
...DON'T TALK ABOUT DESTINY TO ME!! AND DEFINITELY DON'T TELL ME I'M CUTE!!
DON'T SAY PROVOC-ATIVE THINGS IF YOU'RE NOT INTER-ESTED, YOU FOOL!!
JINK JI JINK JINK JI JINK JI JINK
...
I'M GOING HOME.
HEY, CUTIE!
?
YOU DOING ANYTHING RIGHT NOW?
?!

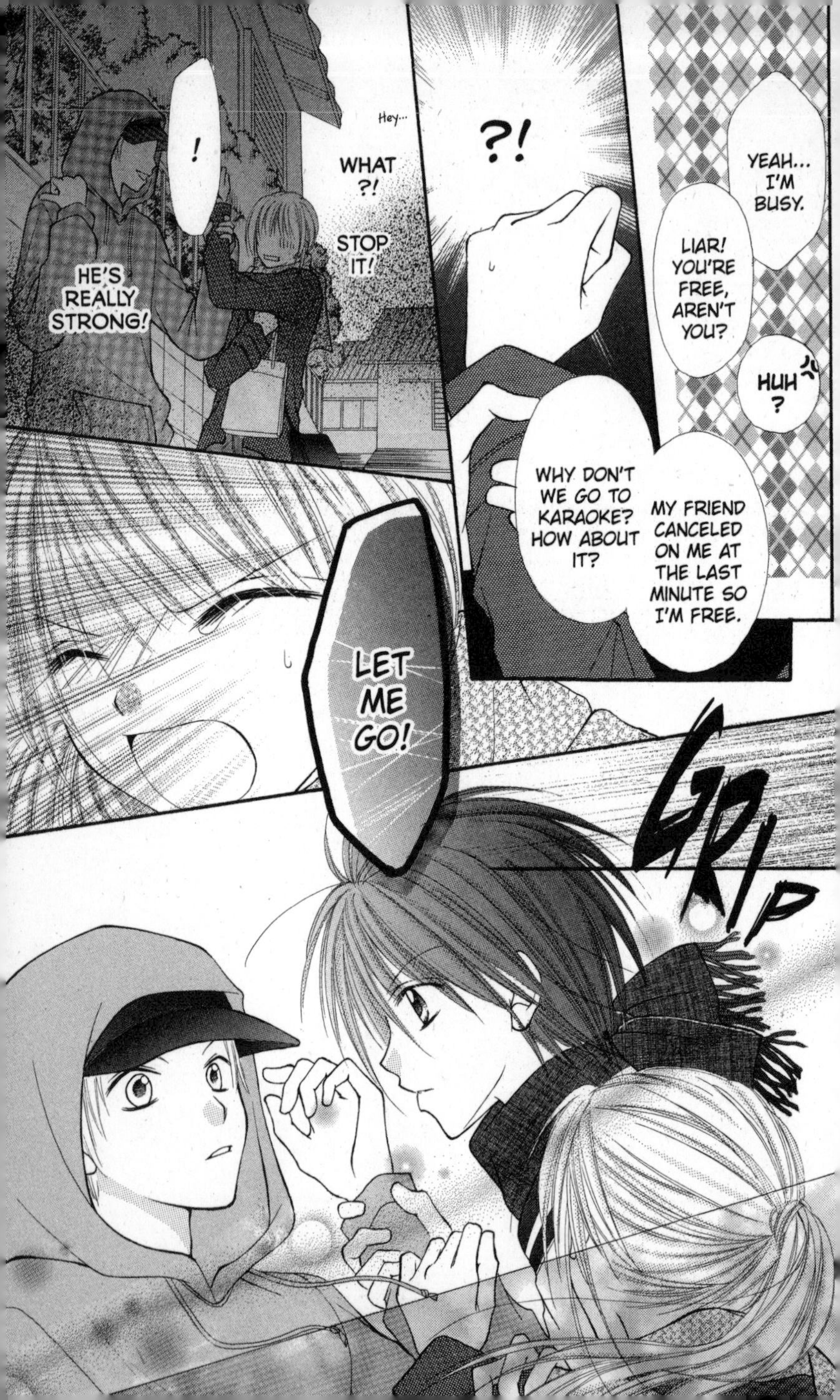
YEAH... I'M BUSY.
LIAR! YOU'RE FREE, AREN'T YOU?
HUH?
MY FRIEND CANCELED ON ME AT THE LAST MINUTE SO I'M FREE.
WHY DON'T WE GO TO KARAOKE? HOW ABOUT IT?
?!
Hey...
WHAT ?!
!
STOP IT!
HE'S REALLY STRONG!
LET ME GO!
GRIP

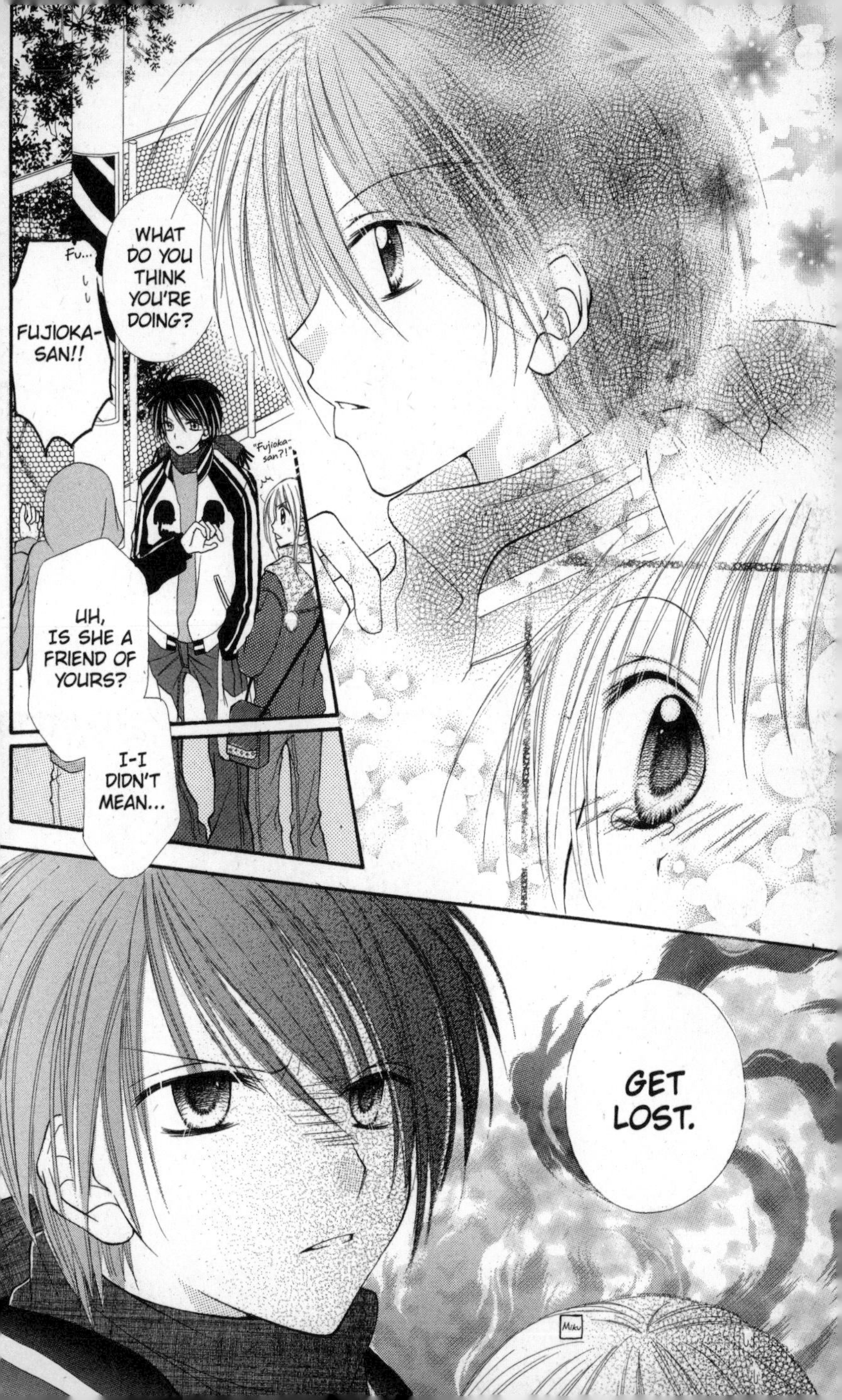
WHAT DO YOU THINK YOU'RE DOING?
Fu...
FUJIOKA-SAN!!
"Fujioka-san?!"
UH, IS SHE A FRIEND OF YOURS?
I-I DIDN'T MEAN...
GET LOST.
Miku

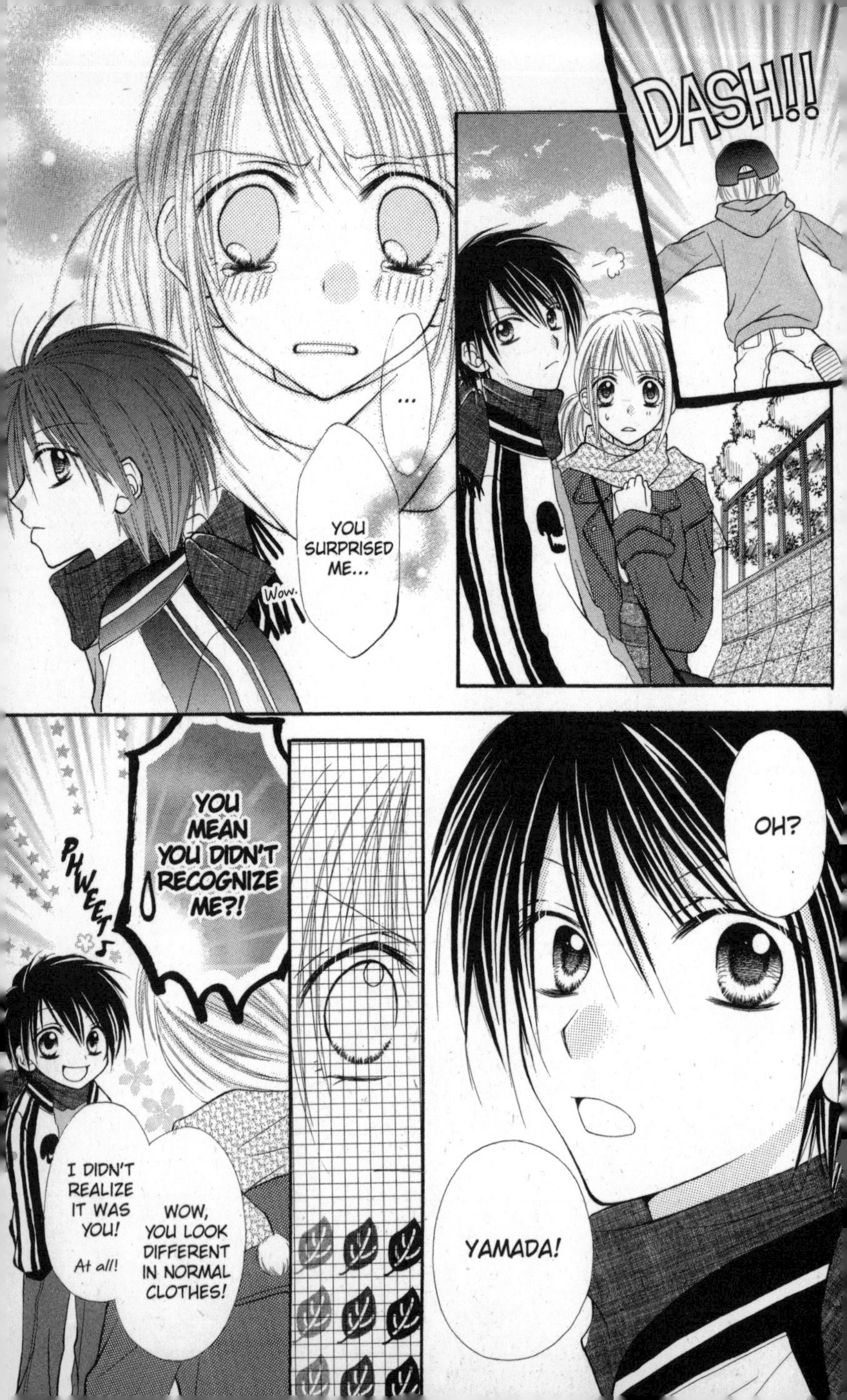
DASH!!
...
YOU SURPRISED ME...
Wow.
OH?
YAMADA!
YOU MEAN YOU DIDN'T RECOGNIZE ME?!
PHWEET
WOW, YOU LOOK DIFFERENT IN NORMAL CLOTHES!
I DIDN'T REALIZE IT WAS YOU!
At all!

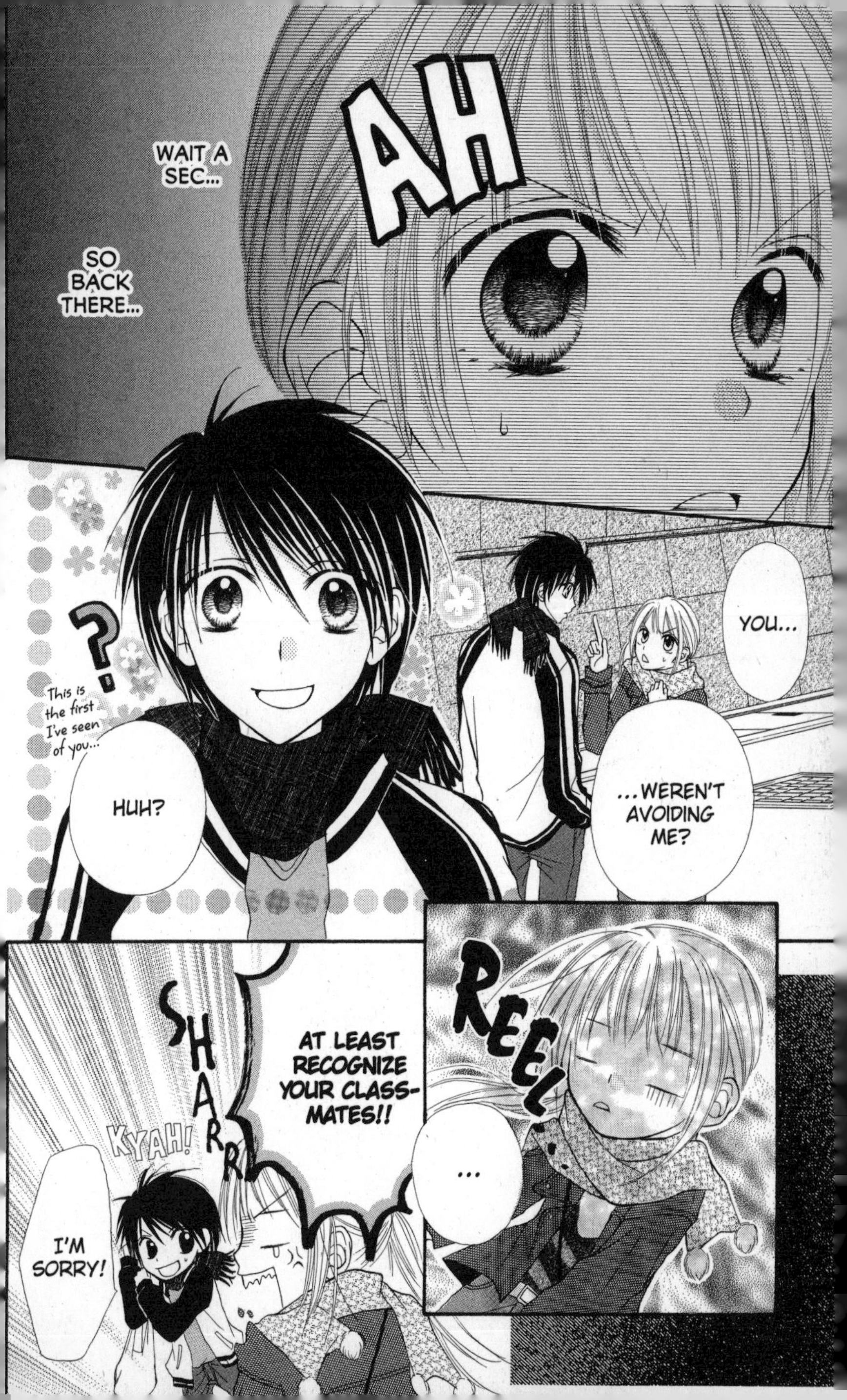
AH
WAIT A SEC...
SO BACK THERE...
YOU...
...WEREN'T AVOIDING ME?
HUH?
?
This is the first I've seen of you...
REEL
...
AT LEAST RECOGNIZE YOUR CLASS-MATES!!
SHARRR
KYAH!
I'M SORRY!

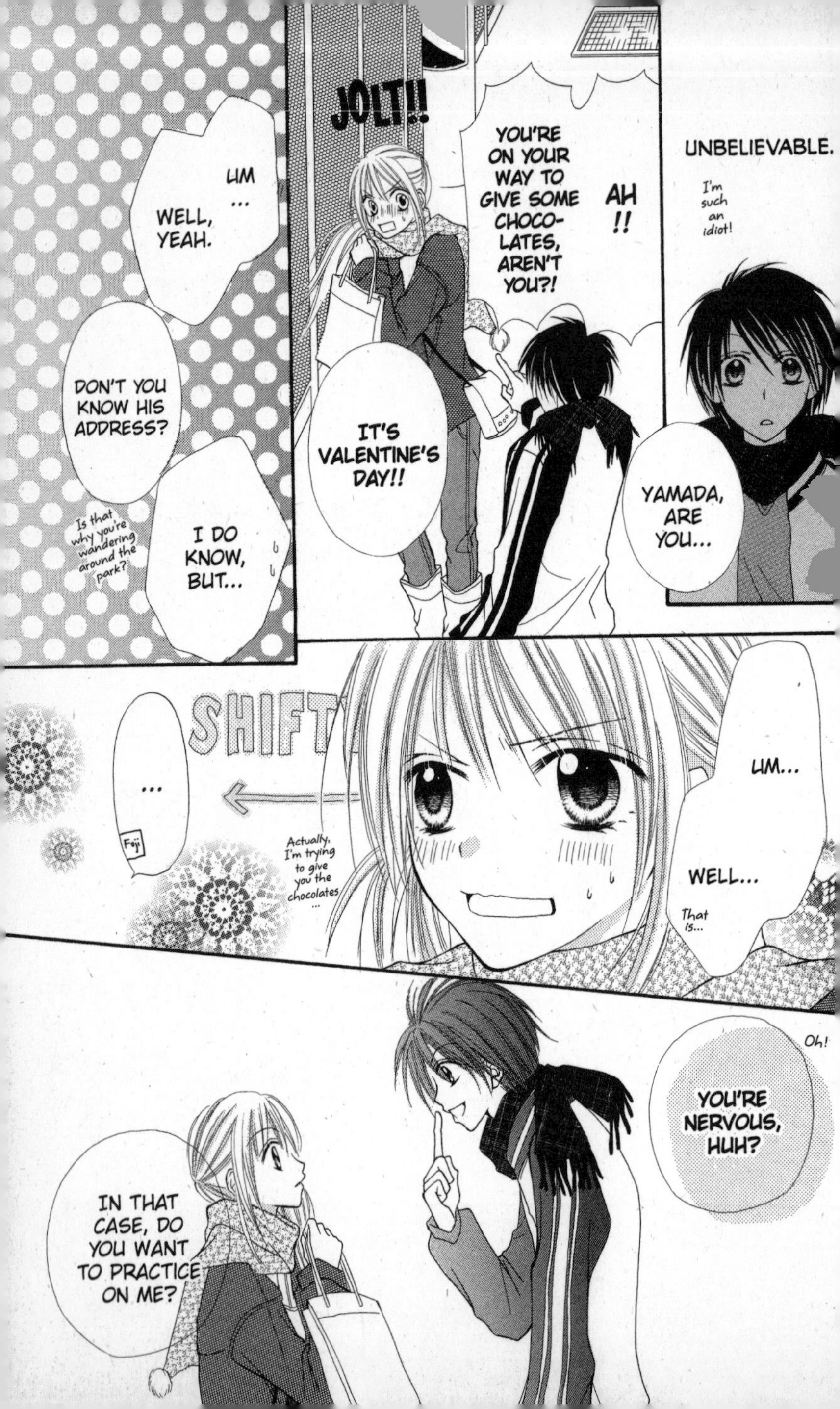
UNBELIEVABLE.
I'm such an idiot!
YAMADA, ARE YOU...
JOLT!!
YOU'RE ON YOUR WAY TO GIVE SOME CHOCO-LATES, AREN'T YOU?!
AH!!
IT'S VALENTINE'S DAY!!
UM... WELL, YEAH.
DON'T YOU KNOW HIS ADDRESS?
Is that why you're wandering around the park?
I DO KNOW, BUT...
UM...
WELL...
That is...
Actually, I'm trying to give you the chocolates...
SHIFT
...
Fuji
Oh!
YOU'RE NERVOUS, HUH?
IN THAT CASE, DO YOU WANT TO PRACTICE ON ME?

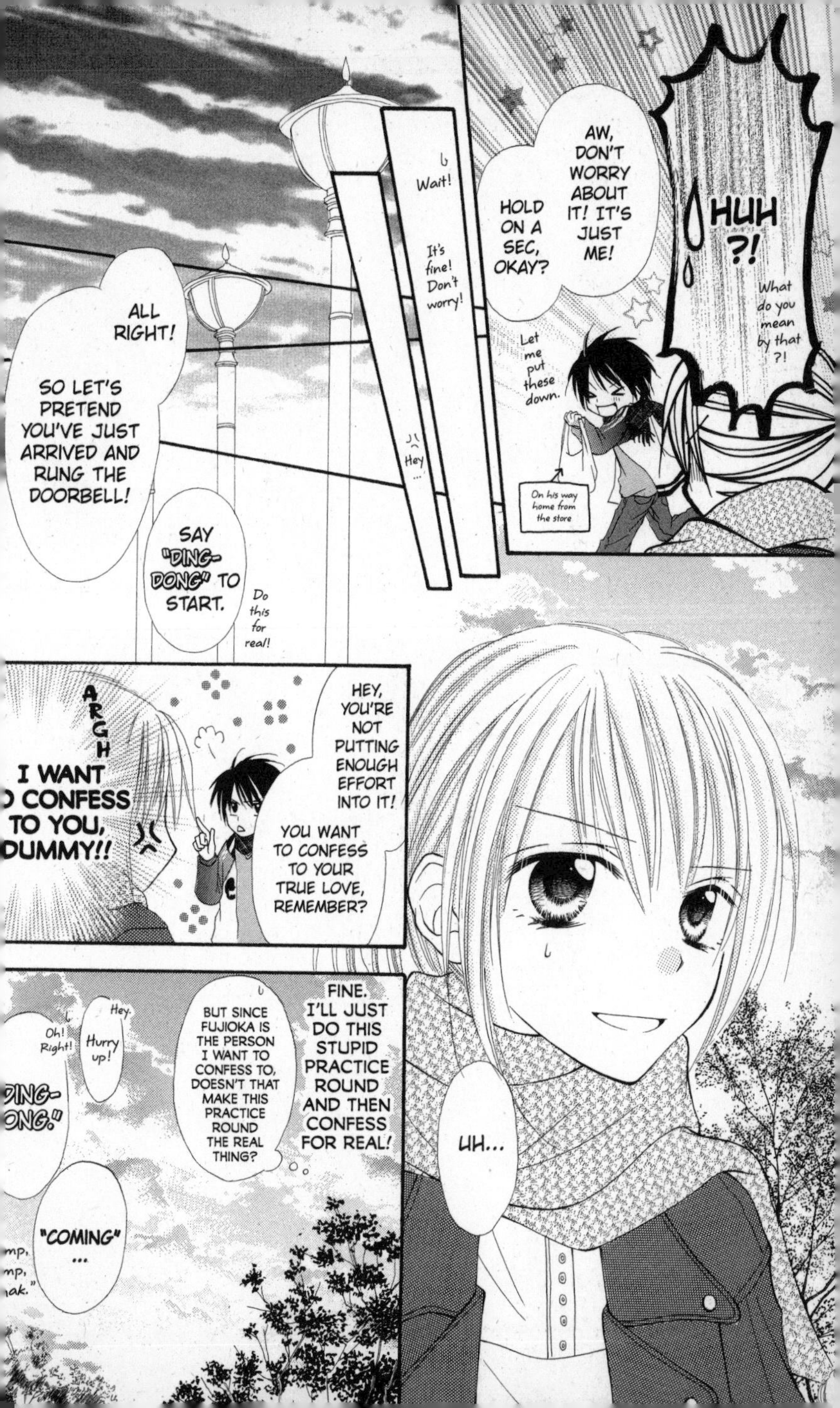
HUH ?!
What do you mean by that ?!
AW, DON'T WORRY ABOUT IT! IT'S JUST ME!
HOLD ON A SEC, OKAY?
Let me put these down.
On his way home from the store
Wait!
It's fine! Don't worry!
Hey...
ALL RIGHT!
SO LET'S PRETEND YOU'VE JUST ARRIVED AND RUNG THE DOORBELL!
SAY "DING-DONG" TO START.
Do this for real!
UH...
HEY, YOU'RE NOT PUTTING ENOUGH EFFORT INTO IT!
YOU WANT TO CONFESS TO YOUR TRUE LOVE, REMEMBER?
ARGH
I WANT O CONFESS TO YOU, DUMMY!!
FINE. I'LL JUST DO THIS STUPID PRACTICE ROUND AND THEN CONFESS FOR REAL!
BUT SINCE FUJIOKA IS THE PERSON I WANT TO CONFESS TO, DOESN'T THAT MAKE THIS PRACTICE ROUND THE REAL THING?
Hey. Hurry up!
Oh! Right!
"COMING" ...

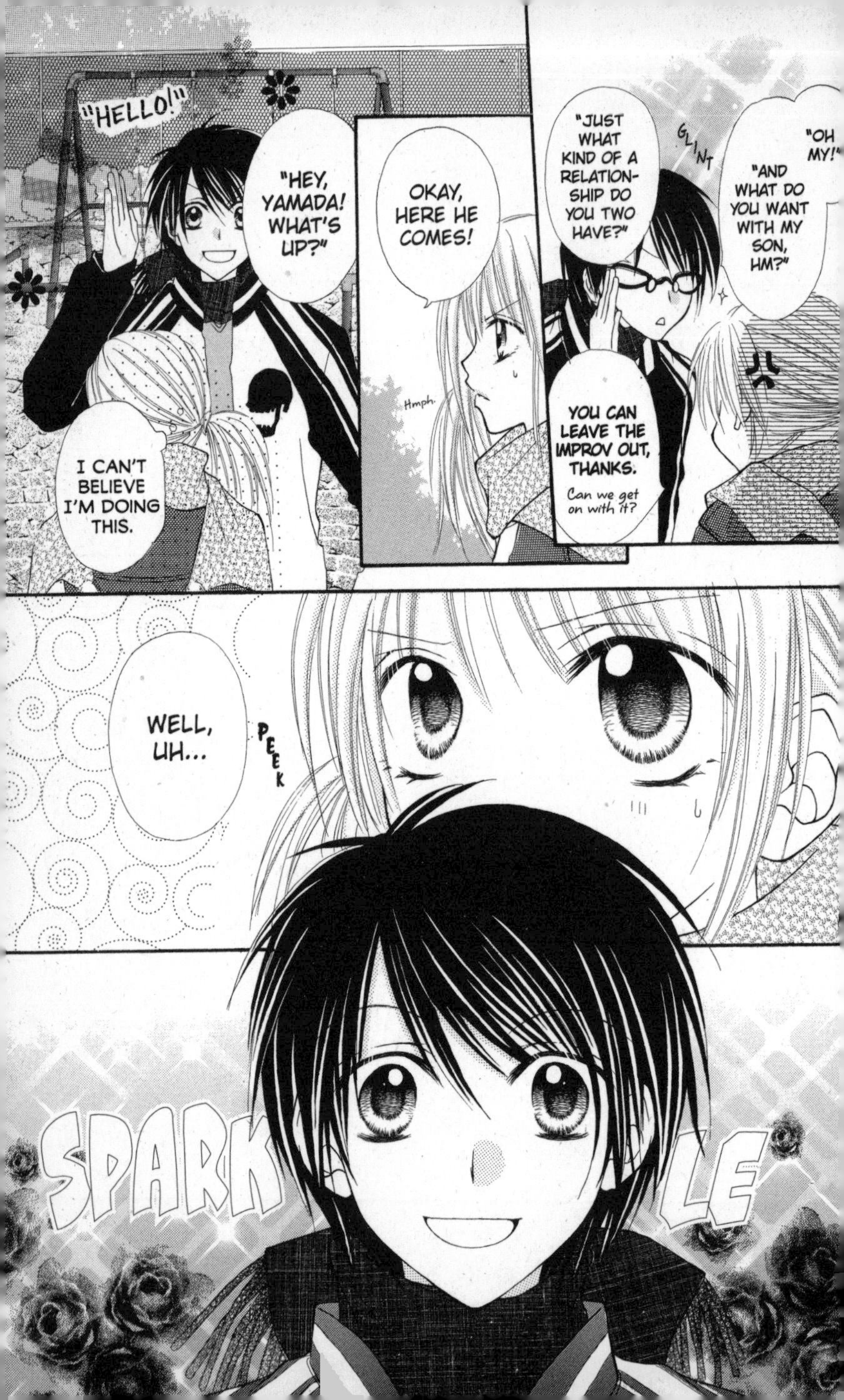
"OH MY!"
"AND WHAT DO YOU WANT WITH MY SON, HM?"
GLINT
"JUST WHAT KIND OF A RELATIONSHIP DO YOU TWO HAVE?"
YOU CAN LEAVE THE IMPROV OUT, THANKS.
Can we get on with it?
OKAY, HERE HE COMES!
Hmph.
"HEY, YAMADA! WHAT'S UP?"
"HELLO!"
I CAN'T BELIEVE I'M DOING THIS.
PEEK
WELL, UH...
SPARKLE

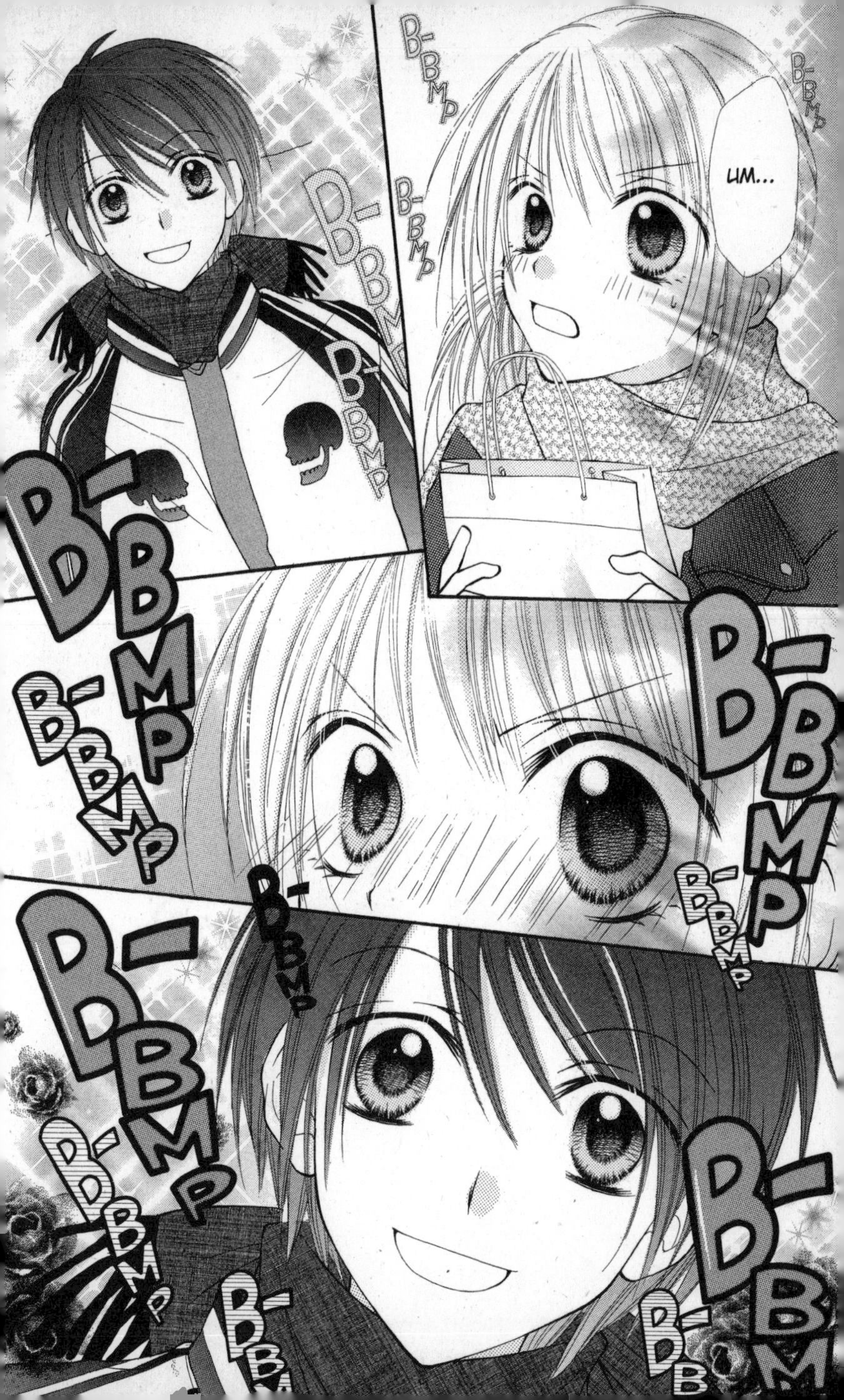
B-BMP
B-BMP
UM...
B-BMP
B-BMP
B-BMP
B-BMP
B-BMP
B-BMP
B-BMP
B-BMP
B-BMP
B-BMP
B-BMP

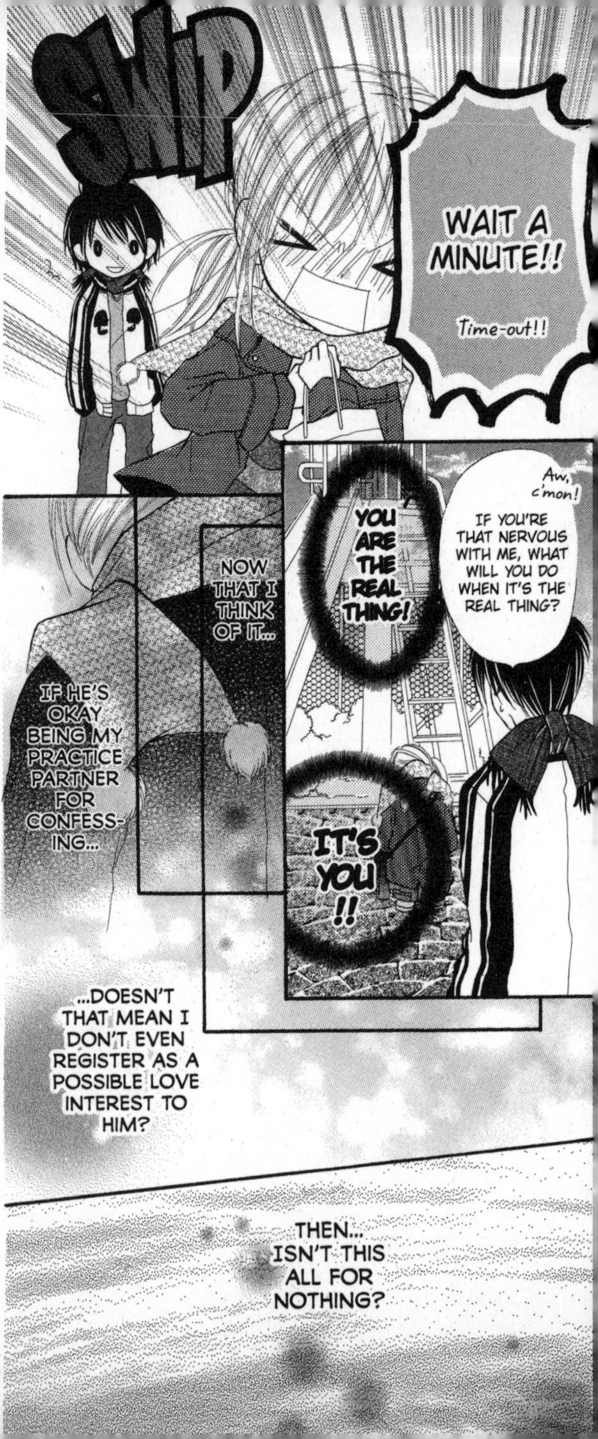
SWHIP
WAIT A MINUTE!!
Time-out!!
Aw, c'mon!
IF YOU'RE THAT NERVOUS WITH ME, WHAT WILL YOU DO WHEN IT'S THE REAL THING?
YOU ARE THE REAL THING!
IT'S YOU!!
NOW THAT I THINK OF IT...
IF HE'S OKAY BEING MY PRACTICE PARTNER FOR CONFESS-ING...
...DOESN'T THAT MEAN I DON'T EVEN REGISTER AS A POSSIBLE LOVE INTEREST TO HIM?
THEN... ISN'T THIS ALL FOR NOTHING?

4

Next up... A lot of people have asked me to have an open house at my studio, but since that won't be possible, I thought I'd describe it a bit for you.

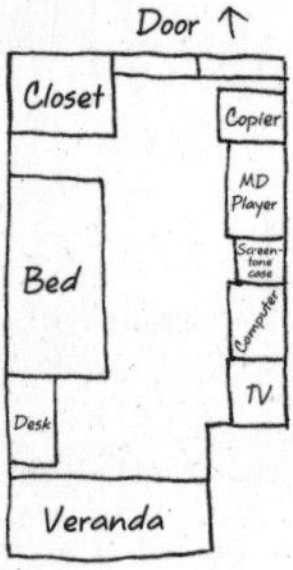
Door ↑
Closet
Copier
MD Player
Screen-tone case
Bed
Computer
TV
Desk
Veranda

So this is my studio...which is also my apartment, so everything is kind of crammed in. Well, I don't mind the limited space when it's just me, but when my assistants are here, it's so squished you can't turn this way or that. I'm really sorry about that... It's just too crowded in here for me plus 2-4 assistants...

I've never had a TV or computer in my room before now, and I'm finding it's really not a good thing. There's too much temptation to slack off and not do my work. (laugh) Having a TV in my room has suddenly and dramatically increased the amount of time I watch it.

I want to binge on video games! I want to binge on watching DVDs too!

I so wish I didn't have to do work...

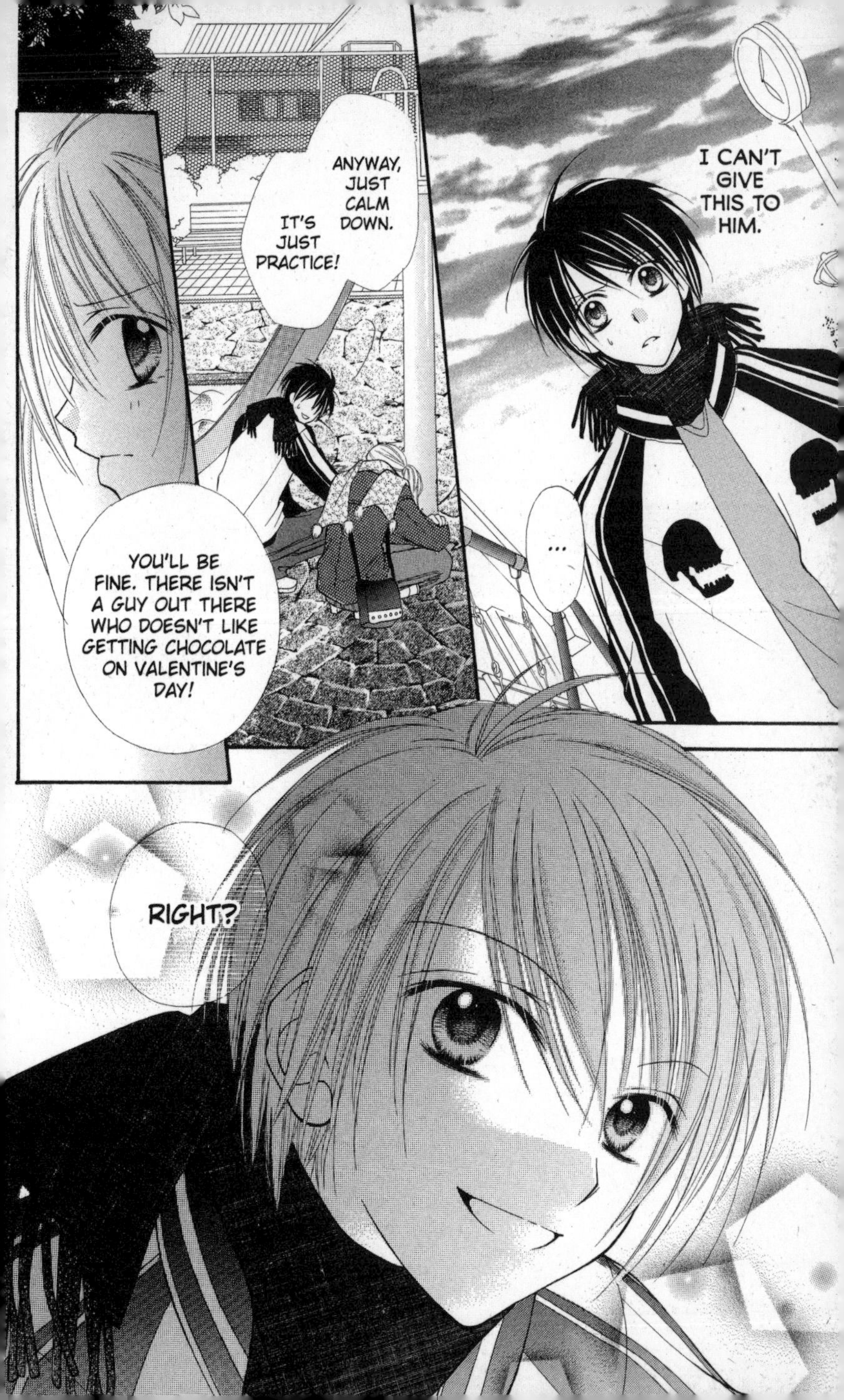

I CAN'T GIVE THIS TO HIM.
...
ANYWAY, JUST CALM DOWN.
IT'S JUST PRACTICE!
YOU'LL BE FINE. THERE ISN'T A GUY OUT THERE WHO DOESN'T LIKE GETTING CHOCOLATE ON VALENTINE'S DAY!
RIGHT?

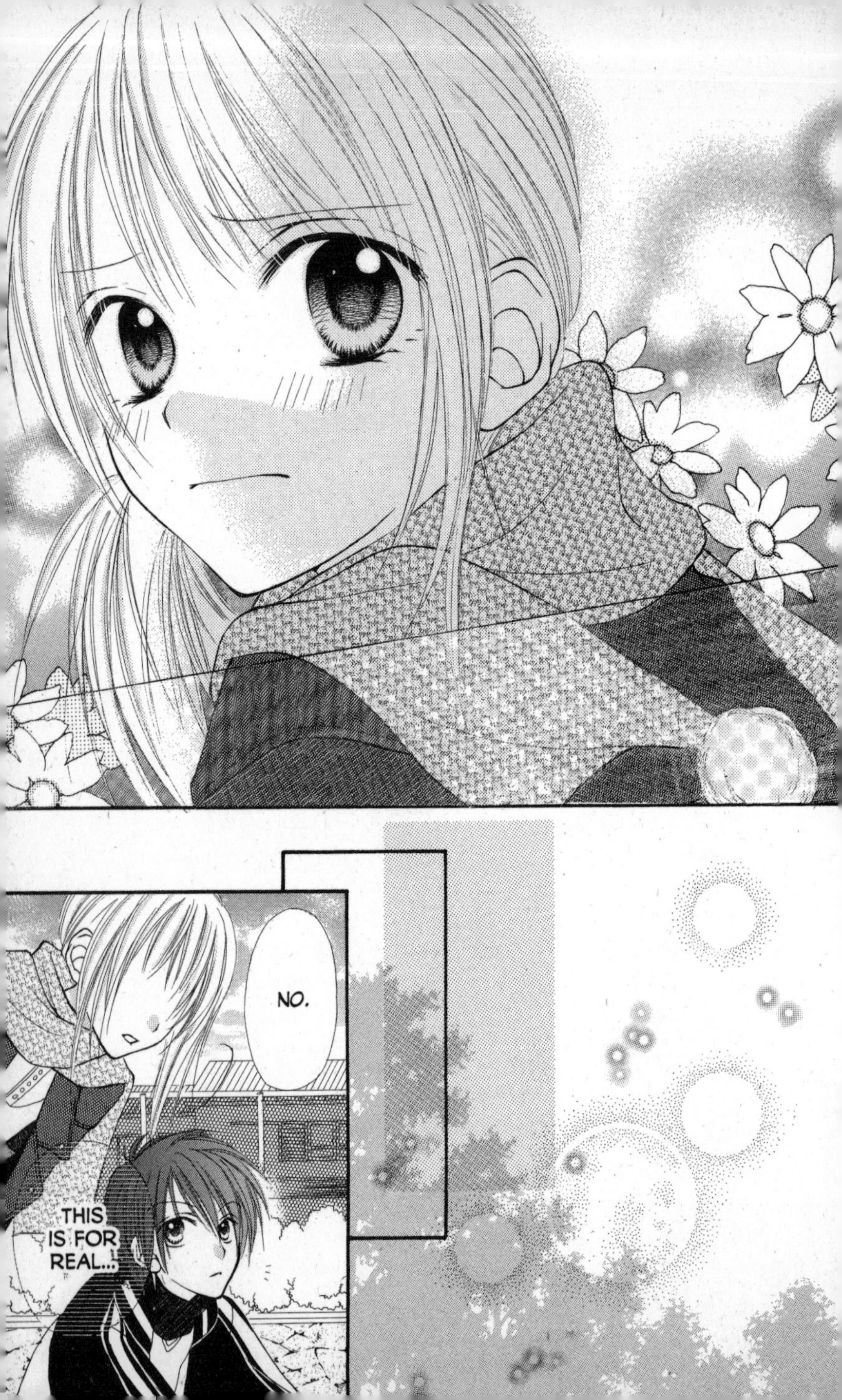
NO.
THIS IS FOR REAL...

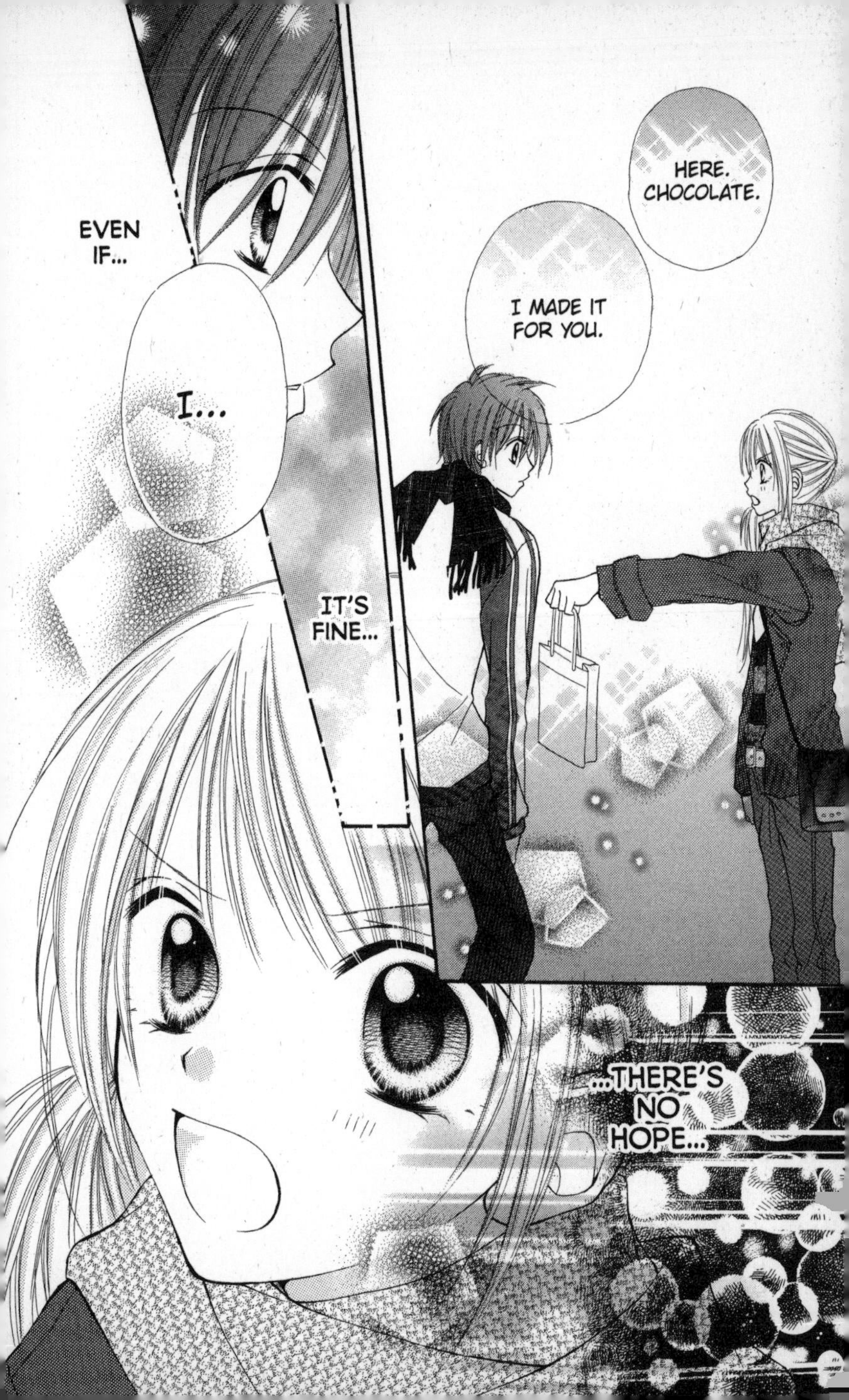
HERE. CHOCOLATE.
I MADE IT FOR YOU.
EVEN IF...
I...
IT'S FINE...
...THERE'S NO HOPE...

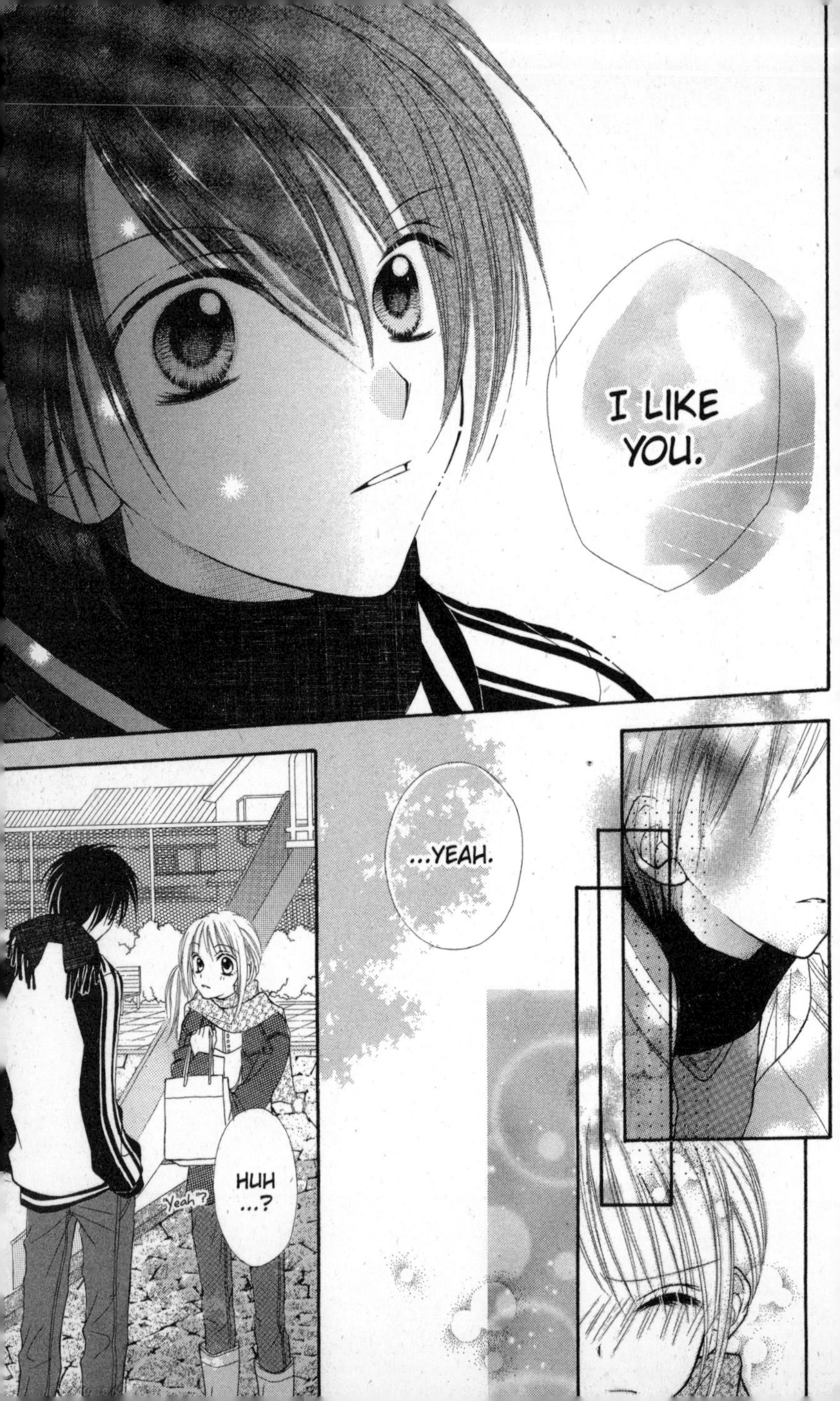
I LIKE YOU.
...YEAH.
"Yeah"?
HUH ...?

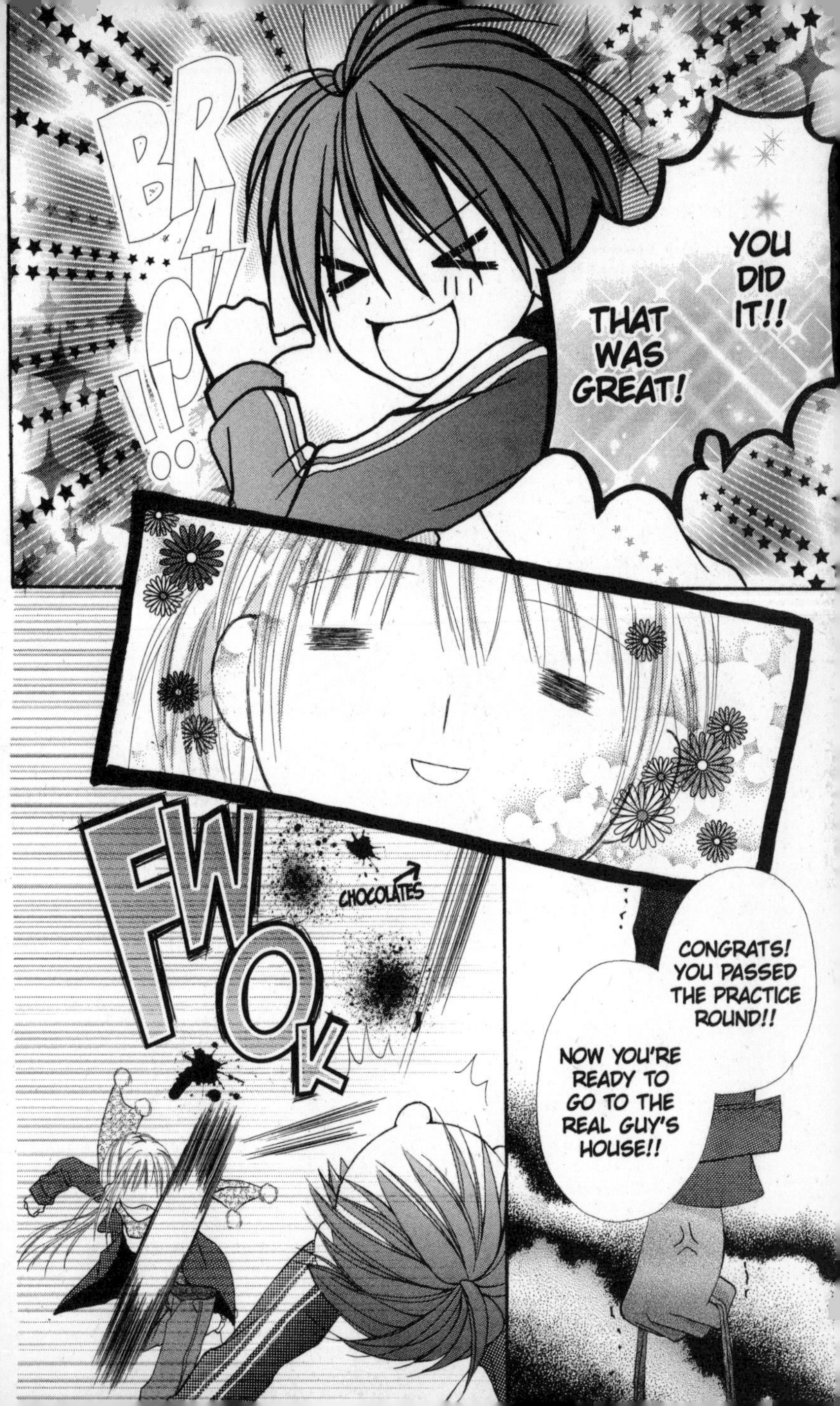
BRAVO!!
YOU DID IT!!
THAT WAS GREAT!
CONGRATS! YOU PASSED THE PRACTICE ROUND!!
NOW YOU'RE READY TO GO TO THE REAL GUY'S HOUSE!!
FWOK
CHOCOLATES

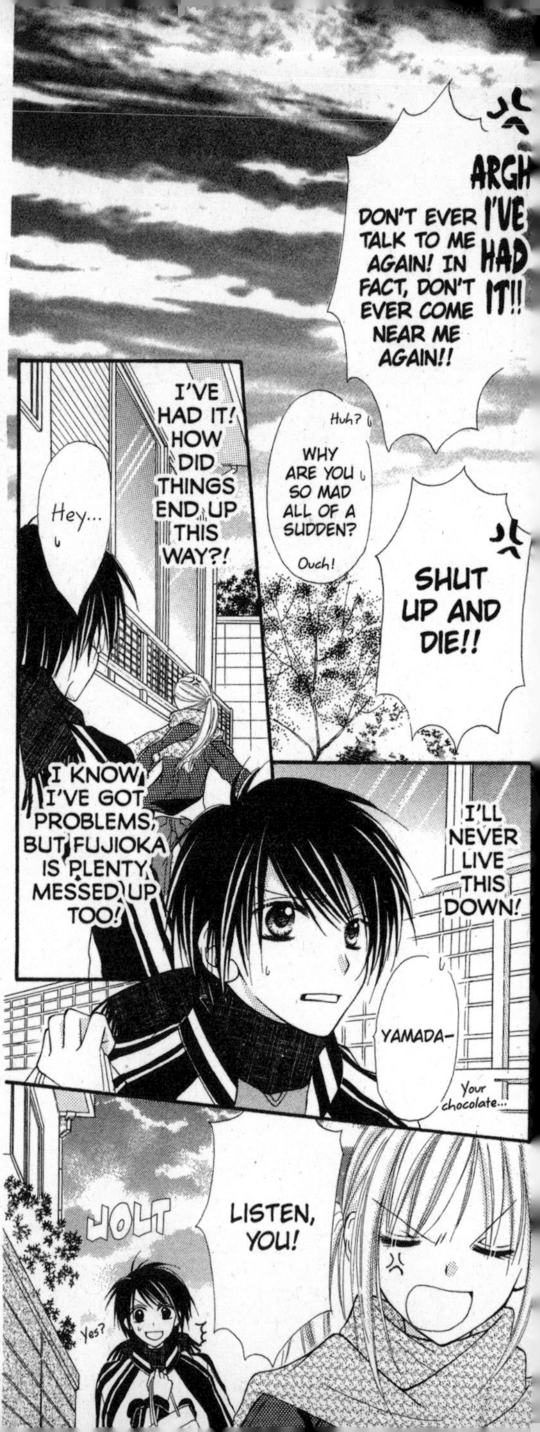
ARGH I'VE HAD IT!!
DON'T EVER TALK TO ME AGAIN! IN FACT, DON'T EVER COME NEAR ME AGAIN!!
SHUT UP AND DIE!!
Huh?
WHY ARE YOU SO MAD ALL OF A SUDDEN?
Ouch!
I'LL NEVER LIVE THIS DOWN!
YAMADA-
Your chocolate...
I'VE HAD IT! HOW DID THINGS END UP THIS WAY?!
Hey...
I KNOW I'VE GOT PROBLEMS, BUT FUJIOKA IS PLENTY MESSED UP TOO!
LISTEN, YOU!
JOLT
Yes?

5

When I play video games alone in my room, I sometimes get really upset when I'm losing—which isn't all that unusual, of course! However, once when I kept on losing...

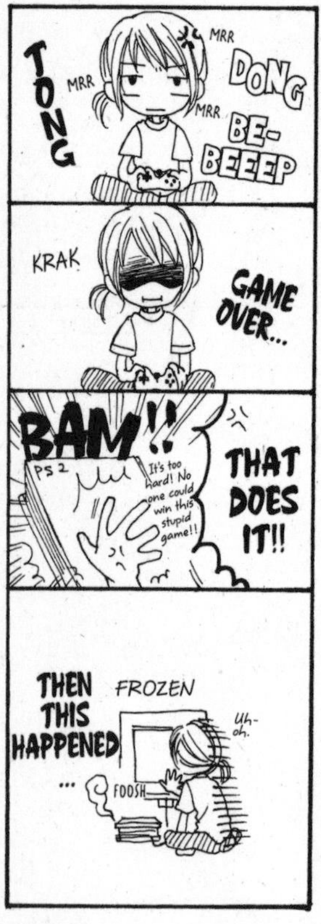
TONG
MRR
MRR
MRR
DONG
BE-BEEEP
KRAK
GAME OVER...
BAM!!
PS2
It's too hard! No one could win this stupid game!!
THAT DOES IT!!
THEN THIS HAPPENED...
FROZEN
Uh-oh.
FOOSH

When my PlayStation 2 froze up like that, it was as if the shock caused my brain to freeze up too. It took me a full 5 minutes to comprehend what had happened. Heh heh...

Now that I've cleared *Final Fantasy VIII*, I'm going back and playing *VII*. Yes, I am defying the flow of the ages.

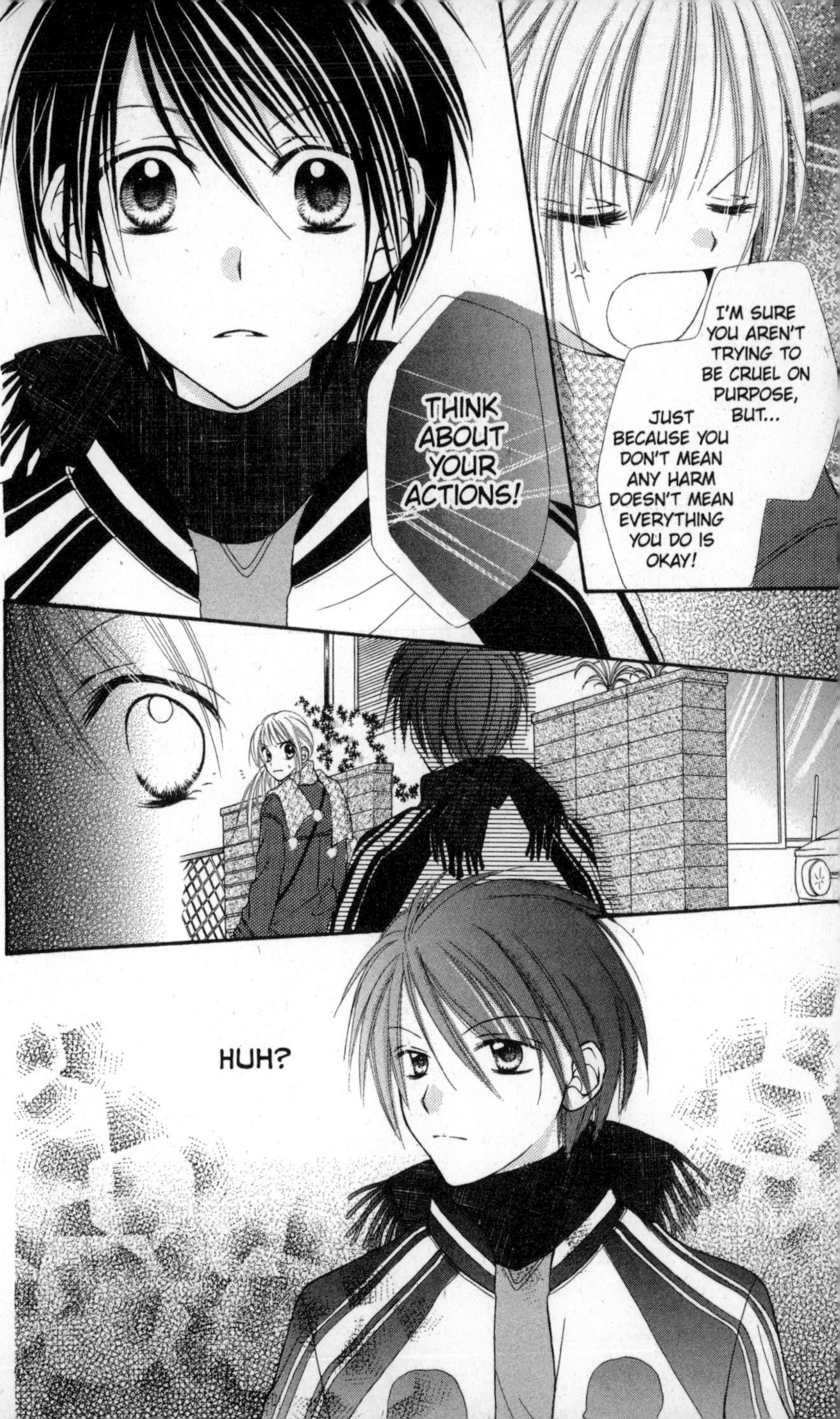
I'M SURE YOU AREN'T TRYING TO BE CRUEL ON PURPOSE, BUT...
JUST BECAUSE YOU DON'T MEAN ANY HARM DOESN'T MEAN EVERYTHING YOU DO IS OKAY!
THINK ABOUT YOUR ACTIONS!
HUH?

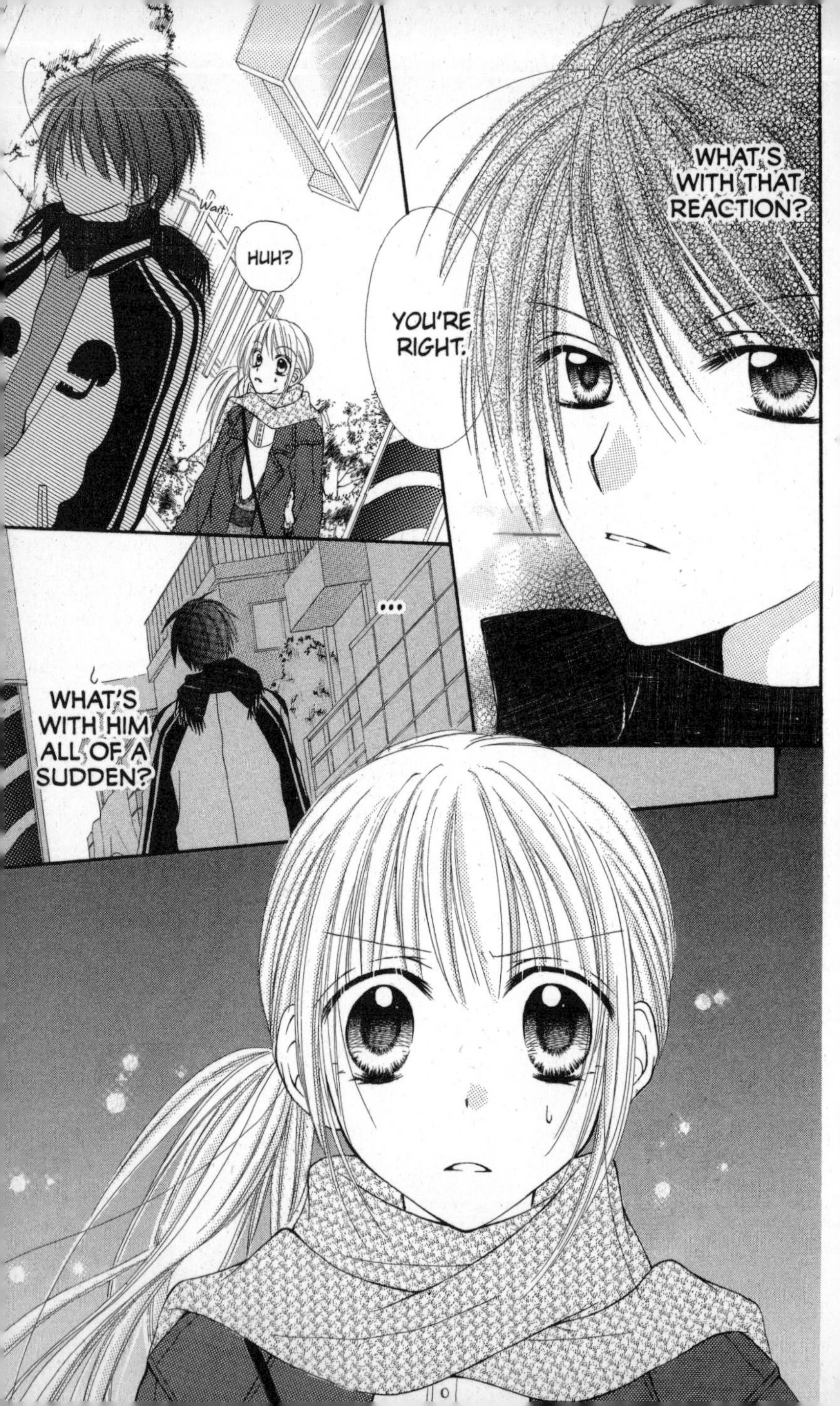
WHAT'S WITH THAT REACTION?
YOU'RE RIGHT.
Wait...
HUH?
...
WHAT'S WITH HIM ALL OF A SUDDEN?

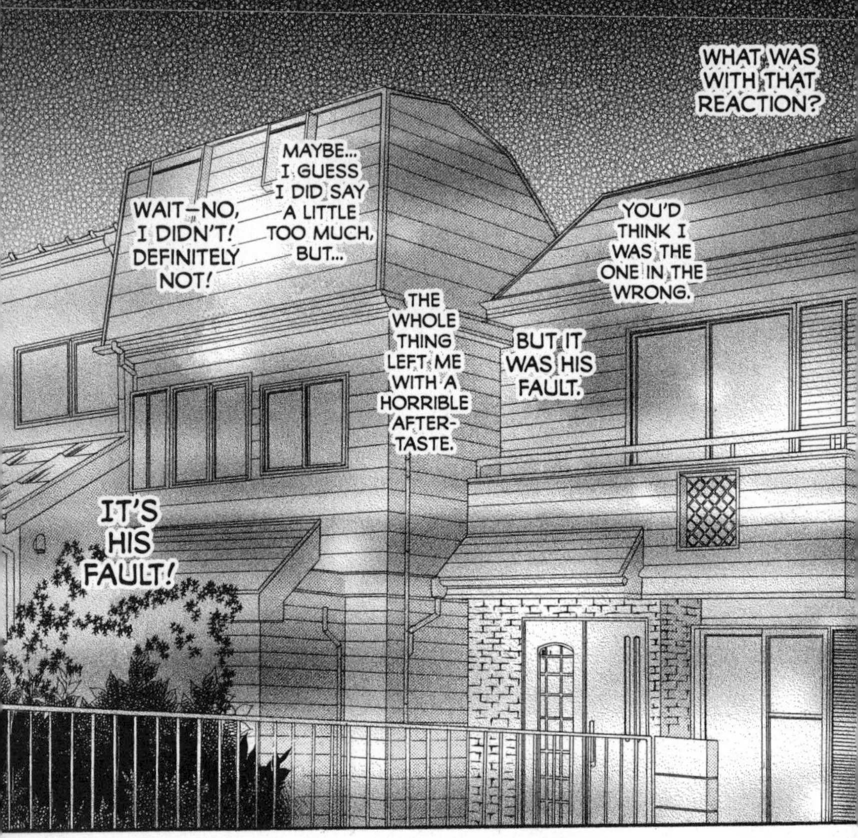
WHAT WAS WITH THAT REACTION?
YOU'D THINK I WAS THE ONE IN THE WRONG.
BUT IT WAS HIS FAULT.
THE WHOLE THING LEFT ME WITH A HORRIBLE AFTER-TASTE.
MAYBE... I GUESS I DID SAY A LITTLE TOO MUCH, BUT...
WAIT—NO, I DIDN'T! DEFINITELY NOT!
IT'S HIS FAULT!

SMALL TALK ②

I miraculously finished chapter 3 several hours before the deadline! I drew 31 pages in ten days. It was the first time I'd ever done so many so fast, but in exchange, I caused trouble for a lot of people. I'm sorry... And thank you so much...!!

Starting about three days before the deadline, I'd basically draw nonstop without even pausing to eat a proper meal. After I finally mailed the completed manuscript off, I was so exhausted I just went straight to sleep without eating at all. So when I woke up, I was in an anemic haze and gorged myself on everything within arm's reach.

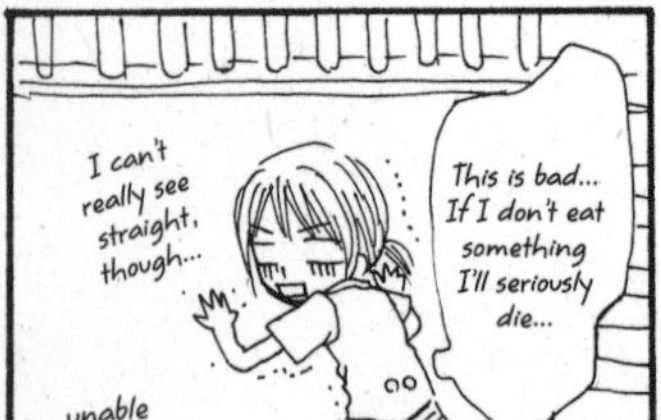
This is bad... If I don't eat something I'll seriously die...
I can't really see straight, though...
unable to walk normally
staircase

← I was seriously on the verge of death making my way to the kitc

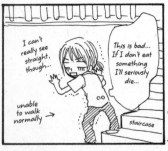

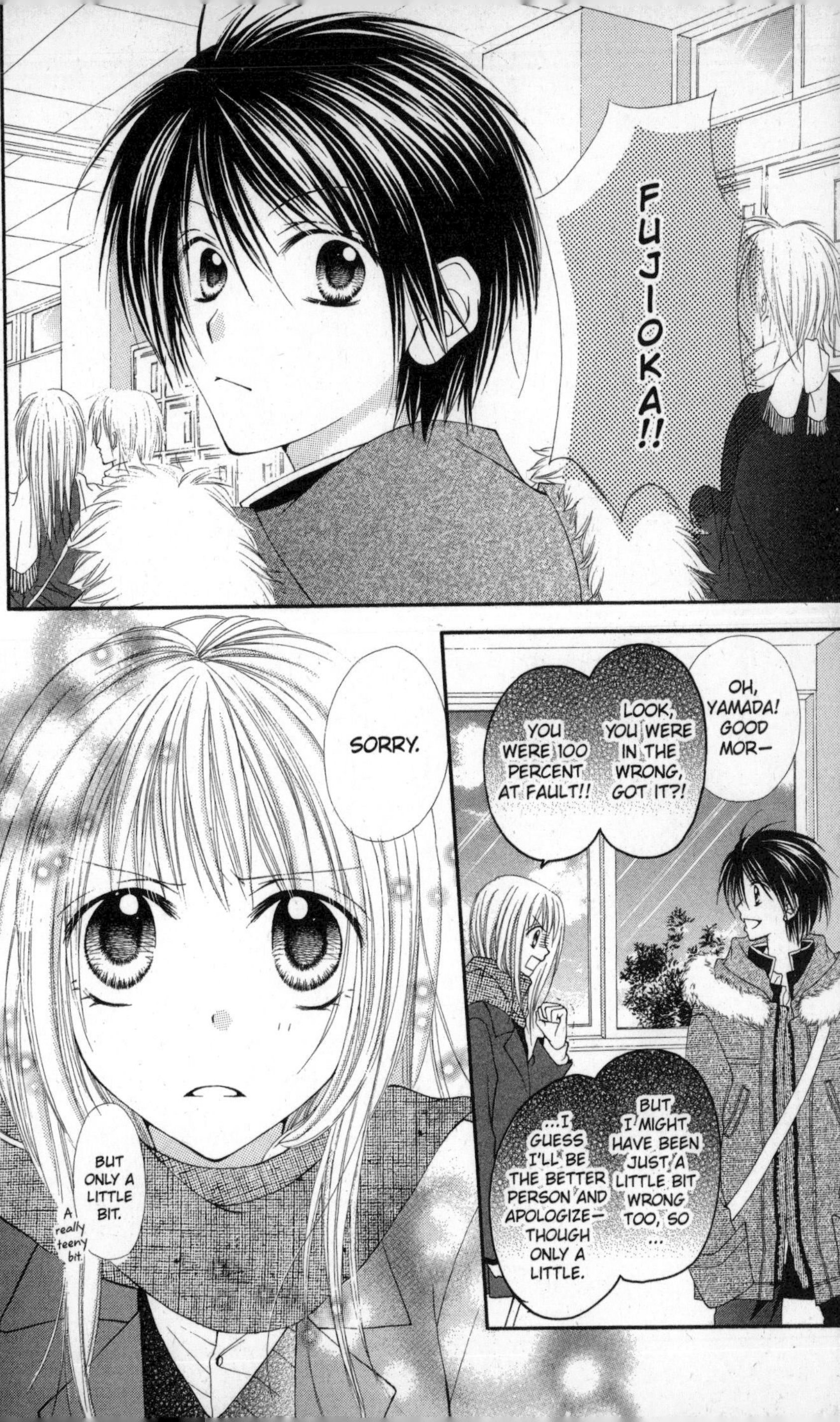
FUJIOKA!!
OH, YAMADA! GOOD MOR—
LOOK, YOU WERE IN THE WRONG, GOT IT?!
YOU WERE 100 PERCENT AT FAULT!!
BUT I MIGHT HAVE BEEN JUST A LITTLE BIT WRONG TOO, SO ...
...I GUESS I'LL BE THE BETTER PERSON AND APOLOGIZE—THOUGH ONLY A LITTLE.
SORRY.
BUT ONLY A LITTLE BIT.
A really teeny bit.

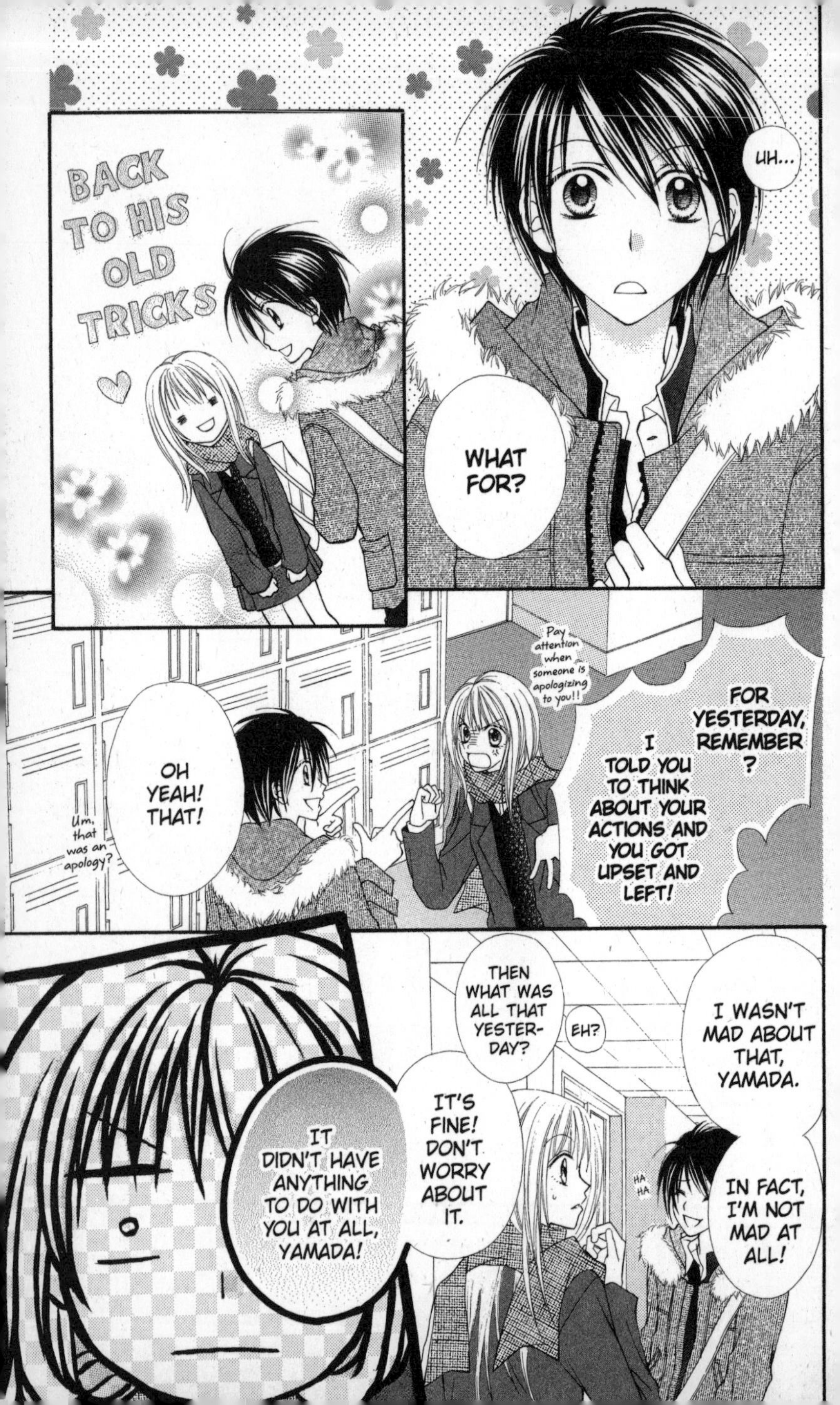
UH...
WHAT FOR?
BACK TO HIS OLD TRICKS
FOR YESTERDAY, REMEMBER? I TOLD YOU TO THINK ABOUT YOUR ACTIONS AND YOU GOT UPSET AND LEFT!
Pay attention when someone is apologizing to you!!
OH YEAH! THAT!
Um, that was an apology?
I WASN'T MAD ABOUT THAT, YAMADA.
IN FACT, I'M NOT MAD AT ALL!
HA HA
EH?
THEN WHAT WAS ALL THAT YESTER-DAY?
IT'S FINE! DON'T WORRY ABOUT IT.
IT DIDN'T HAVE ANYTHING TO DO WITH YOU AT ALL, YAMADA!

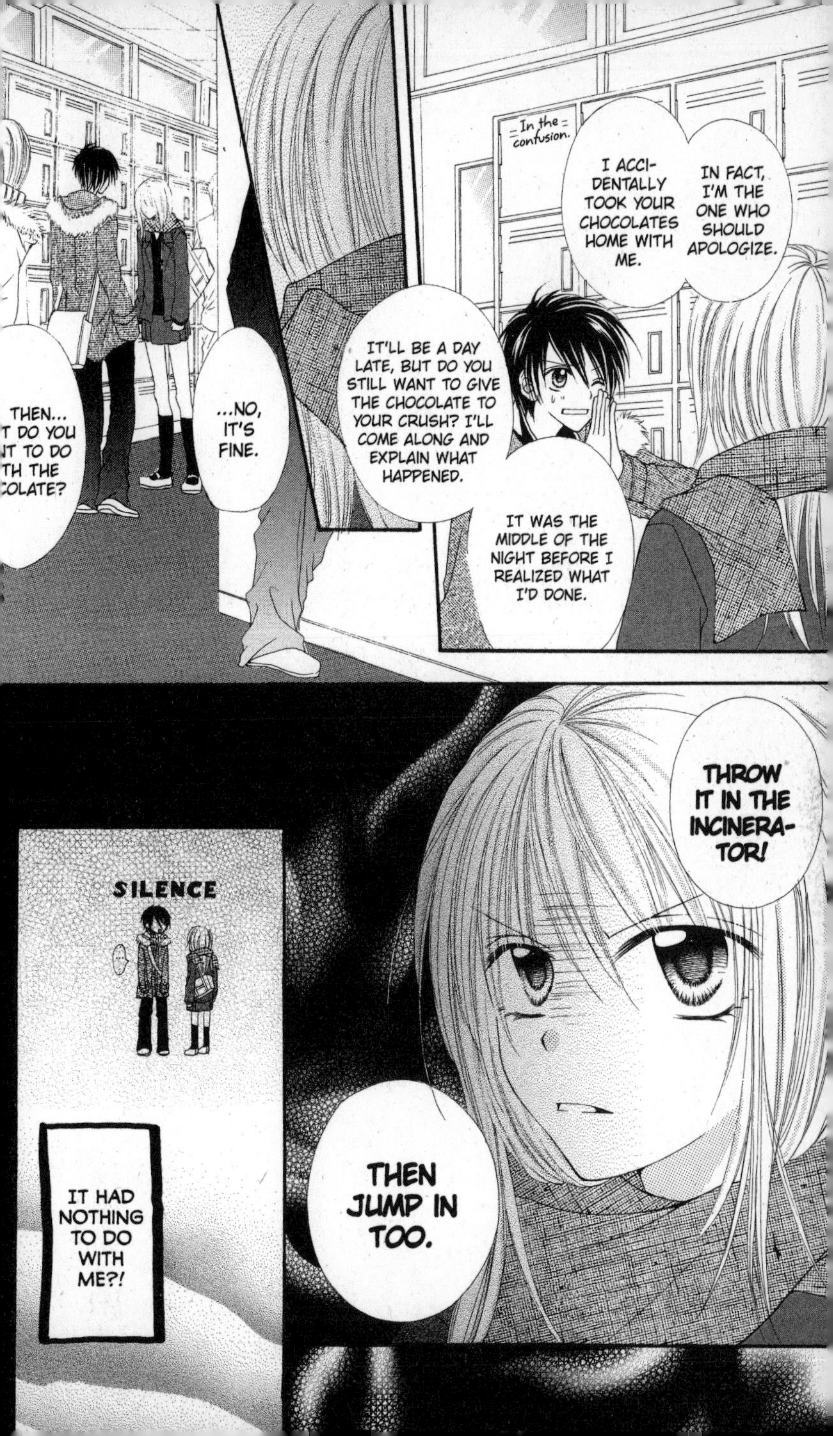
IN FACT, I'M THE ONE WHO SHOULD APOLOGIZE.
I ACCIDENTALLY TOOK YOUR CHOCOLATES HOME WITH ME.
In the confusion.
IT WAS THE MIDDLE OF THE NIGHT BEFORE I REALIZED WHAT I'D DONE.
IT'LL BE A DAY LATE, BUT DO YOU STILL WANT TO GIVE THE CHOCOLATE TO YOUR CRUSH? I'LL COME ALONG AND EXPLAIN WHAT HAPPENED.
...NO, IT'S FINE.
THEN... T DO YOU IT TO DO TH THE COLATE?
THROW IT IN THE INCINERATOR!
THEN JUMP IN TOO.
SILENCE
IT HAD NOTHING TO DO WITH ME?!

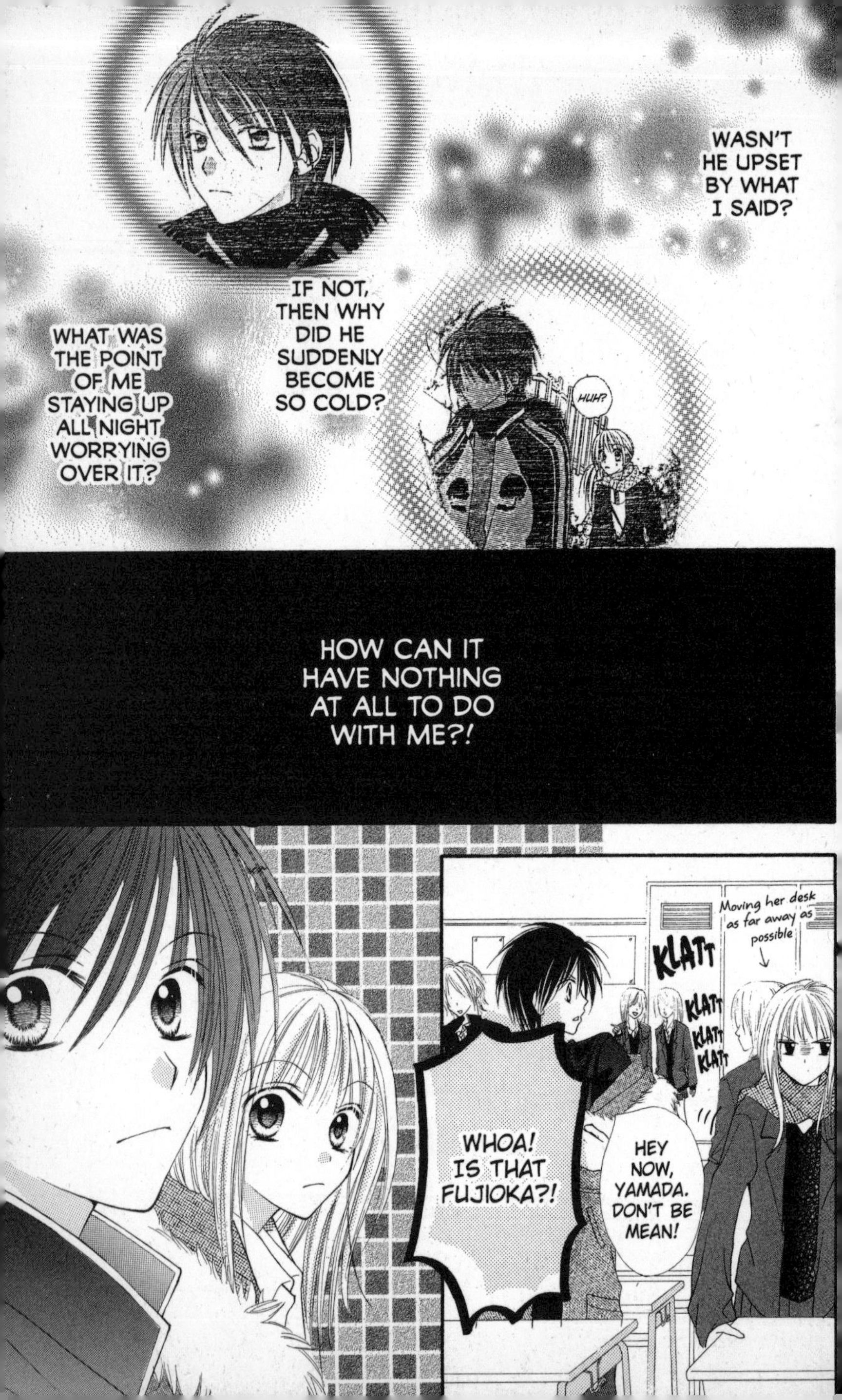
WASN'T HE UPSET BY WHAT I SAID?
IF NOT, THEN WHY DID HE SUDDENLY BECOME SO COLD?
HUH?
WHAT WAS THE POINT OF ME STAYING UP ALL NIGHT WORRYING OVER IT?
HOW CAN IT HAVE NOTHING AT ALL TO DO WITH ME?!
Moving her desk as far away as possible
KLATT
KLATT
KLATT
KLATT
HEY NOW, YAMADA. DON'T BE MEAN!
WHOA! IS THAT FUJIOKA?!

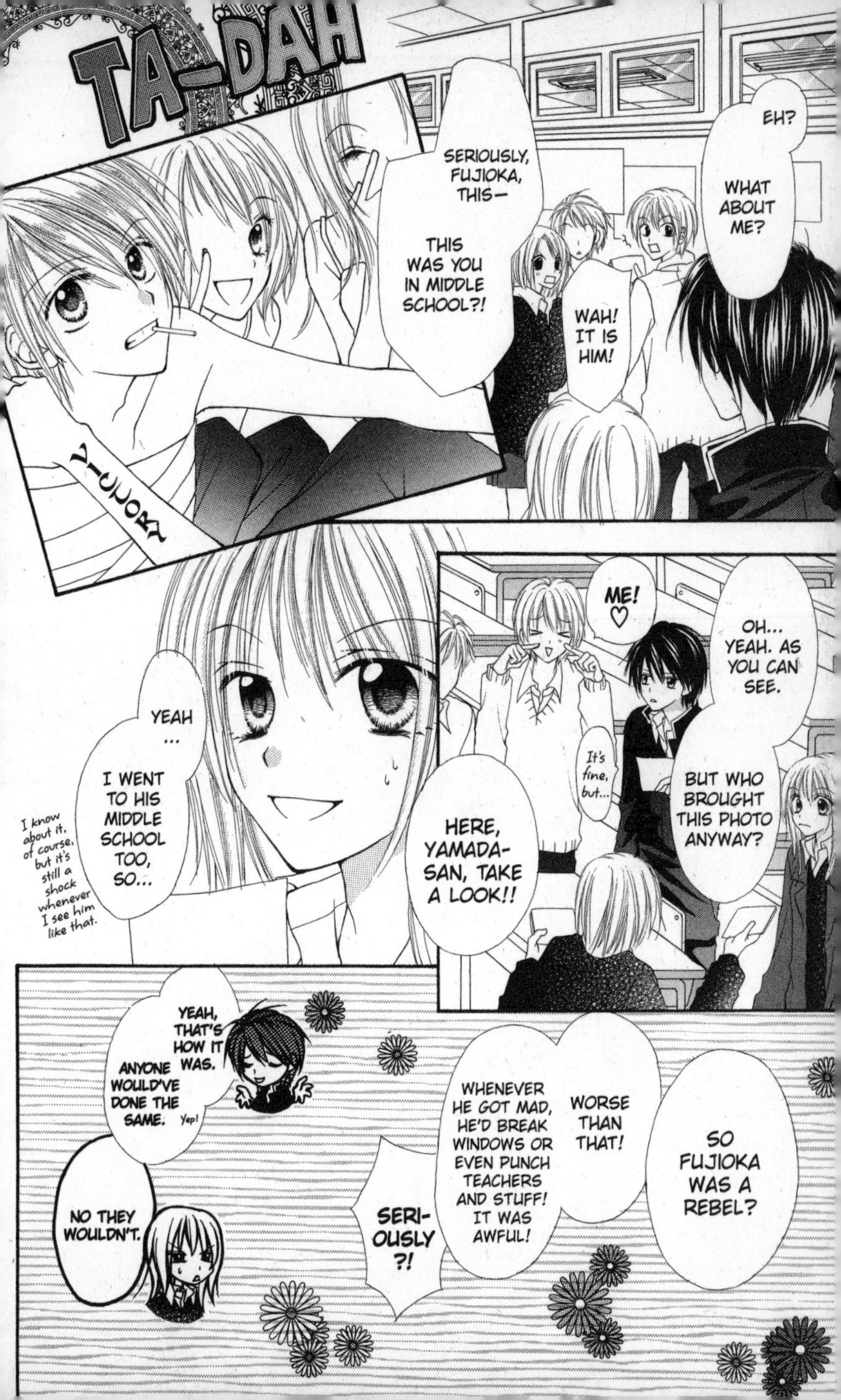
EH?
WHAT ABOUT ME?
SERIOUSLY, FUJIOKA, THIS—
THIS WAS YOU IN MIDDLE SCHOOL?!
WAH! IT IS HIM!
TA-DAH
OH... YEAH. AS YOU CAN SEE.
ME! ♡
BUT WHO BROUGHT THIS PHOTO ANYWAY?
It's fine, but...
HERE, YAMADA-SAN, TAKE A LOOK!!
YEAH ...
I WENT TO HIS MIDDLE SCHOOL TOO, SO...
I know about it, of course, but it's still a shock whenever I see him like that.
SO FUJIOKA WAS A REBEL?
WORSE THAN THAT!
WHENEVER HE GOT MAD, HE'D BREAK WINDOWS OR EVEN PUNCH TEACHERS AND STUFF! IT WAS AWFUL!
SERI-OUSLY?!
YEAH, THAT'S HOW IT WAS.
ANYONE WOULD'VE DONE THE SAME.
Yep!
NO THEY WOULDN'T.

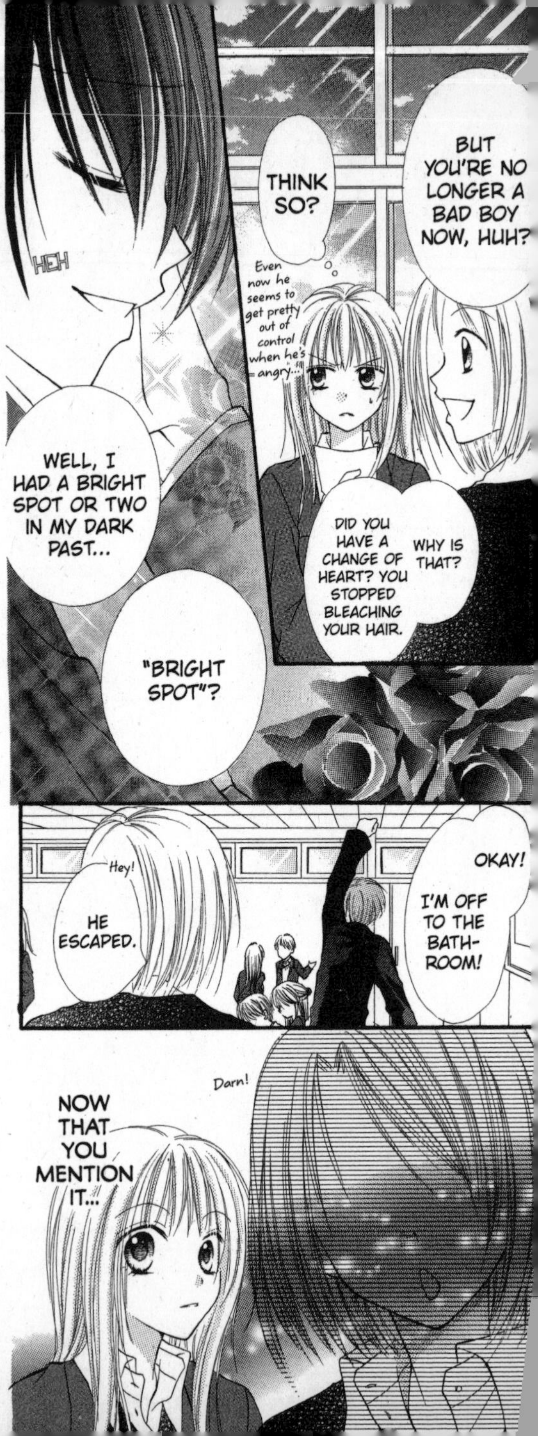
BUT YOU'RE NO LONGER A BAD BOY NOW, HUH?
THINK SO?
Even now he seems to get pretty out of control when he's angry...
WHY IS THAT?
DID YOU HAVE A CHANGE OF HEART? YOU STOPPED BLEACHING YOUR HAIR.
HEH
WELL, I HAD A BRIGHT SPOT OR TWO IN MY DARK PAST...
"BRIGHT SPOT"?
OKAY!
I'M OFF TO THE BATH-ROOM!
Hey!
HE ESCAPED.
Darn!
NOW THAT YOU MENTION IT...

6

Waah... I'm doing some color work right now and I just accidentally spilled some colored ink all over my pillow!! I went to wash the pillowcase out immediately, but unsurprisingly, it left a stain. (cry) What's worse, the color I spilled was yellow...so now it looks like I wet the bed or something... Argh!!

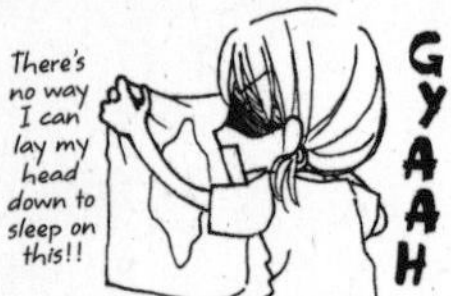
There's no way I can lay my head down to sleep on this!!
GYAAH

Naturally, the pillow itself looked thoroughly bed-wetted too...

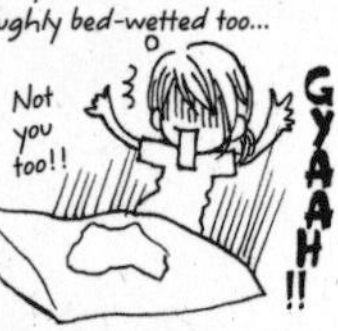
Not you too!!
GYAAH!!

I guess I'll have to buy a new pillow... Sorry for talking about this weird topic. I've been spacing out too much lately. When I was on the train recently, I got so drowsy that it soon became a ride to the realms of Deepest Sleep. When I finally awoke, I'd long since passed my stop and found myself at the very end of the line. And stupid me didn't even realize it wasn't my usual station until I'd walked all the way up to the ticket gate. I really fear for my future.

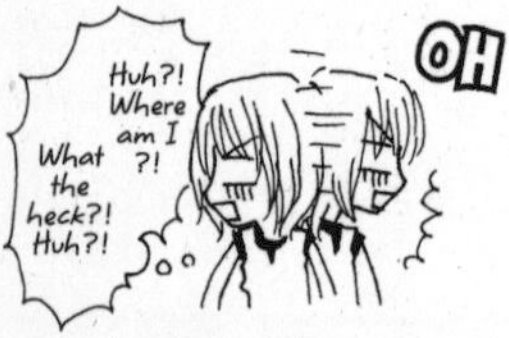
OH
Huh?! Where am I ?!
What the heck?! Huh?!

A spacey-looking person who suddenly started freaking out must've really looked like a shady character, huh? Ha ha ha. Well, it's a good thing I'm such a dork that I found this manga-like behavior of mine pretty amusing. Heh heh!

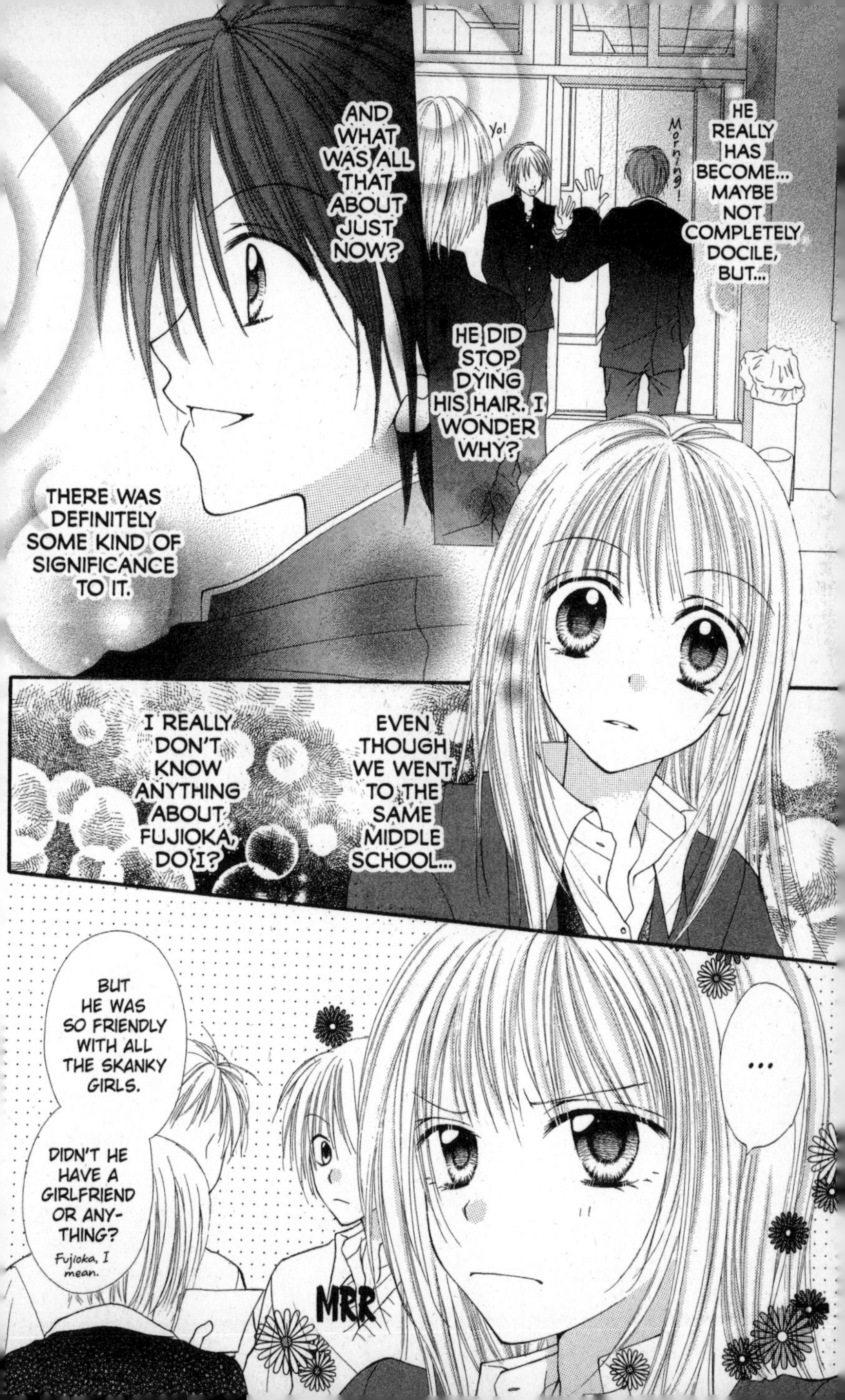
HE REALLY HAS BECOME... MAYBE NOT COMPLETELY DOCILE, BUT...
Morning!
Yo!
AND WHAT WAS ALL THAT ABOUT JUST NOW?
HE DID STOP DYING HIS HAIR. I WONDER WHY?
THERE WAS DEFINITELY SOME KIND OF SIGNIFICANCE TO IT.
EVEN THOUGH WE WENT TO THE SAME MIDDLE SCHOOL...
I REALLY DON'T KNOW ANYTHING ABOUT FUJIOKA, DO I?
...
BUT HE WAS SO FRIENDLY WITH ALL THE SKANKY GIRLS.
DIDN'T HE HAVE A GIRLFRIEND OR ANY-THING?
Fujioka, I mean.
MRR

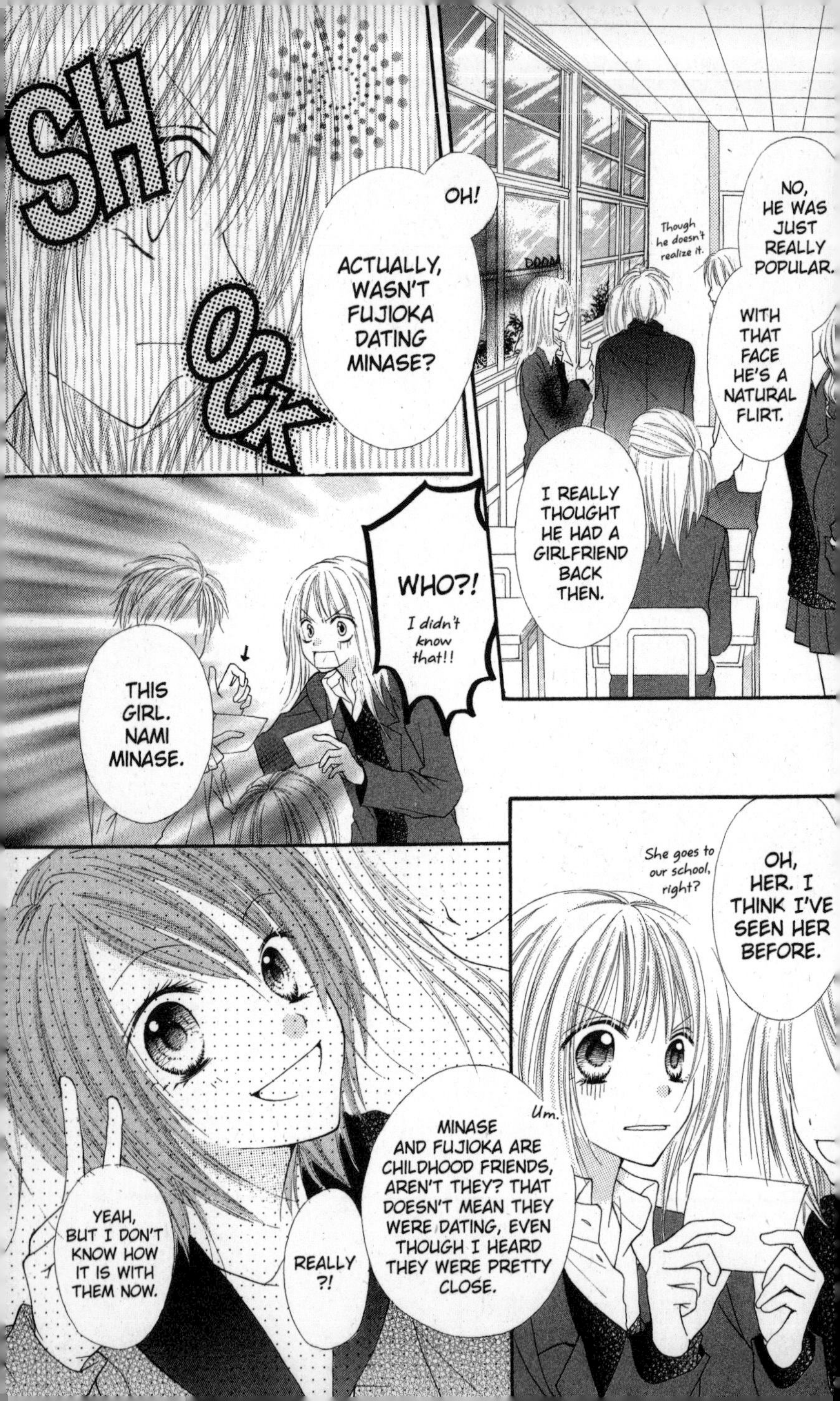
NO, HE WAS JUST REALLY POPULAR.
Though he doesn't realize it.
WITH THAT FACE HE'S A NATURAL FLIRT.
DOOM
I REALLY THOUGHT HE HAD A GIRLFRIEND BACK THEN.
OH!
ACTUALLY, WASN'T FUJIOKA DATING MINASE?
SHOCK
WHO?!
I didn't know that!!
THIS GIRL. NAMI MINASE.
OH, HER. I THINK I'VE SEEN HER BEFORE.
She goes to our school, right?
Um.
MINASE AND FUJIOKA ARE CHILDHOOD FRIENDS, AREN'T THEY? THAT DOESN'T MEAN THEY WERE DATING, EVEN THOUGH I HEARD THEY WERE PRETTY CLOSE.
REALLY?!
YEAH, BUT I DON'T KNOW HOW IT IS WITH THEM NOW.

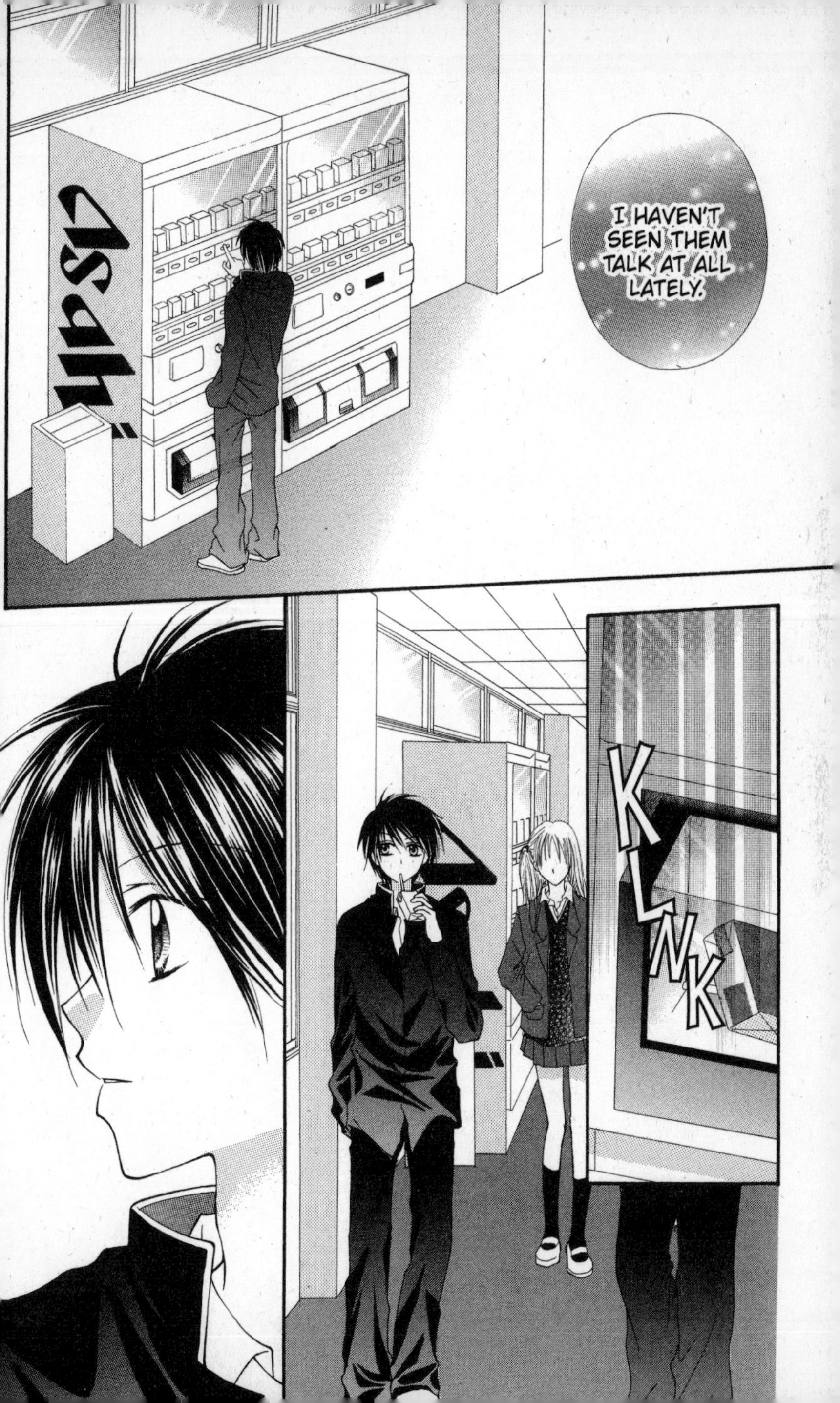
I HAVEN'T SEEN THEM TALK AT ALL LATELY.
Asahi
KLNK

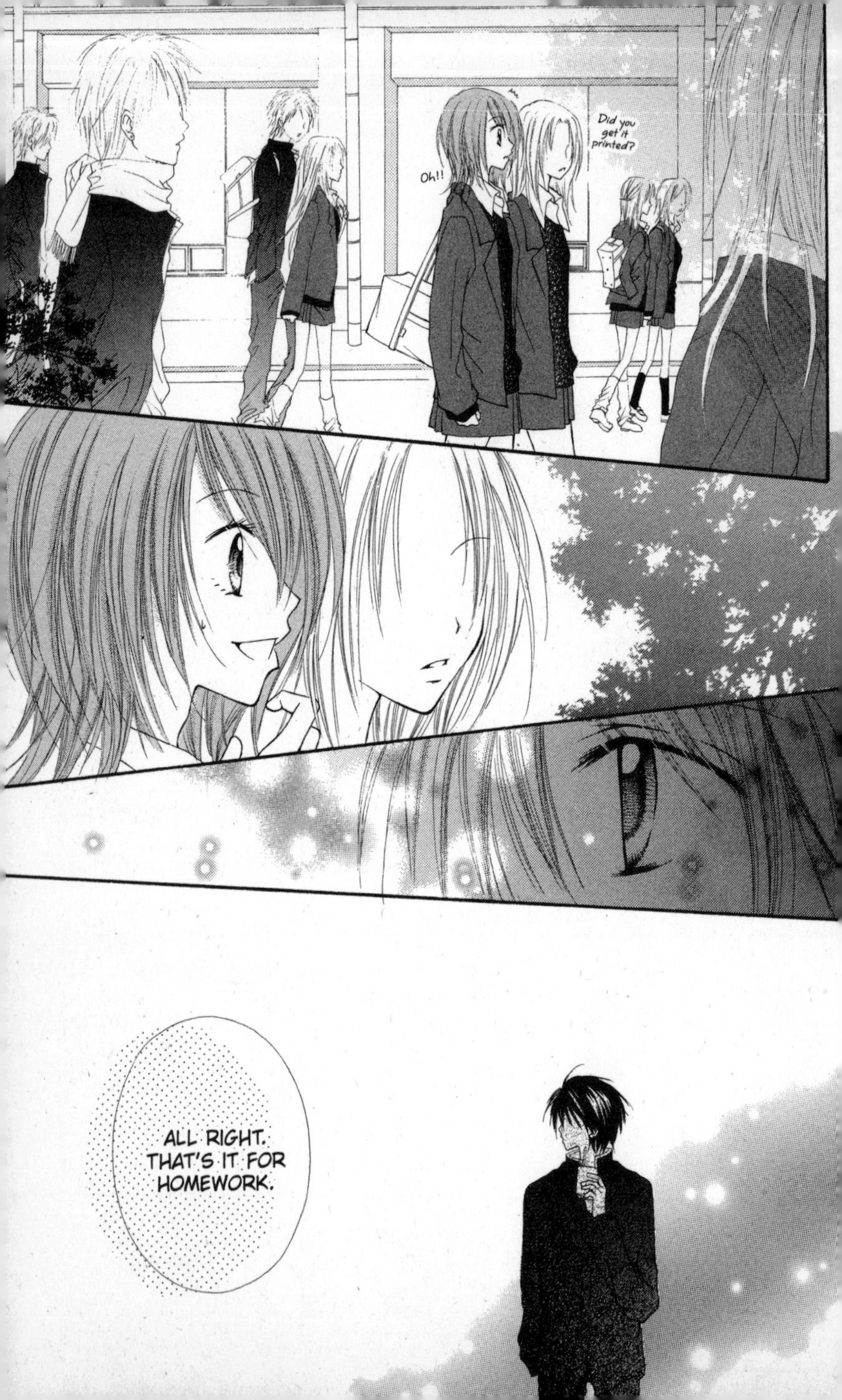
Did you get it printed?
Oh!!
ALL RIGHT. THAT'S IT FOR HOMEWORK.

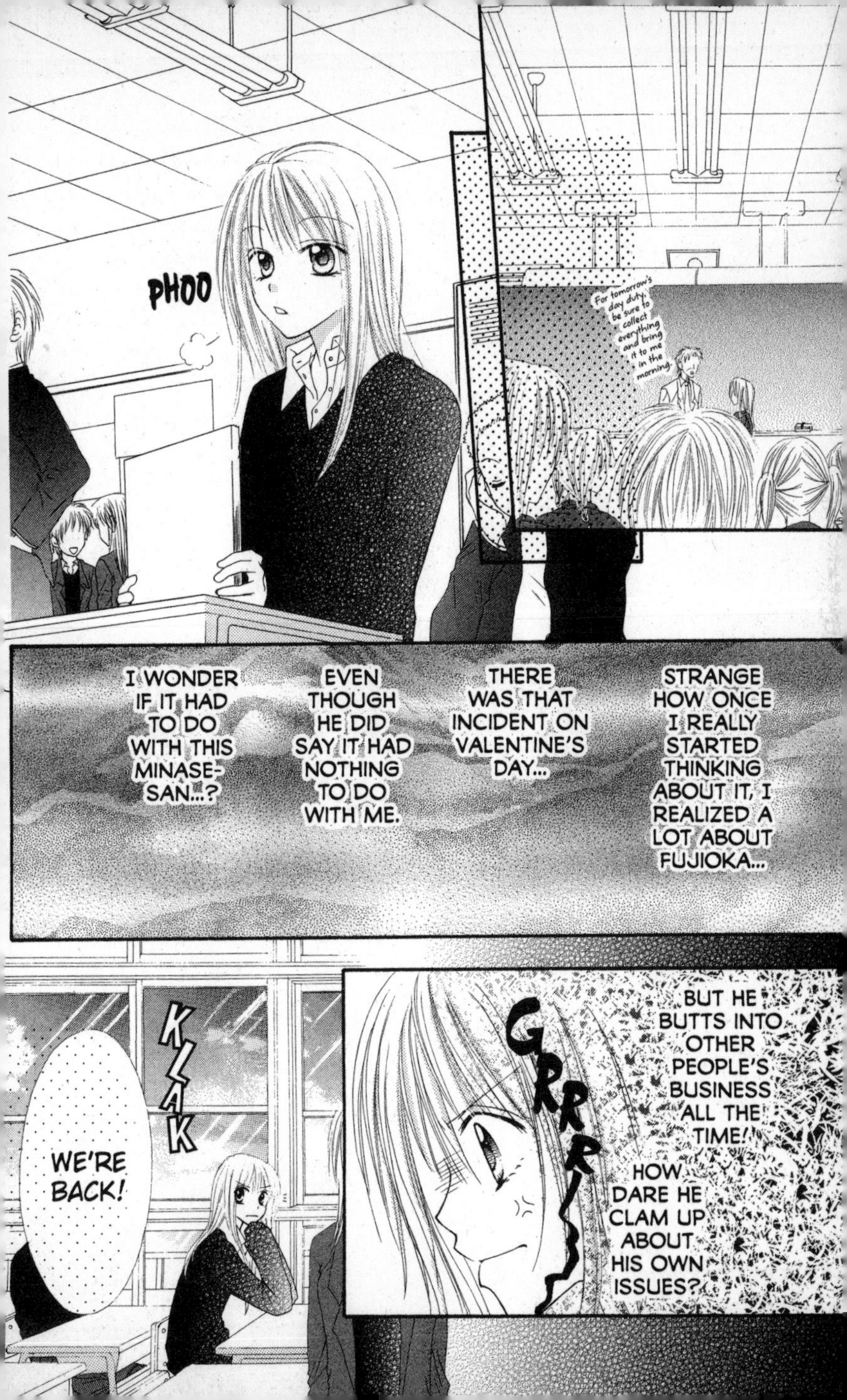
For tomorrow's day duty, be sure to collect everything and bring it to me in the morning.
PHOO
STRANGE HOW ONCE I REALLY STARTED THINKING ABOUT IT, I REALIZED A LOT ABOUT FUJIOKA...
THERE WAS THAT INCIDENT ON VALENTINE'S DAY...
EVEN THOUGH HE DID SAY IT HAD NOTHING TO DO WITH ME.
I WONDER IF IT HAD TO DO WITH THIS MINASE-SAN...?
BUT HE BUTTS INTO OTHER PEOPLE'S BUSINESS ALL THE TIME!
GRRR
HOW DARE HE CLAM UP ABOUT HIS OWN ISSUES?
KLAK
WE'RE BACK!

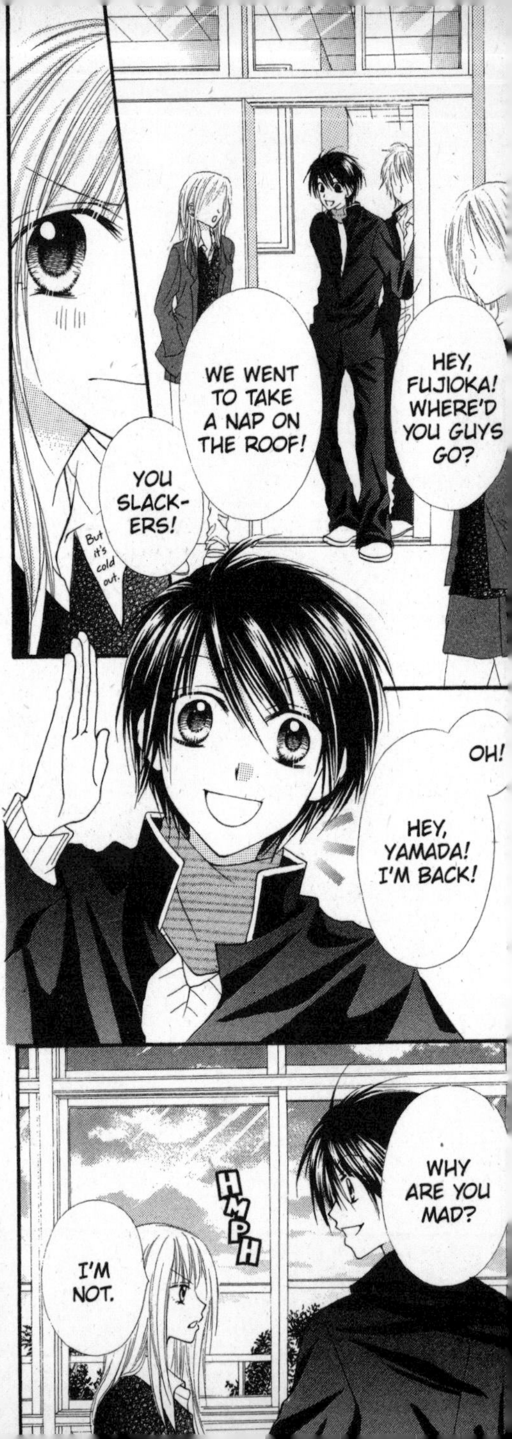
HEY, FUJIOKA! WHERE'D YOU GUYS GO?
WE WENT TO TAKE A NAP ON THE ROOF!
YOU SLACKERS!
But it's cold out.
OH!
HEY, YAMADA! I'M BACK!
WHY ARE YOU MAD?
HMPH
I'M NOT.

7

Oh yeah! In addition to the sleeping-on-the-train incident, there was another case of my "Do you think you're a manga character?!" problem. ↓

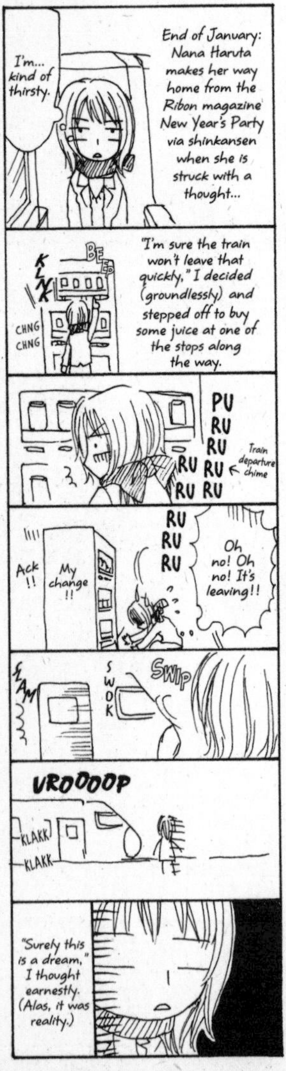
End of January: Nana Haruta makes her way home from the Ribon magazine New Year's Party via shinkansen when she is struck with a thought...
I'm... kind of thirsty.
"I'm sure the train won't leave that quickly," I decided (groundlessly) and stepped off to buy some juice at one of the stops along the way.
BEEP
KLNK
CHNG CHNG
Train departure chime
PU RU RU RU RU RU RU RU
Oh no! Oh no! It's leaving!!
RU RU RU
My change!!
Ack!!
SWIP
SWOK
SLAM
UROOOOP
KLAKK
KLAKK
"Surely this is a dream," I thought earnestly. (Alas, it was reality.)

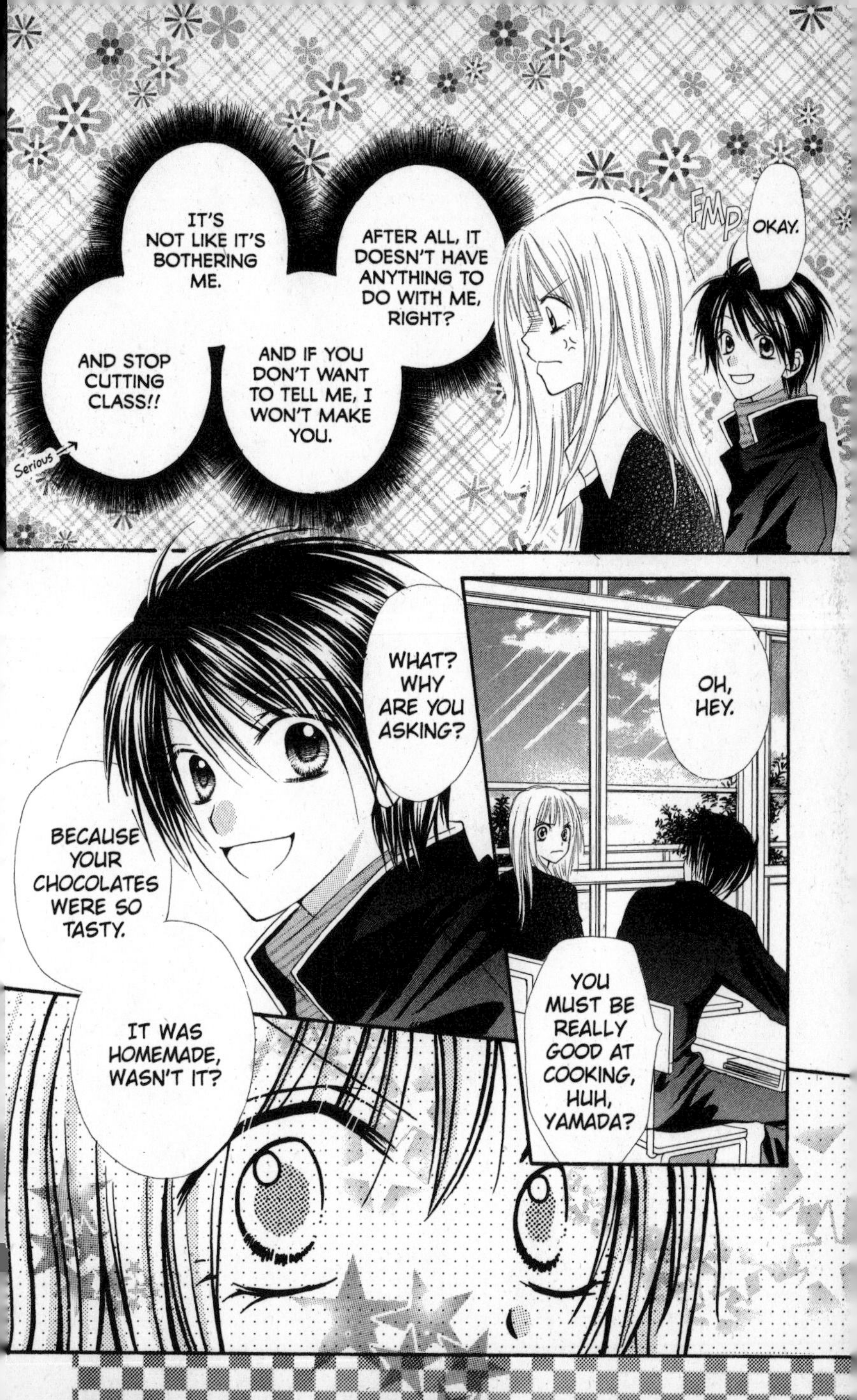
IT'S NOT LIKE IT'S BOTHERING ME.
AFTER ALL, IT DOESN'T HAVE ANYTHING TO DO WITH ME, RIGHT?
AND IF YOU DON'T WANT TO TELL ME, I WON'T MAKE YOU.
AND STOP CUTTING CLASS!!
Serious
FMP
OKAY.
OH, HEY.
YOU MUST BE REALLY GOOD AT COOKING, HUH, YAMADA?
WHAT? WHY ARE YOU ASKING?
BECAUSE YOUR CHOCOLATES WERE SO TASTY.
IT WAS HOMEMADE, WASN'T IT?

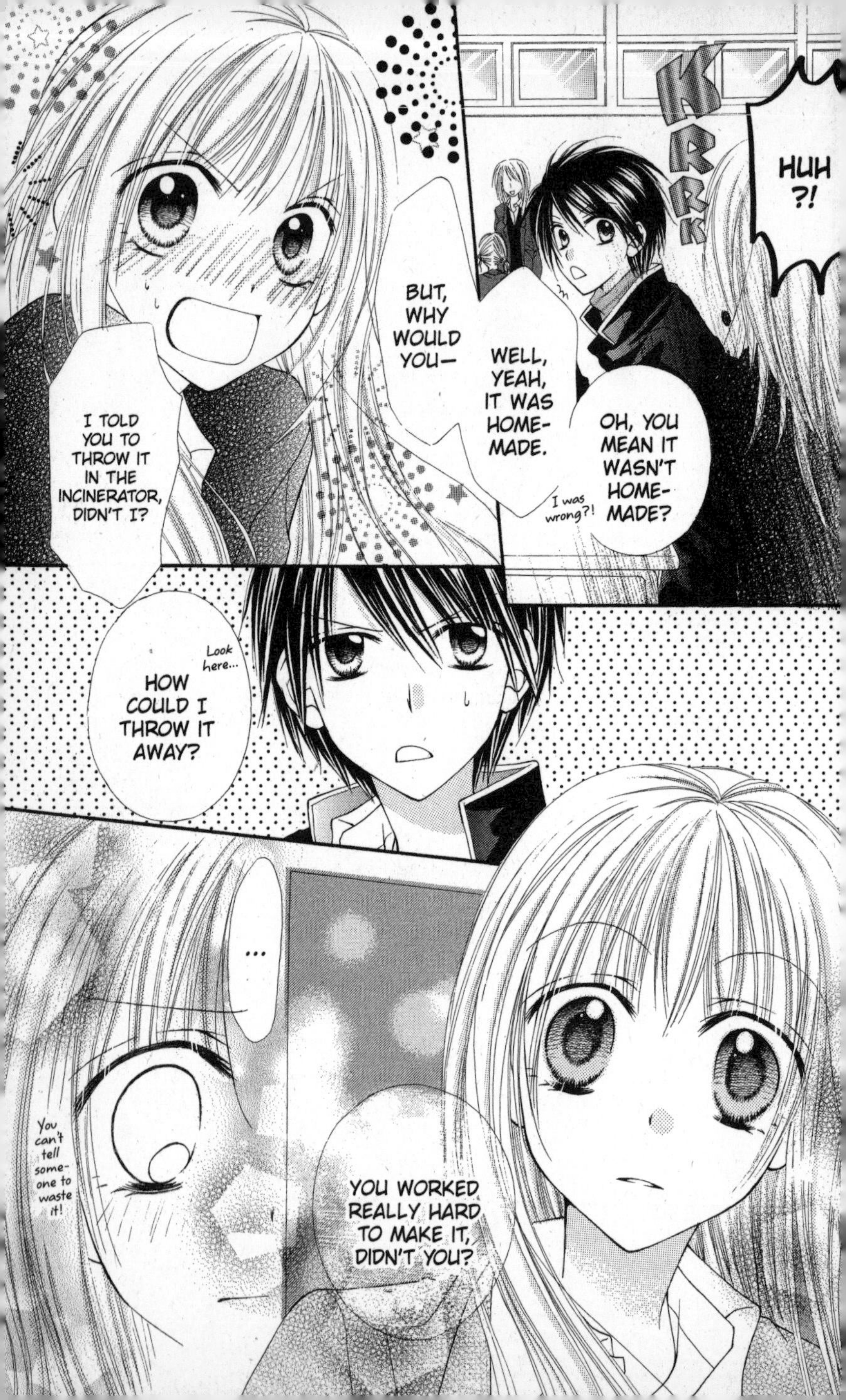
KRRK
HUH ?!
OH, YOU MEAN IT WASN'T HOME-MADE?
I was wrong?!
WELL, YEAH, IT WAS HOME-MADE.
BUT, WHY WOULD YOU—
I TOLD YOU TO THROW IT IN THE INCINERATOR, DIDN'T I?
Look here...
HOW COULD I THROW IT AWAY?
YOU WORKED REALLY HARD TO MAKE IT, DIDN'T YOU?
...
You can't tell some-one to waste it!

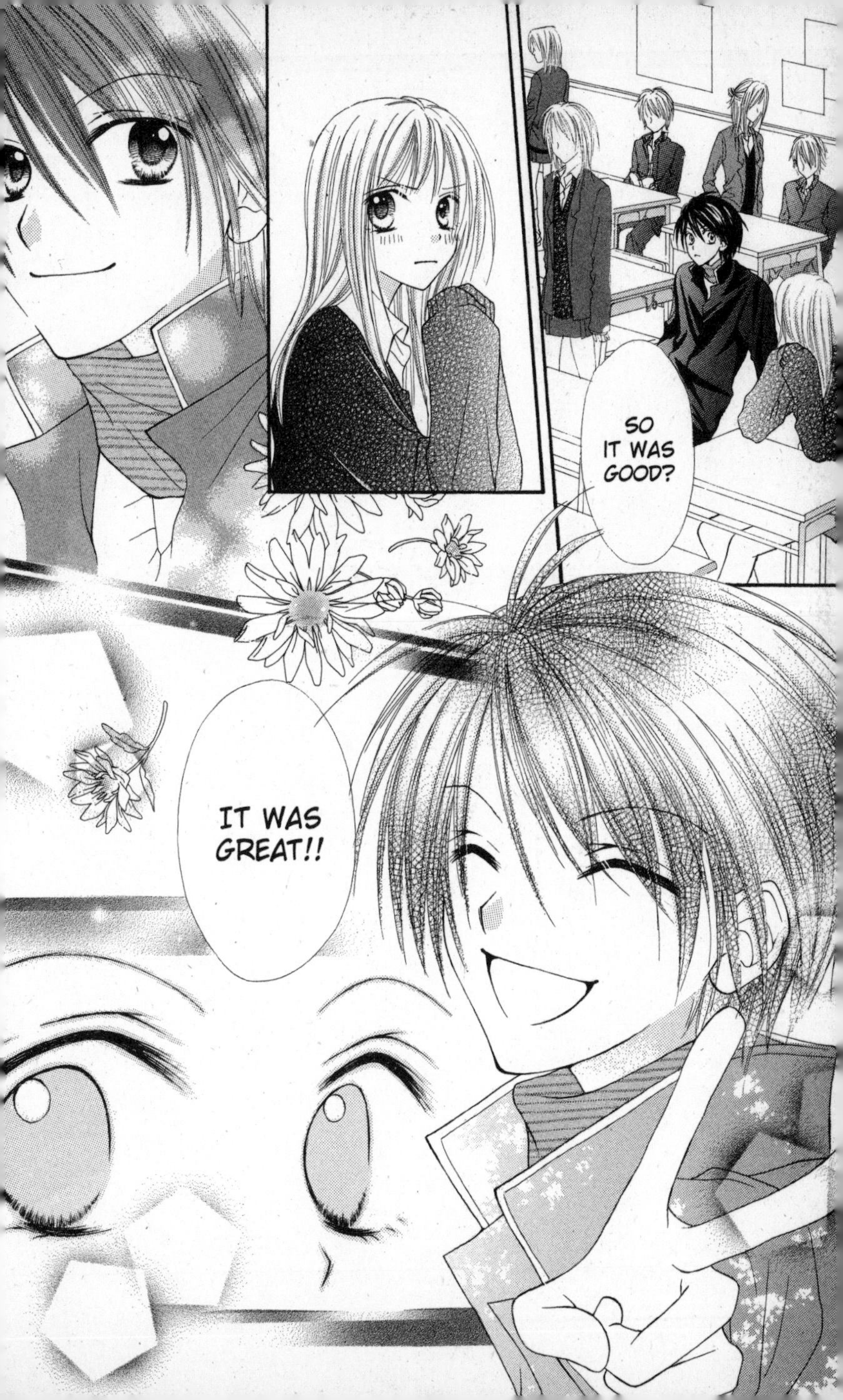
SO IT WAS GOOD?
IT WAS GREAT!!

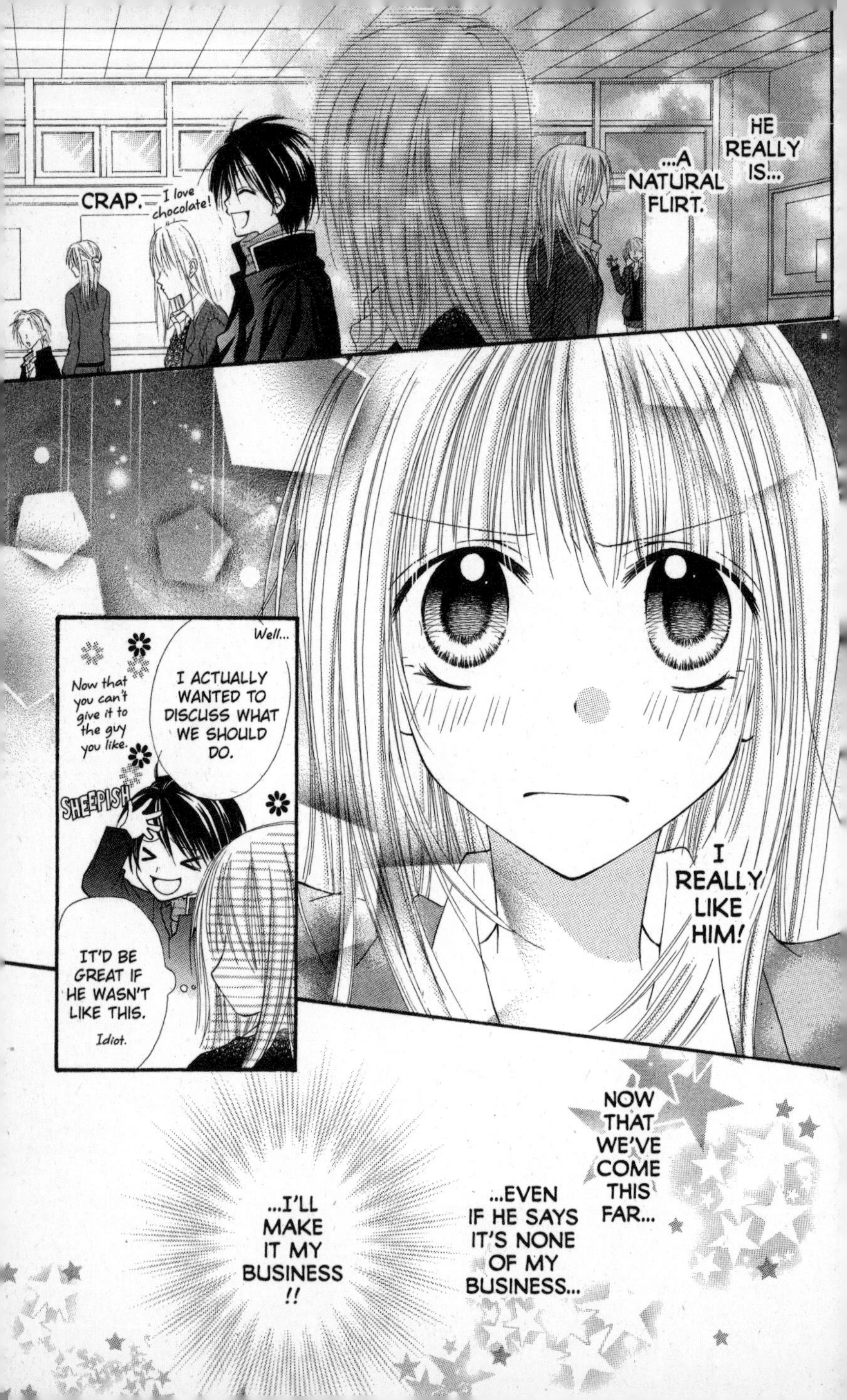
HE REALLY IS...
...A NATURAL FLIRT.
I love chocolate!
CRAP.
I REALLY LIKE HIM!
Well...
I ACTUALLY WANTED TO DISCUSS WHAT WE SHOULD DO.
Now that you can't give it to the guy you like.
SHEEPISH
IT'D BE GREAT IF HE WASN'T LIKE THIS.
Idiot.
NOW THAT WE'VE COME THIS FAR...
...EVEN IF HE SAYS IT'S NONE OF MY BUSINESS...
...I'LL MAKE IT MY BUSINESS!!

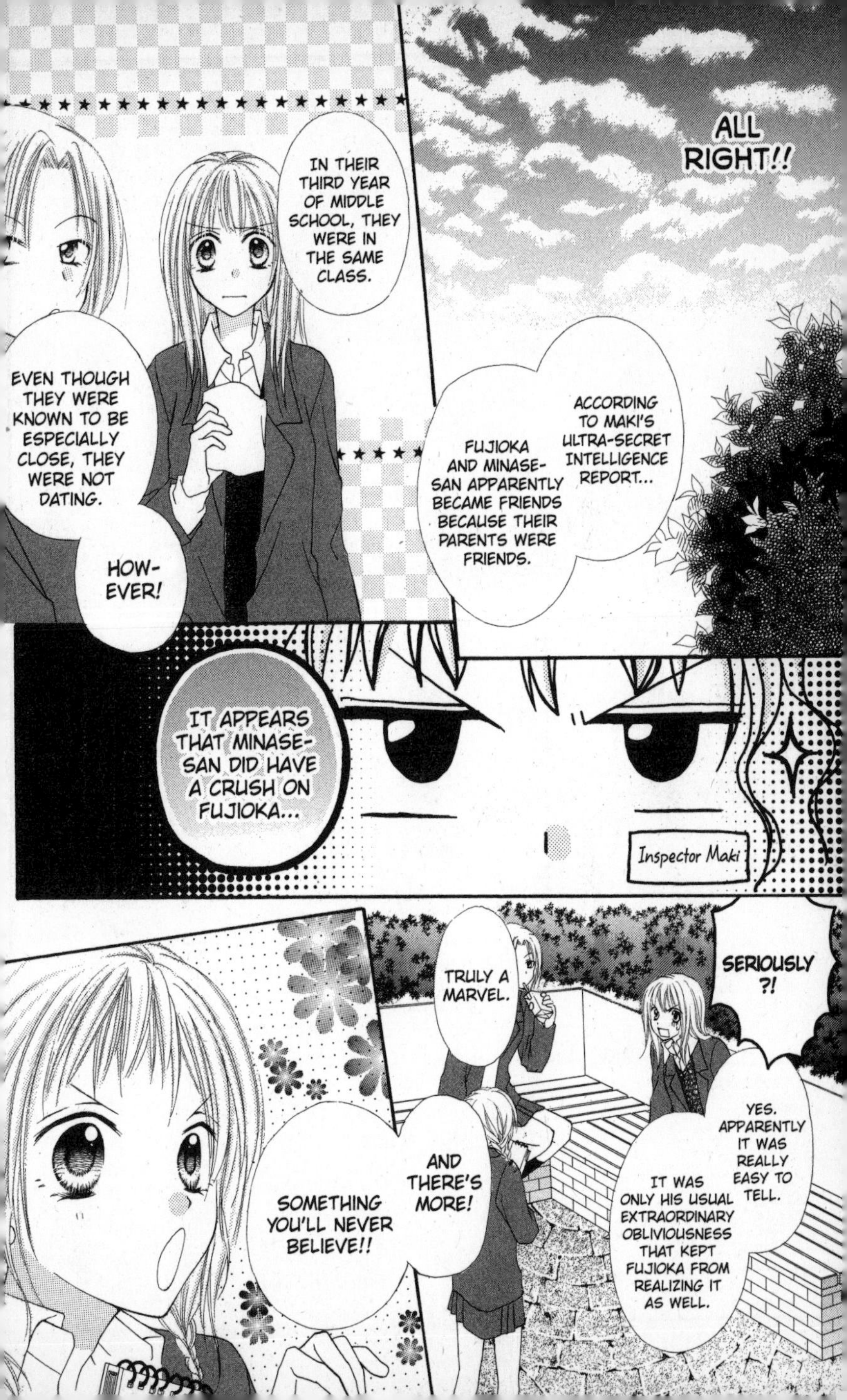
ALL RIGHT!!
ACCORDING TO MAKI'S ULTRA-SECRET INTELLIGENCE REPORT...
FUJIOKA AND MINASE-SAN APPARENTLY BECAME FRIENDS BECAUSE THEIR PARENTS WERE FRIENDS.
IN THEIR THIRD YEAR OF MIDDLE SCHOOL, THEY WERE IN THE SAME CLASS.
EVEN THOUGH THEY WERE KNOWN TO BE ESPECIALLY CLOSE, THEY WERE NOT DATING.
HOW-EVER!
IT APPEARS THAT MINASE-SAN DID HAVE A CRUSH ON FUJIOKA...
Inspector Maki
SERIOUSLY?!
TRULY A MARVEL.
YES. APPARENTLY IT WAS REALLY EASY TO TELL.
IT WAS ONLY HIS USUAL EXTRAORDINARY OBLIVIOUSNESS THAT KEPT FUJIOKA FROM REALIZING IT AS WELL.
AND THERE'S MORE!
SOMETHING YOU'LL NEVER BELIEVE!!

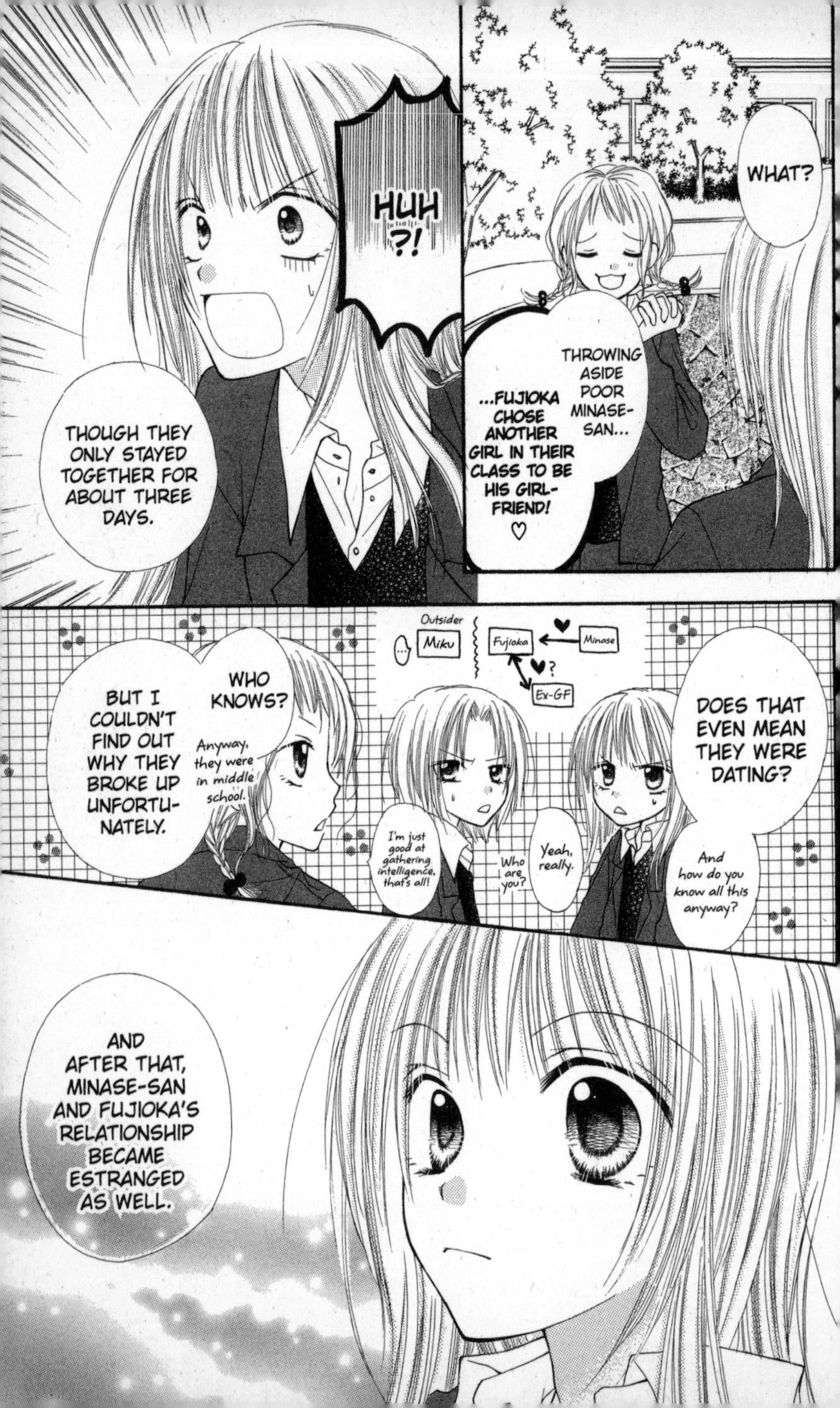
WHAT?
THROWING ASIDE POOR MINASE-SAN...
...FUJIOKA CHOSE ANOTHER GIRL IN THEIR CLASS TO BE HIS GIRL-FRIEND! ♡
HUH ?!
THOUGH THEY ONLY STAYED TOGETHER FOR ABOUT THREE DAYS.
DOES THAT EVEN MEAN THEY WERE DATING?
And how do you know all this anyway?
Minase
Fujioka
Ex-GF
Outsider
Miku
...
Yeah, really.
Who are you?
I'm just good at gathering intelligence, that's all!
WHO KNOWS?
Anyway, they were in middle school.
BUT I COULDN'T FIND OUT WHY THEY BROKE UP UNFORTU-NATELY.
AND AFTER THAT, MINASE-SAN AND FUJIOKA'S RELATIONSHIP BECAME ESTRANGED AS WELL.

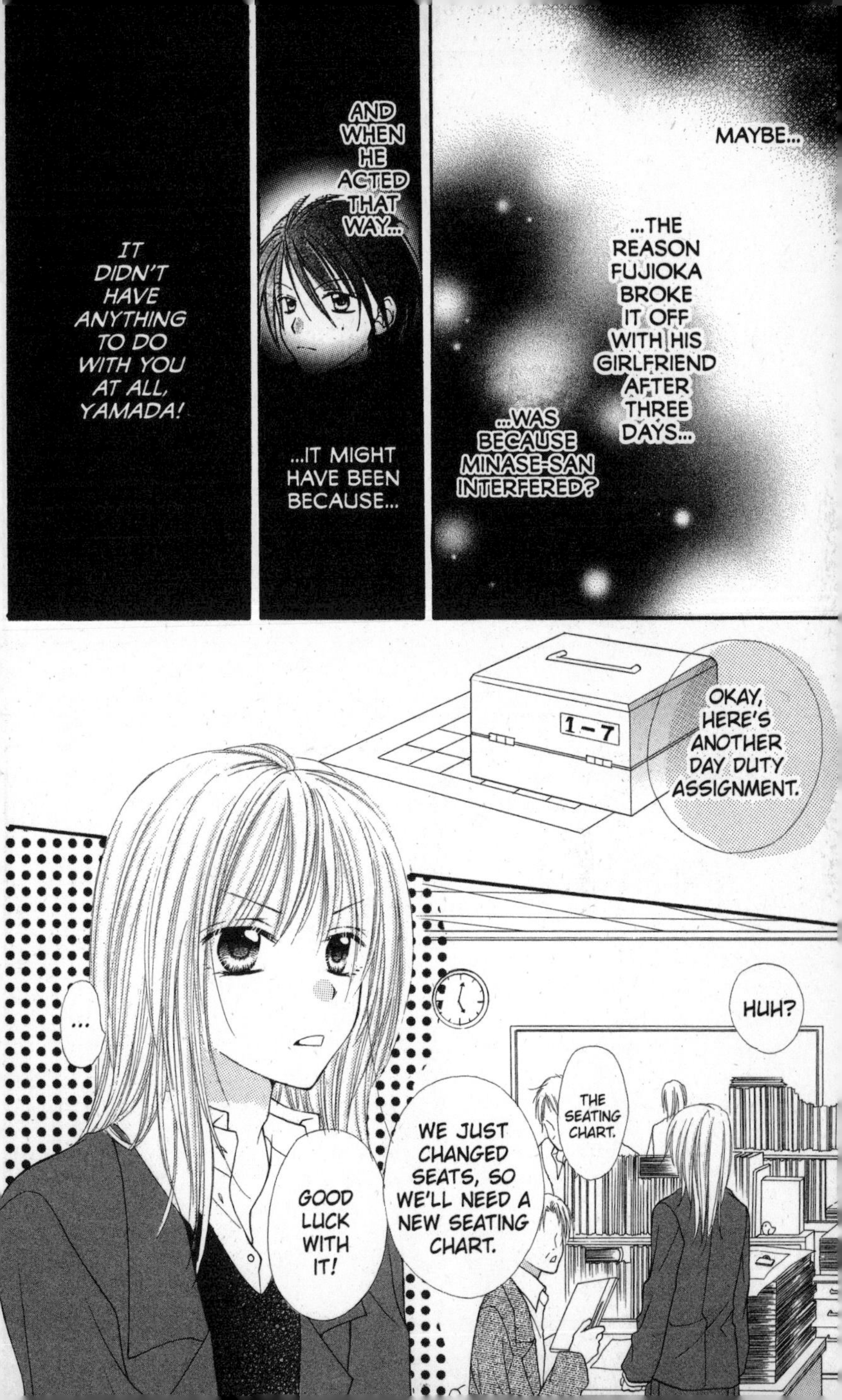
MAYBE...
...THE REASON FUJIOKA BROKE IT OFF WITH HIS GIRLFRIEND AFTER THREE DAYS...
...WAS BECAUSE MINASE-SAN INTERFERED?
AND WHEN HE ACTED THAT WAY...
...IT MIGHT HAVE BEEN BECAUSE...
IT DIDN'T HAVE ANYTHING TO DO WITH YOU AT ALL, YAMADA!
1-7
OKAY, HERE'S ANOTHER DAY DUTY ASSIGNMENT.
HUH?
THE SEATING CHART.
WE JUST CHANGED SEATS, SO WE'LL NEED A NEW SEATING CHART.
GOOD LUCK WITH IT!
...

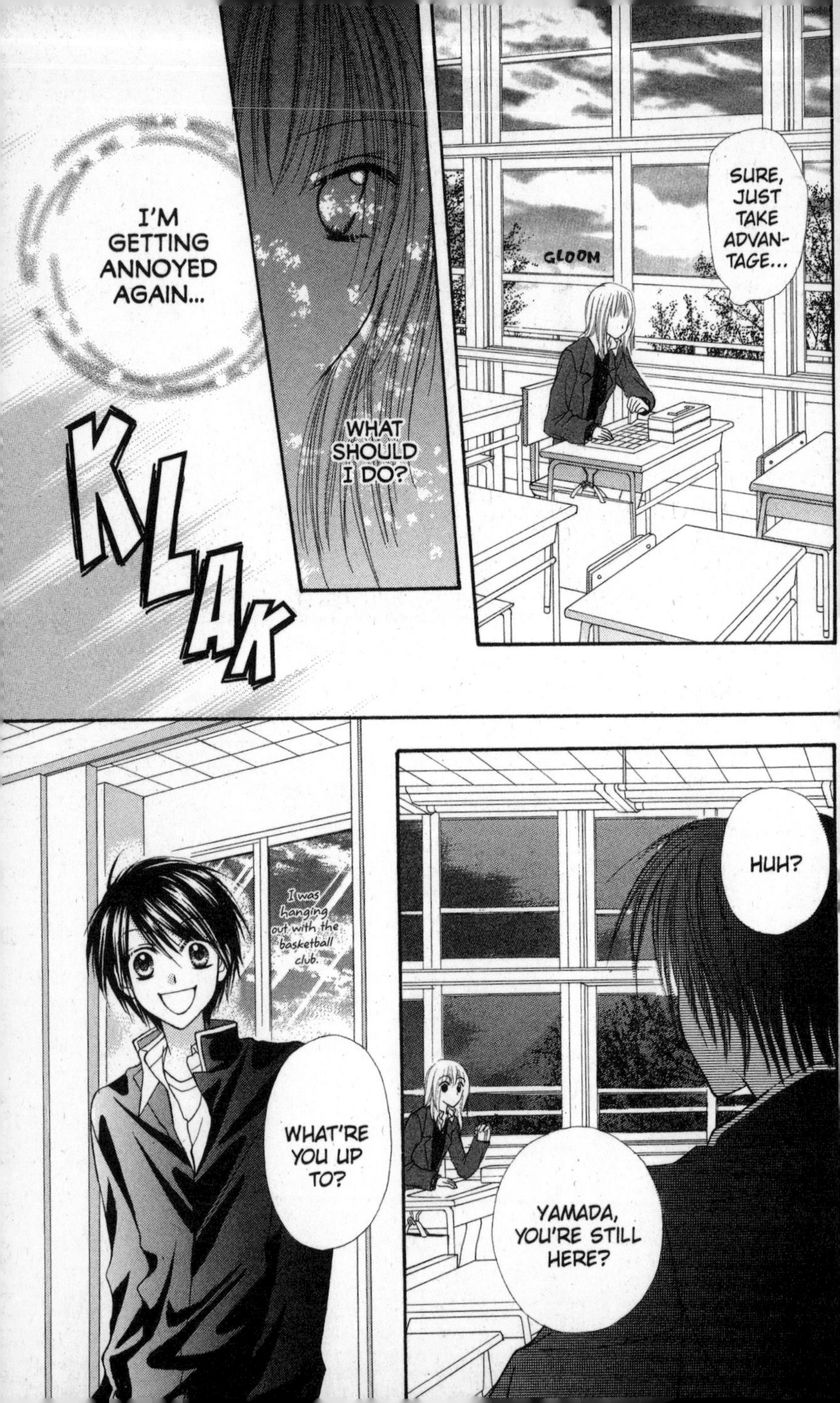
SURE, JUST TAKE ADVANTAGE...
GLOOM
WHAT SHOULD I DO?
I'M GETTING ANNOYED AGAIN...
KLAK
HUH?
YAMADA, YOU'RE STILL HERE?
WHAT'RE YOU UP TO?
I was hanging out with the basketball club.

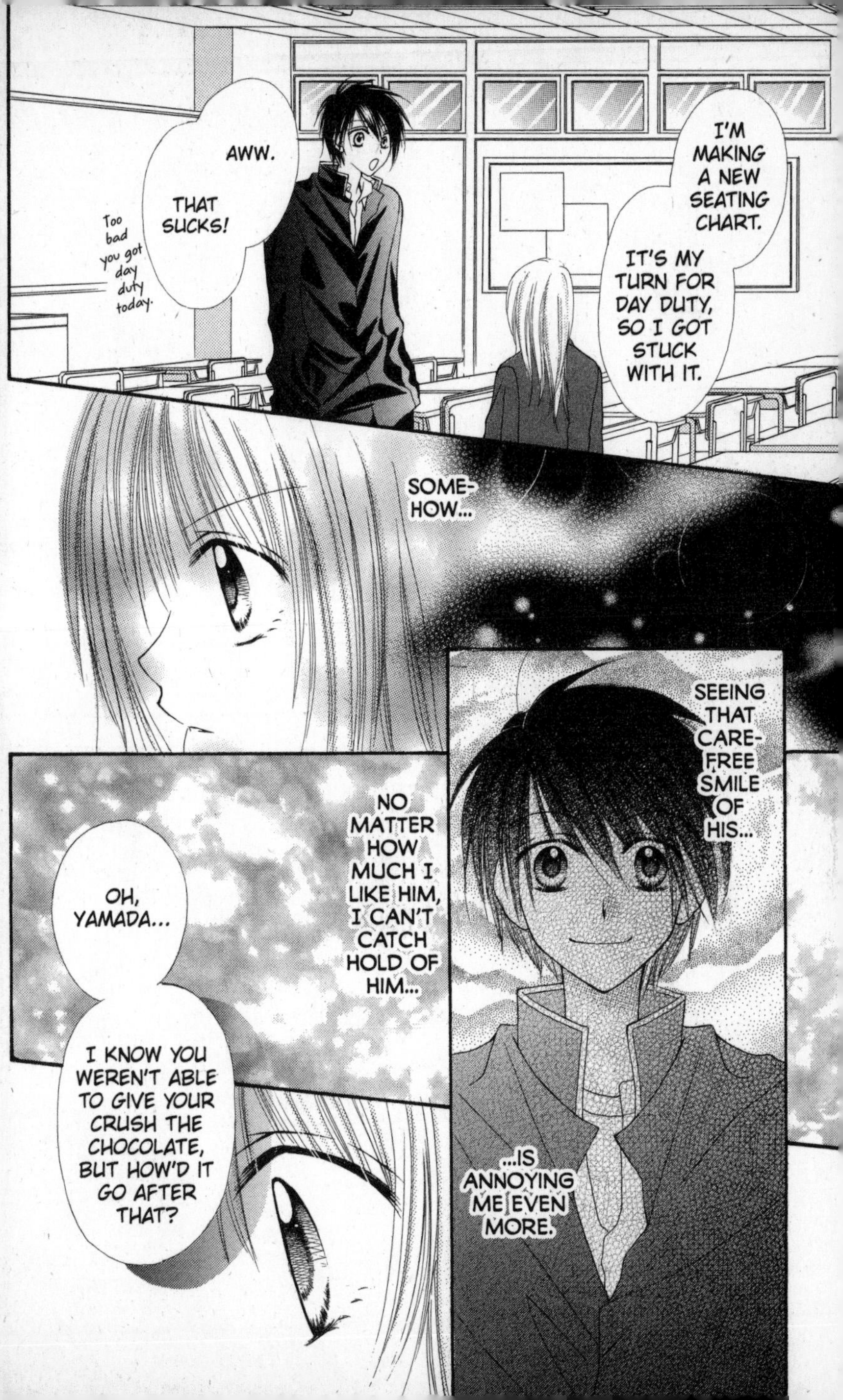
I'M MAKING A NEW SEATING CHART.
IT'S MY TURN FOR DAY DUTY, SO I GOT STUCK WITH IT.
AWW.
THAT SUCKS!
Too bad you got day duty today.
SOME-HOW...
SEEING THAT CARE-FREE SMILE OF HIS...
NO MATTER HOW MUCH I LIKE HIM, I CAN'T CATCH HOLD OF HIM...
...IS ANNOYING ME EVEN MORE.
OH, YAMADA...
I KNOW YOU WEREN'T ABLE TO GIVE YOUR CRUSH THE CHOCOLATE, BUT HOW'D IT GO AFTER THAT?

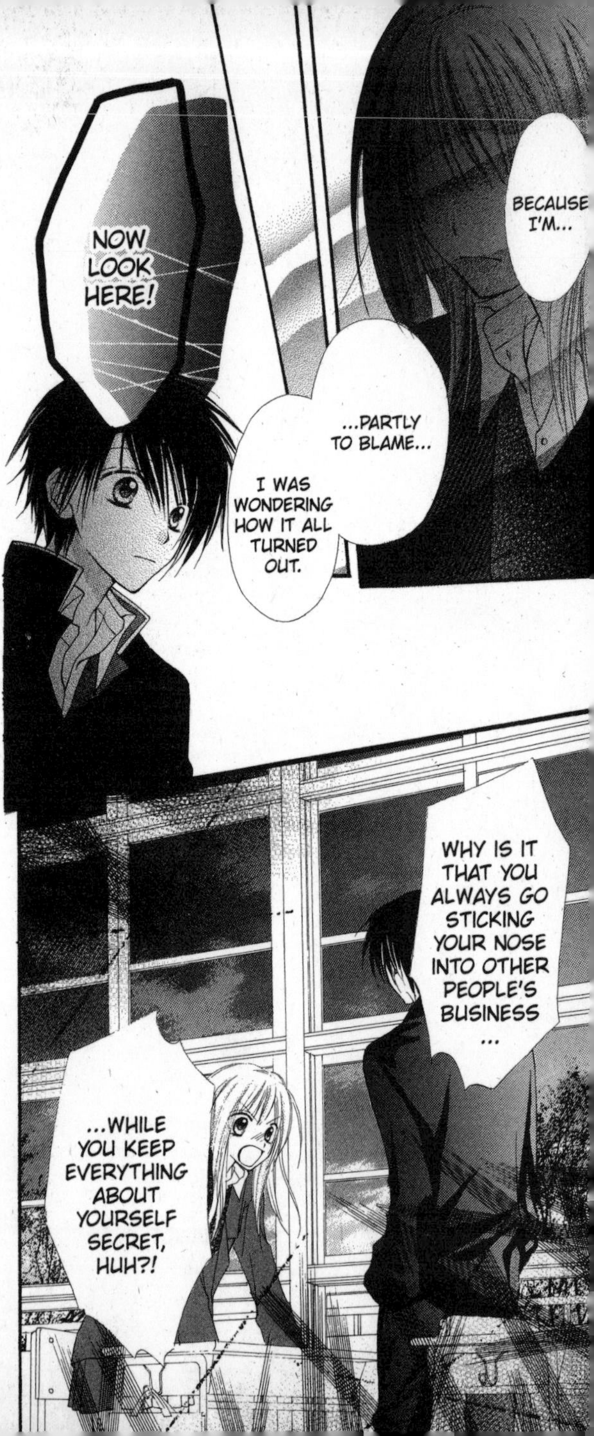
BECAUSE I'M...
...PARTLY TO BLAME...
I WAS WONDERING HOW IT ALL TURNED OUT.
NOW LOOK HERE!
WHY IS IT THAT YOU ALWAYS GO STICKING YOUR NOSE INTO OTHER PEOPLE'S BUSINESS ...
...WHILE YOU KEEP EVERYTHING ABOUT YOURSELF SECRET, HUH?!

8

Ahh! While I was in the middle of writing these sidebars (there are 14), my editor changed again! The reason I say "again" is because—since my debut as a mangaka three and a half years ago—I've had five different editors working with me! It's actually pretty interesting, so let me describe them for you:

Debut to September 2001 — Kiwazou-san
↓
October 2001–June 2002 — Ouji-san
↓
July 2002–June 2003 — T-san
↓
July 2003–June 2004 — K-san
↓
July 2004 to present — Morii-san

My first editor took care of me for over a year, but after that, everyone else each bid me adieu after less than a year. That's just too often! I'm guessing that the editors themselves said:

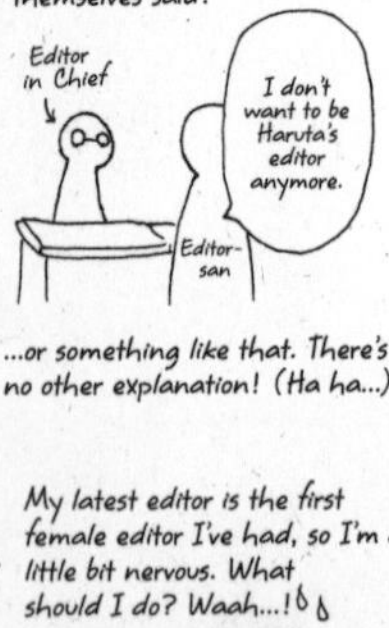
Editor in Chief
I don't want to be Haruta's editor anymore.
Editor-san

...or something like that. There's no other explanation! (Ha ha...)

My latest editor is the first female editor I've had, so I'm a little bit nervous. What should I do? Waah...!

I'll become a ninja! Maybe not.

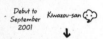

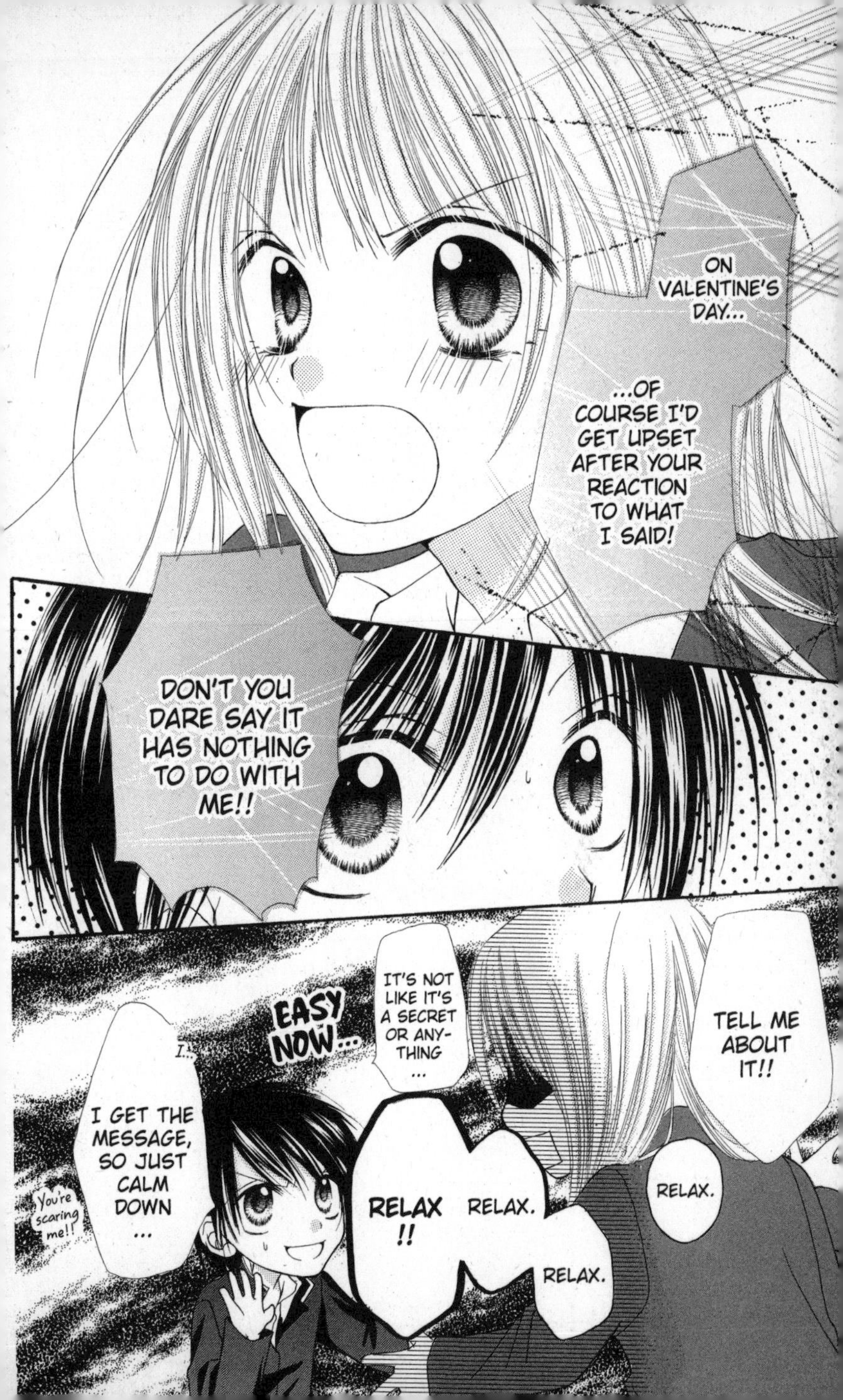
ON VALENTINE'S DAY...
...OF COURSE I'D GET UPSET AFTER YOUR REACTION TO WHAT I SAID!
DON'T YOU DARE SAY IT HAS NOTHING TO DO WITH ME!!
TELL ME ABOUT IT!!
IT'S NOT LIKE IT'S A SECRET OR ANYTHING ...
EASY NOW...
I...
I GET THE MESSAGE, SO JUST CALM DOWN ...
You're scaring me!!
RELAX.
RELAX !!
RELAX.
RELAX.

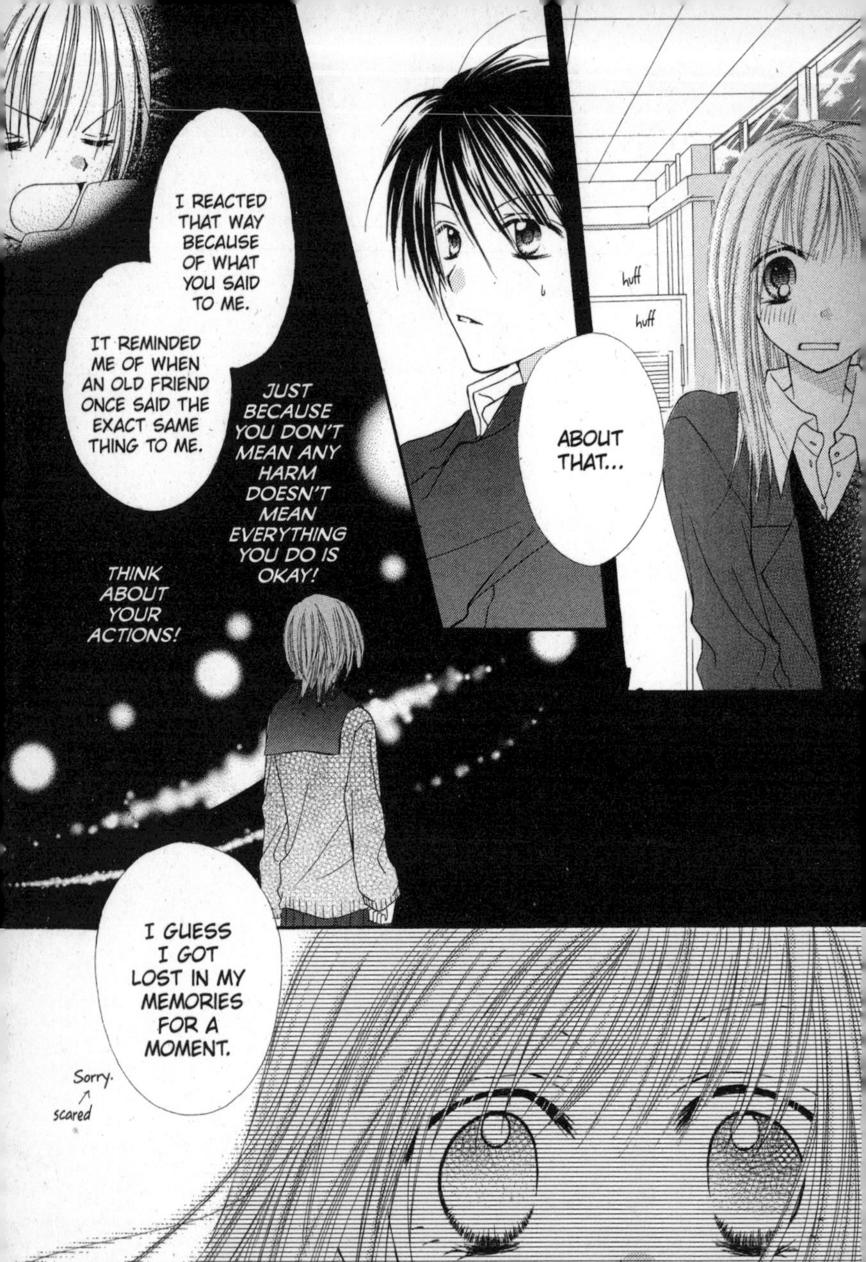
huff
huff
ABOUT THAT...
I REACTED THAT WAY BECAUSE OF WHAT YOU SAID TO ME.
IT REMINDED ME OF WHEN AN OLD FRIEND ONCE SAID THE EXACT SAME THING TO ME.
JUST BECAUSE YOU DON'T MEAN ANY HARM DOESN'T MEAN EVERYTHING YOU DO IS OKAY!
THINK ABOUT YOUR ACTIONS!
I GUESS I GOT LOST IN MY MEMORIES FOR A MOMENT.
Sorry.
scared

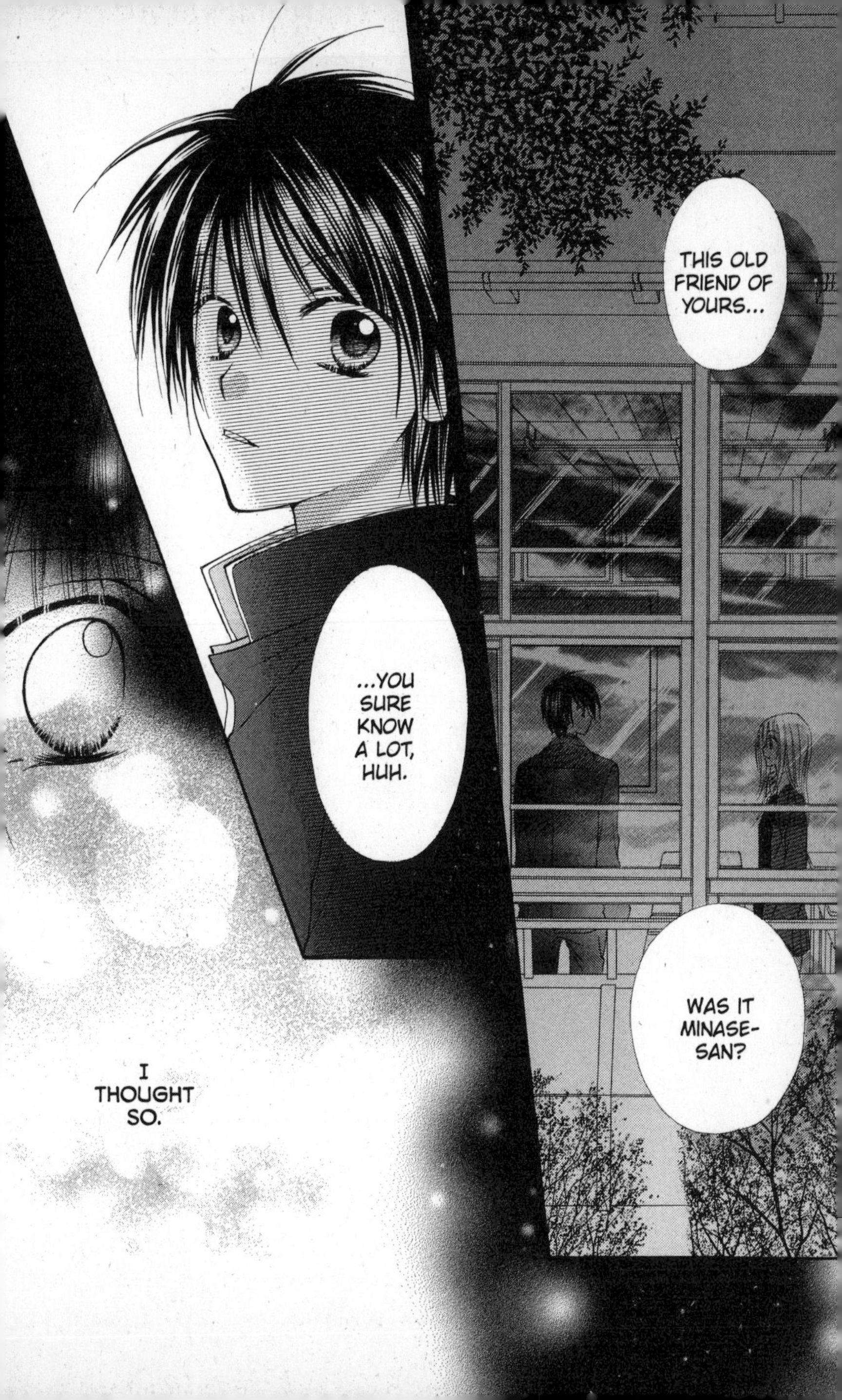
THIS OLD FRIEND OF YOURS...
WAS IT MINASE-SAN?
...YOU SURE KNOW A LOT, HUH.
I THOUGHT SO.

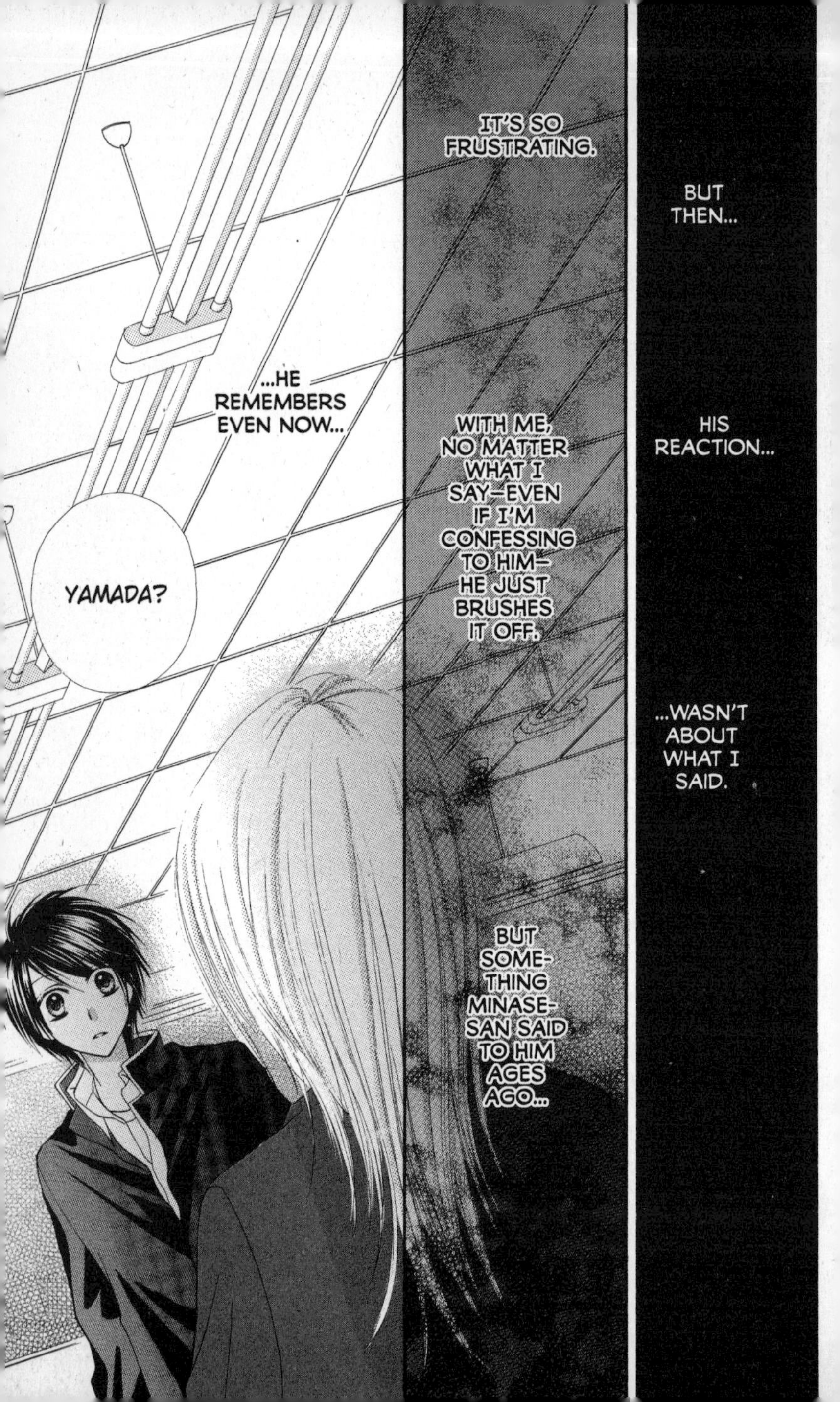
BUT THEN...
HIS REACTION...
...WASN'T ABOUT WHAT I SAID.
IT'S SO FRUSTRATING.
WITH ME, NO MATTER WHAT I SAY—EVEN IF I'M CONFESSING TO HIM—HE JUST BRUSHES IT OFF.
BUT SOME-THING MINASE-SAN SAID TO HIM AGES AGO...
...HE REMEMBERS EVEN NOW...
YAMADA?

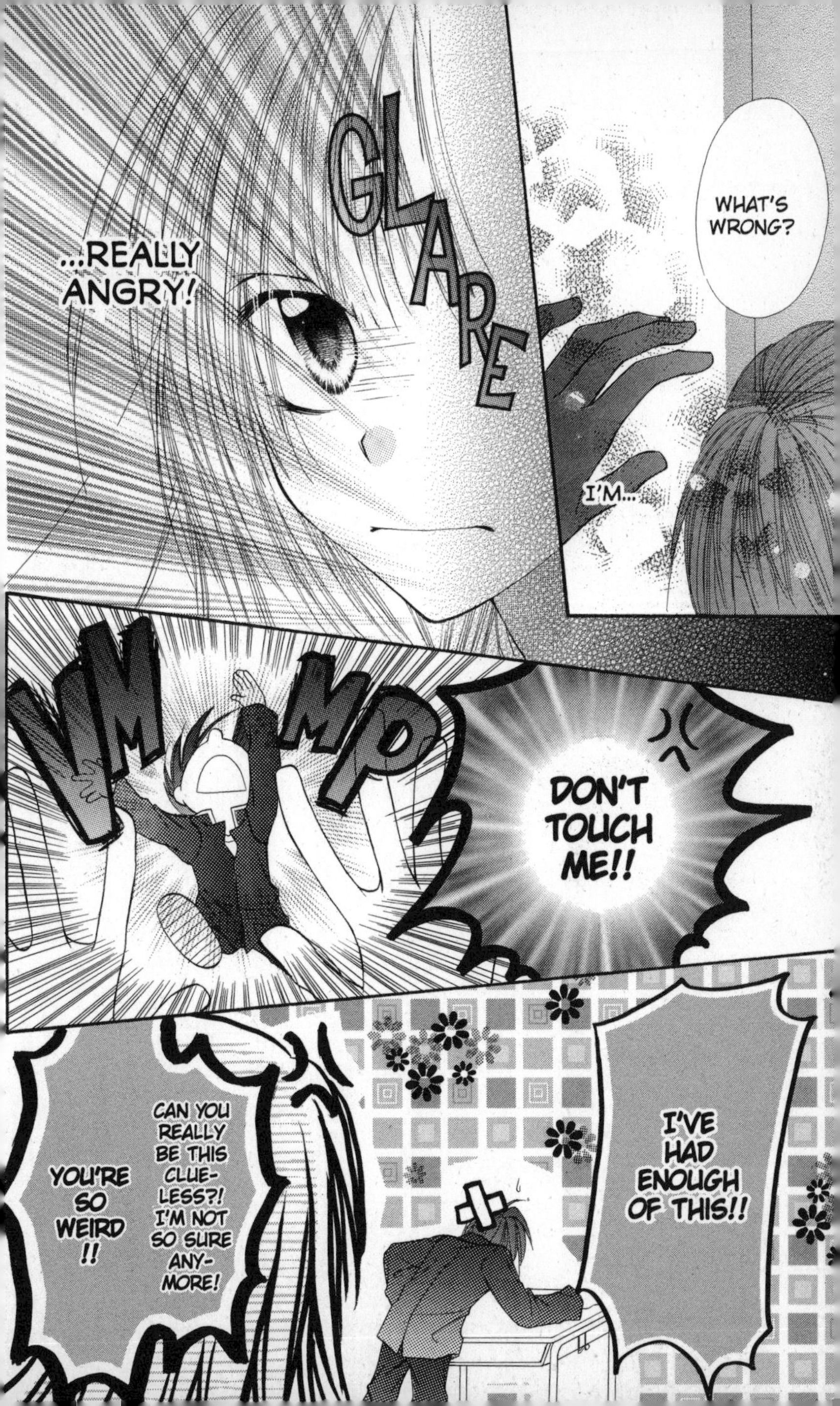
WHAT'S WRONG?
I'M...
GLARE
...REALLY ANGRY!
DON'T TOUCH ME!!
WM MP
I'VE HAD ENOUGH OF THIS!!
CAN YOU REALLY BE THIS CLUE-LESS?! I'M NOT SO SURE ANY-MORE!
YOU'RE SO WEIRD!!

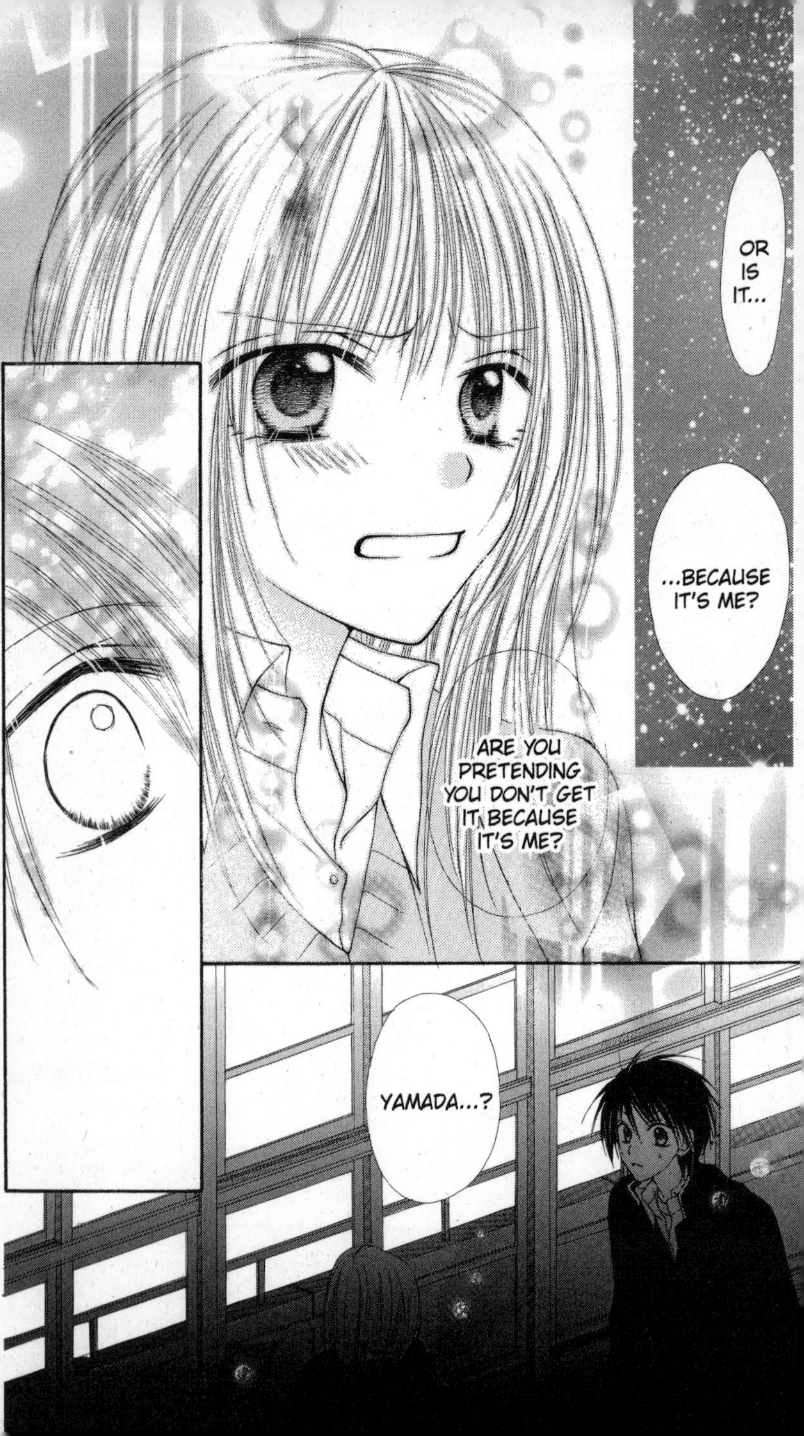
OR IS IT...
...BECAUSE IT'S ME?
ARE YOU PRETENDING YOU DON'T GET IT BECAUSE IT'S ME?
YAMADA...?

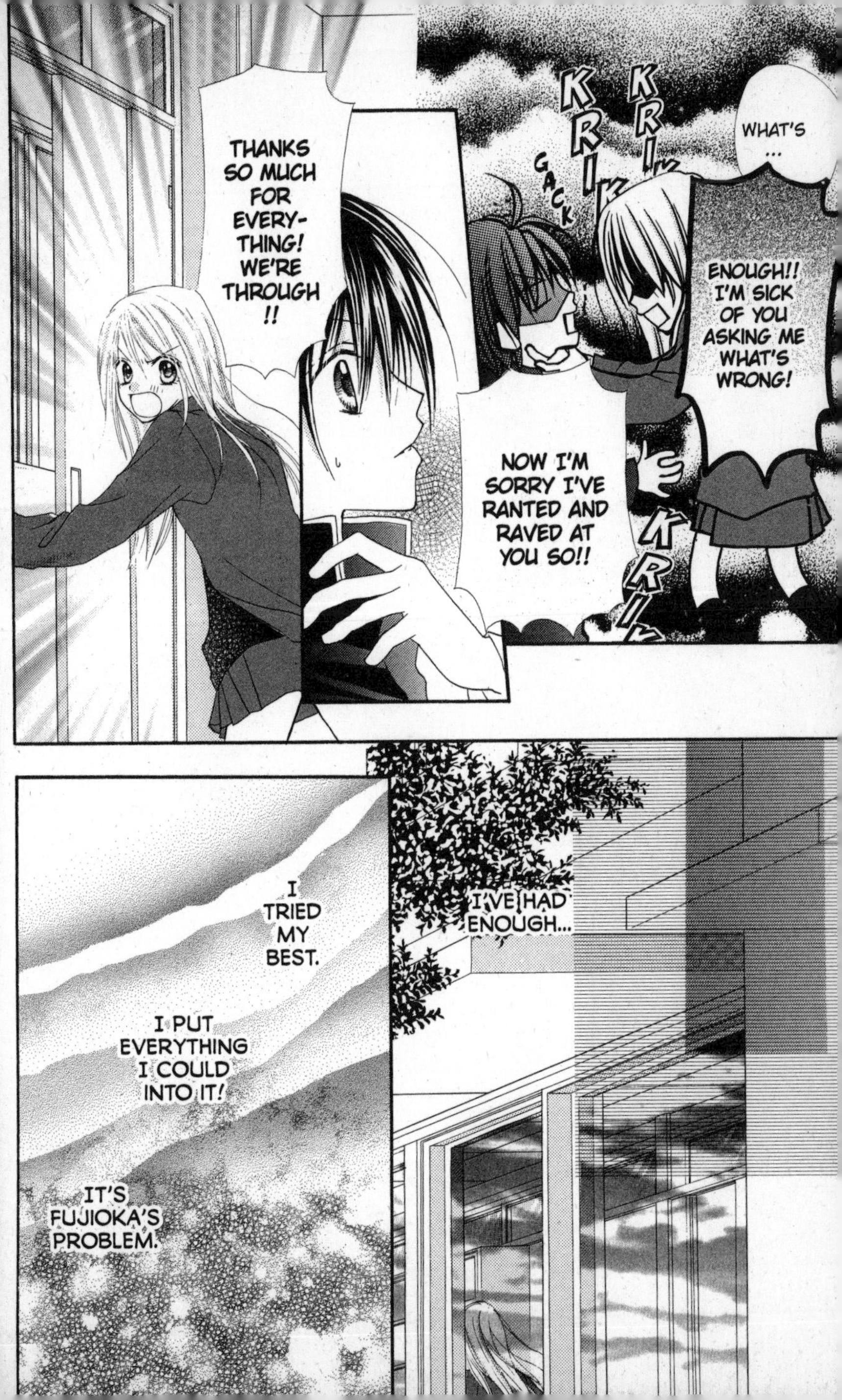
WHAT'S ...
KRIK KRIK
GACK
ENOUGH!! I'M SICK OF YOU ASKING ME WHAT'S WRONG!
KRIK
NOW I'M SORRY I'VE RANTED AND RAVED AT YOU SO!!
THANKS SO MUCH FOR EVERY-THING! WE'RE THROUGH !!
I'VE HAD ENOUGH...
I TRIED MY BEST.
I PUT EVERYTHING I COULD INTO IT!
IT'S FUJIOKA'S PROBLEM.

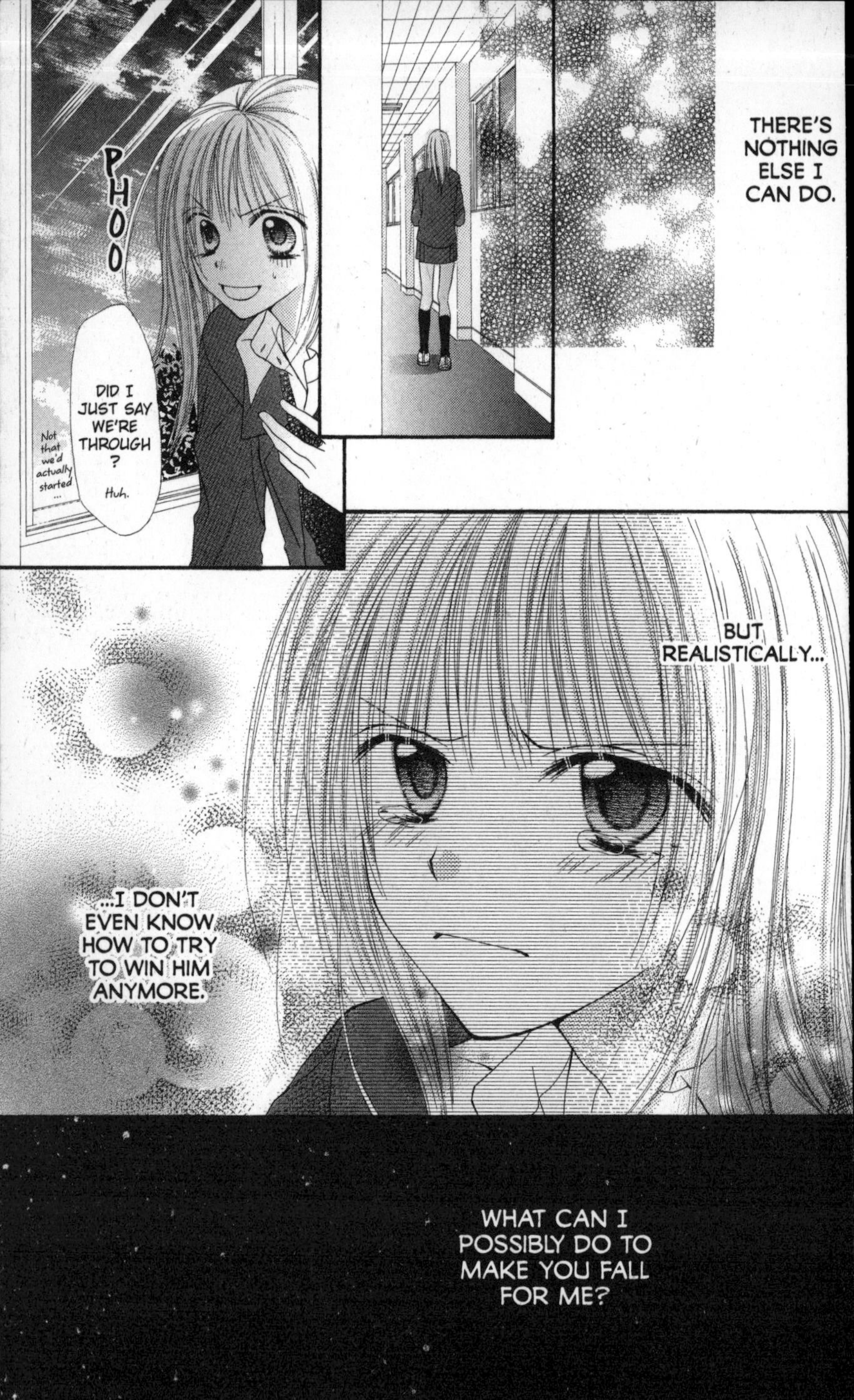
THERE'S NOTHING ELSE I CAN DO.
PHOO
DID I JUST SAY WE'RE THROUGH? Huh.
Not that we'd actually started...
BUT REALISTICALLY...
...I DON'T EVEN KNOW HOW TO TRY TO WIN HIM ANYMORE.
WHAT CAN I POSSIBLY DO TO MAKE YOU FALL FOR ME?

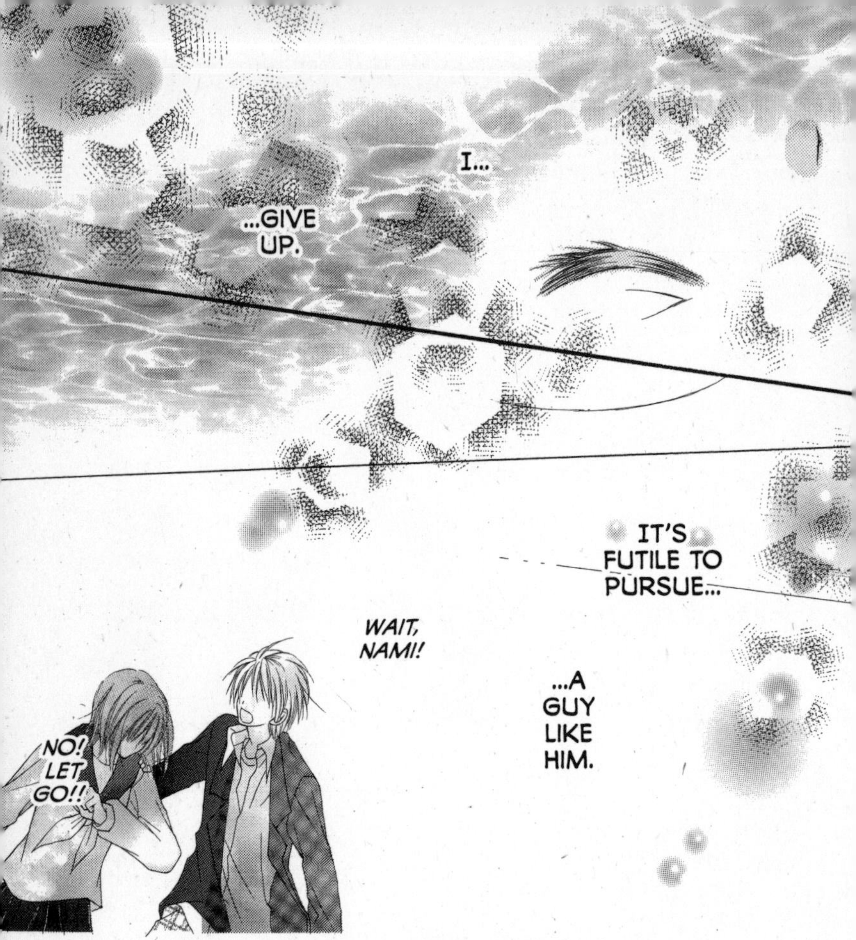
I...
...GIVE UP.
IT'S FUTILE TO PURSUE...
...A GUY LIKE HIM.
WAIT, NAMI!
NO! LET GO!!

SMALL TALK ③

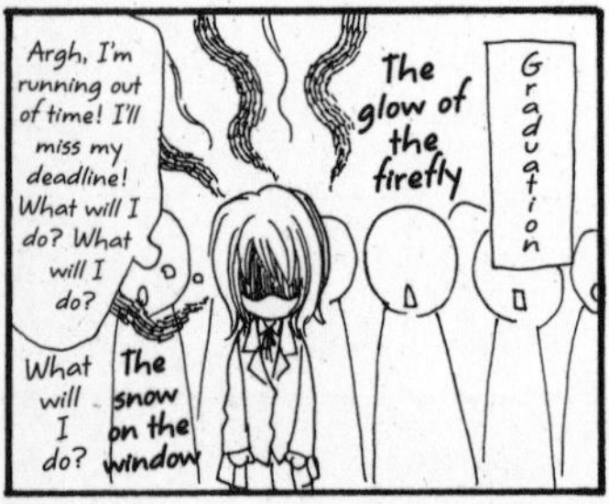
Graduation
The glow of the firefly
Argh, I'm running out of time! I'll miss my deadline! What will I do? What will I do?
The snow on the window
What will I do?

I wonder why chapter 4 ended up being 40 pages... What's worse, the deadline for it and my high school graduation were on the same day! (laugh) Ah ha ha, running off right after the ceremony totally wasn't like me either. A toast to me, who got strange looks from people who didn't know my circumstances and thought, "What's her problem?"

Well, no point in dwelling on the past... Eh heh heh! (cry)

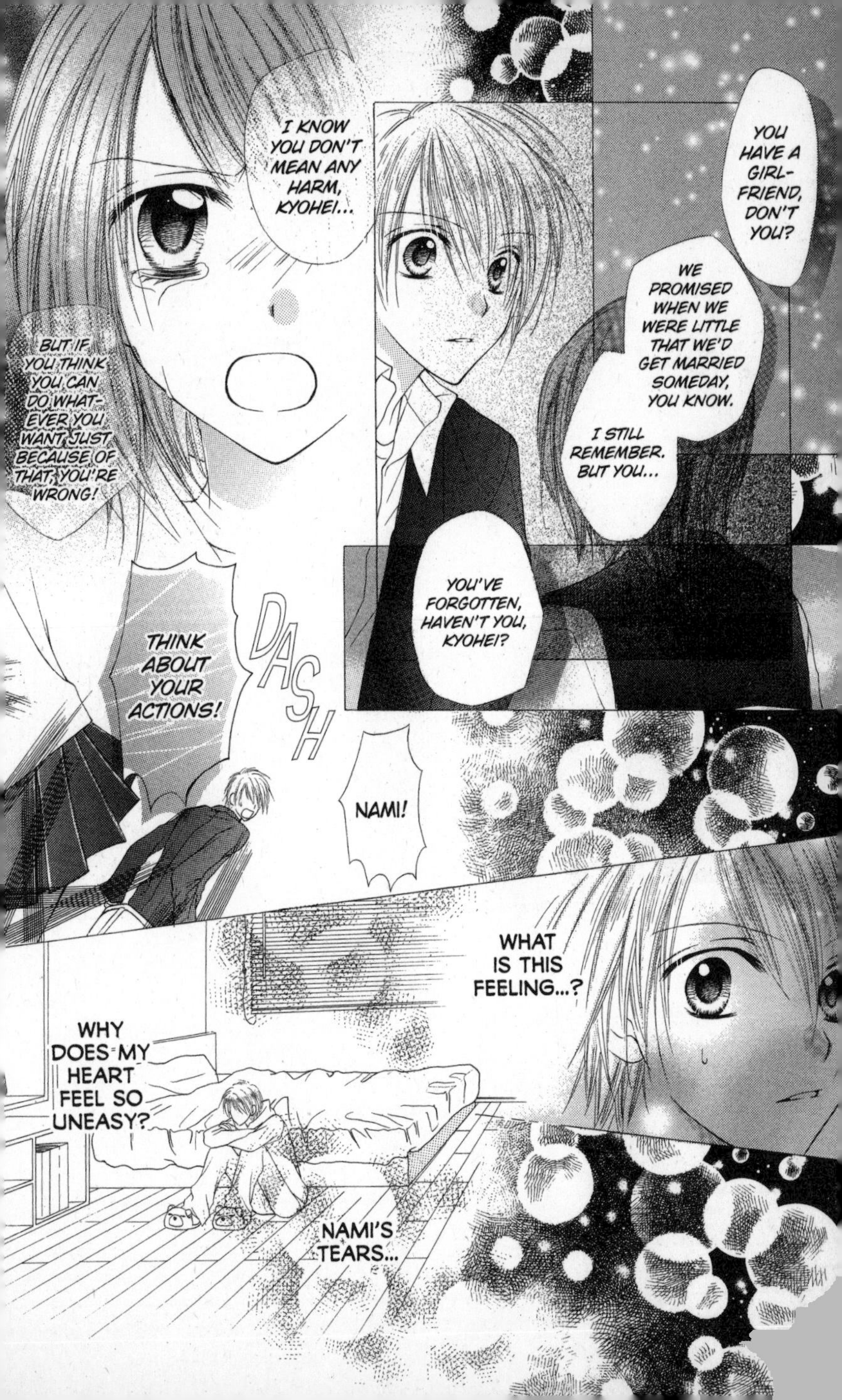
YOU HAVE A GIRL-FRIEND, DON'T YOU?
WE PROMISED WHEN WE WERE LITTLE THAT WE'D GET MARRIED SOMEDAY, YOU KNOW.
I STILL REMEMBER. BUT YOU...
YOU'VE FORGOTTEN, HAVEN'T YOU, KYOHEI?
I KNOW YOU DON'T MEAN ANY HARM, KYOHEI...
BUT IF YOU THINK YOU CAN DO WHAT-EVER YOU WANT JUST BECAUSE OF THAT, YOU'RE WRONG!
THINK ABOUT YOUR ACTIONS!
DASH
NAMI!
WHAT IS THIS FEELING...?
WHY DOES MY HEART FEEL SO UNEASY?
NAMI'S TEARS...

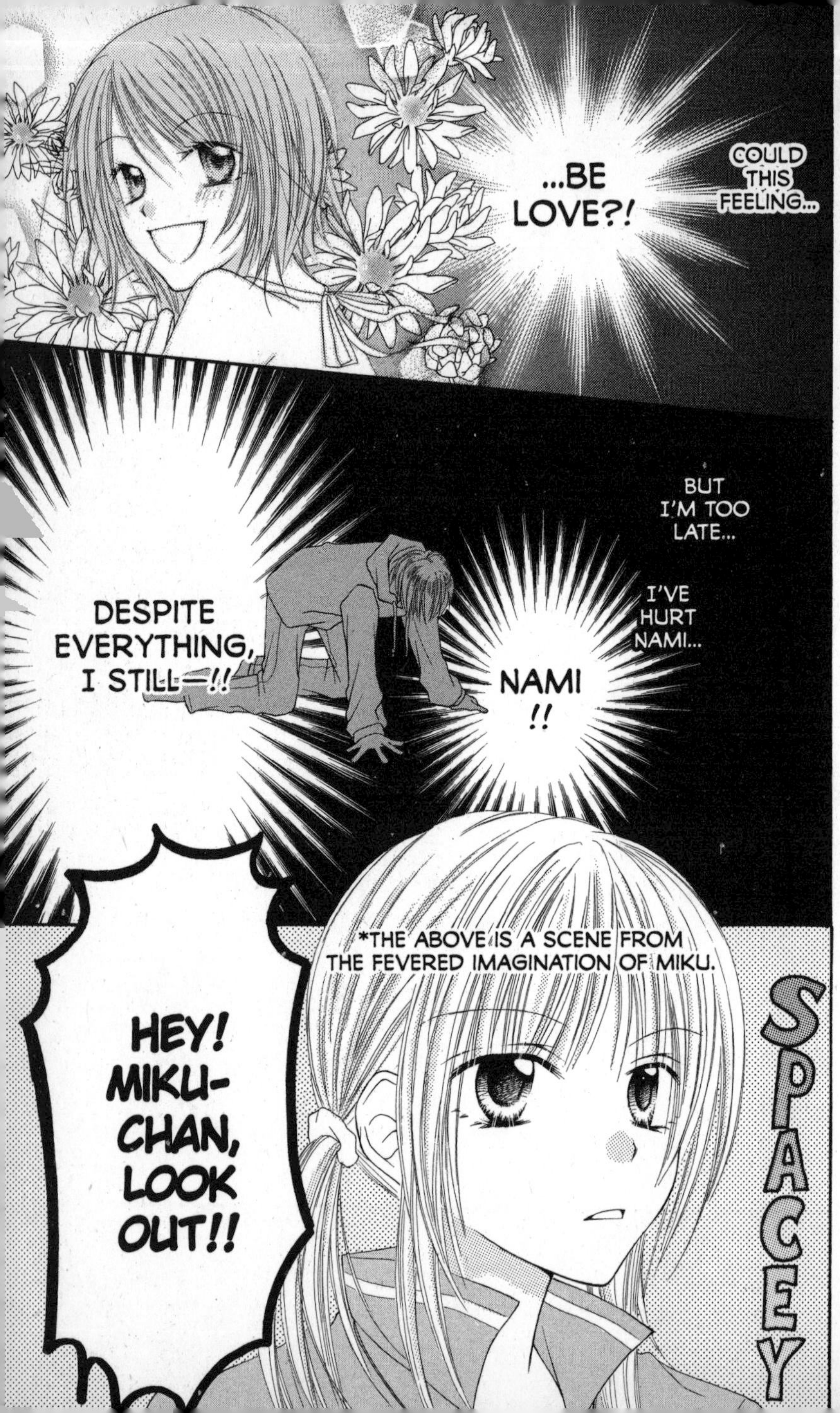
COULD THIS FEELING...
...BE LOVE?!
BUT I'M TOO LATE...
I'VE HURT NAMI...
NAMI!!
DESPITE EVERYTHING, I STILL—!!
SPACEY
*THE ABOVE IS A SCENE FROM THE FEVERED IMAGINATION OF MIKU.
HEY! MIKU-CHAN, LOOK OUT!!

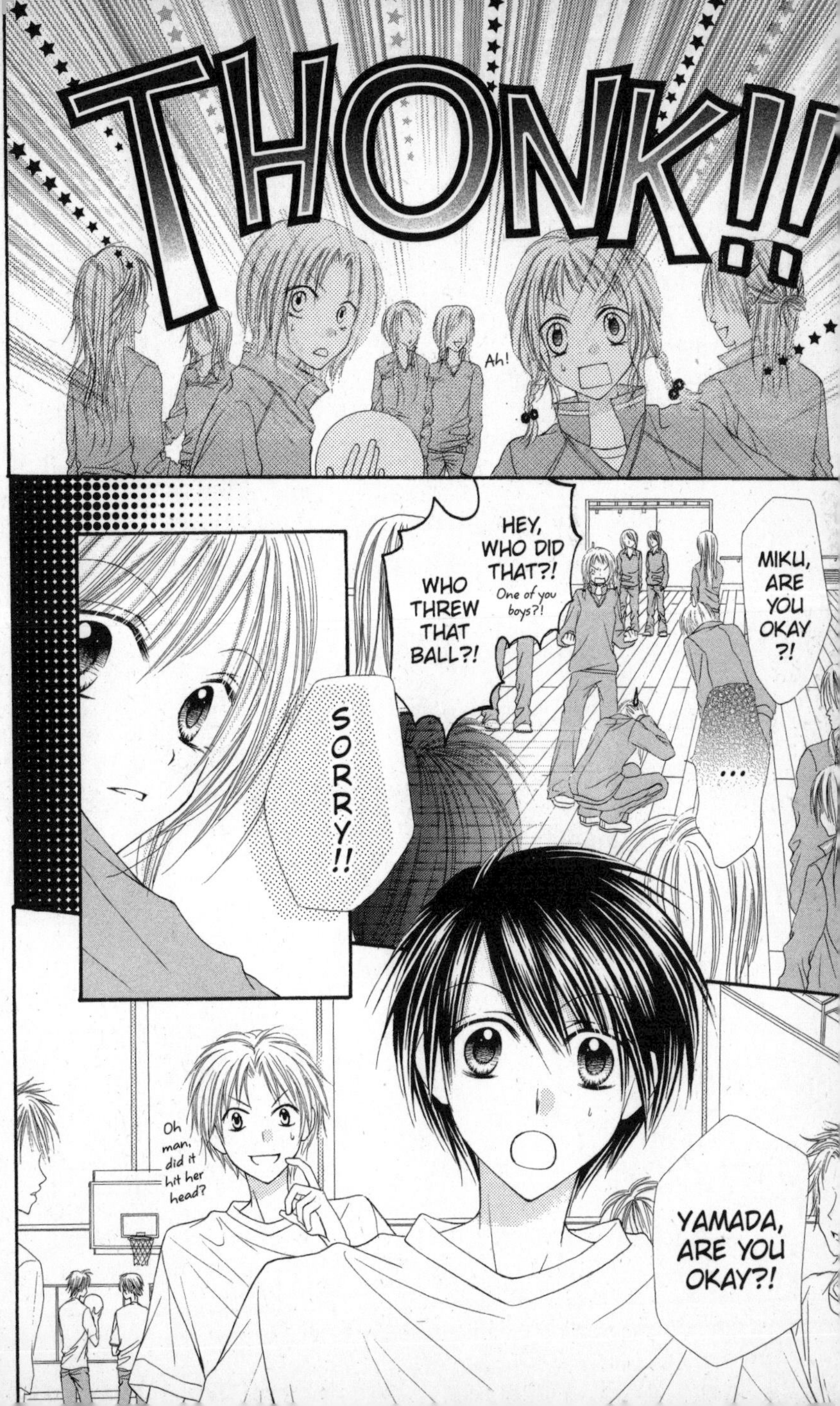
THONK!!
Ah!
MIKU, ARE YOU OKAY?!
HEY, WHO DID THAT?!
One of you boys?!
WHO THREW THAT BALL?!
...
SORRY!!
YAMADA, ARE YOU OKAY?!
Oh man, did it hit her head?

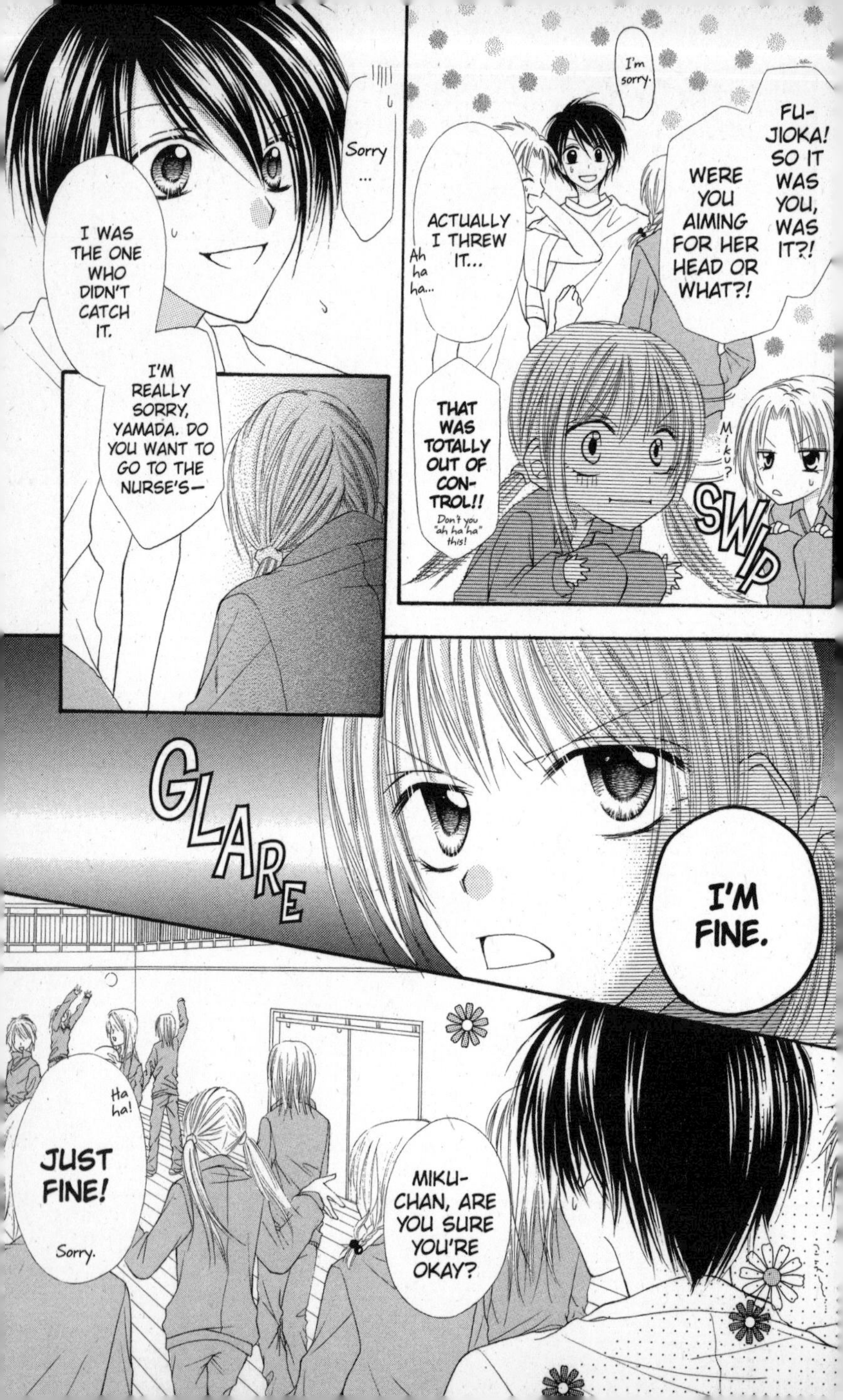
I'm sorry.
FUJIOKA! SO IT WAS YOU, WAS IT?!
WERE YOU AIMING FOR HER HEAD OR WHAT?!
ACTUALLY I THREW IT...
Ah ha ha...
THAT WAS TOTALLY OUT OF CONTROL!!
Don't you "ah ha ha" this!
Miku?
SWIP
Sorry...
I WAS THE ONE WHO DIDN'T CATCH IT.
I'M REALLY SORRY, YAMADA. DO YOU WANT TO GO TO THE NURSE'S—
GLARE
I'M FINE.
MIKU-CHAN, ARE YOU SURE YOU'RE OKAY?
Ha ha!
JUST FINE!
Sorry.

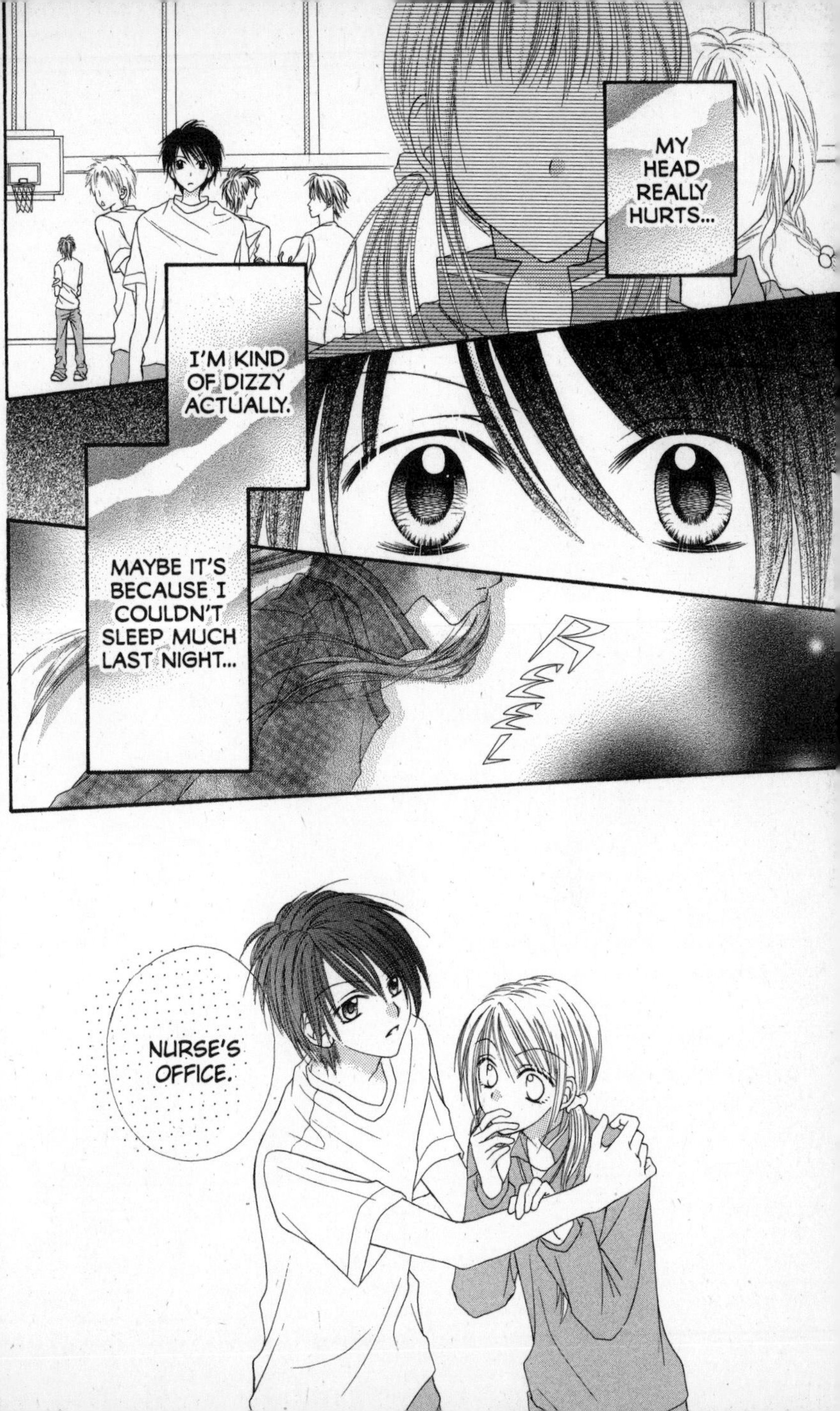
MY HEAD REALLY HURTS...
I'M KIND OF DIZZY ACTUALLY.
MAYBE IT'S BECAUSE I COULDN'T SLEEP MUCH LAST NIGHT...
REEEL
NURSE'S OFFICE.

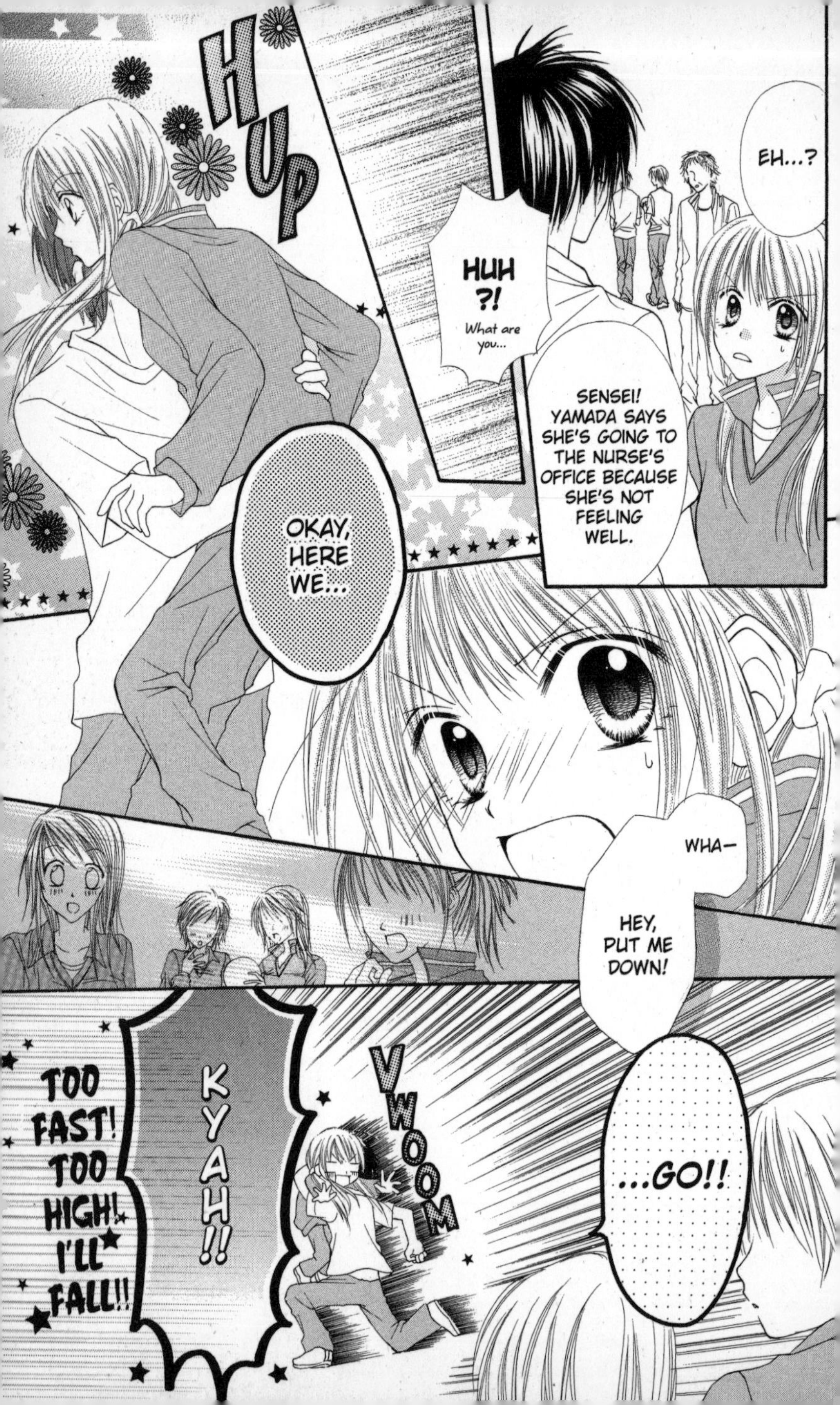
EH...?
SENSEI! YAMADA SAYS SHE'S GOING TO THE NURSE'S OFFICE BECAUSE SHE'S NOT FEELING WELL.
HUH ?!
What are you...
HUP
OKAY, HERE WE...
WHA—
HEY, PUT ME DOWN!
...GO!!
VWOOM
KYAH!!
TOO FAST! TOO HIGH! I'LL FALL!!

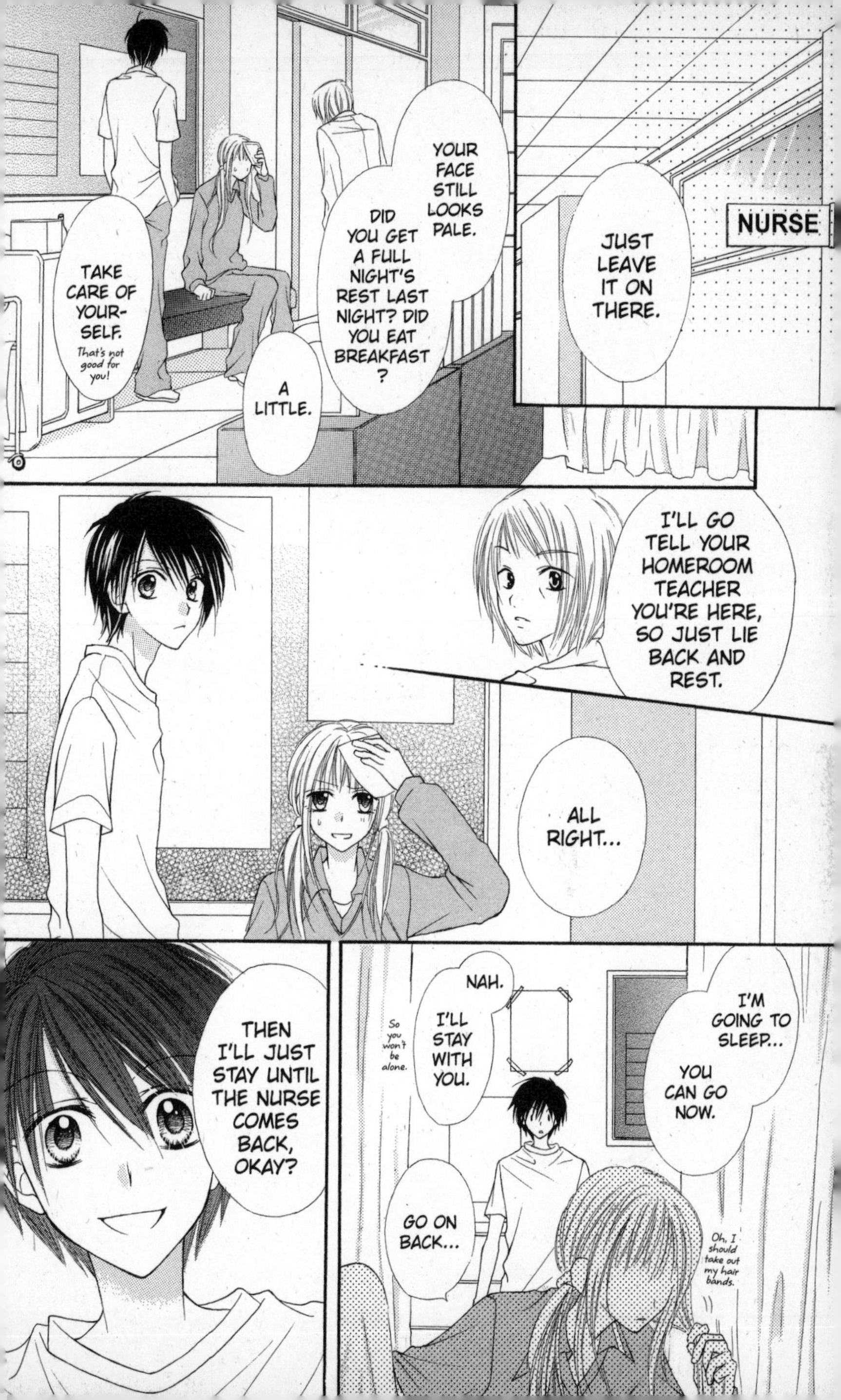
NURSE
JUST LEAVE IT ON THERE.
YOUR FACE STILL LOOKS PALE.
DID YOU GET A FULL NIGHT'S REST LAST NIGHT? DID YOU EAT BREAKFAST?
A LITTLE.
TAKE CARE OF YOUR-SELF.
That's not good for you!
I'LL GO TELL YOUR HOMEROOM TEACHER YOU'RE HERE, SO JUST LIE BACK AND REST.
ALL RIGHT...
I'M GOING TO SLEEP...
YOU CAN GO NOW.
Oh, I should take out my hair bands.
NAH.
I'LL STAY WITH YOU.
So you won't be alone.
GO ON BACK...
THEN I'LL JUST STAY UNTIL THE NURSE COMES BACK, OKAY?

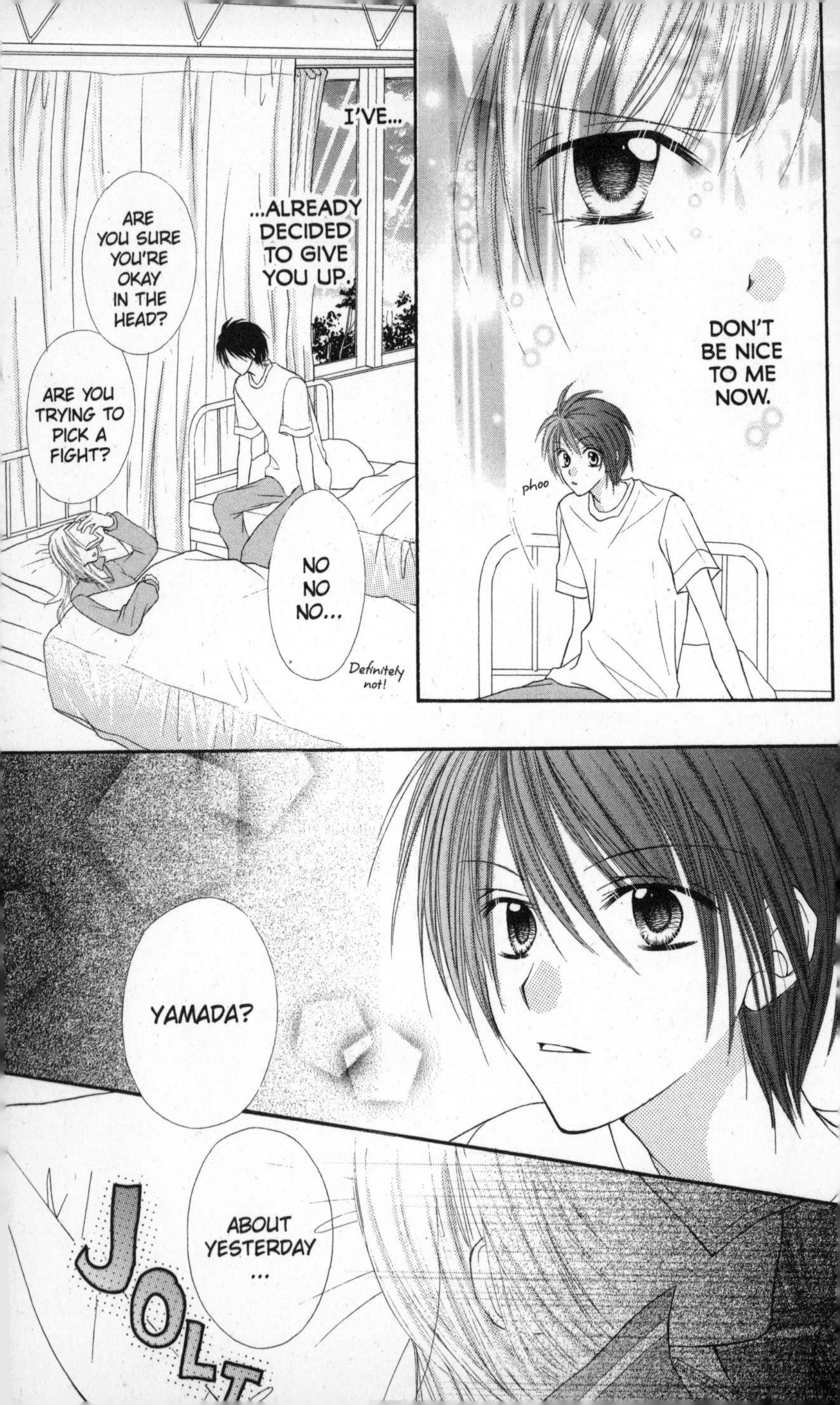
DON'T BE NICE TO ME NOW.
phoo
I'VE...
...ALREADY DECIDED TO GIVE YOU UP.
ARE YOU SURE YOU'RE OKAY IN THE HEAD?
ARE YOU TRYING TO PICK A FIGHT?
NO NO NO...
Definitely not!
YAMADA?
ABOUT YESTERDAY ...
JOLT

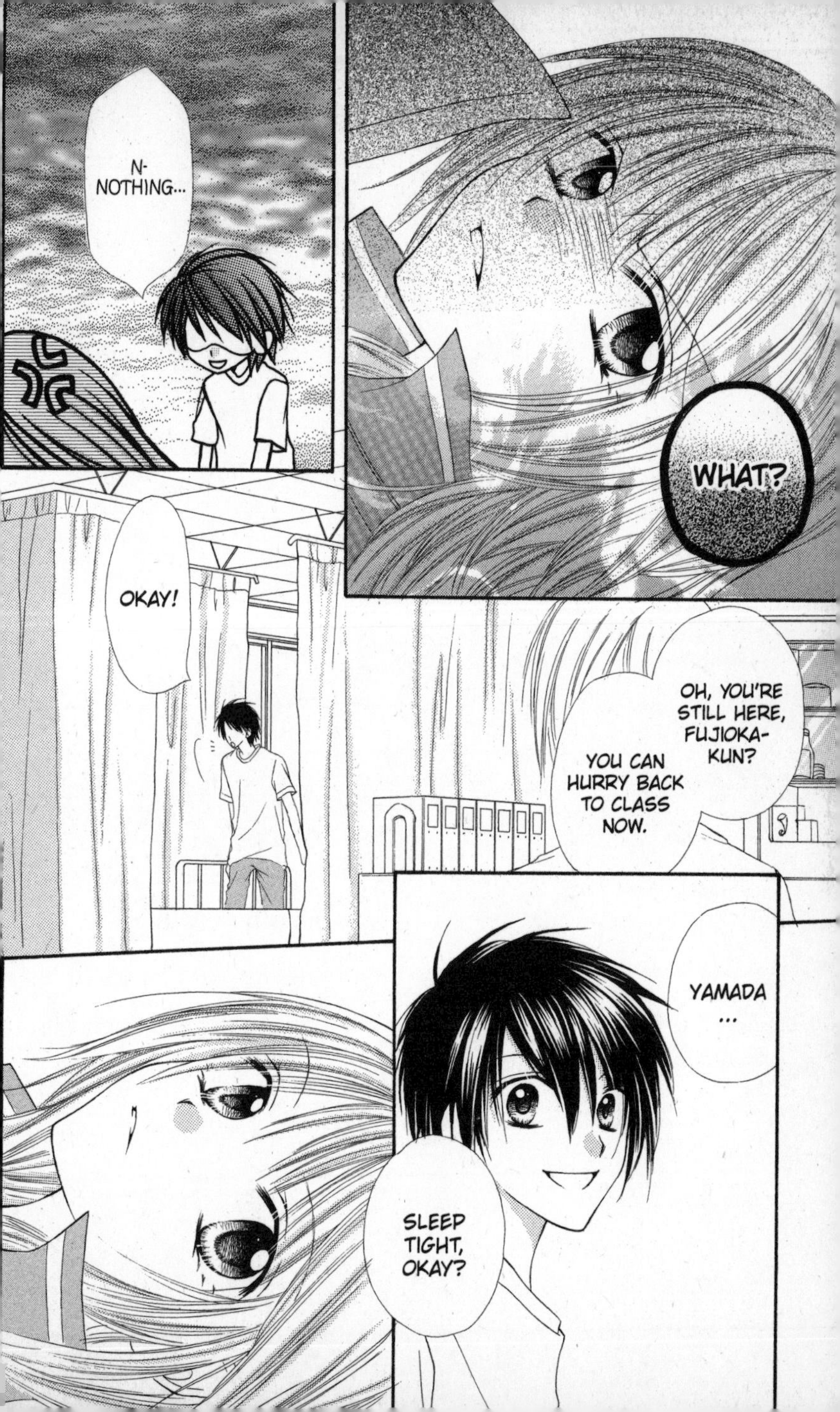
WHAT?
N-NOTHING...
OH, YOU'RE STILL HERE, FUJIOKA-KUN?
YOU CAN HURRY BACK TO CLASS NOW.
OKAY!
YAMADA...
SLEEP TIGHT, OKAY?

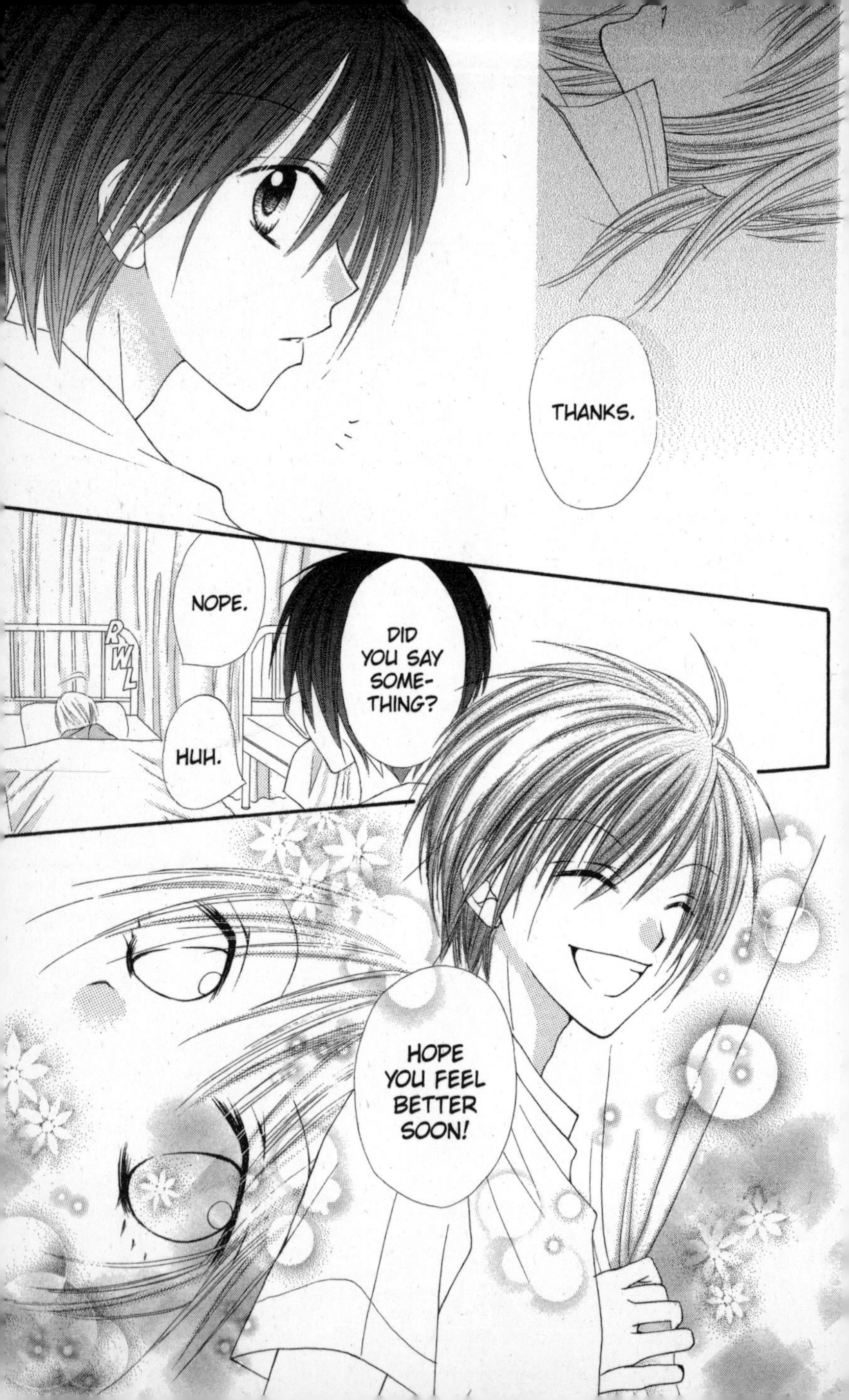
THANKS.
DID YOU SAY SOME-THING?
NOPE.
RWL
HUH.
HOPE YOU FEEL BETTER SOON!

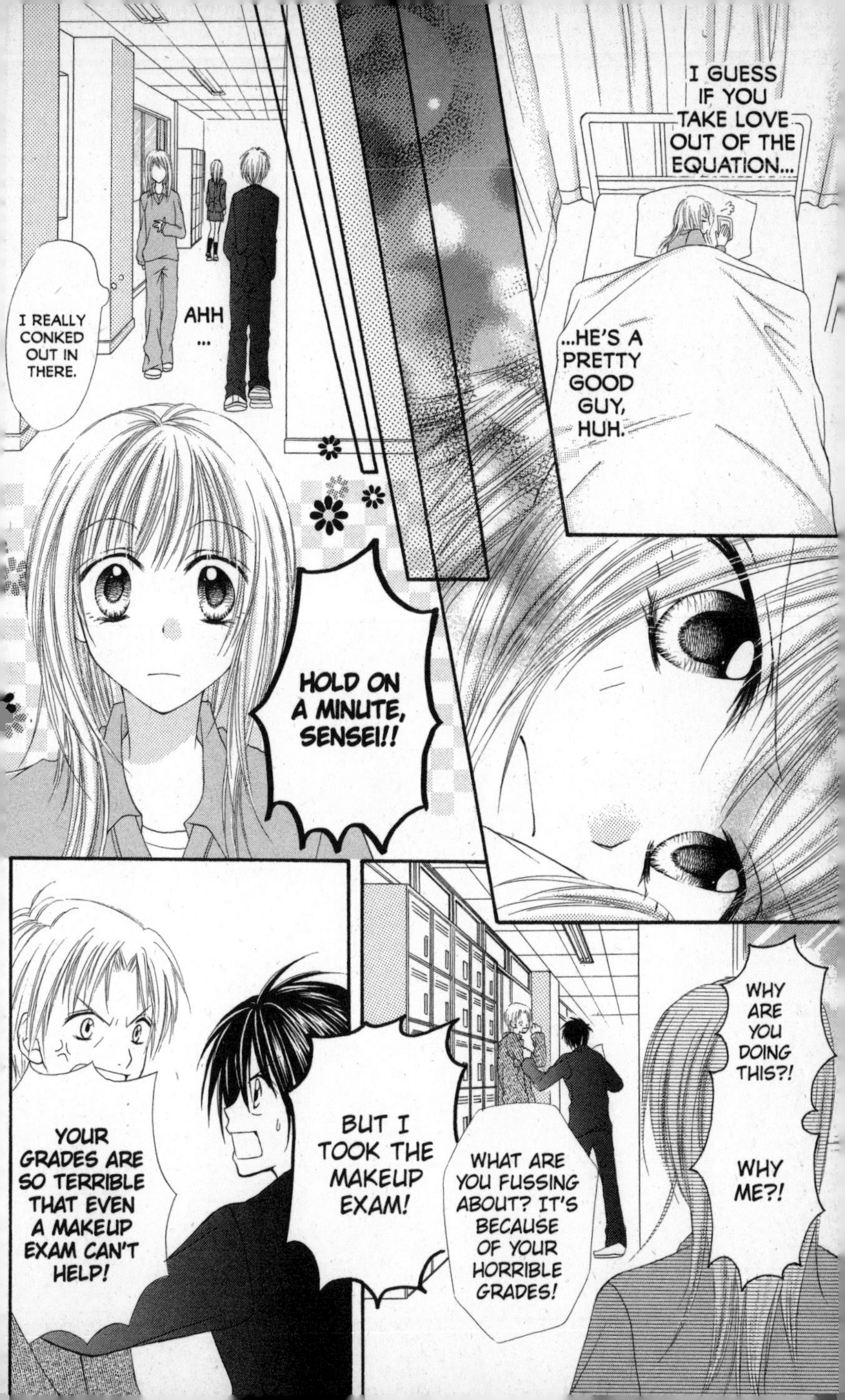
I GUESS IF YOU TAKE LOVE OUT OF THE EQUATION...
...HE'S A PRETTY GOOD GUY, HUH.
AHH ...
I REALLY CONKED OUT IN THERE.
HOLD ON A MINUTE, SENSEI!!
WHY ARE YOU DOING THIS?!
WHY ME?!
WHAT ARE YOU FUSSING ABOUT? IT'S BECAUSE OF YOUR HORRIBLE GRADES!
BUT I TOOK THE MAKEUP EXAM!
YOUR GRADES ARE SO TERRIBLE THAT EVEN A MAKEUP EXAM CAN'T HELP!

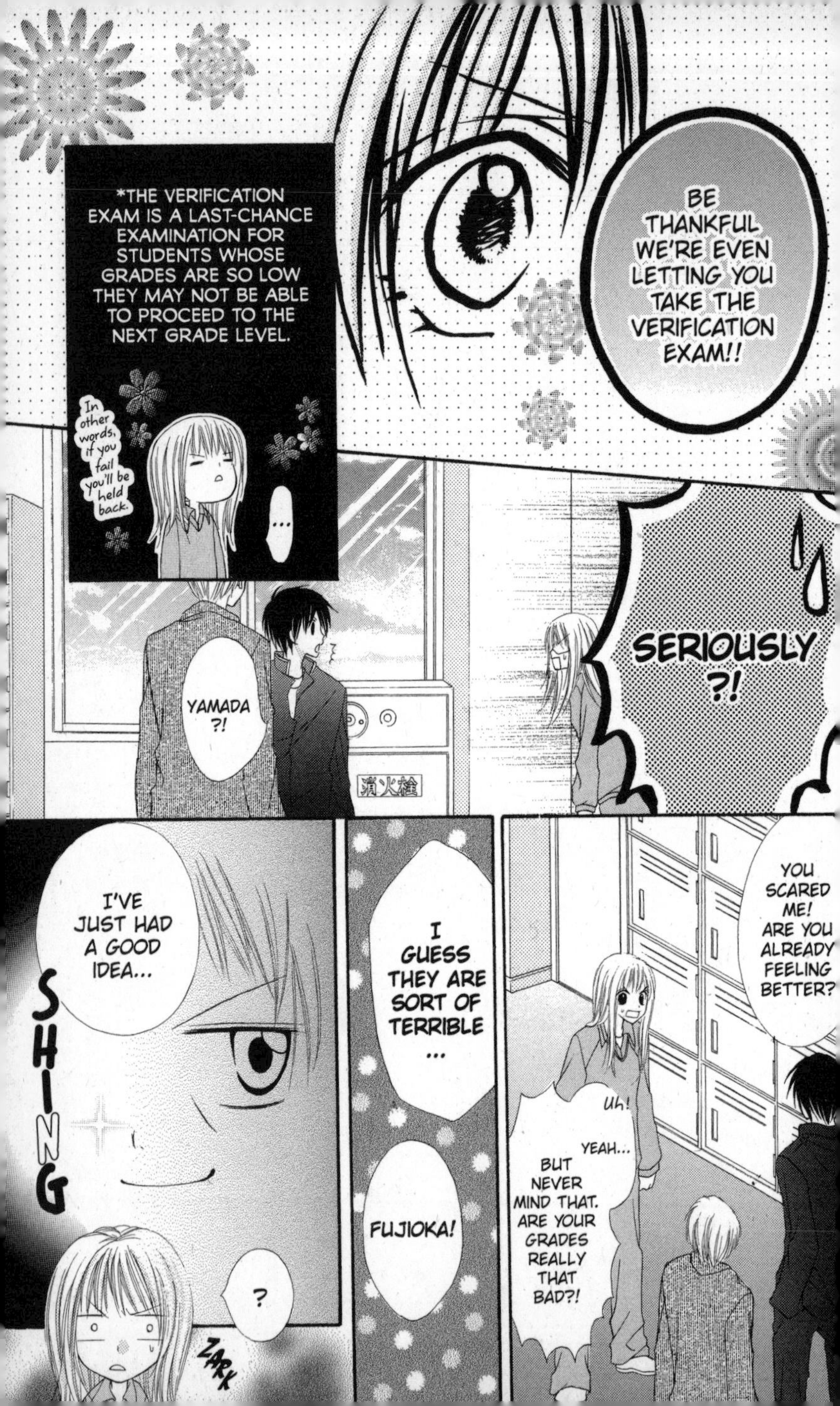

BE THANKFUL WE'RE EVEN LETTING YOU TAKE THE VERIFICATION EXAM!!
*THE VERIFICATION EXAM IS A LAST-CHANCE EXAMINATION FOR STUDENTS WHOSE GRADES ARE SO LOW THEY MAY NOT BE ABLE TO PROCEED TO THE NEXT GRADE LEVEL.
In other words, if you fail you'll be held back.
...
SERIOUSLY?!
YAMADA?!
YOU SCARED ME! ARE YOU ALREADY FEELING BETTER?
Uh!
YEAH...
BUT NEVER MIND THAT. ARE YOUR GRADES REALLY THAT BAD?!
I GUESS THEY ARE SORT OF TERRIBLE...
FUJIOKA!
I'VE JUST HAD A GOOD IDEA...
SHING
?
ZARK

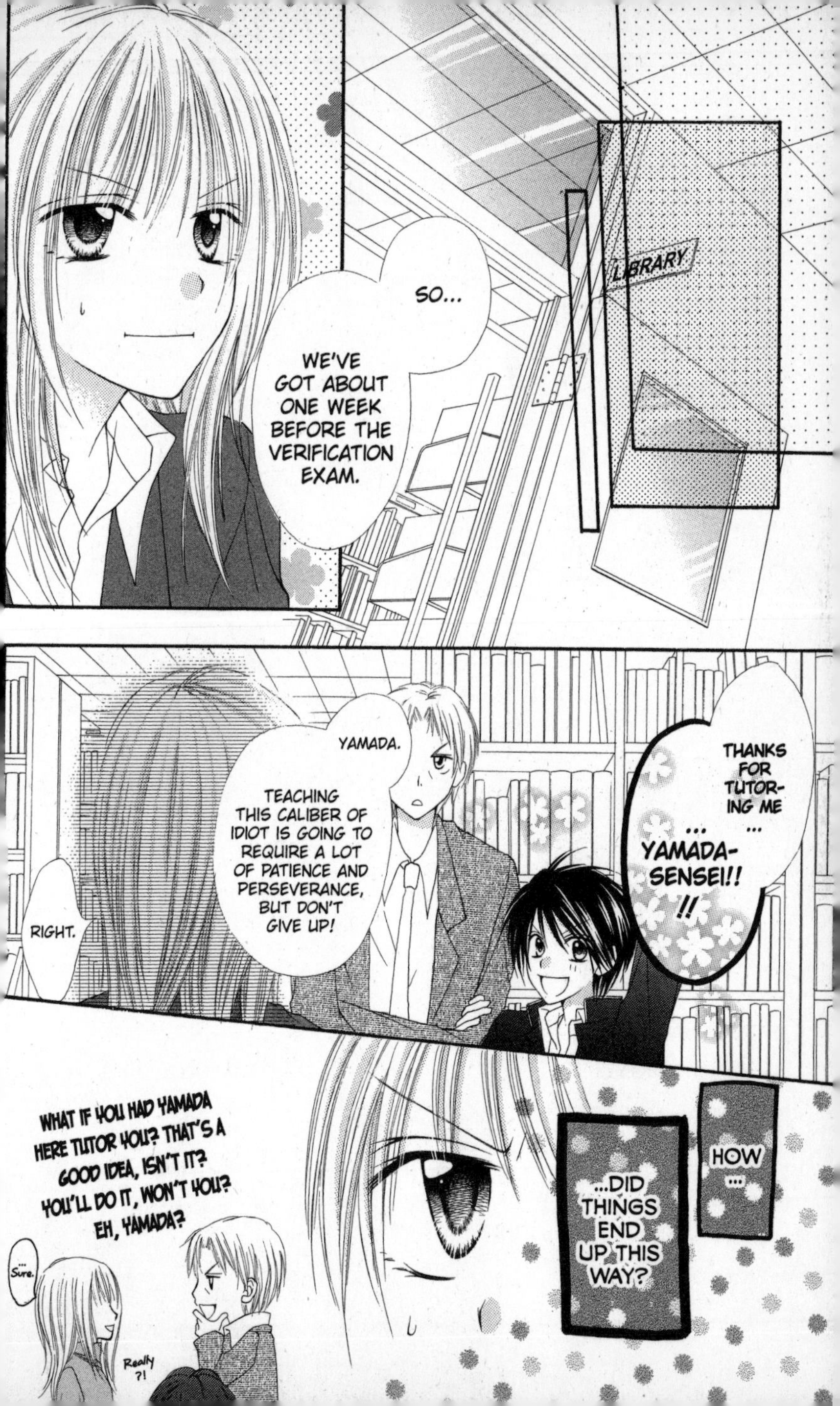
LIBRARY
SO...
WE'VE GOT ABOUT ONE WEEK BEFORE THE VERIFICATION EXAM.
THANKS FOR TUTOR-ING ME ...
... YAMADA-SENSEI!! !!
YAMADA.
TEACHING THIS CALIBER OF IDIOT IS GOING TO REQUIRE A LOT OF PATIENCE AND PERSEVERANCE, BUT DON'T GIVE UP!
RIGHT.
HOW ...
...DID THINGS END UP THIS WAY?
WHAT IF YOU HAD YAMADA HERE TUTOR YOU? THAT'S A GOOD IDEA, ISN'T IT? YOU'LL DO IT, WON'T YOU? EH, YAMADA?
... Sure.
Really ?!

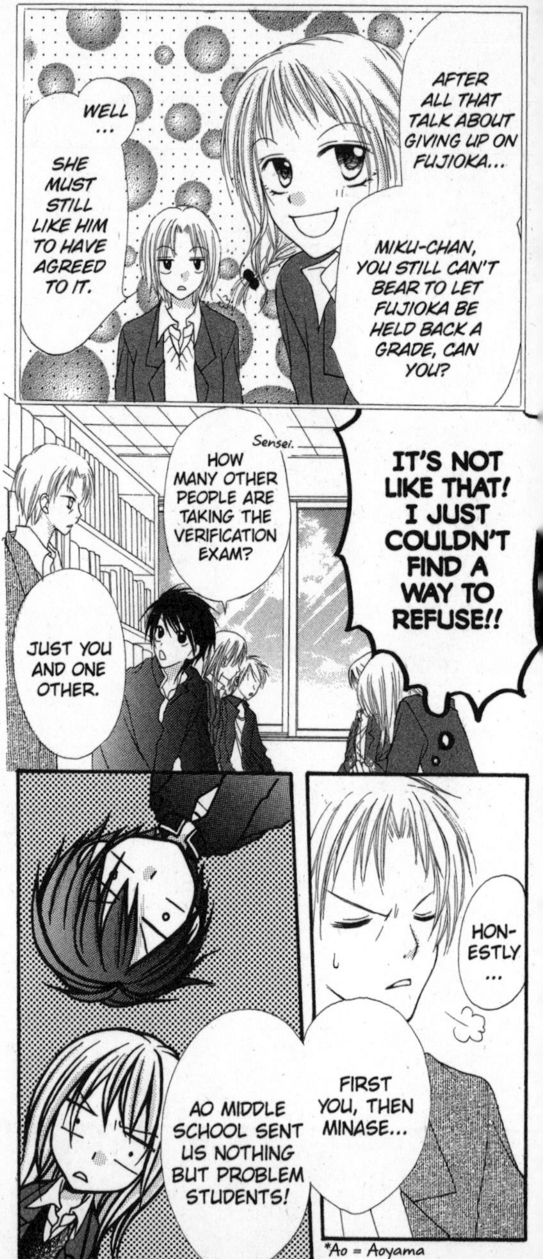
AFTER ALL THAT TALK ABOUT GIVING UP ON FUJIOKA...
MIKU-CHAN, YOU STILL CAN'T BEAR TO LET FUJIOKA BE HELD BACK A GRADE, CAN YOU?
WELL ...
SHE MUST STILL LIKE HIM TO HAVE AGREED TO IT.
IT'S NOT LIKE THAT! I JUST COULDN'T FIND A WAY TO REFUSE!!
Sensei.
HOW MANY OTHER PEOPLE ARE TAKING THE VERIFICATION EXAM?
JUST YOU AND ONE OTHER.
HON-ESTLY ...
FIRST YOU, THEN MINASE...
AO MIDDLE SCHOOL SENT US NOTHING BUT PROBLEM STUDENTS!

*Ao = Aoyama

9

I just realized I went off on a tangent instead of answering readers' questions. So let's get on to the next one! Let's see... Here's a question: "How did you pick your characters' names?"

I talked about this once in the magazine too, but for Miku, I used the name of one of my friends from high school. Though their names are the same, the manga Miku and the real Miku-tsun are completely different in personality, appearance, and so on.

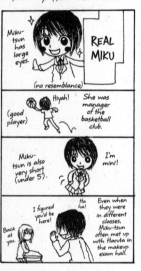

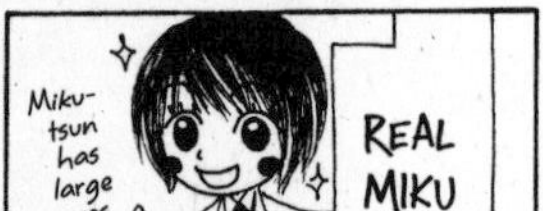
Miku-tsun has large eyes.
REAL MIKU
(no resemblance)
Hiyah!
She was manager of the basketball club.
(good player)
Miku-tsun is also very short (under 5').
I'm mini!
Ha ha!
Even when they were in different classes, Miku-tsun often met up with Haruta in the makeup exam hall.
I figured you'd be here!
Back at you.

These days, the real Miku-tsun is working part-time at a convenience store that's close to school. Apparently she's been reading Cactus every month in the copy of Ribon they leave out for customers to look through. Please buy it and read it properly!

Miku-tsun and I were in the same class during our first year of high school, but she didn't realize until third year that I was a mangaka. She looked so surprised when she found out I was "Nana Haruta." Guess that's to be expected.

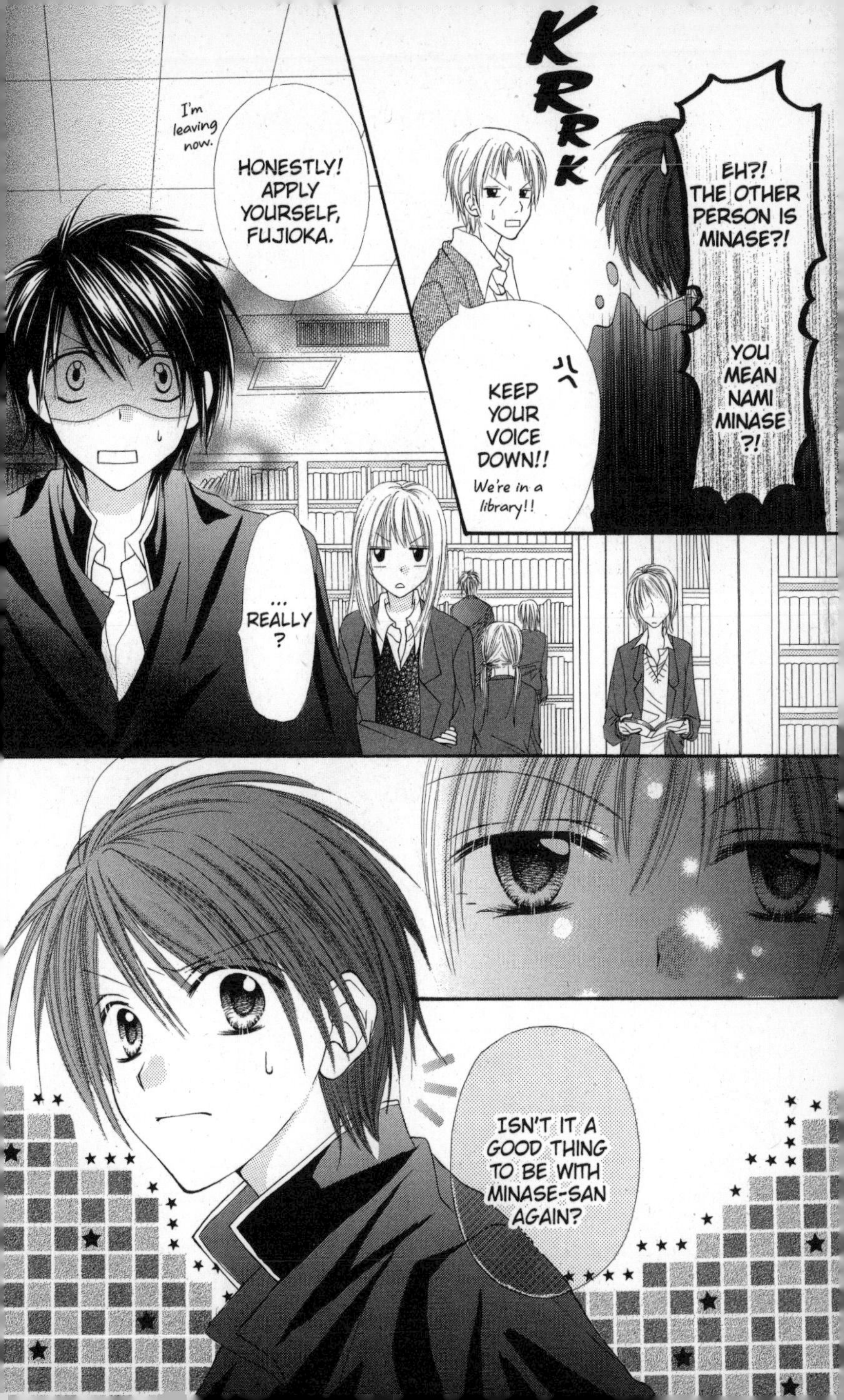
KRRK
EH?! THE OTHER PERSON IS MINASE?!
YOU MEAN NAMI MINASE ?!
KEEP YOUR VOICE DOWN!!
We're in a library!!
I'm leaving now.
HONESTLY! APPLY YOURSELF, FUJIOKA.
... REALLY ?
ISN'T IT A GOOD THING TO BE WITH MINASE-SAN AGAIN?

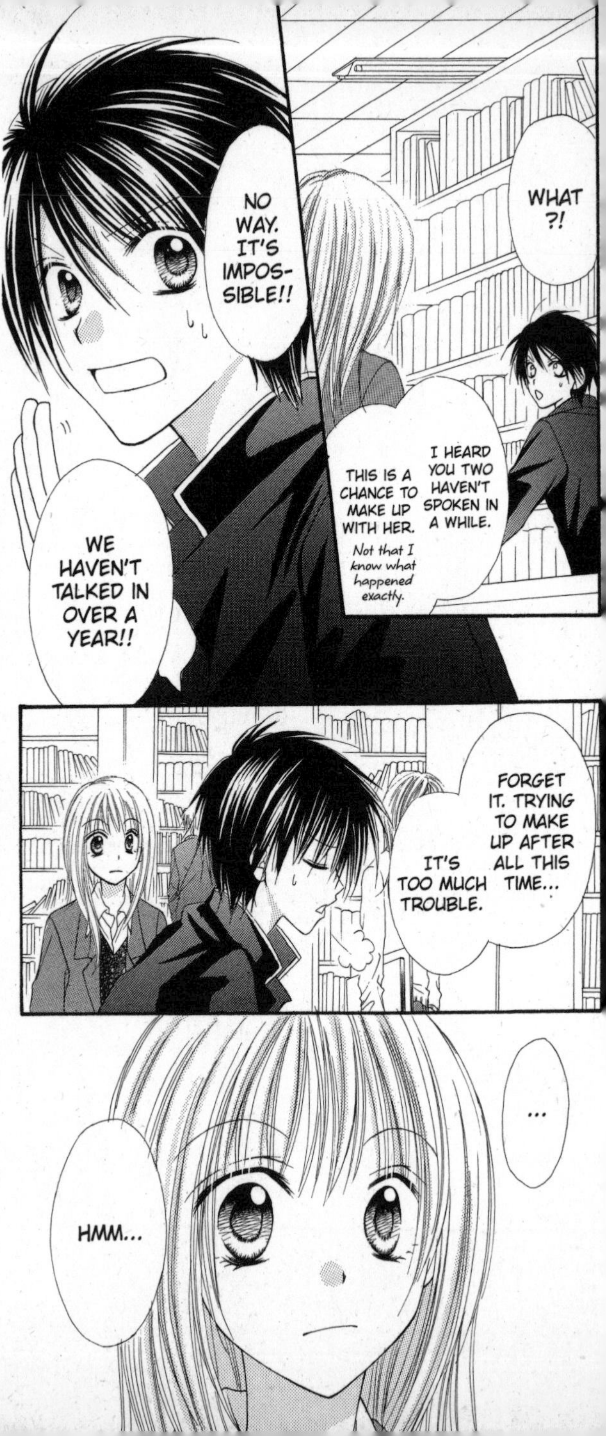
WHAT ?!
I HEARD YOU TWO HAVEN'T SPOKEN IN A WHILE.
THIS IS A CHANCE TO MAKE UP WITH HER.
Not that I know what happened exactly.
NO WAY. IT'S IMPOSSIBLE!!
WE HAVEN'T TALKED IN OVER A YEAR!!
FORGET IT. TRYING TO MAKE UP AFTER ALL THIS TIME...
IT'S TOO MUCH TROUBLE.
...
HMM...

10

Continuing on from 9... As for Fujioka's name, it really wasn't anything special. Since my name has a low stroke count, I wanted to give him a family name that used lots of strokes. Also, I just kind of like the kanji for "fuji." I wonder why...

In the case of Minase-san ↓

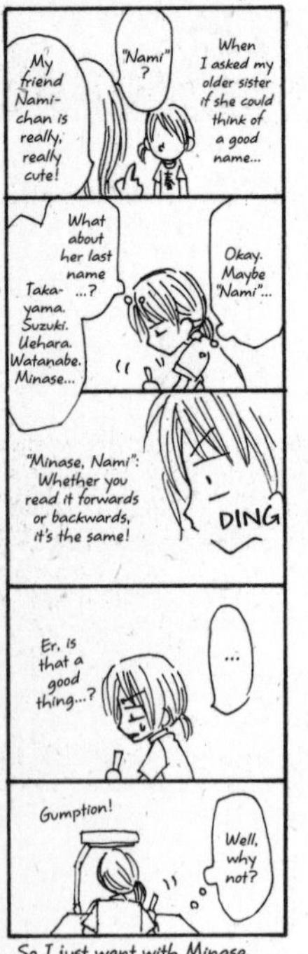
When I asked my older sister if she could think of a good name...
"Nami" ?
My friend Nami-chan is really, really cute!
Okay. Maybe "Nami"...
What about her last name ...?
Taka-yama. Suzuki. Uehara. Watanabe. Minase...
DING
"Minase, Nami": Whether you read it forwards or backwards, it's the same!
...
Er, is that a good thing...?
Well, why not?
Gumption!

So I just went with Minase.

In *Ribon's* fan mail page, there was a reader who pointed out that Minase-san's name was a palindrome. Heh, you were really paying attention, huh. That makes me so happy!

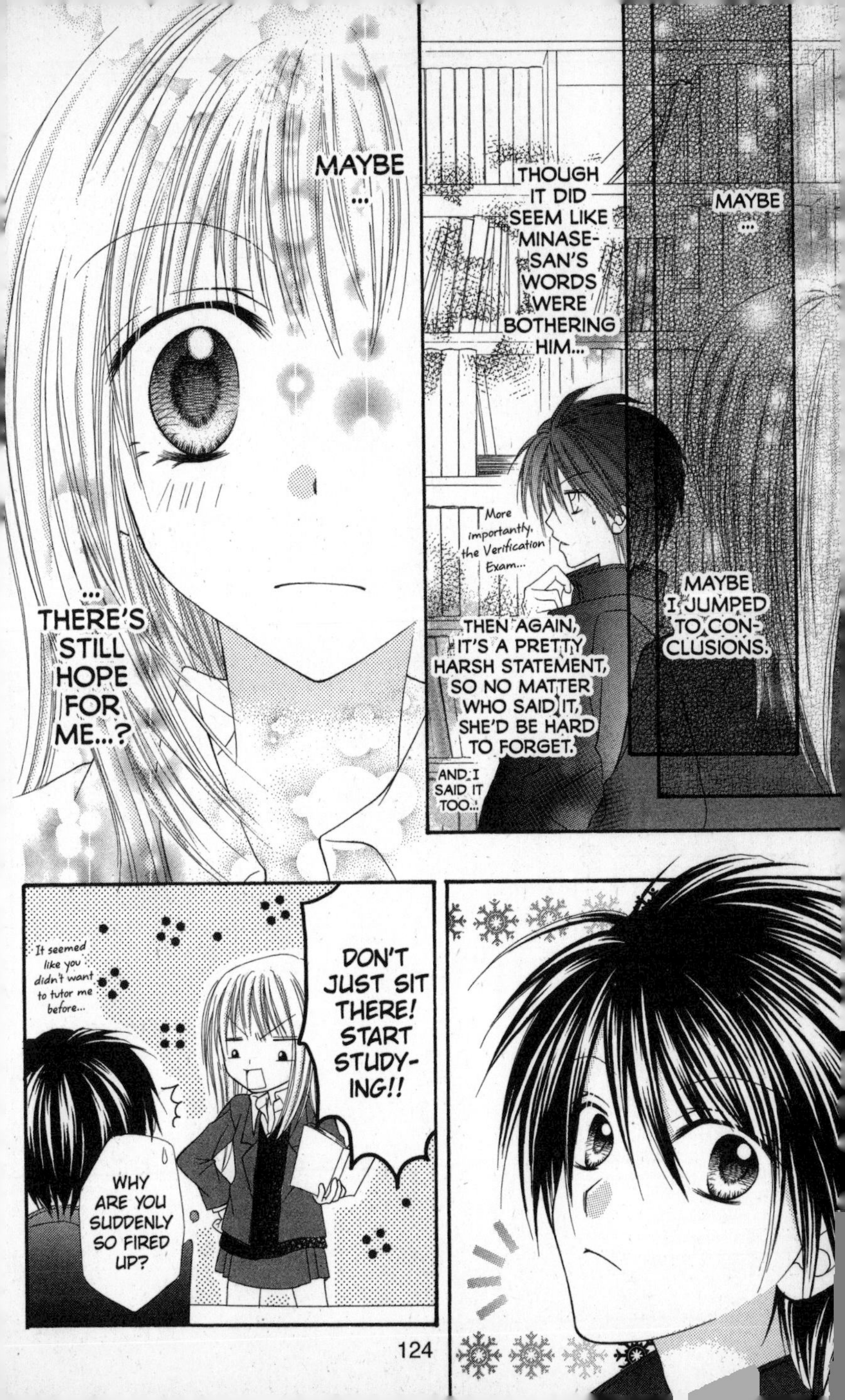
MAYBE ...
THOUGH IT DID SEEM LIKE MINASE-SAN'S WORDS WERE BOTHERING HIM...
MAYBE I JUMPED TO CONCLUSIONS.
More importantly, the Verification Exam...
THEN AGAIN, IT'S A PRETTY HARSH STATEMENT, SO NO MATTER WHO SAID IT, SHE'D BE HARD TO FORGET.
AND I SAID IT TOO...
MAYBE ...
... THERE'S STILL HOPE FOR ME...?
DON'T JUST SIT THERE! START STUDYING!!
It seemed like you didn't want to tutor me before...
WHY ARE YOU SUDDENLY SO FIRED UP?

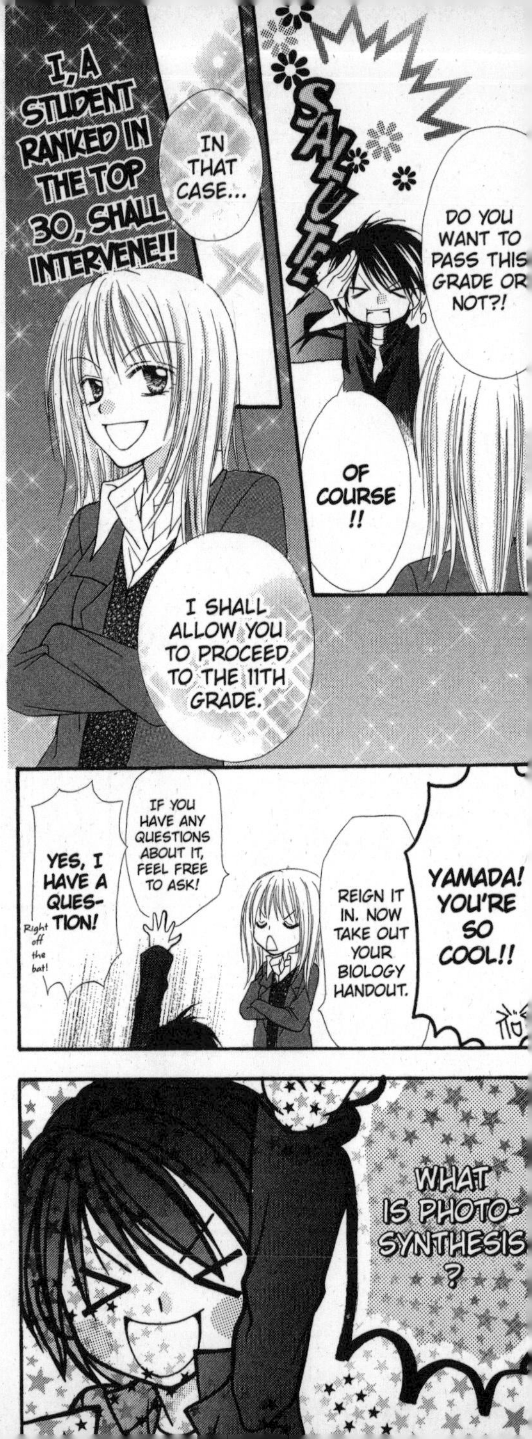
DO YOU WANT TO PASS THIS GRADE OR NOT?!
SALUTE
OF COURSE!!
IN THAT CASE...
I, A STUDENT RANKED IN THE TOP 30, SHALL INTERVENE!!
I SHALL ALLOW YOU TO PROCEED TO THE 11TH GRADE.
YAMADA! YOU'RE SO COOL!!
REIGN IT IN. NOW TAKE OUT YOUR BIOLOGY HANDOUT.
IF YOU HAVE ANY QUESTIONS ABOUT IT, FEEL FREE TO ASK!
YES, I HAVE A QUES-TION!
Right off the bat!
WHAT IS PHOTO-SYNTHESIS?

11

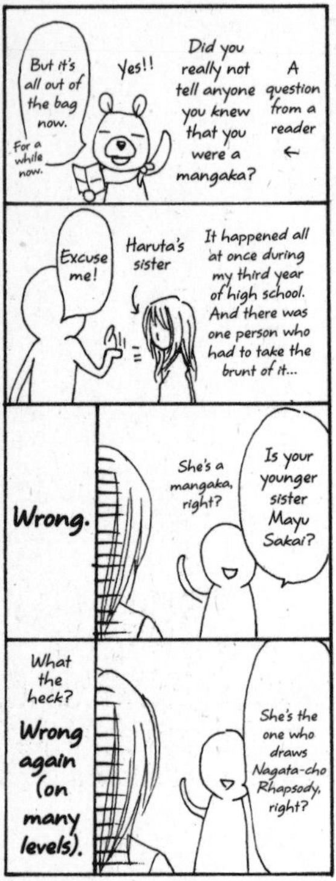
A question from a reader ←
Did you really not tell anyone you knew that you were a mangaka?
Yes!!
But it's all out of the bag now.
For a while now.
It happened all at once during my third year of high school. And there was one person who had to take the brunt of it...
Haruta's sister
Excuse me!
Is your younger sister Mayu Sakai?
She's a mangaka, right?
Wrong.
She's the one who draws Nagata-cho Rhapsody, right?
What the heck?
Wrong again (on many levels).

Why on earth did that person think I was Mayu-pon Sakai...?! And while we're at it, Mayu-pon's manga is called Nagata-cho Strawberry...! It is serialized in the same magazine as Cactus, but still...!!

I've become good friends with Mayu-pon Sakai-sensei. In fact, in Strawberry volume 3, she even gave her readers a preview of my work by letting me collaborate on the bonus section with her. I'll just say it's a very unusual work. "Unusual how?" you ask? Well, you'll just have to go read it to find out! Sorry. I'm a foolish idiot!

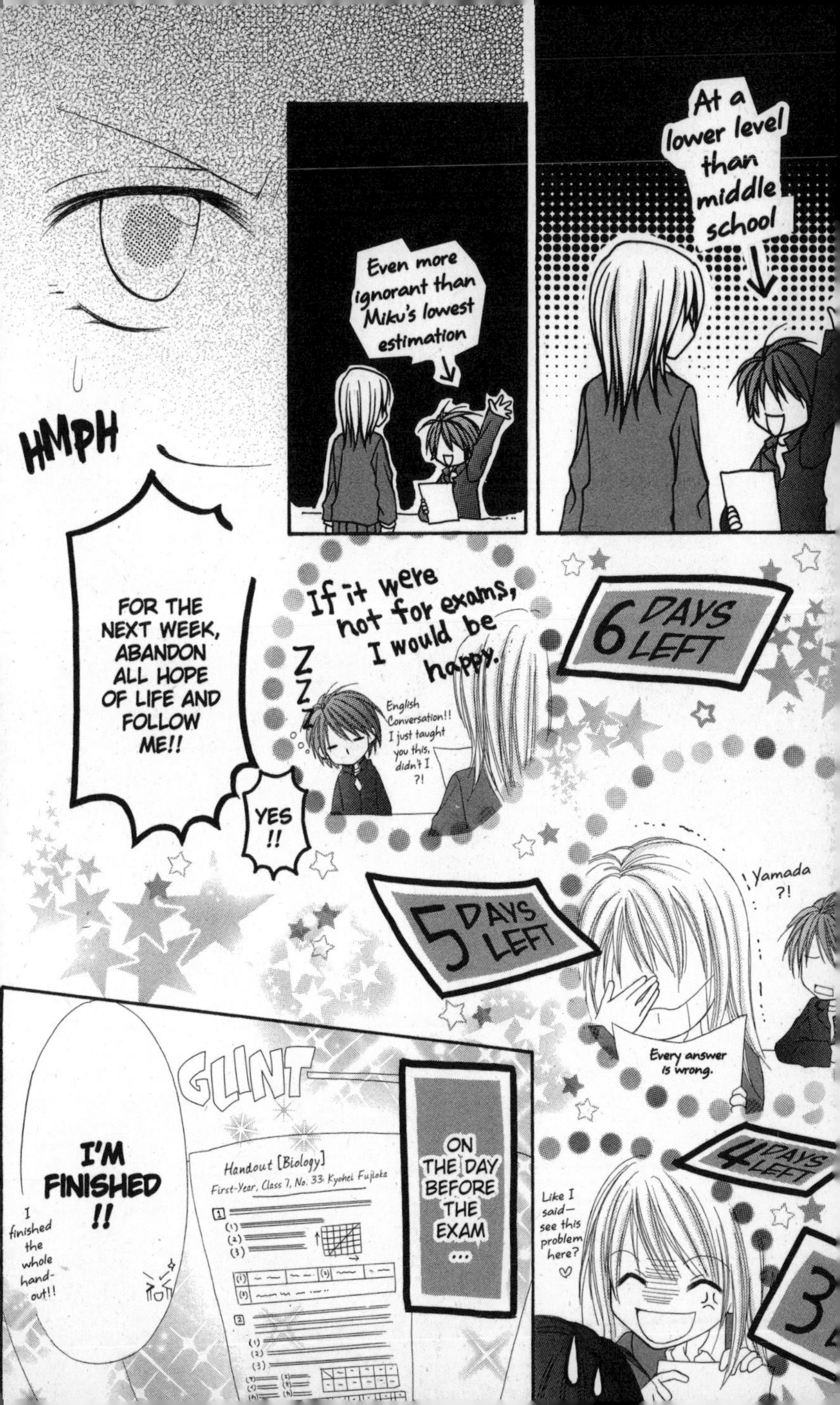
At a lower level than middle school
Even more ignorant than Miku's lowest estimation
HMPH
FOR THE NEXT WEEK, ABANDON ALL HOPE OF LIFE AND FOLLOW ME!!
YES!!
6 DAYS LEFT
If it were not for exams, I would be happy.
ZZZ
English Conversation!! I just taught you this, didn't I?!
5 DAYS LEFT
Yamada ?!
Every answer is wrong.
4 DAYS LEFT
Like I said— see this problem here?
3
ON THE DAY BEFORE THE EXAM...
GLINT
Handout [Biology]
First-Year, Class 7, No. 33: Kyohei Fujioka
I'M FINISHED!!
I finished the whole hand-out!!

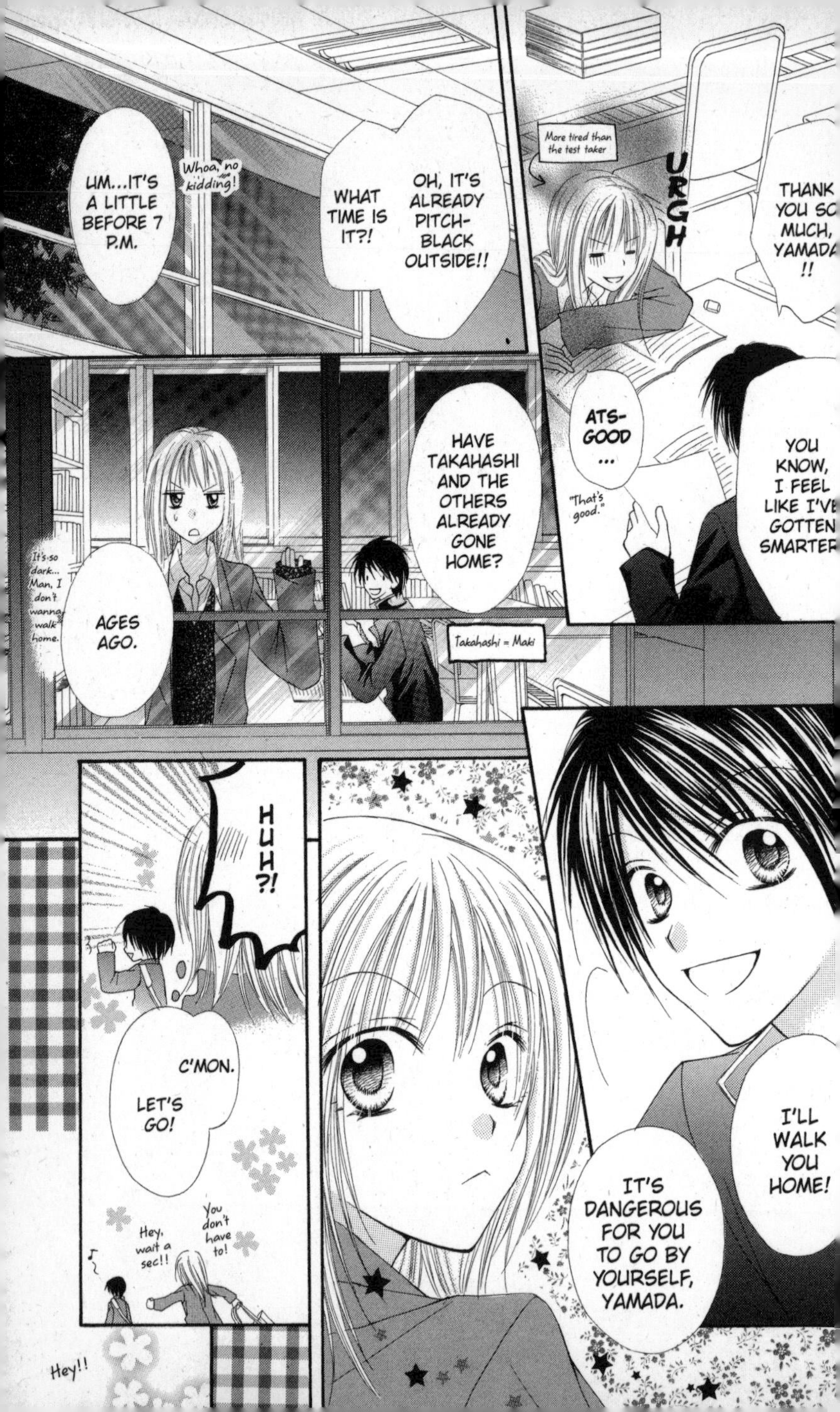
More tired than the test taker
URGH
THANK YOU SO MUCH, YAMADA !!
OH, IT'S ALREADY PITCH-BLACK OUTSIDE!!
WHAT TIME IS IT?!
Whoa, no kidding!
UM...IT'S A LITTLE BEFORE 7 P.M.
YOU KNOW, I FEEL LIKE I'VE GOTTEN SMARTER
ATS-GOOD ...
"That's good."
HAVE TAKAHASHI AND THE OTHERS ALREADY GONE HOME?
Takahashi = Maki
AGES AGO.
It's so dark... Man, I don't wanna walk home.
I'LL WALK YOU HOME!
IT'S DANGEROUS FOR YOU TO GO BY YOURSELF, YAMADA.
HUH?!
C'MON.
LET'S GO!
You don't have to!
Hey, wait a sec!!
Hey!!

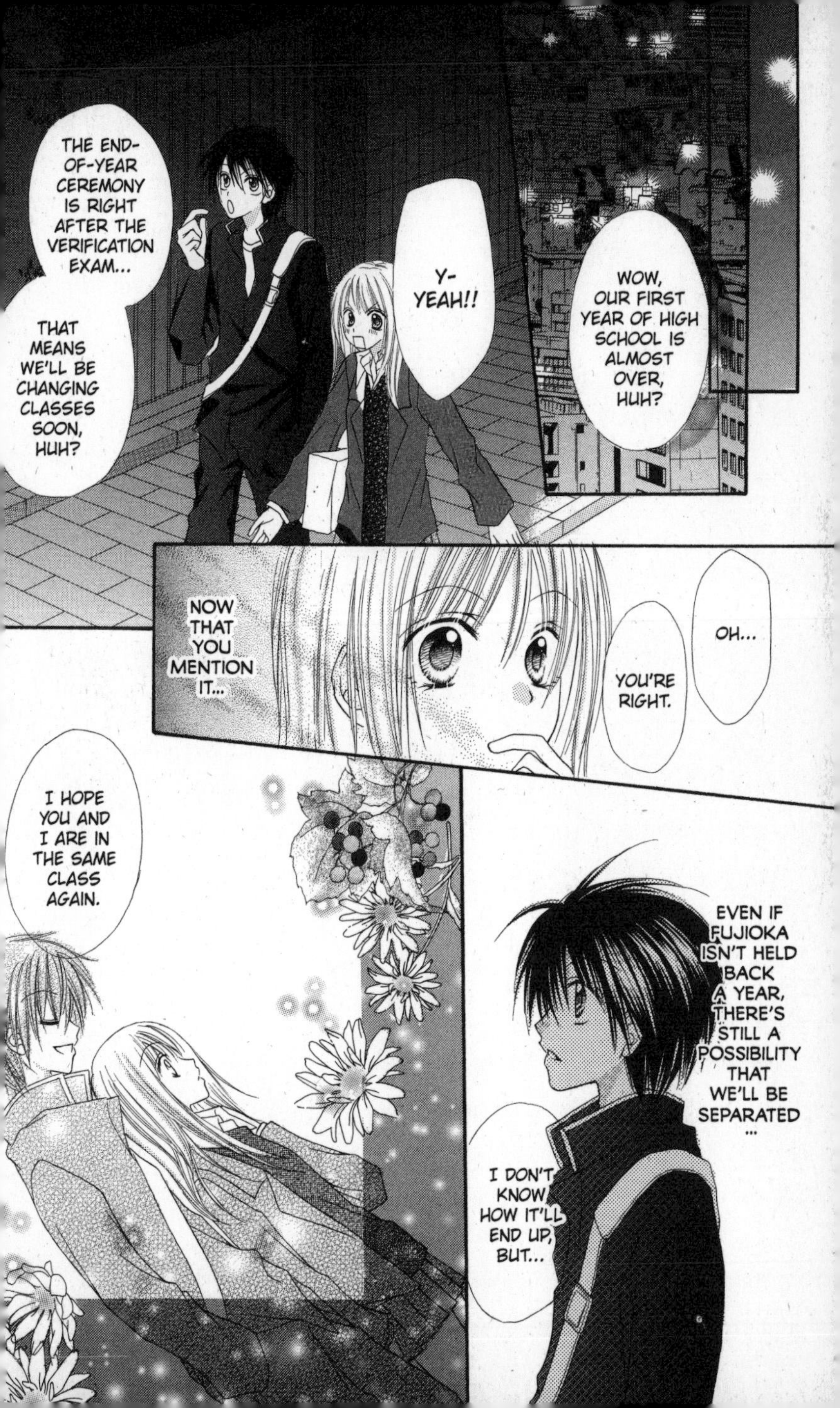
WOW, OUR FIRST YEAR OF HIGH SCHOOL IS ALMOST OVER, HUH?
Y-YEAH!!
THE END-OF-YEAR CEREMONY IS RIGHT AFTER THE VERIFICATION EXAM...
THAT MEANS WE'LL BE CHANGING CLASSES SOON, HUH?
OH...
YOU'RE RIGHT.
NOW THAT YOU MENTION IT...
EVEN IF FUJIOKA ISN'T HELD BACK A YEAR, THERE'S STILL A POSSIBILITY THAT WE'LL BE SEPARATED...
I DON'T KNOW HOW IT'LL END UP, BUT...
I HOPE YOU AND I ARE IN THE SAME CLASS AGAIN.

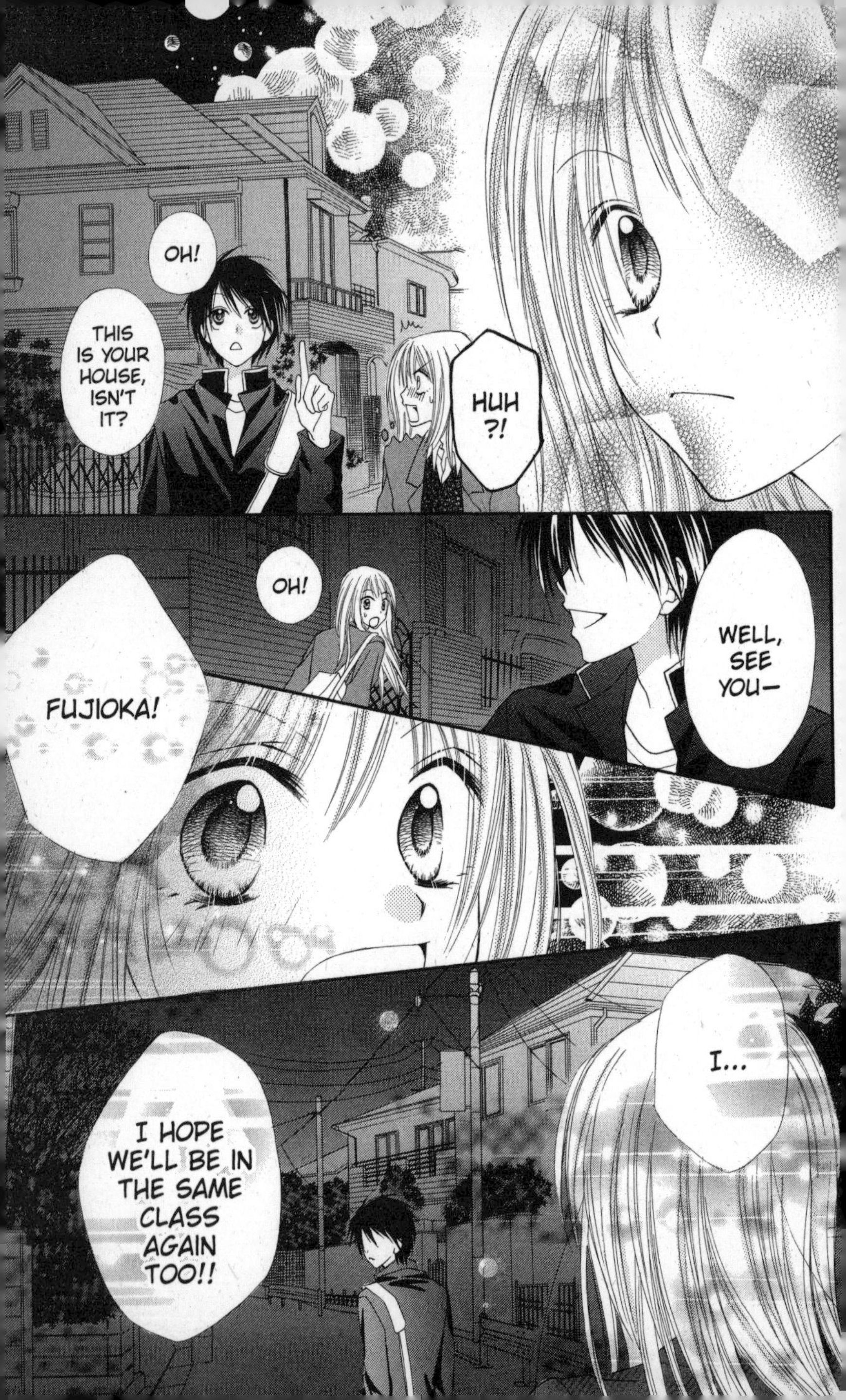
OH!
THIS IS YOUR HOUSE, ISN'T IT?
HUH ?!
WELL, SEE YOU—
OH!
FUJIOKA!
I...
I HOPE WE'LL BE IN THE SAME CLASS AGAIN TOO!!

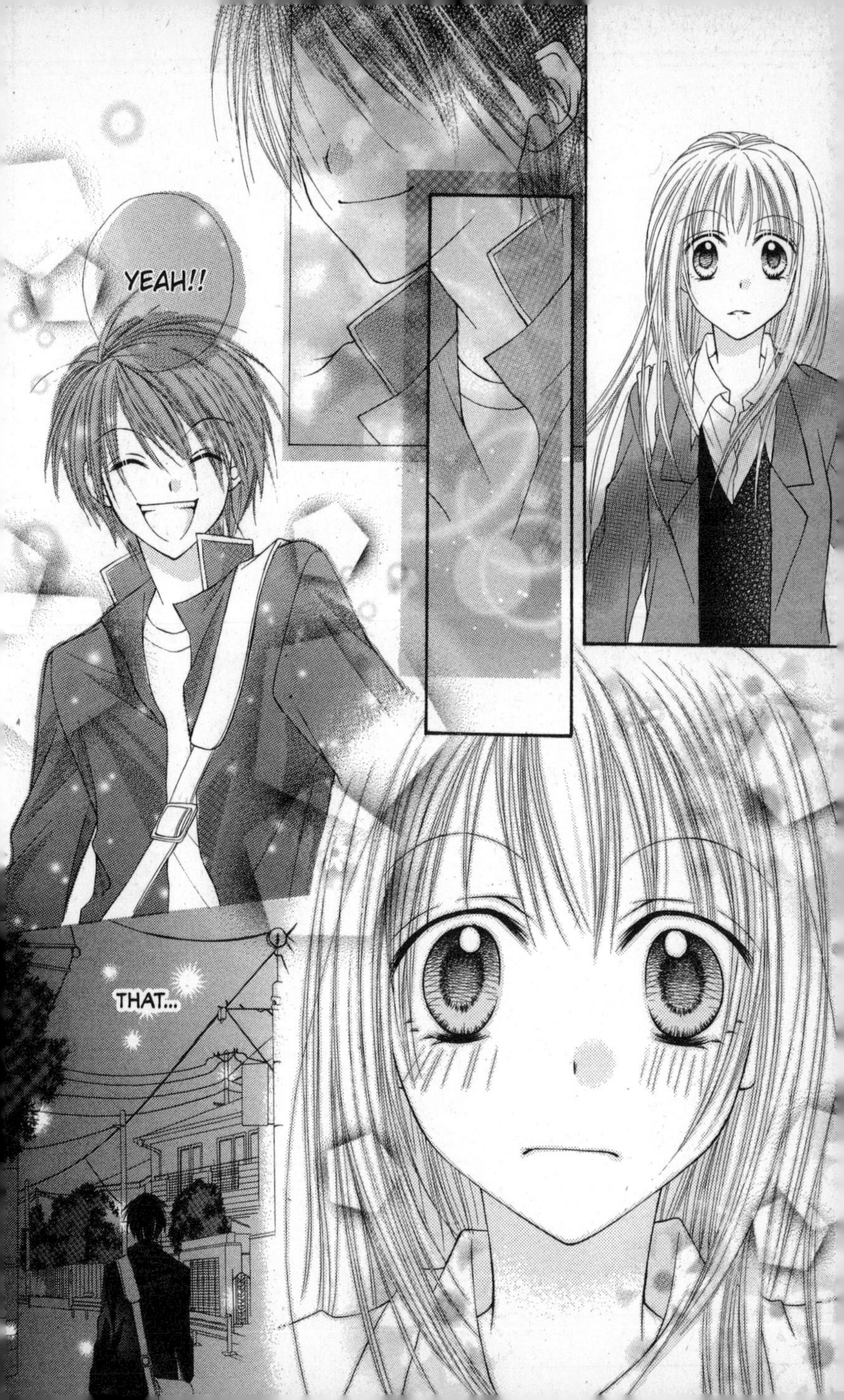
YEAH!!
THAT...

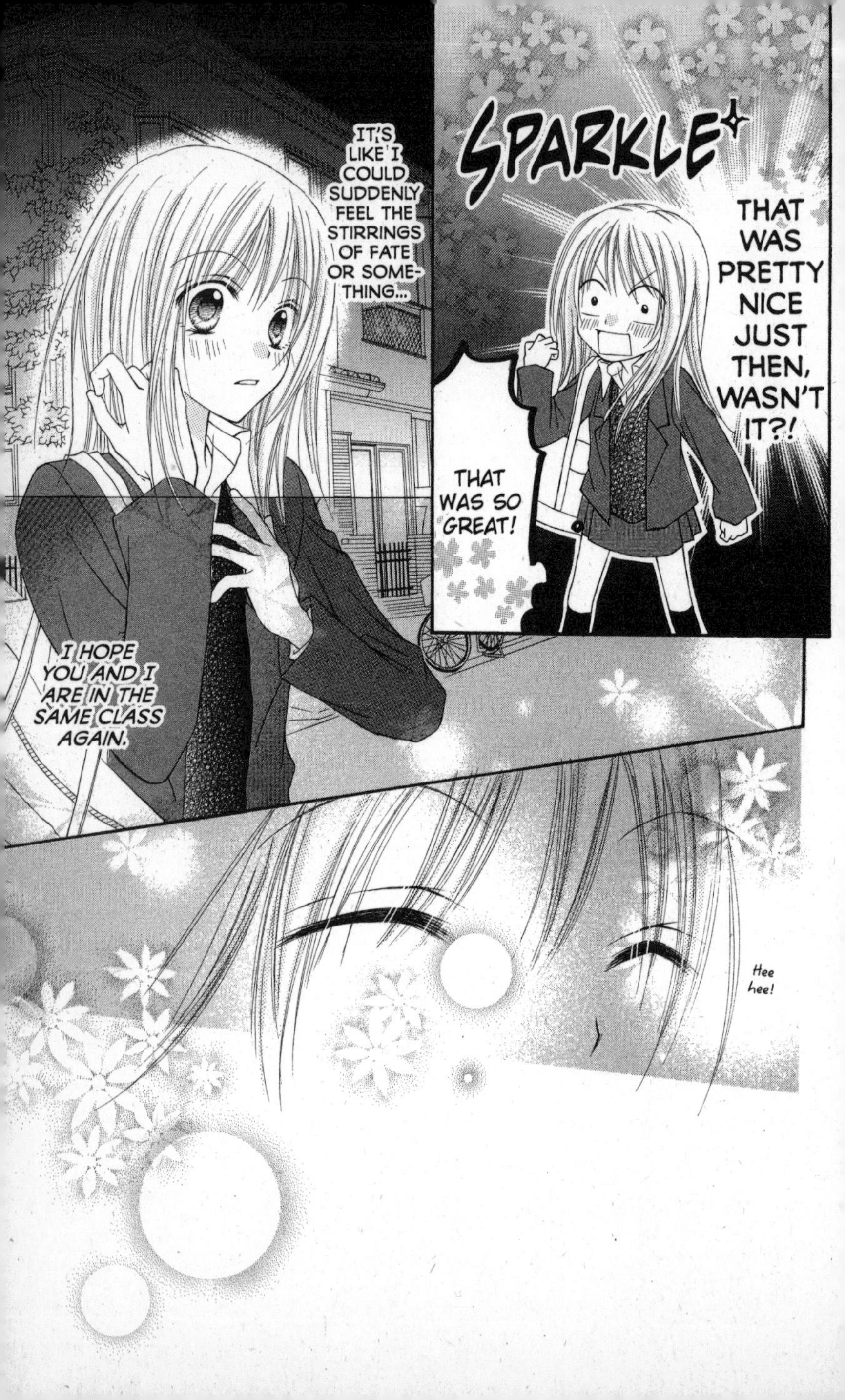
SPARKLE
THAT WAS PRETTY NICE JUST THEN, WASN'T IT?!
THAT WAS SO GREAT!
IT'S LIKE I COULD SUDDENLY FEEL THE STIRRINGS OF FATE OR SOME-THING...
I HOPE YOU AND I ARE IN THE SAME CLASS AGAIN.
Hee hee!

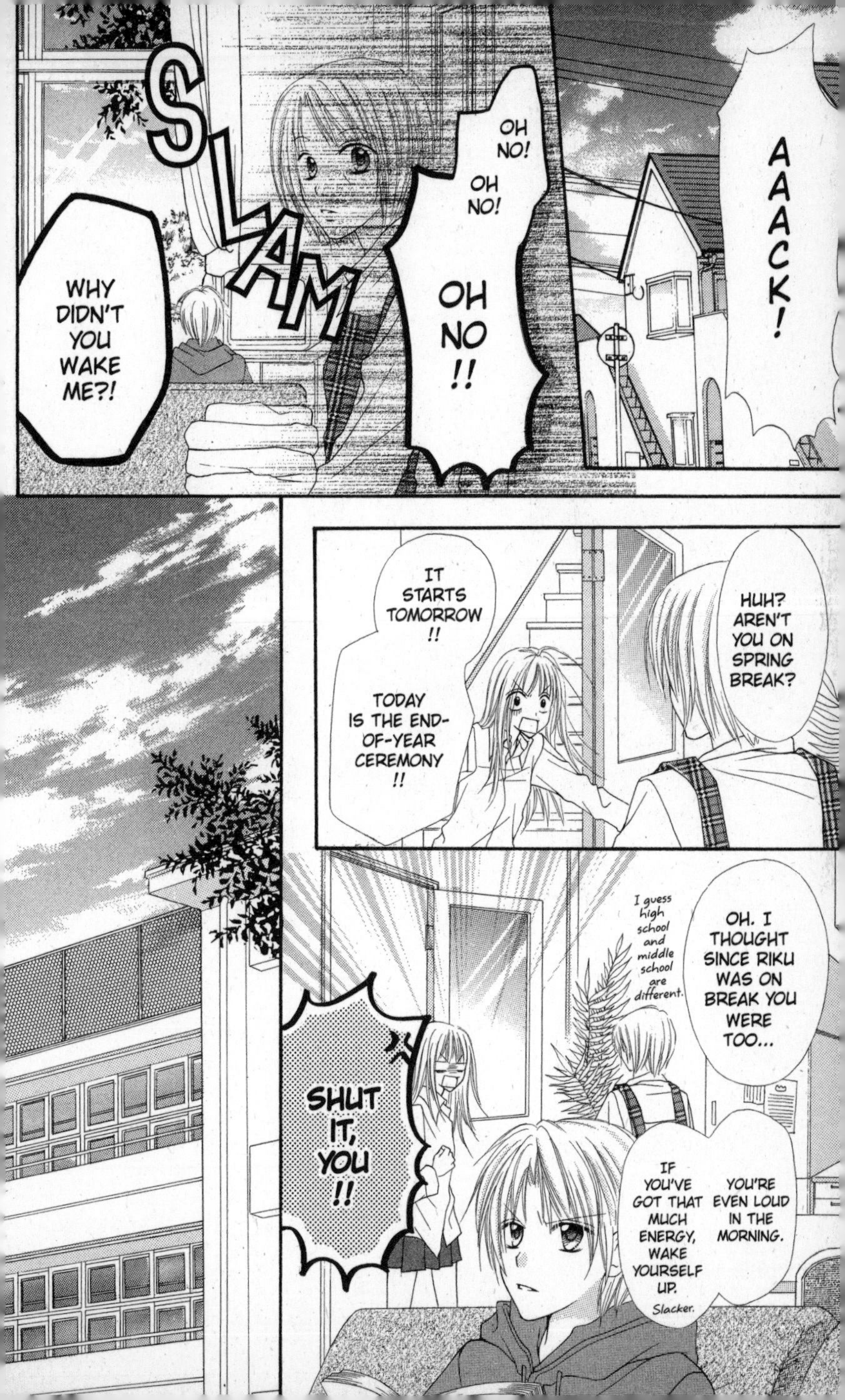
AAACK!
OH NO! OH NO! OH NO!!
SLAM
WHY DIDN'T YOU WAKE ME?!
HUH? AREN'T YOU ON SPRING BREAK?
IT STARTS TOMORROW!!
TODAY IS THE END-OF-YEAR CEREMONY!!
OH. I THOUGHT SINCE RIKU WAS ON BREAK YOU WERE TOO...
I guess high school and middle school are different.
YOU'RE EVEN LOUD IN THE MORNING.
IF YOU'VE GOT THAT MUCH ENERGY, WAKE YOURSELF UP.
Slacker.
SHUT IT, YOU!!

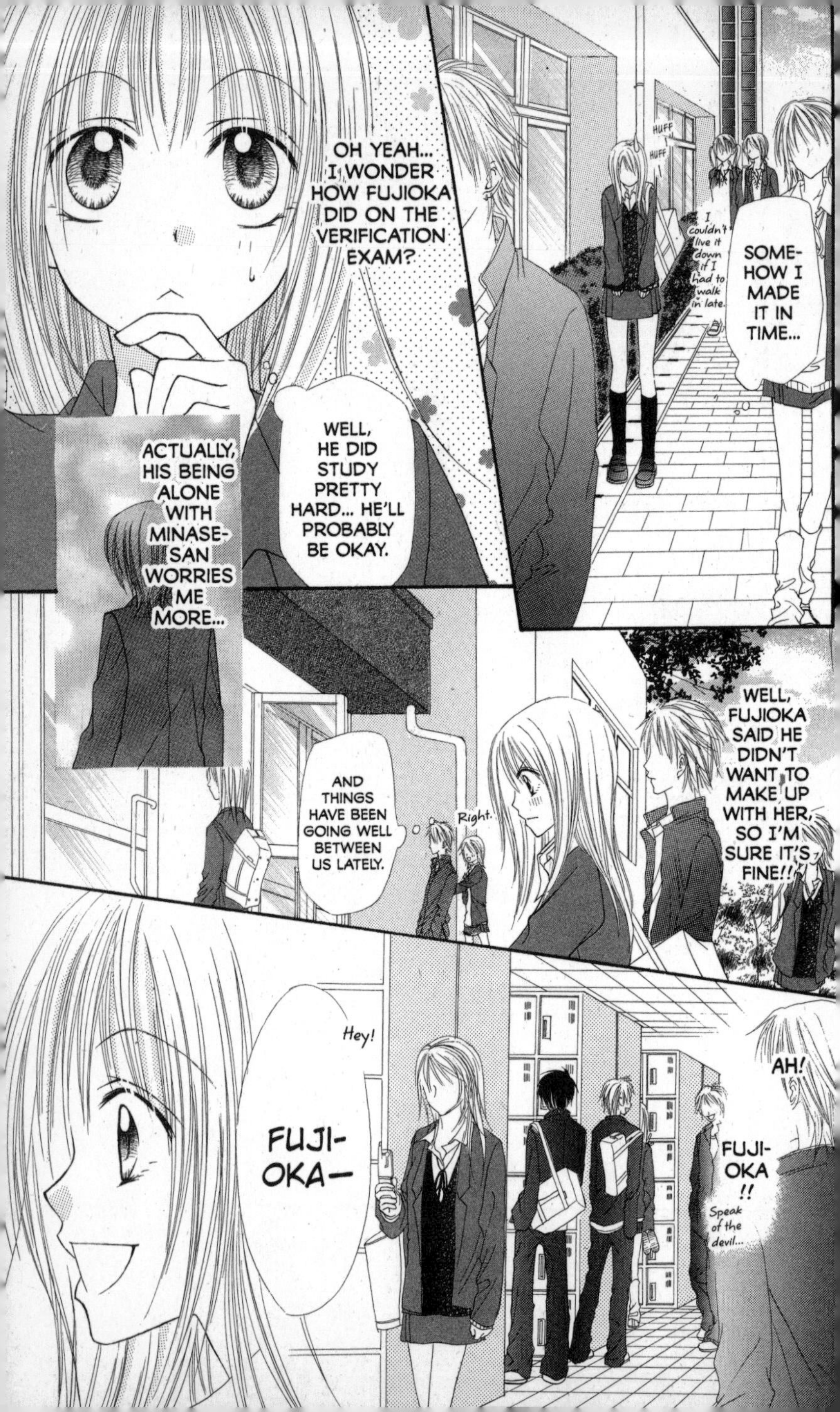
HUFF
HUFF
I couldn't live it down if I had to walk in late.
SOME-HOW I MADE IT IN TIME...
OH YEAH... I WONDER HOW FUJIOKA DID ON THE VERIFICATION EXAM?
WELL, HE DID STUDY PRETTY HARD... HE'LL PROBABLY BE OKAY.
ACTUALLY, HIS BEING ALONE WITH MINASE-SAN WORRIES ME MORE...
WELL, FUJIOKA SAID HE DIDN'T WANT TO MAKE UP WITH HER, SO I'M SURE IT'S FINE!!
AND THINGS HAVE BEEN GOING WELL BETWEEN US LATELY.
Right.
AH!
FUJI-OKA!!
Speak of the devil...
Hey!
FUJI-OKA—

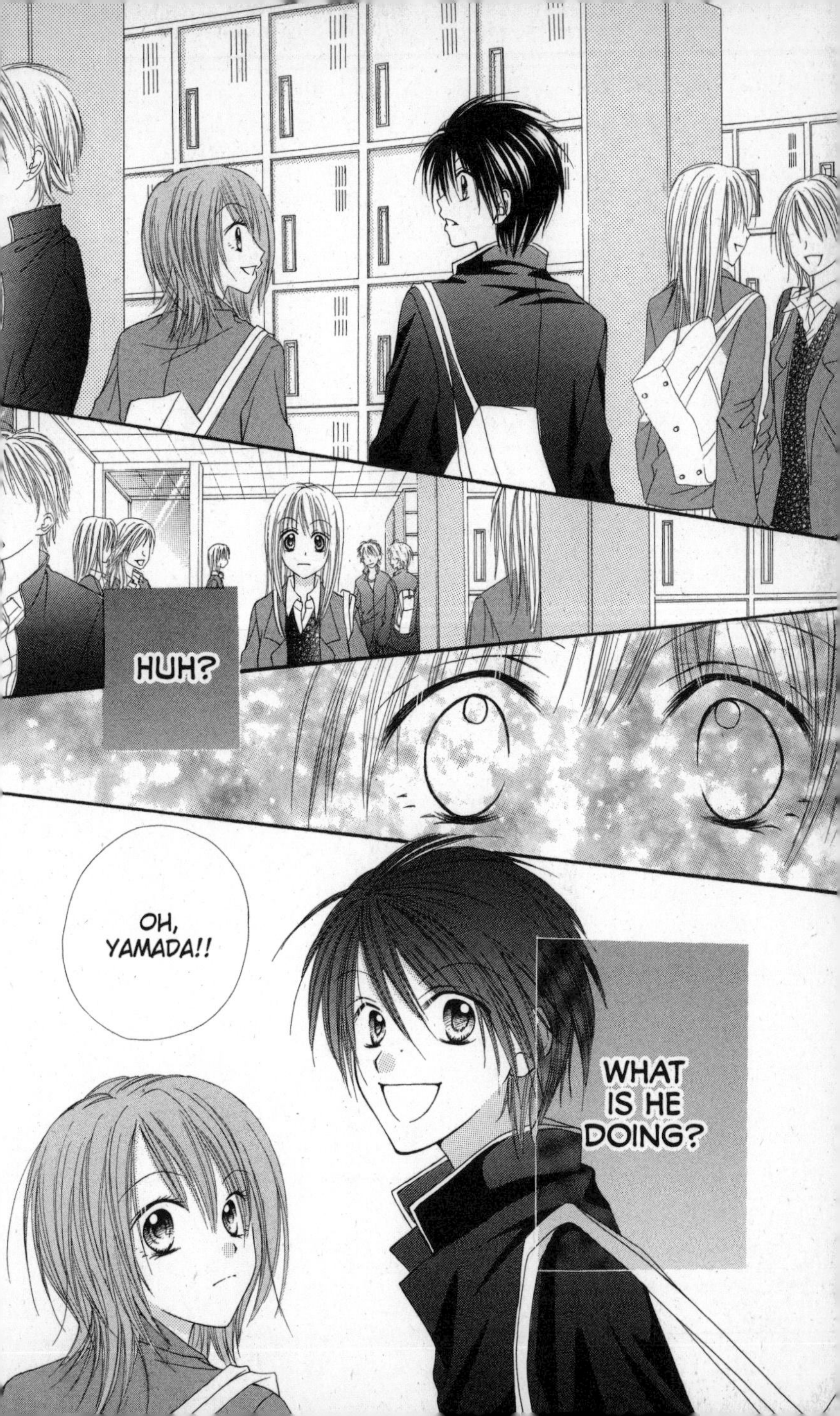
HUH?
WHAT IS HE DOING?
OH, YAMADA!!

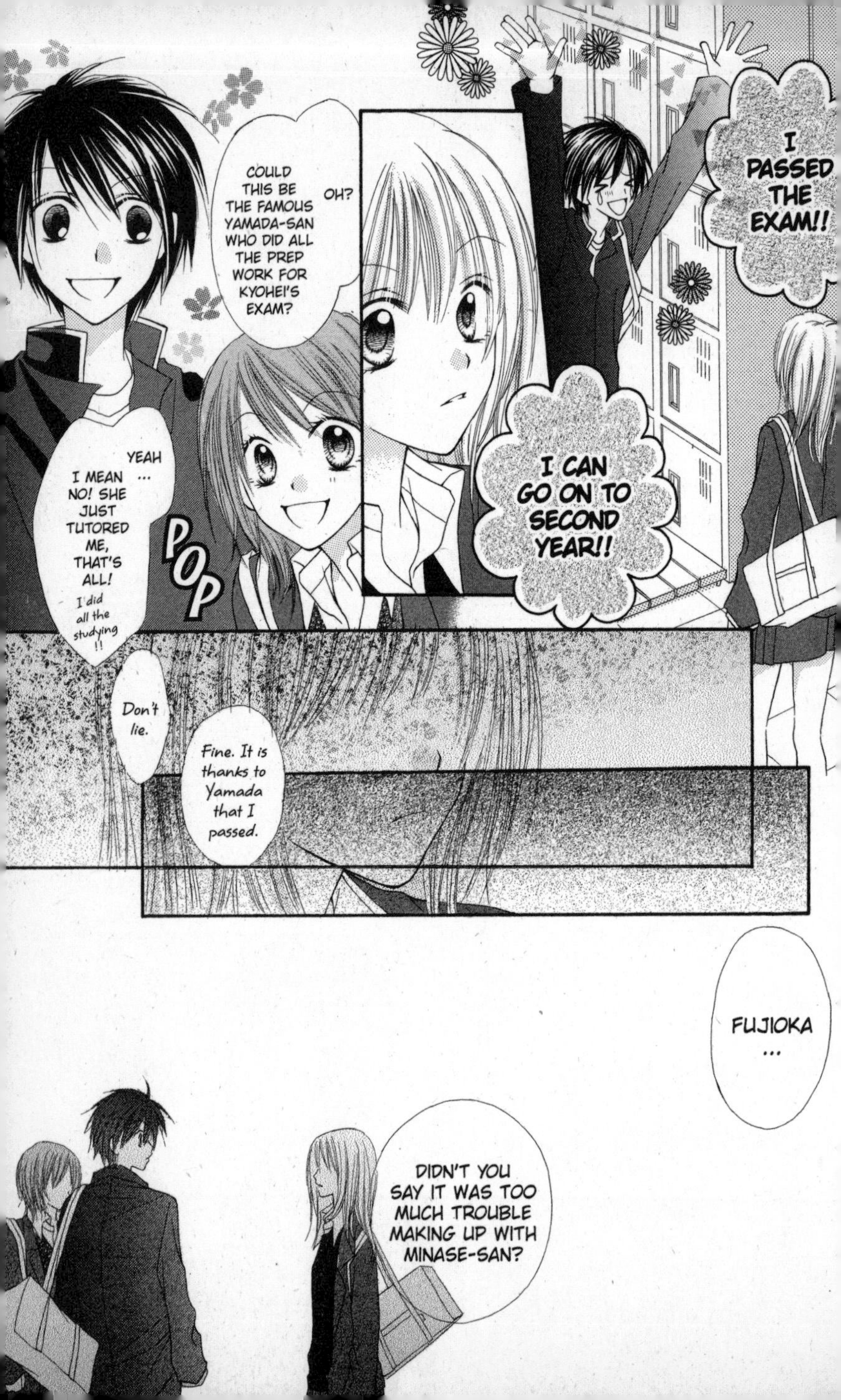
I PASSED THE EXAM!!
I CAN GO ON TO SECOND YEAR!!
OH?
COULD THIS BE THE FAMOUS YAMADA-SAN WHO DID ALL THE PREP WORK FOR KYOHEI'S EXAM?
YEAH ... I MEAN NO! SHE JUST TUTORED ME, THAT'S ALL!
I did all the studying !!
POP
Don't lie.
Fine. It is thanks to Yamada that I passed.
FUJIOKA ...
DIDN'T YOU SAY IT WAS TOO MUCH TROUBLE MAKING UP WITH MINASE-SAN?

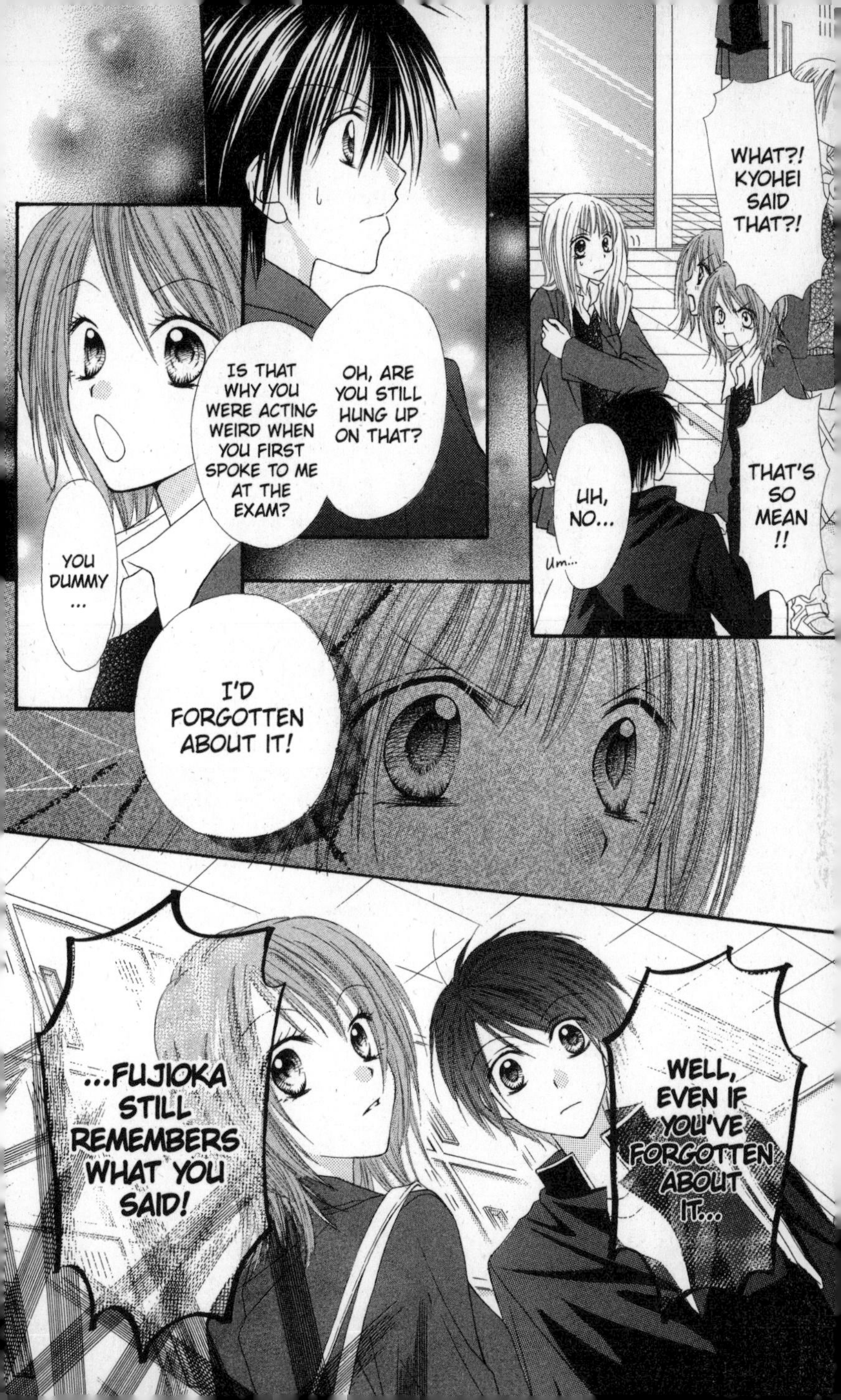
WHAT?! KYOHEI SAID THAT?!
THAT'S SO MEAN!!
UH, NO...
Um...
OH, ARE YOU STILL HUNG UP ON THAT?
IS THAT WHY YOU WERE ACTING WEIRD WHEN YOU FIRST SPOKE TO ME AT THE EXAM?
YOU DUMMY...
I'D FORGOTTEN ABOUT IT!
WELL, EVEN IF YOU'VE FORGOTTEN ABOUT IT...
...FUJIOKA STILL REMEMBERS WHAT YOU SAID!

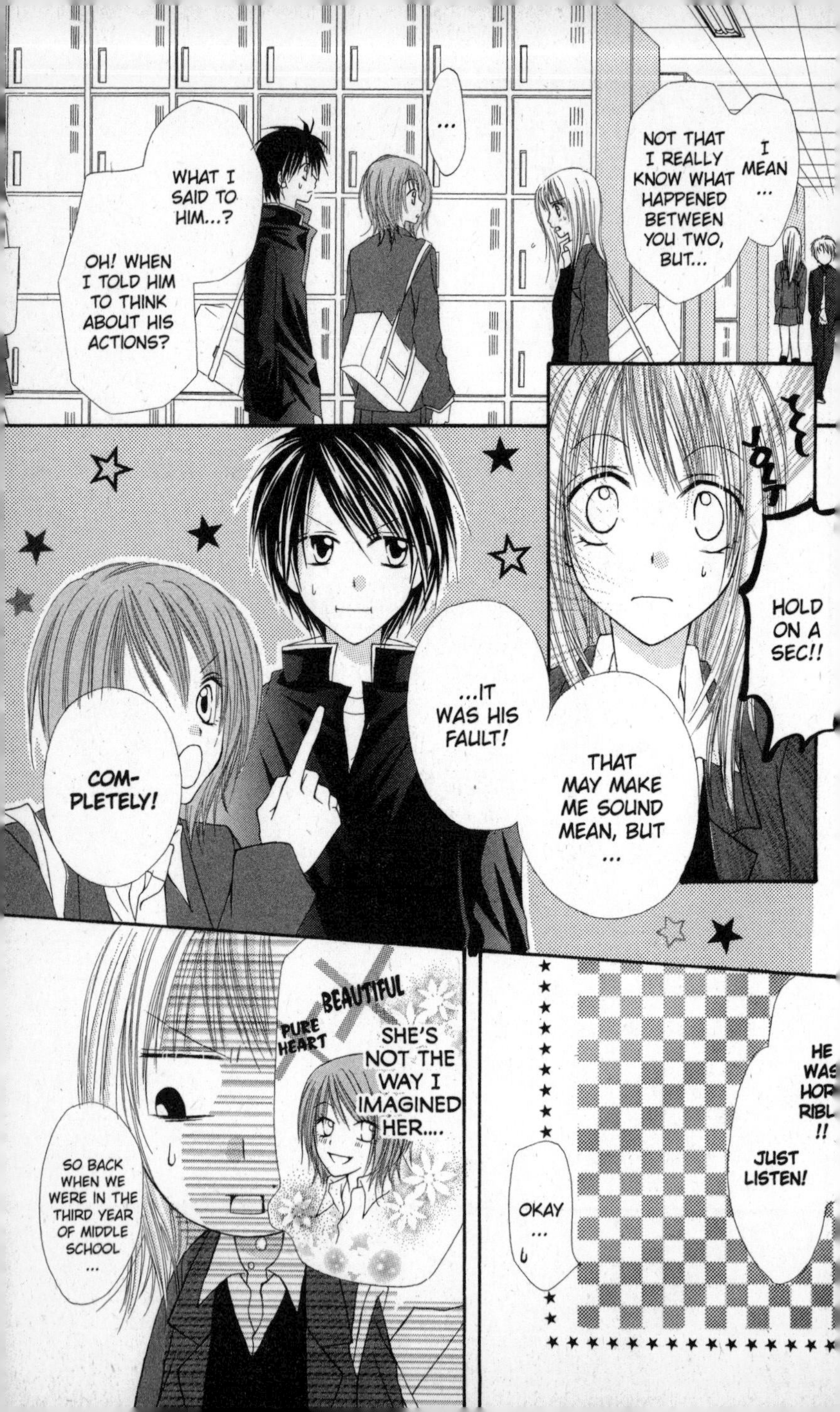
I MEAN ...
NOT THAT I REALLY KNOW WHAT HAPPENED BETWEEN YOU TWO, BUT...
...
WHAT I SAID TO HIM...?
OH! WHEN I TOLD HIM TO THINK ABOUT HIS ACTIONS?
HOLD ON A SEC!!
THAT MAY MAKE ME SOUND MEAN, BUT ...
...IT WAS HIS FAULT!
COM-PLETELY!
HE WAS HOR RIBL !!
JUST LISTEN!
OKAY ...
SHE'S NOT THE WAY I IMAGINED HER....
BEAUTIFUL
PURE HEART
SO BACK WHEN WE WERE IN THE THIRD YEAR OF MIDDLE SCHOOL ...

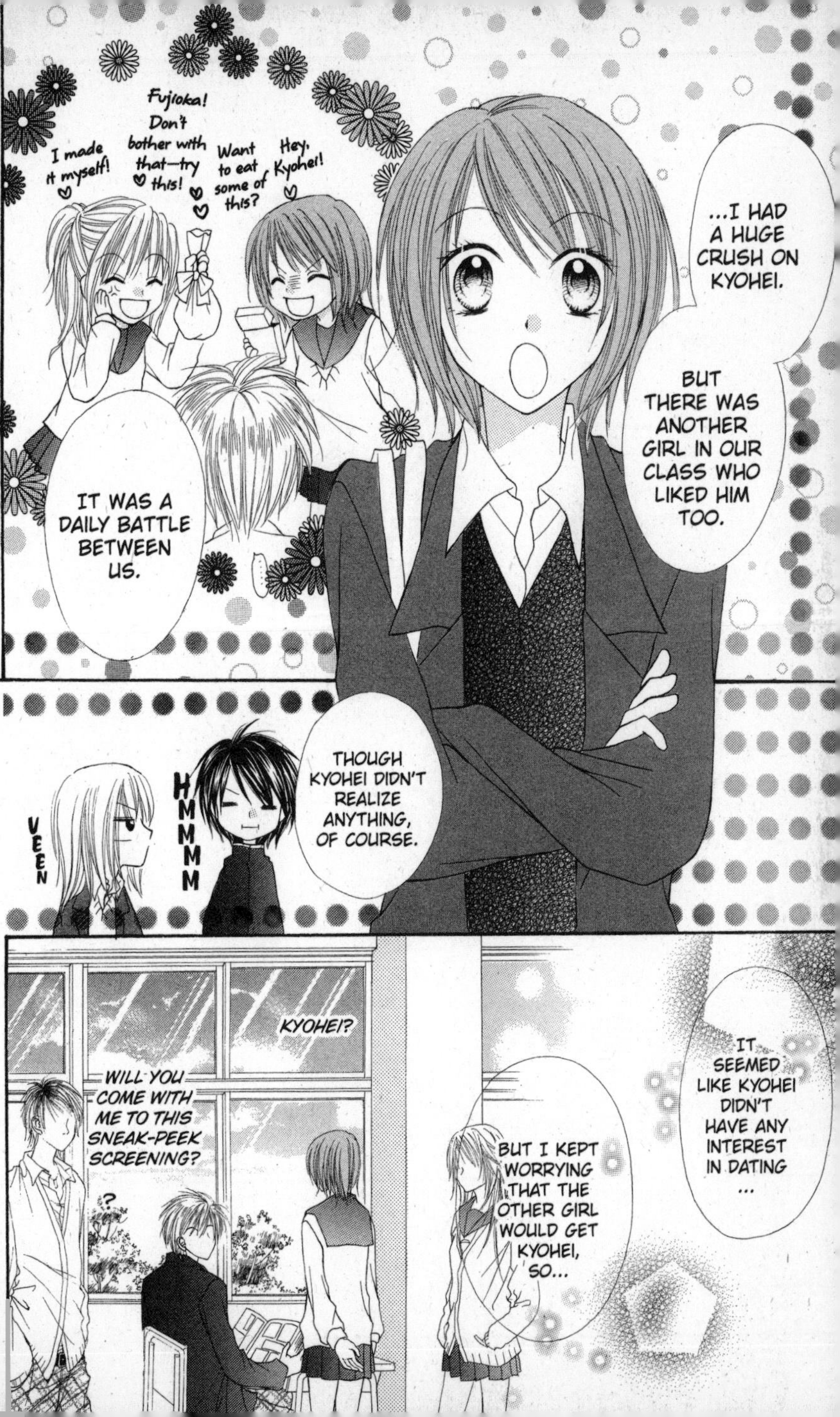
...I HAD A HUGE CRUSH ON KYOHEI.
BUT THERE WAS ANOTHER GIRL IN OUR CLASS WHO LIKED HIM TOO.
Hey, Kyohei!
Want to eat some of this?
Fujioka! Don't bother with that—try this!
I made it myself!
IT WAS A DAILY BATTLE BETWEEN US.
THOUGH KYOHEI DIDN'T REALIZE ANYTHING, OF COURSE.
HMMMM
VEEN
IT SEEMED LIKE KYOHEI DIDN'T HAVE ANY INTEREST IN DATING...
BUT I KEPT WORRYING THAT THE OTHER GIRL WOULD GET KYOHEI, SO...
KYOHEI?
WILL YOU COME WITH ME TO THIS SNEAK-PEEK SCREENING?
?

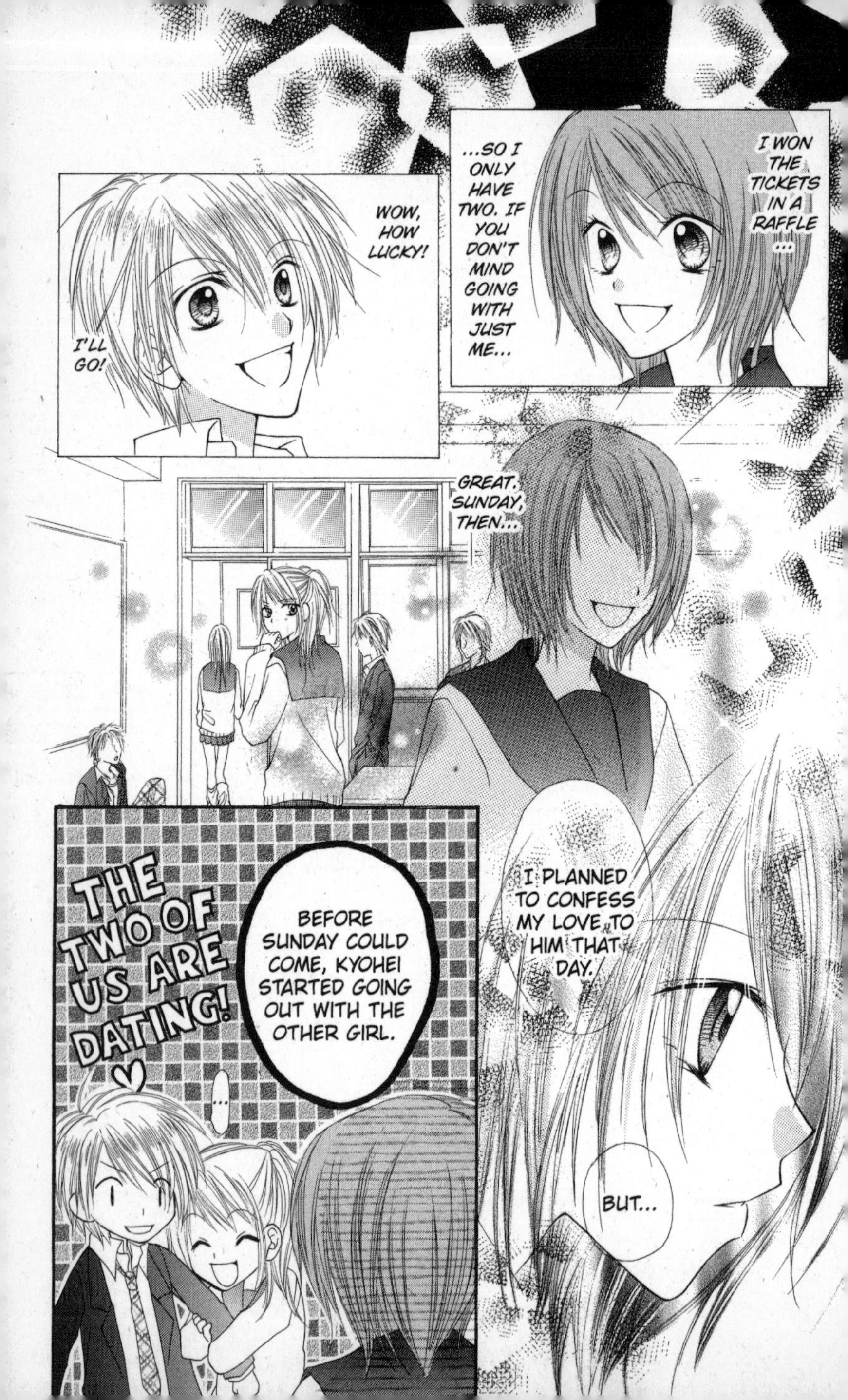
I WON THE TICKETS IN A RAFFLE...
...SO I ONLY HAVE TWO. IF YOU DON'T MIND GOING WITH JUST ME...
WOW, HOW LUCKY!
I'LL GO!
GREAT. SUNDAY, THEN...
I PLANNED TO CONFESS MY LOVE TO HIM THAT DAY.
BUT...
BEFORE SUNDAY COULD COME, KYOHEI STARTED GOING OUT WITH THE OTHER GIRL.
THE TWO OF US ARE DATING!
...

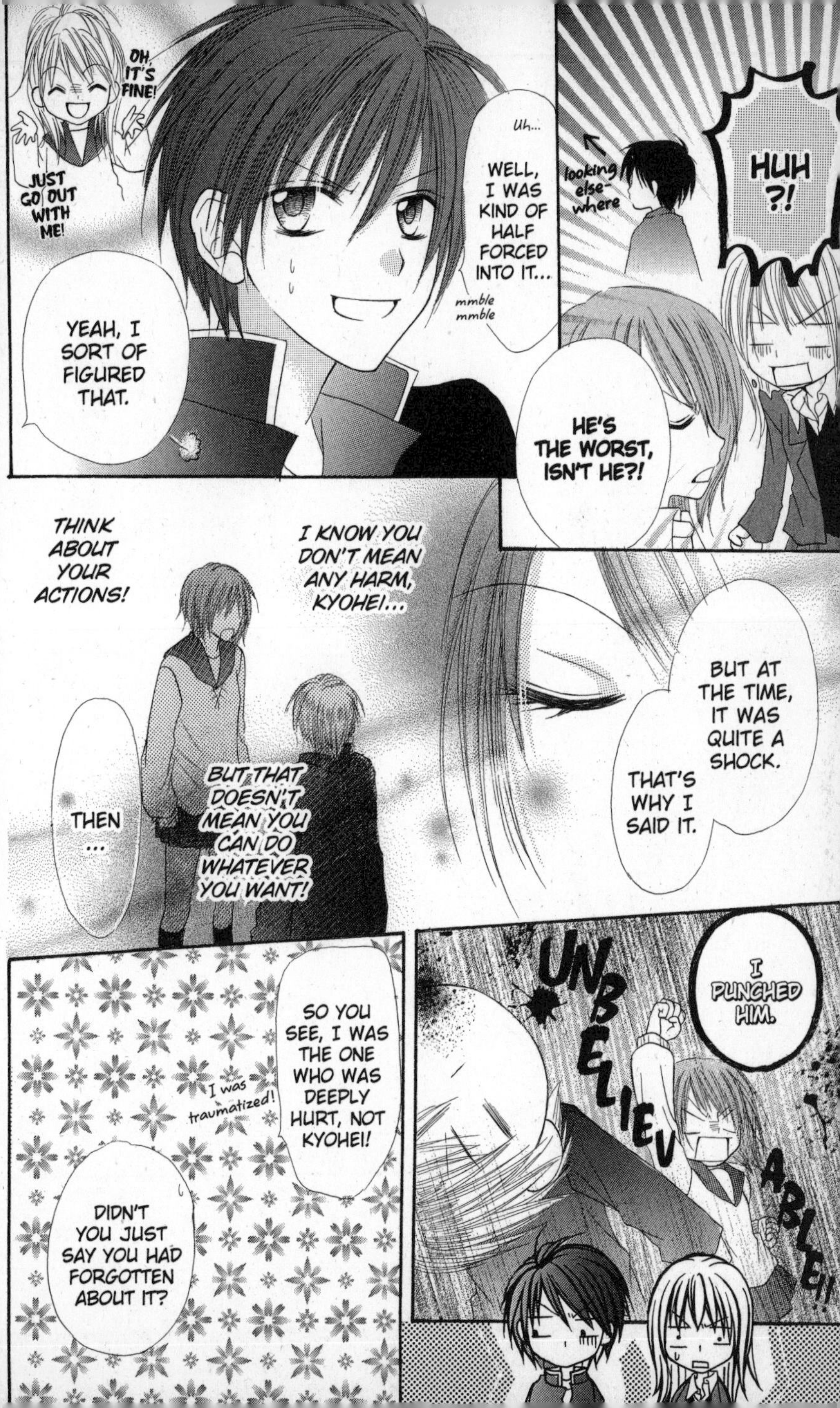
HUH ?!
looking else-where
HE'S THE WORST, ISN'T HE?!
Uh...
WELL, I WAS KIND OF HALF FORCED INTO IT...
mmble mmble
OH, IT'S FINE!
JUST GO OUT WITH ME!
YEAH, I SORT OF FIGURED THAT.
BUT AT THE TIME, IT WAS QUITE A SHOCK.
THAT'S WHY I SAID IT.
I KNOW YOU DON'T MEAN ANY HARM, KYOHEI...
THINK ABOUT YOUR ACTIONS!
BUT THAT DOESN'T MEAN YOU CAN DO WHATEVER YOU WANT!
THEN ...
I PUNCHED HIM.
UNBELIEVABLE!!
SO YOU SEE, I WAS THE ONE WHO WAS DEEPLY HURT, NOT KYOHEI!
I was traumatized!
DIDN'T YOU JUST SAY YOU HAD FORGOTTEN ABOUT IT?

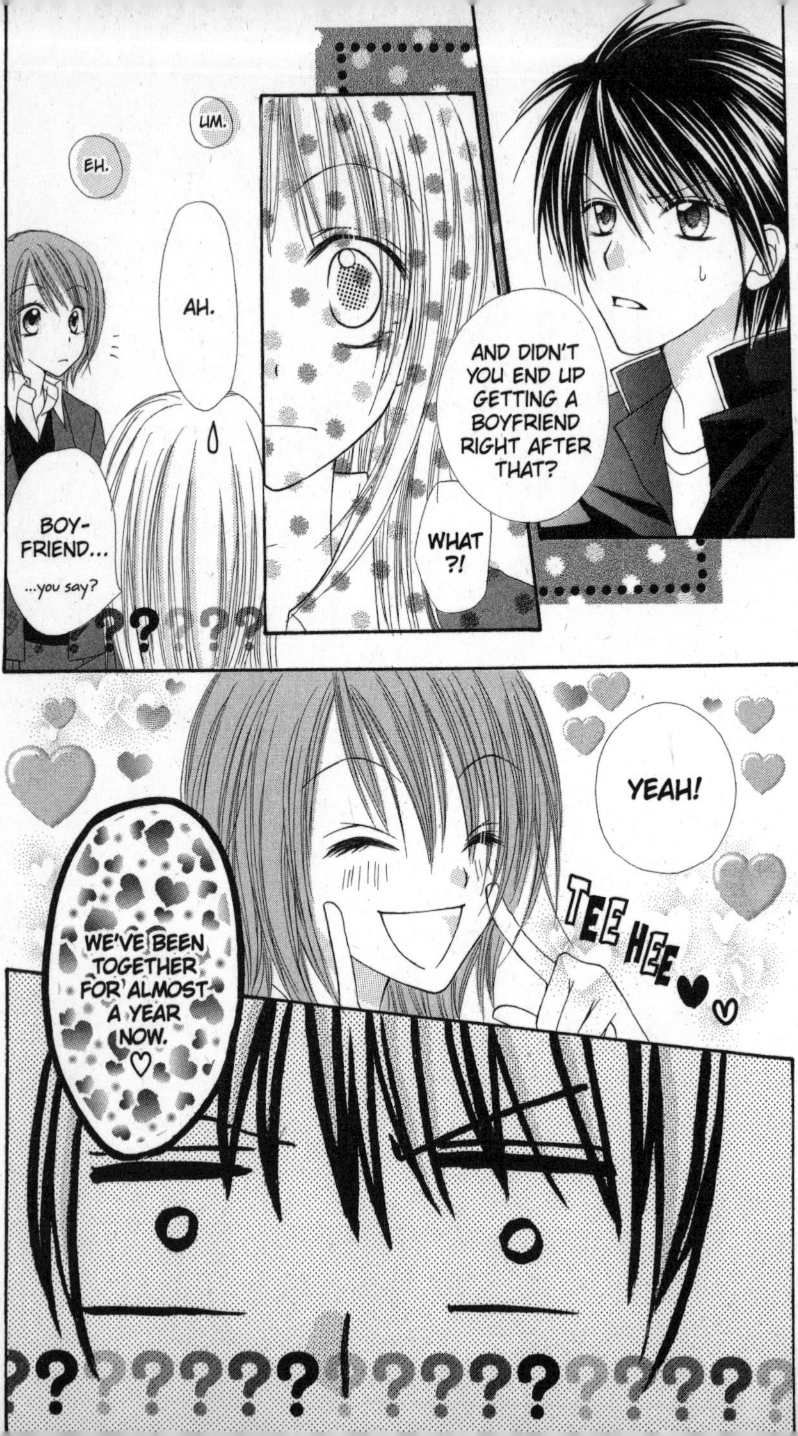
AND DIDN'T YOU END UP GETTING A BOYFRIEND RIGHT AFTER THAT?
WHAT ?!
UM.
EH.
AH.
BOY-FRIEND... ...you say?
YEAH!
TEE HEE ♥ ♡
WE'VE BEEN TOGETHER FOR ALMOST A YEAR NOW. ♡

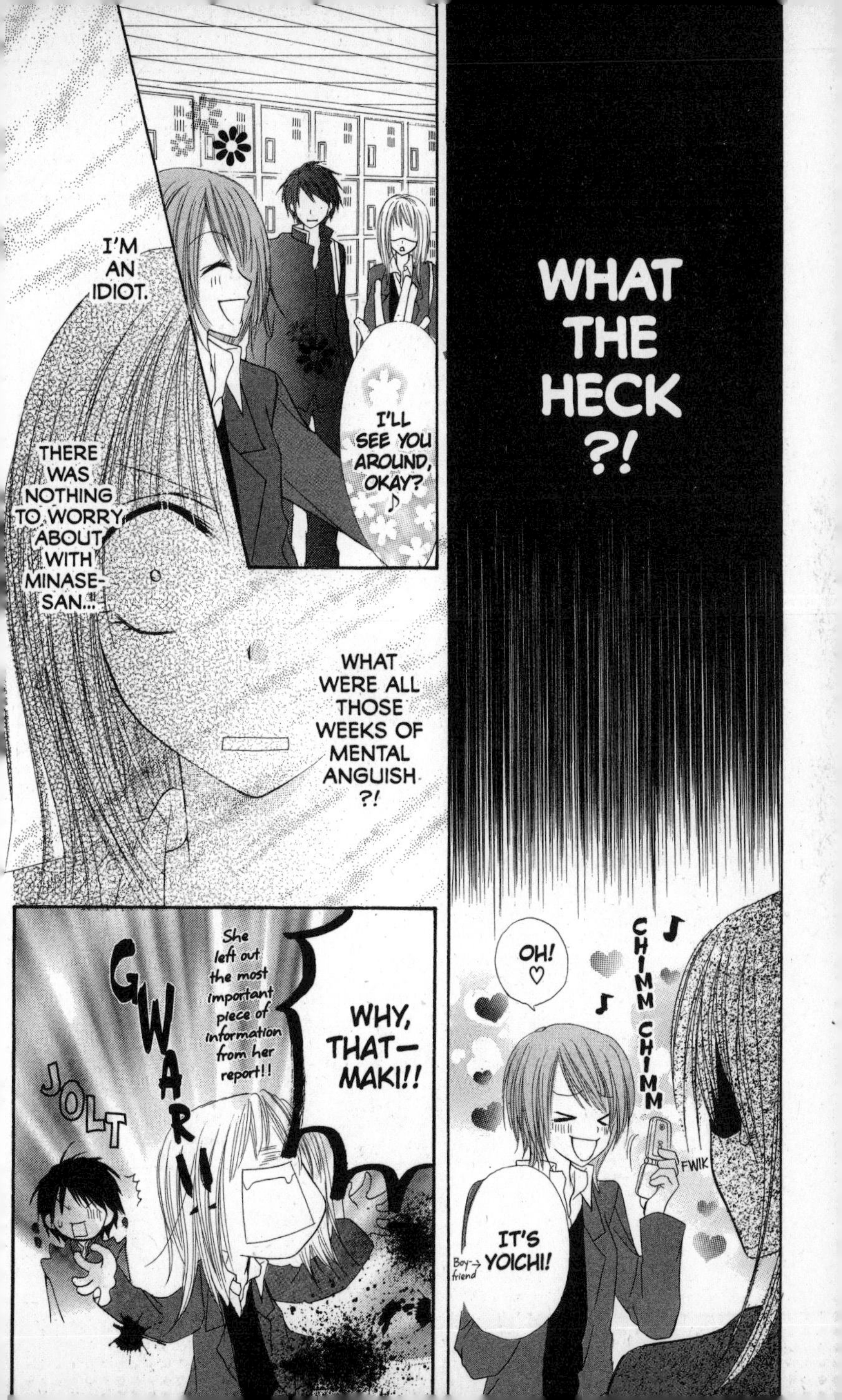
WHAT THE HECK ?!
I'M AN IDIOT.
I'LL SEE YOU AROUND, OKAY? ♪
THERE WAS NOTHING TO WORRY ABOUT WITH MINASE-SAN...
WHAT WERE ALL THOSE WEEKS OF MENTAL ANGUISH ?!
CHIMM CHIMM CHIMM
OH! ♡
FWIK
IT'S YOICHI!
Boy-→ friend
WHY, THAT— MAKI!!
She left out the most important piece of information from her report!!
GWARI
JOLT

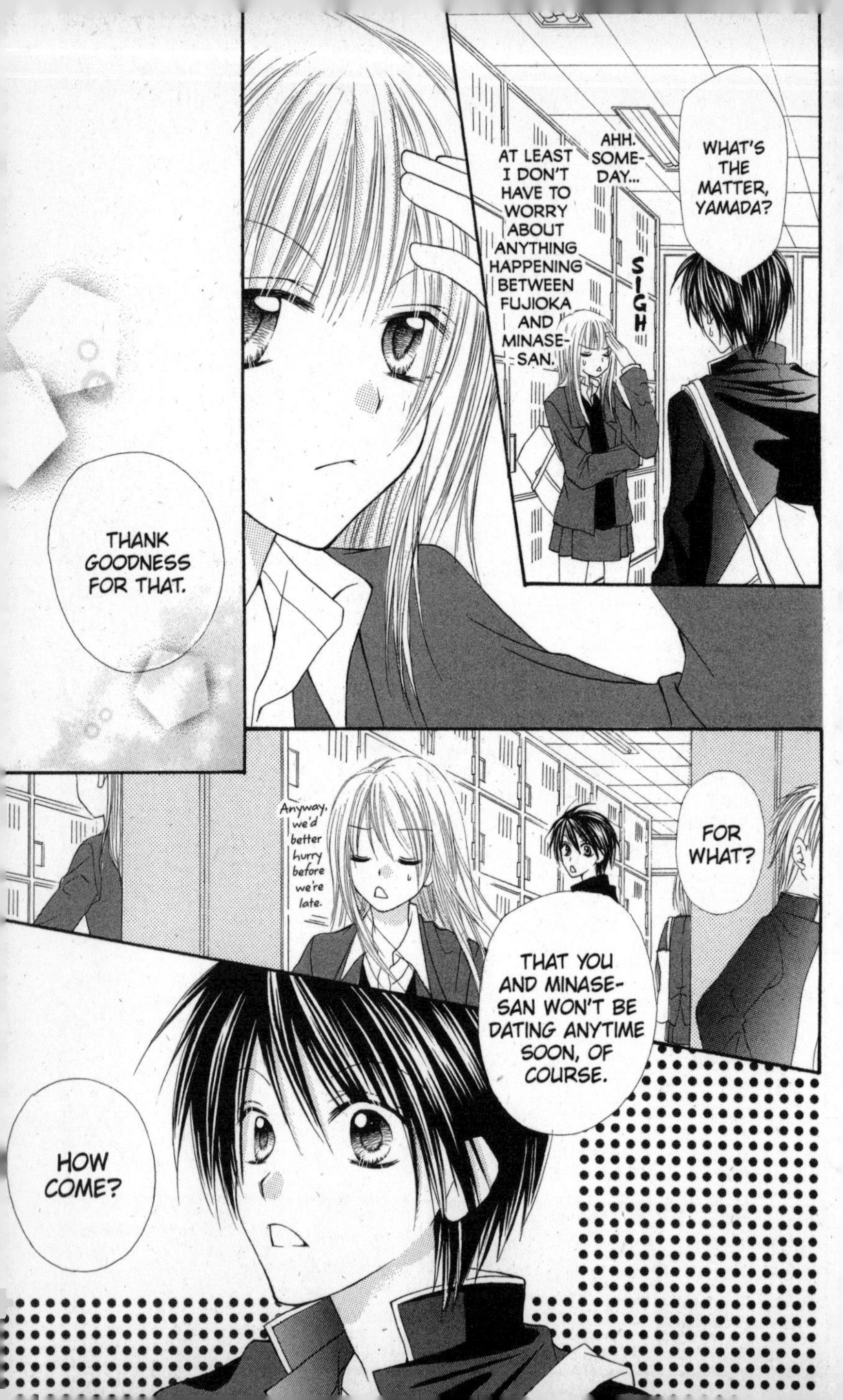
WHAT'S THE MATTER, YAMADA?
SIGH
AHH. SOME-DAY...
AT LEAST I DON'T HAVE TO WORRY ABOUT ANYTHING HAPPENING BETWEEN FUJIOKA AND MINASE-SAN.
THANK GOODNESS FOR THAT.
FOR WHAT?
THAT YOU AND MINASE-SAN WON'T BE DATING ANYTIME SOON, OF COURSE.
Anyway, we'd better hurry before we're late.
HOW COME?

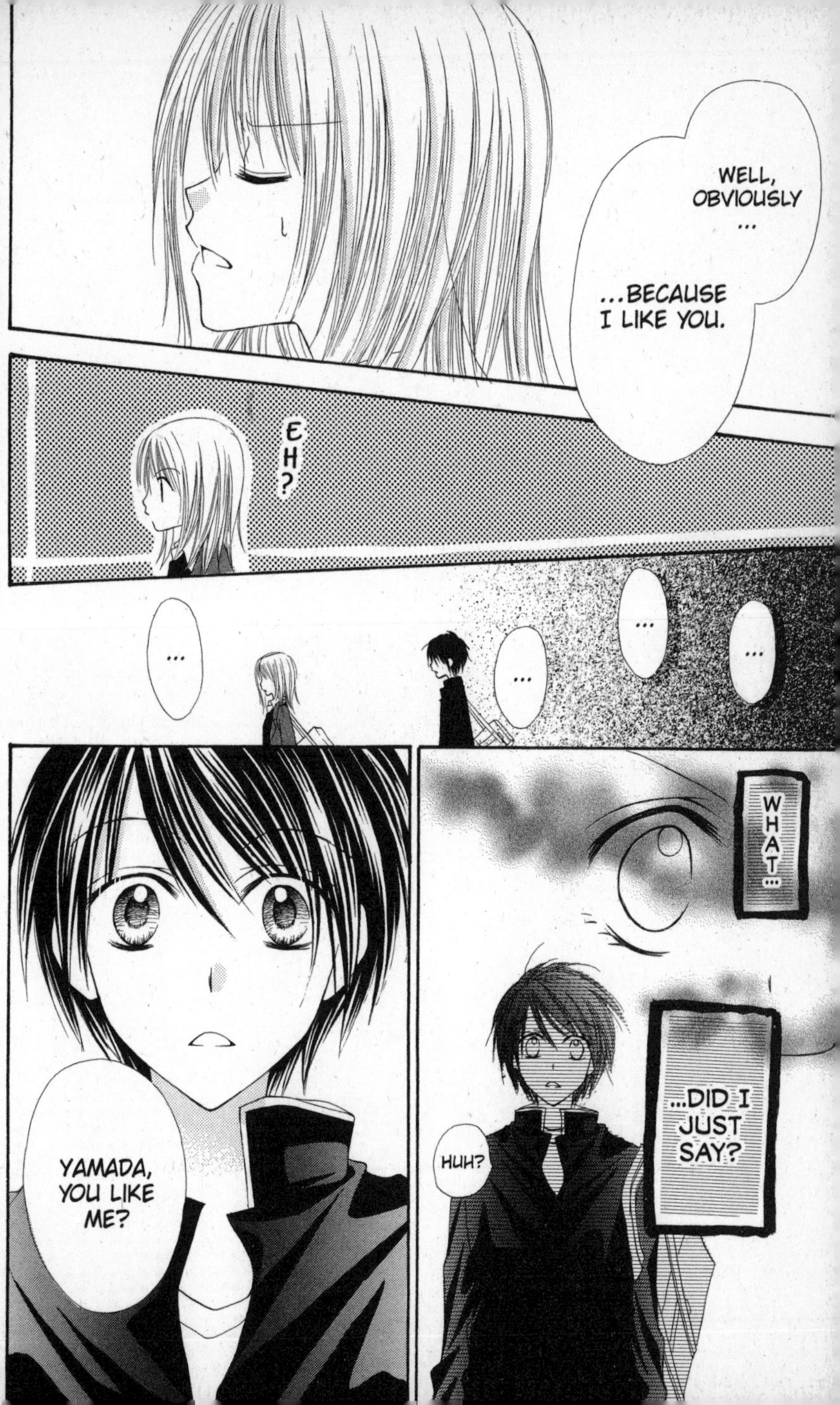
WELL, OBVIOUSLY ...
...BECAUSE I LIKE YOU.
EH?
...
...
...
...
WHAT...
...DID I JUST SAY?
HUH?
YAMADA, YOU LIKE ME?

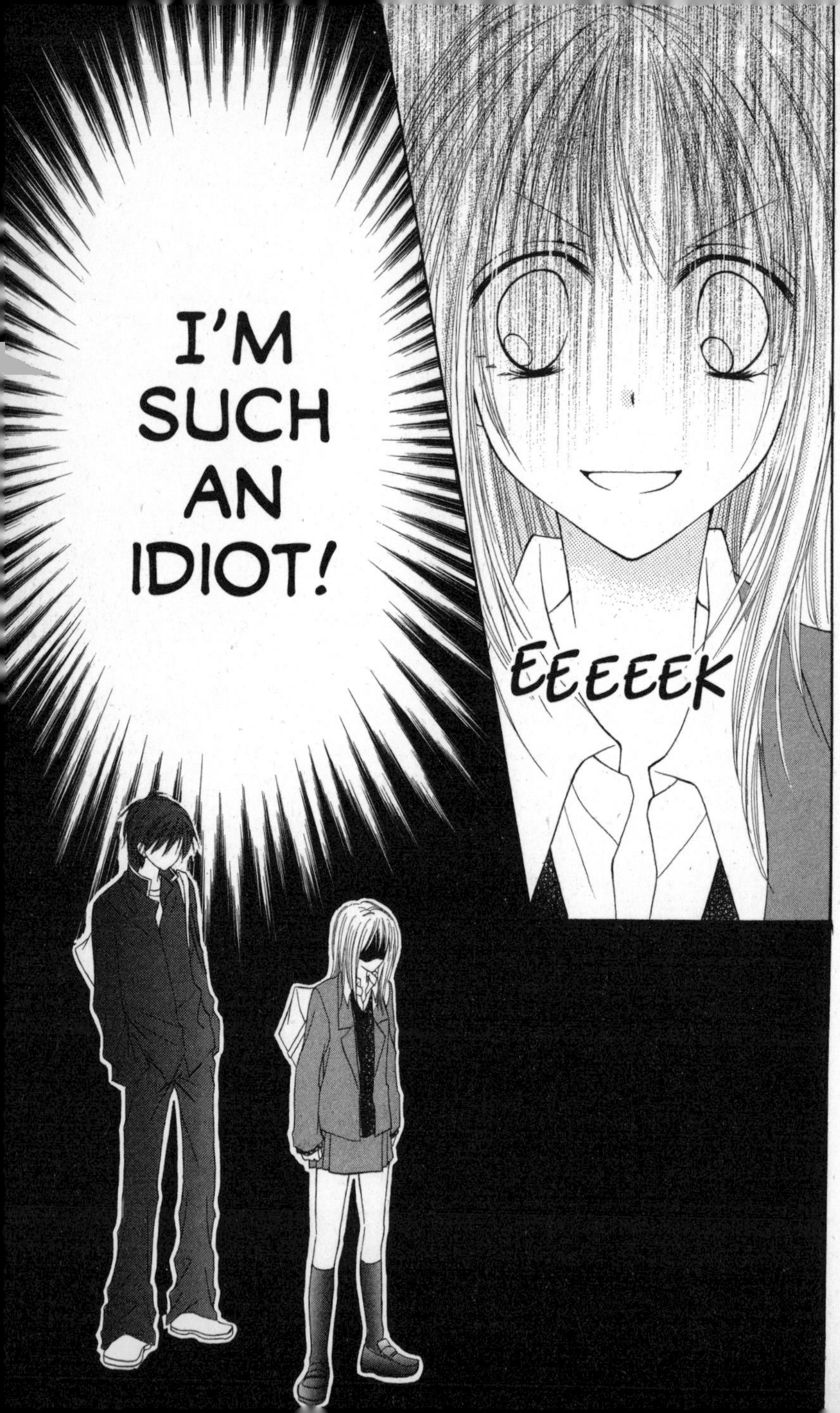
EEEEEK
I'M SUCH AN IDIOT!

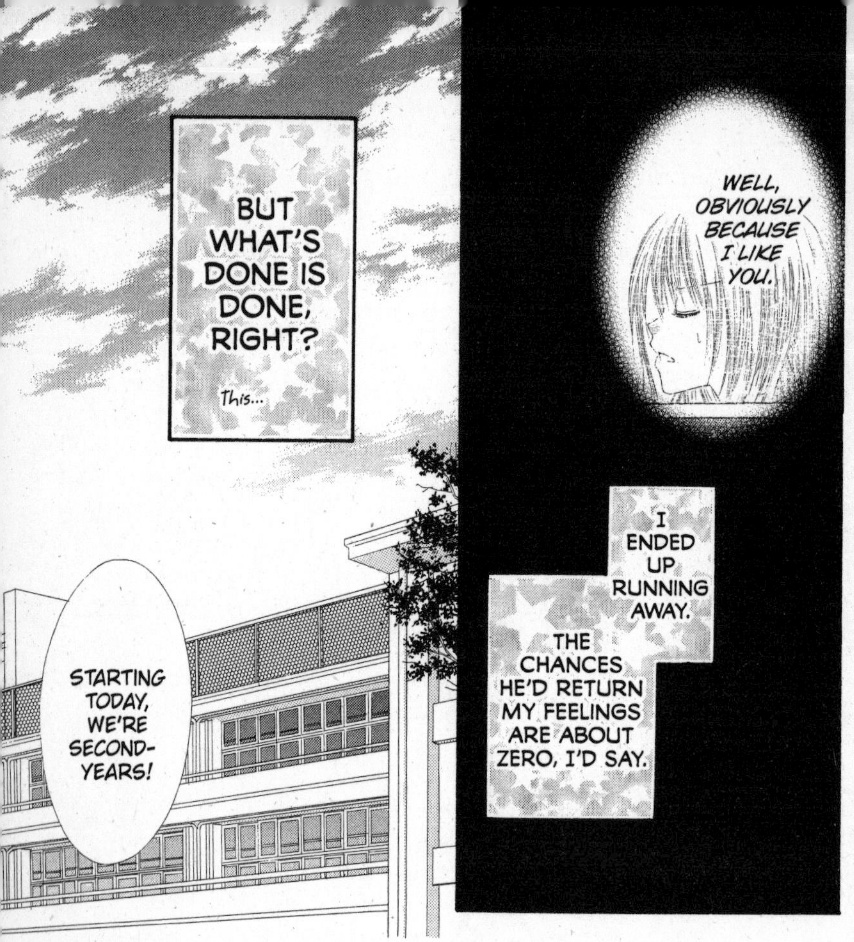
WELL, OBVIOUSLY BECAUSE I LIKE YOU.
I ENDED UP RUNNING AWAY.
THE CHANCES HE'D RETURN MY FEELINGS ARE ABOUT ZERO, I'D SAY.
BUT WHAT'S DONE IS DONE, RIGHT?
This...
STARTING TODAY, WE'RE SECOND-YEARS!

SMALL TALK ④

In chapter 5, Natsukawa-kun appears for the first time. There's a lot I want to say about him, but since chapter 6 is in volume 2, I guess I'd better wait. Until the next volume anyway.

My wonderful assistants had a very favorable reaction to chapter 5.

←
Smooth sailing through chapter 5... Heh heh heh.

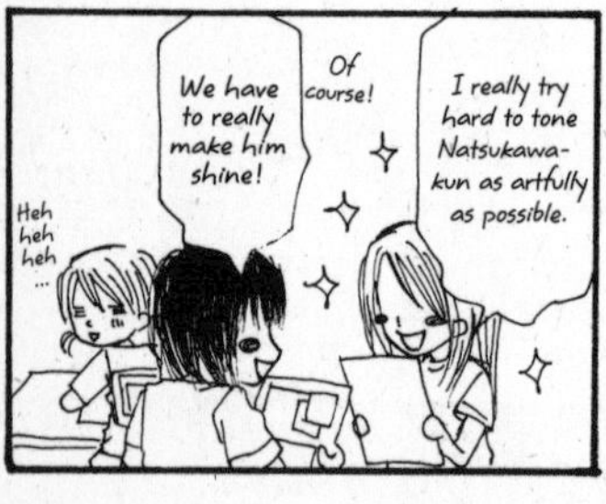
I really try hard to tone Natsukawa-kun as artfully as possible.
Of course!
We have to really make him shine!
Heh heh heh...

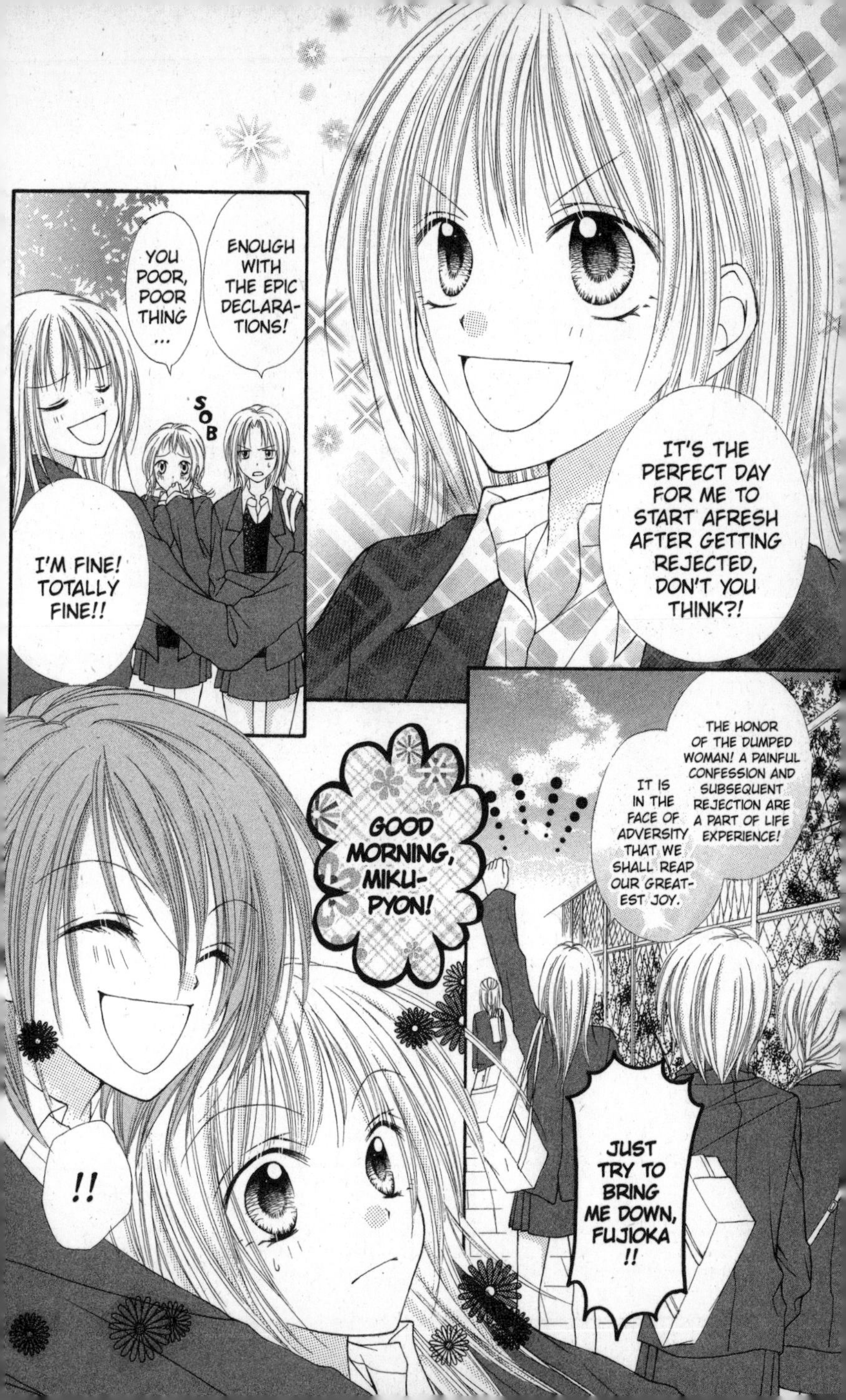
IT'S THE PERFECT DAY FOR ME TO START AFRESH AFTER GETTING REJECTED, DON'T YOU THINK?!
ENOUGH WITH THE EPIC DECLARATIONS!
YOU POOR, POOR THING ...
SOB
I'M FINE! TOTALLY FINE!!
THE HONOR OF THE DUMPED WOMAN! A PAINFUL CONFESSION AND SUBSEQUENT REJECTION ARE A PART OF LIFE EXPERIENCE!
IT IS IN THE FACE OF ADVERSITY THAT WE SHALL REAP OUR GREAT-EST JOY.
JUST TRY TO BRING ME DOWN, FUJIOKA!!
GOOD MORNING, MIKU-PYON!
!!

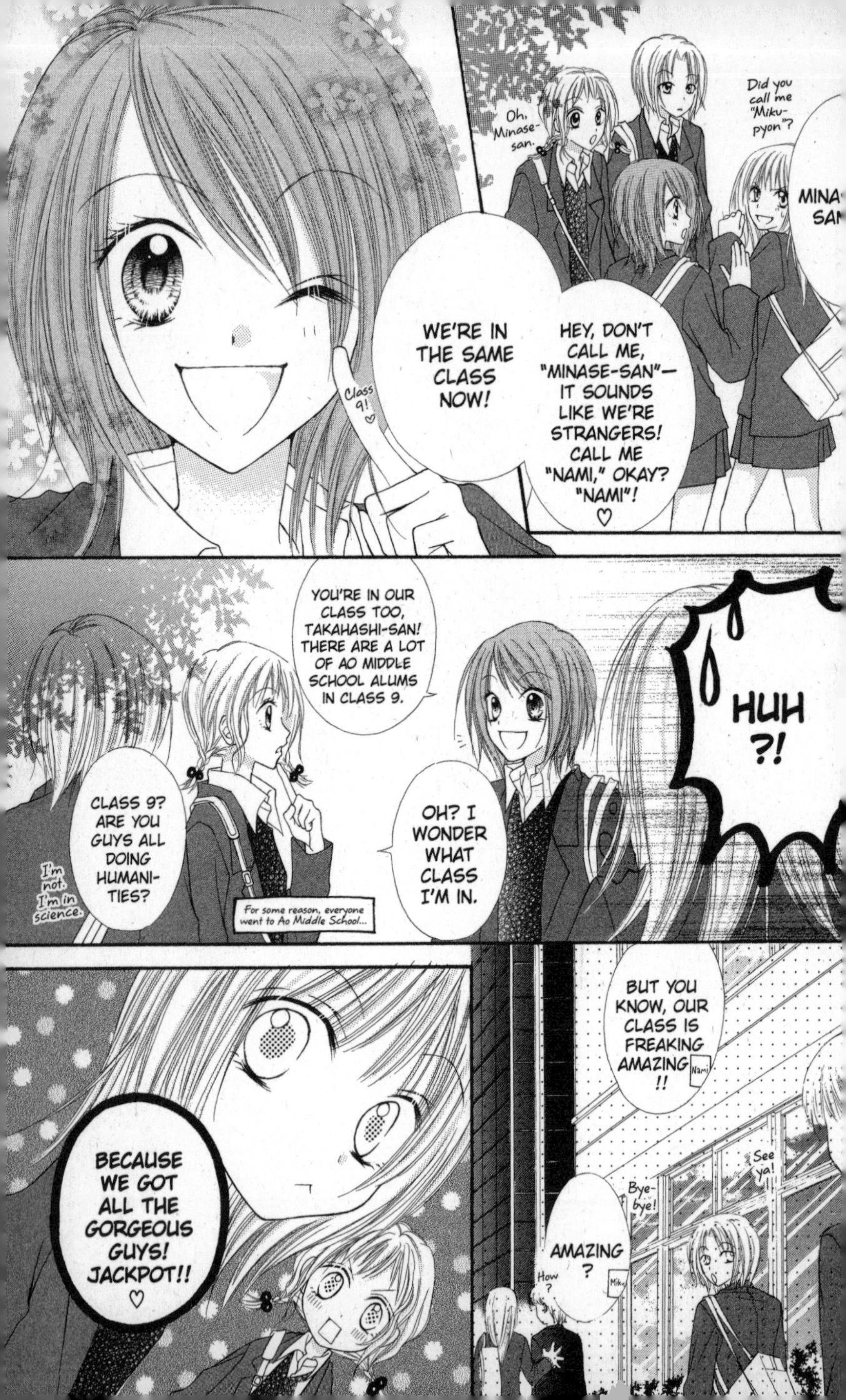

MINA SAN
Did you call me "Miku-pyon"?
Oh, Minase-san.
HEY, DON'T CALL ME, "MINASE-SAN"—IT SOUNDS LIKE WE'RE STRANGERS! CALL ME "NAMI," OKAY? "NAMI"! ♡
WE'RE IN THE SAME CLASS NOW!
Class 9! ♡
HUH ?!
YOU'RE IN OUR CLASS TOO, TAKAHASHI-SAN! THERE ARE A LOT OF AO MIDDLE SCHOOL ALUMS IN CLASS 9.
OH? I WONDER WHAT CLASS I'M IN.
CLASS 9? ARE YOU GUYS ALL DOING HUMANITIES?
I'm not. I'm in science.
For some reason, everyone went to Ao Middle School...
BUT YOU KNOW, OUR CLASS IS FREAKING AMAZING !!
Nami
See ya!
Bye-bye!
AMAZING ?
Miku
How ?
BECAUSE WE GOT ALL THE GORGEOUS GUYS! JACKPOT!! ♡

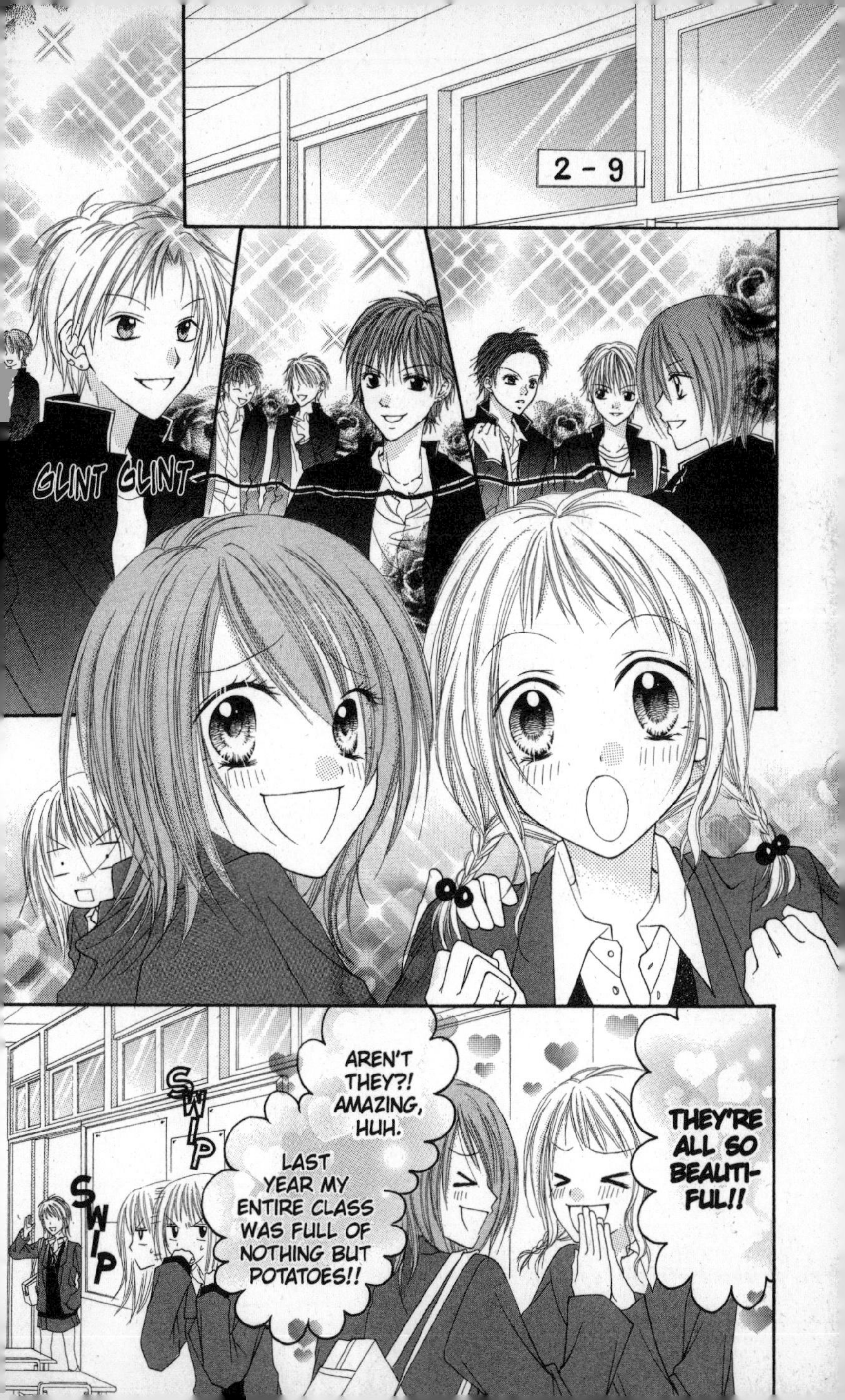
2-9
GLINT GLINT
THEY'RE ALL SO BEAUTI-FUL!!
AREN'T THEY?! AMAZING, HUH.
LAST YEAR MY ENTIRE CLASS WAS FULL OF NOTHING BUT POTATOES!!
SWIP
SWIP

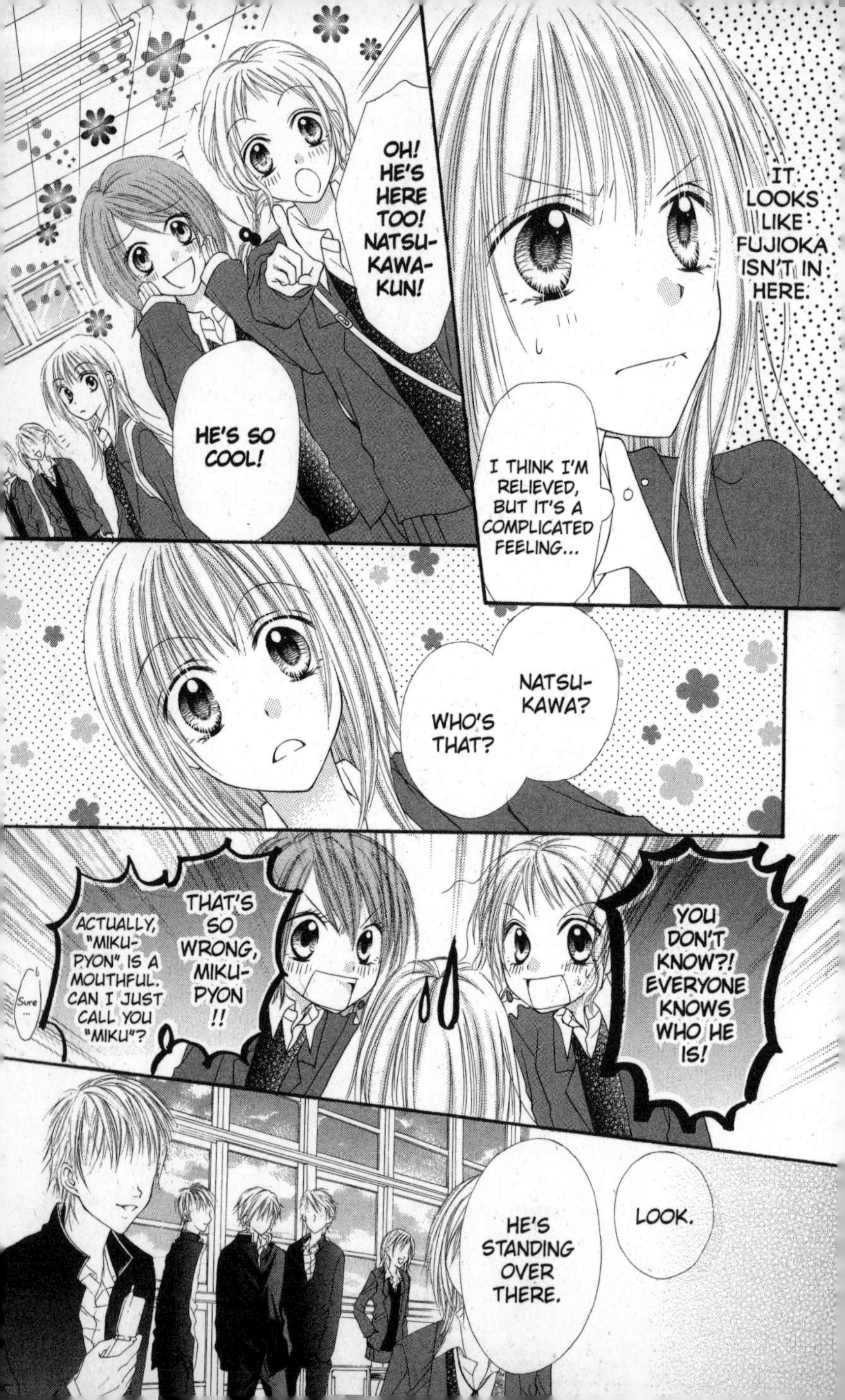
IT LOOKS LIKE FUJIOKA ISN'T IN HERE.
I THINK I'M RELIEVED, BUT IT'S A COMPLICATED FEELING...
OH! HE'S HERE TOO! NATSU-KAWA-KUN!
HE'S SO COOL!
NATSU-KAWA?
WHO'S THAT?
YOU DON'T KNOW?! EVERYONE KNOWS WHO HE IS!
THAT'S SO WRONG, MIKU-PYON!!
ACTUALLY, "MIKU-PYON" IS A MOUTHFUL. CAN I JUST CALL YOU "MIKU"?
Sure...
LOOK.
HE'S STANDING OVER THERE.

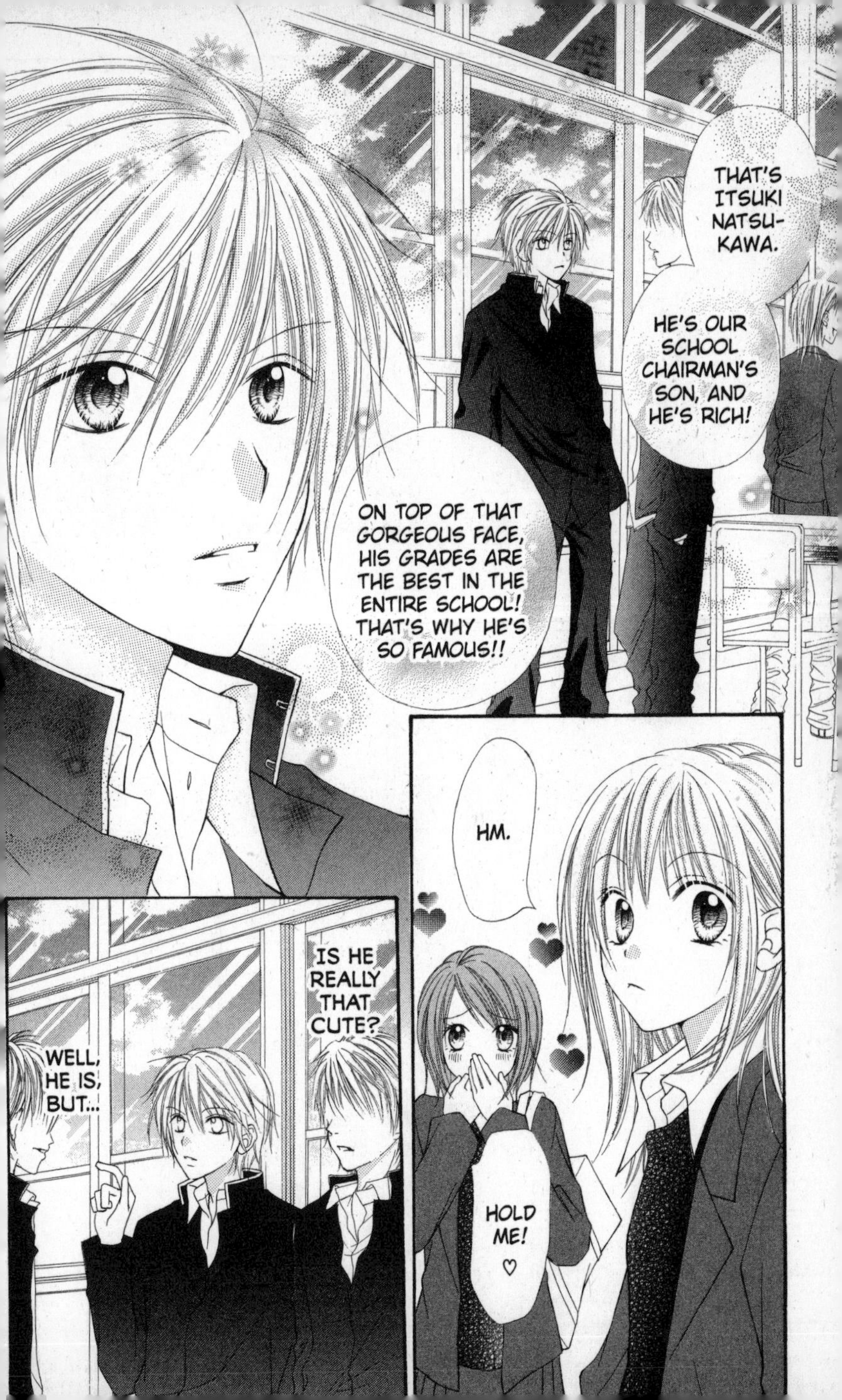
THAT'S ITSUKI NATSU-KAWA.
HE'S OUR SCHOOL CHAIRMAN'S SON, AND HE'S RICH!
ON TOP OF THAT GORGEOUS FACE, HIS GRADES ARE THE BEST IN THE ENTIRE SCHOOL! THAT'S WHY HE'S SO FAMOUS!!
HM.
HOLD ME! ♡
IS HE REALLY THAT CUTE?
WELL, HE IS, BUT...

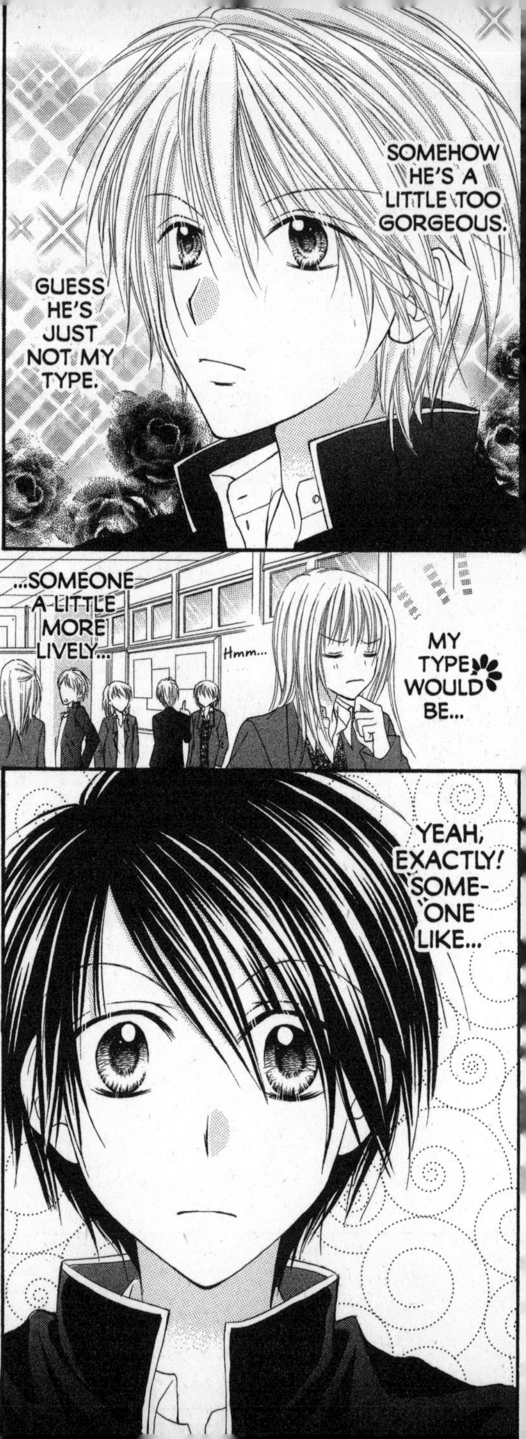
SOMEHOW HE'S A LITTLE TOO GORGEOUS.
GUESS HE'S JUST NOT MY TYPE.
MY TYPE WOULD BE...
Hmm...
...SOMEONE A LITTLE MORE LIVELY...
YEAH, EXACTLY! SOME-ONE LIKE...

12

Oh yeah—so at long last, I traded in my perpetually broken airbrush for a brand-new one.

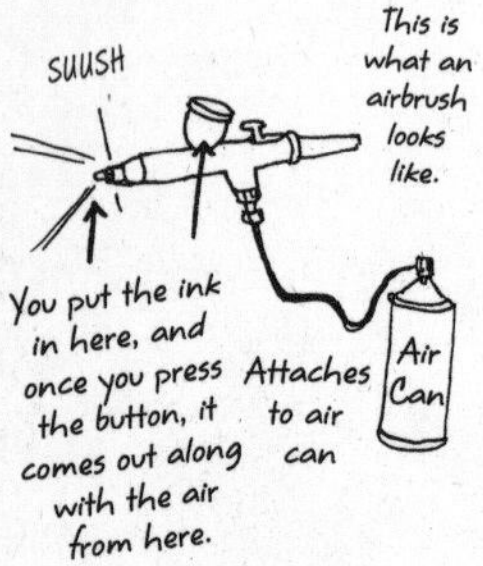
SUUSH
This is what an airbrush looks like.
You put the ink in here, and once you press the button, it comes out along with the air from here.
Attaches to air can
Air Can

If I didn't have one of these, I couldn't vary my coloring technique at all. Basically, an airbrush makes things a lot more convenient. (Yes, so valuable that I just made do with the half-broken one for two years). Even now, I still don't know how to use it fully... It's tough. Perhaps because I treated my first airbrush so carelessly, it ended up breaking in a rather surprising way.

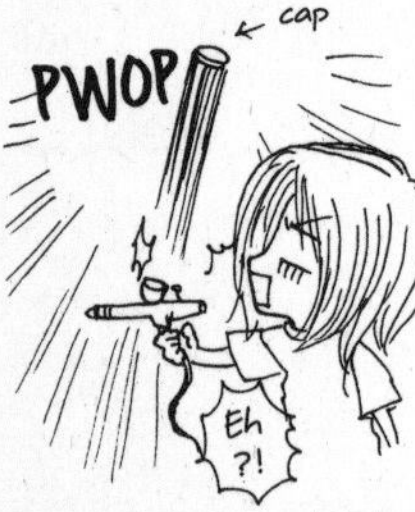
cap
PWOP
Eh ?!

Air came bursting out of a place it wasn't supposed to in a huge blast, and the cap on the ink container came flying off too. I knew then that it was time to lay my old airbrush to rest. It was very sad...because airbrushes are really expensive. (cry) I hope my new one will have a long, healthy life.

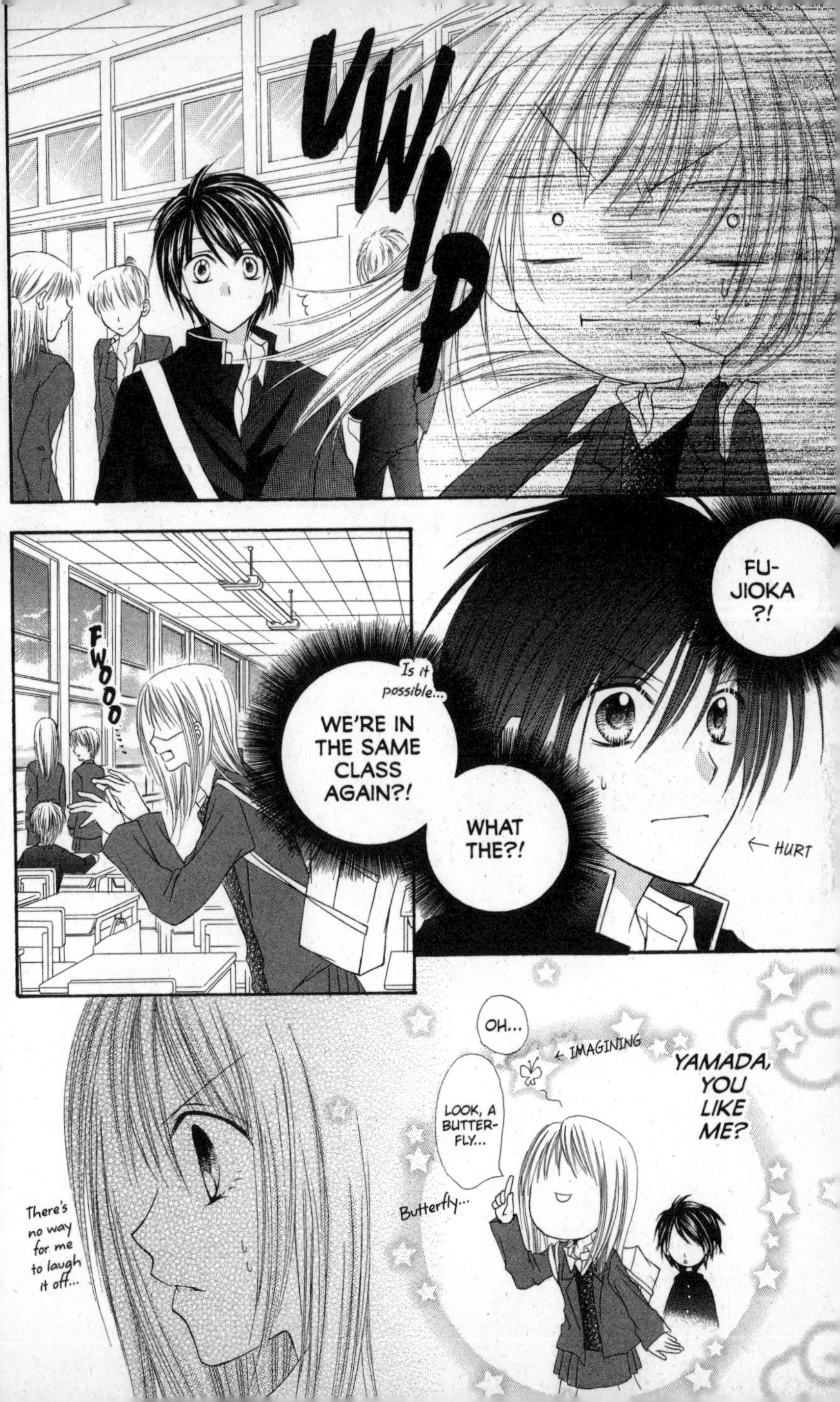
UWIP
FU-JIOKA?!
Is it possible...
WE'RE IN THE SAME CLASS AGAIN?!
WHAT THE?!
← HURT
FWOOO...
YAMADA, YOU LIKE ME?
OH...
← IMAGINING
LOOK, A BUTTER-FLY...
Butterfly...
There's no way for me to laugh it off...

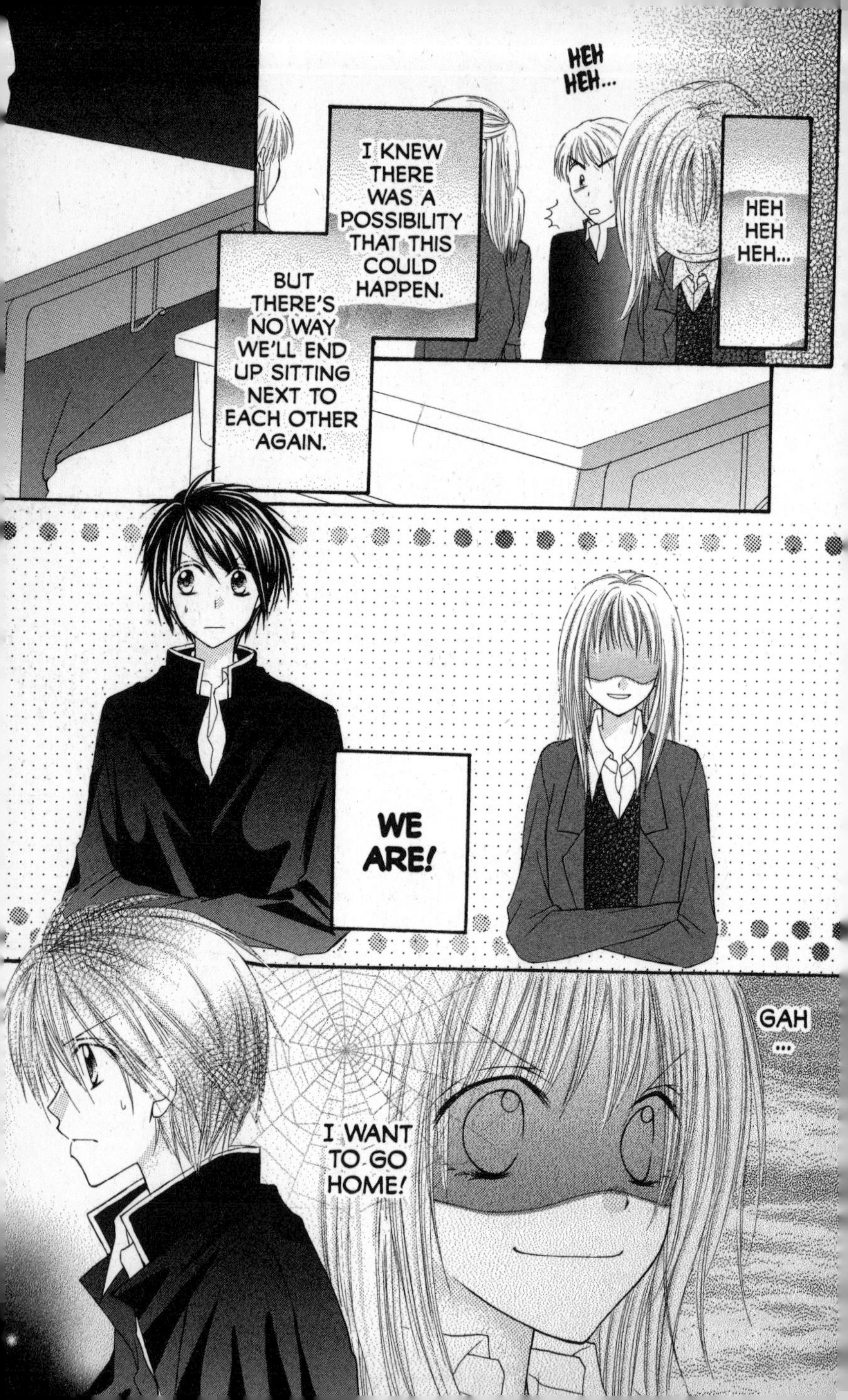
HEH HEH...
HEH HEH HEH...
I KNEW THERE WAS A POSSIBILITY THAT THIS COULD HAPPEN.
BUT THERE'S NO WAY WE'LL END UP SITTING NEXT TO EACH OTHER AGAIN.
WE ARE!
GAH ...
I WANT TO GO HOME!

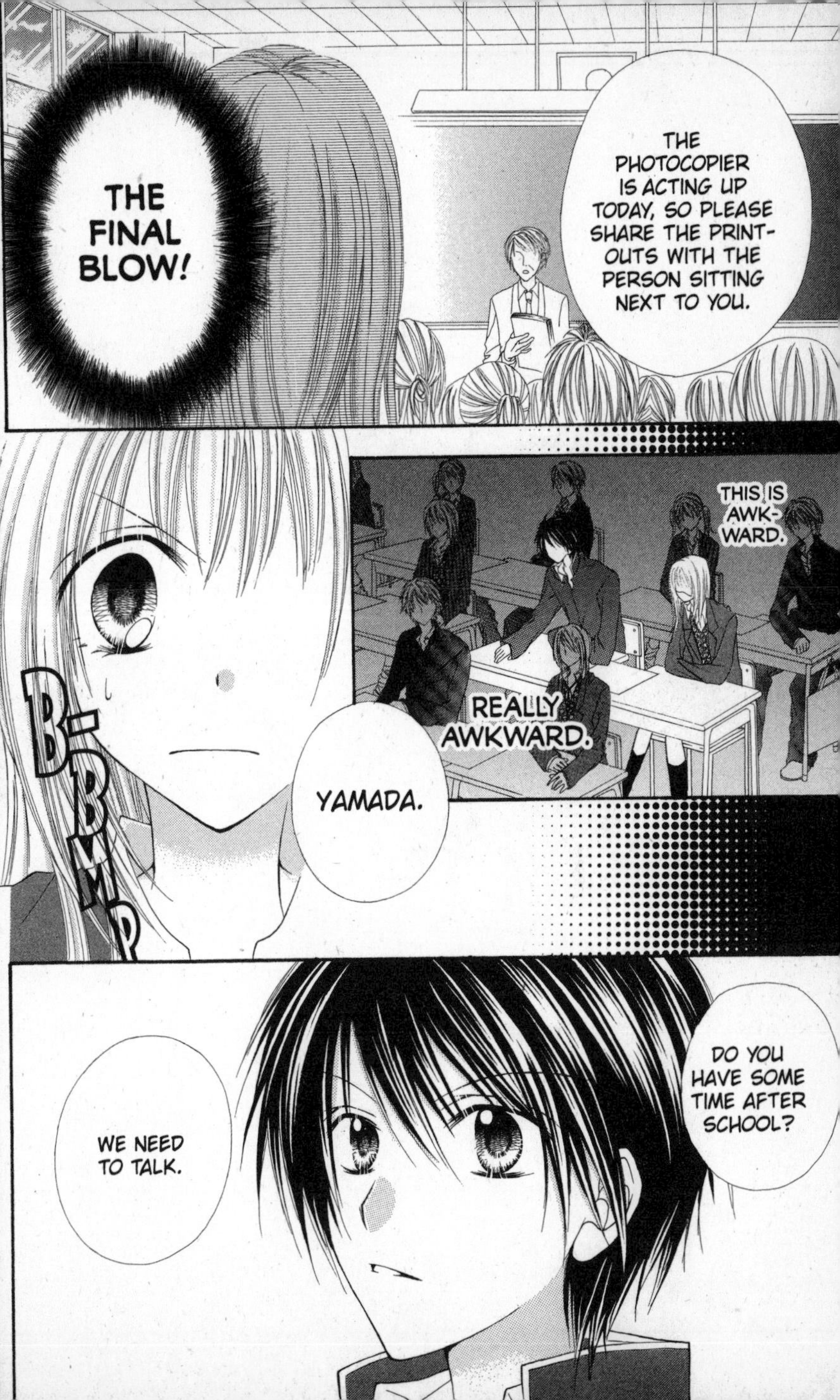
THE PHOTOCOPIER IS ACTING UP TODAY, SO PLEASE SHARE THE PRINT-OUTS WITH THE PERSON SITTING NEXT TO YOU.
THE FINAL BLOW!
THIS IS AWK-WARD.
REALLY AWKWARD.
YAMADA.
B-BUMP
DO YOU HAVE SOME TIME AFTER SCHOOL?
WE NEED TO TALK.

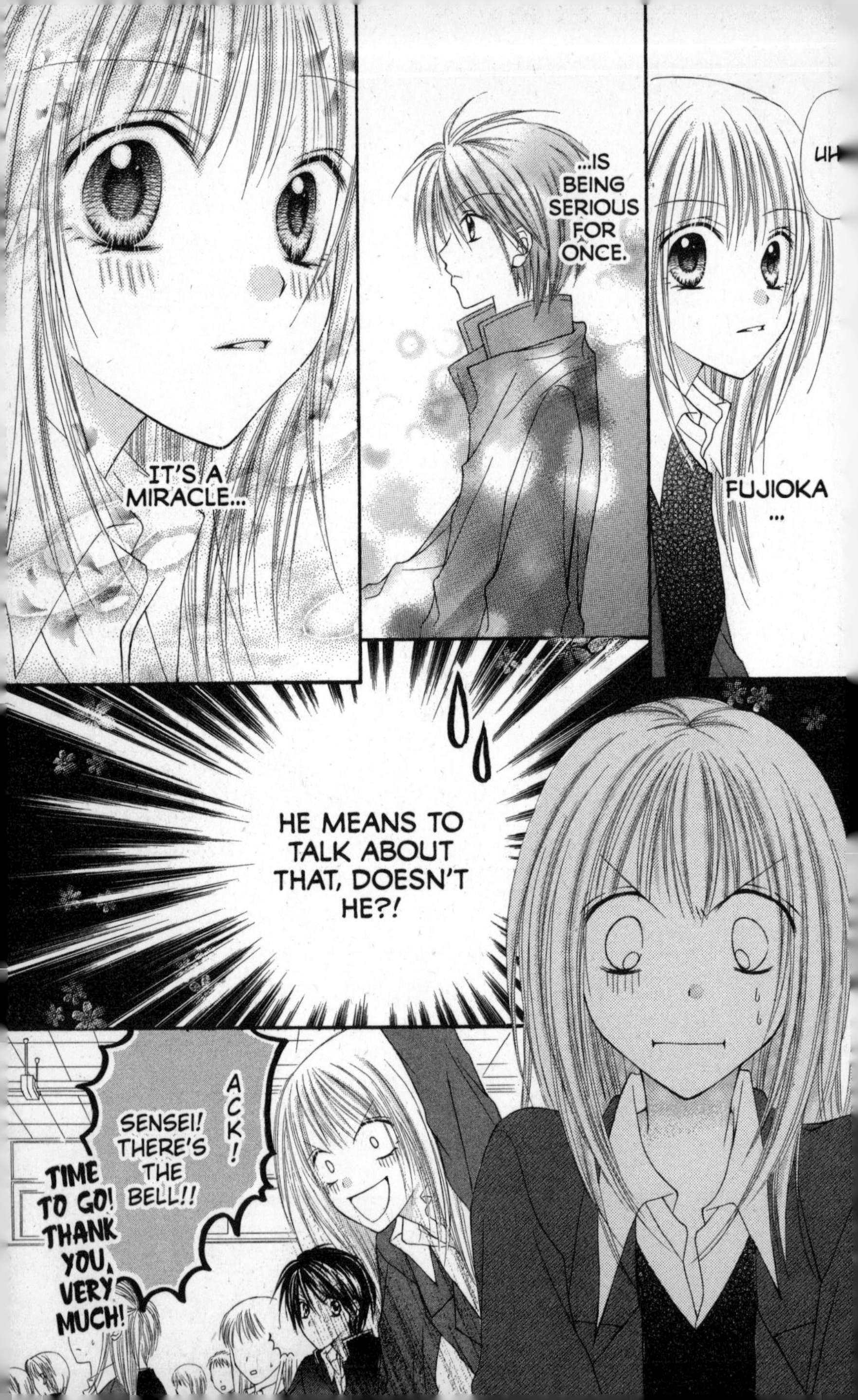
UH
FUJIOKA ...
...IS BEING SERIOUS FOR ONCE.
IT'S A MIRACLE...
HE MEANS TO TALK ABOUT THAT, DOESN'T HE?!
ACK!
SENSEI! THERE'S THE BELL!!
TIME TO GO! THANK YOU, VERY MUCH!

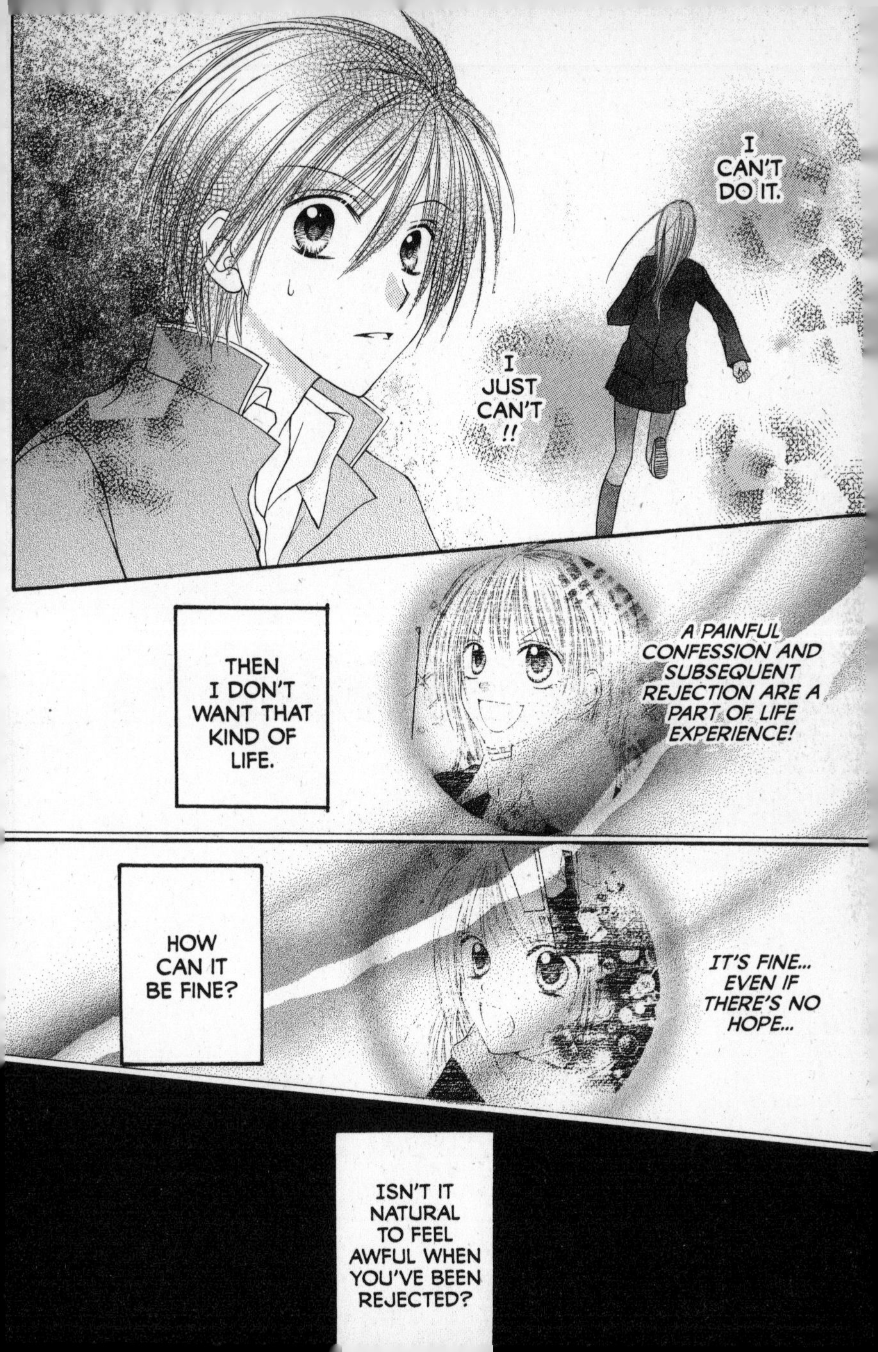
I CAN'T DO IT.
I JUST CAN'T !!
A PAINFUL CONFESSION AND SUBSEQUENT REJECTION ARE A PART OF LIFE EXPERIENCE!
THEN I DON'T WANT THAT KIND OF LIFE.
IT'S FINE... EVEN IF THERE'S NO HOPE...
HOW CAN IT BE FINE?
ISN'T IT NATURAL TO FEEL AWFUL WHEN YOU'VE BEEN REJECTED?

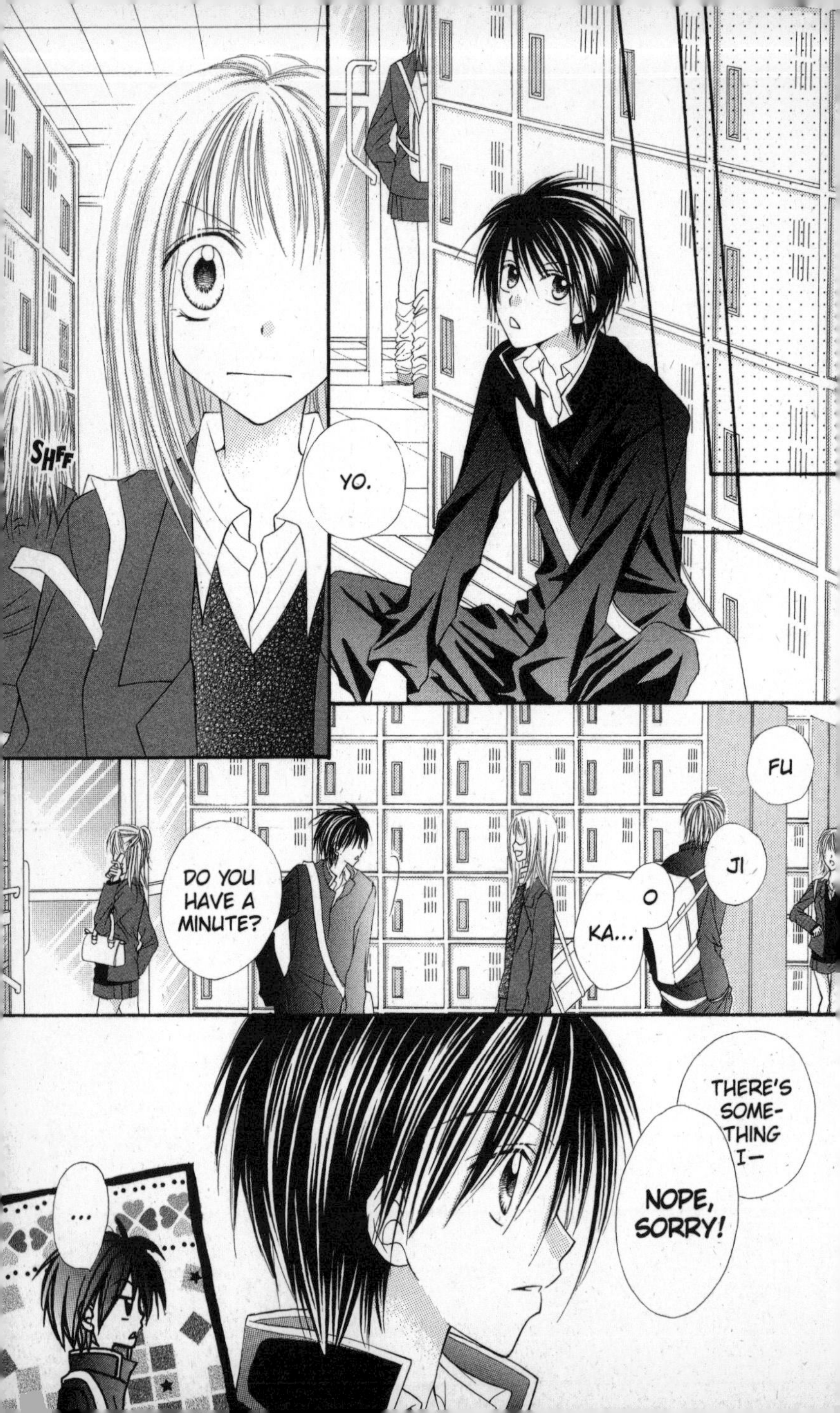
YO.
SHFF
FU
JI
O
KA...
DO YOU HAVE A MINUTE?
THERE'S SOME-THING I—
NOPE, SORRY!
...

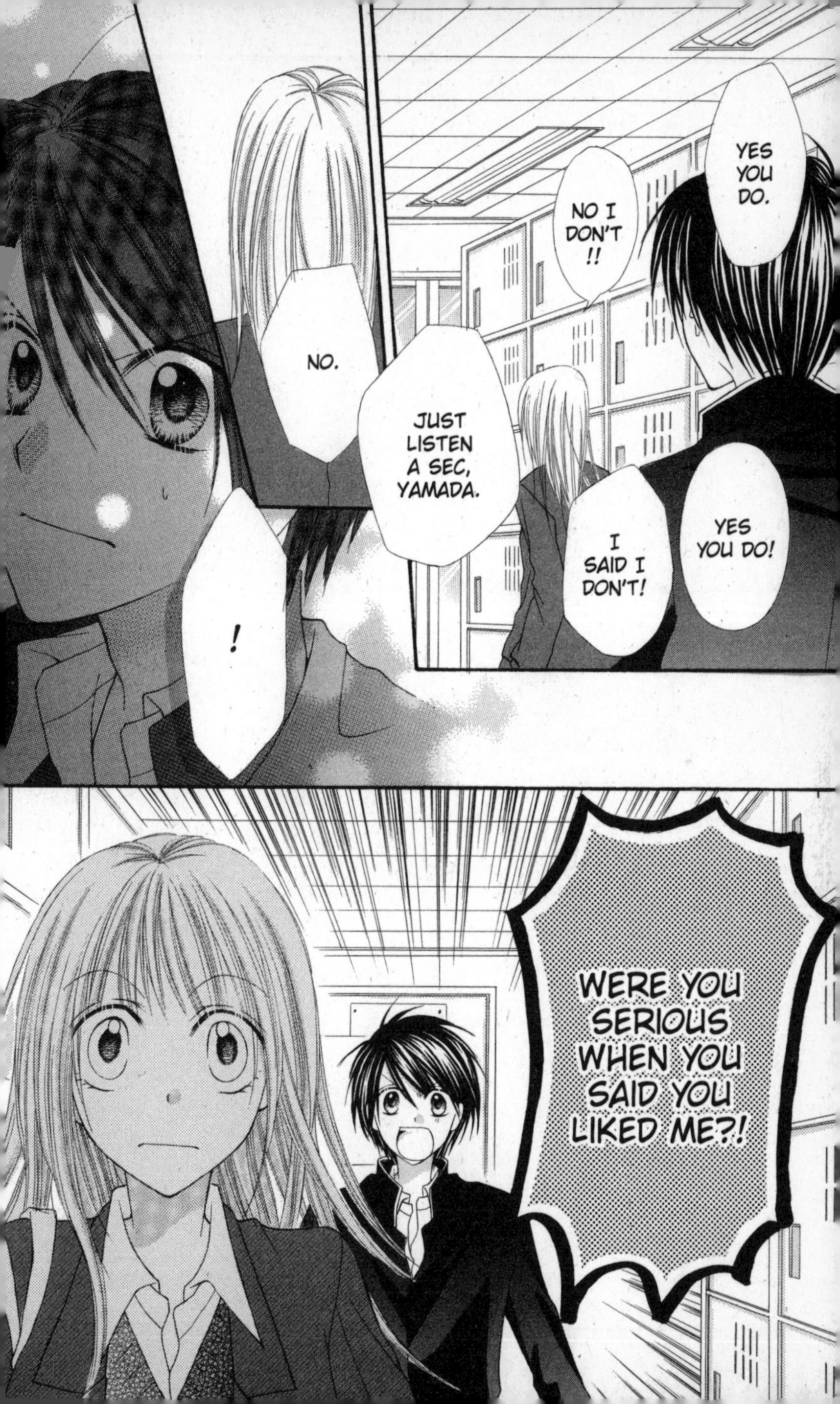

JUST LISTEN A SEC, YAMADA.
NO.
YES YOU DO.
NO I DON'T !!
YES YOU DO!
I SAID I DON'T!
!
WERE YOU SERIOUS WHEN YOU SAID YOU LIKED ME?!

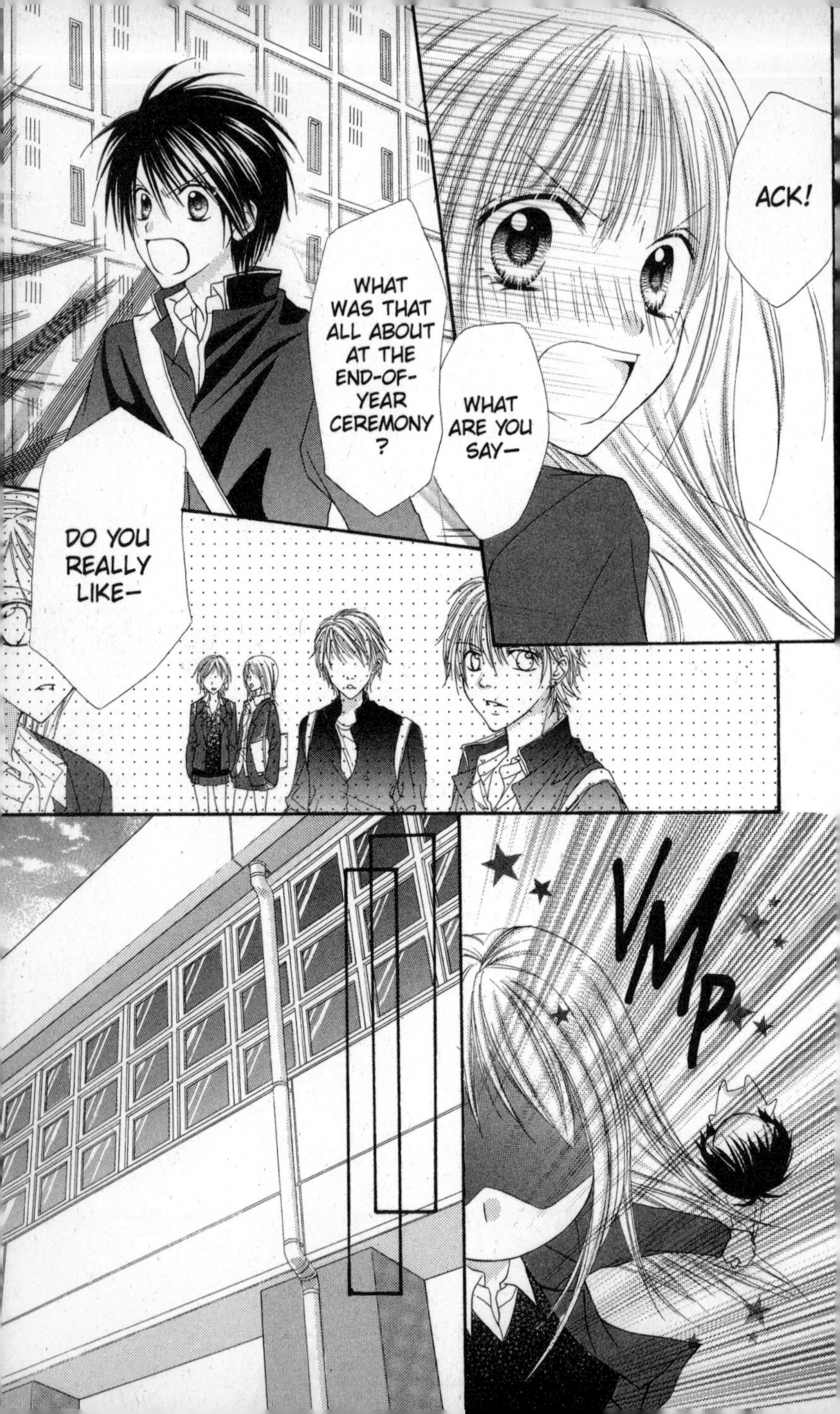
ACK!
WHAT WAS THAT ALL ABOUT AT THE END-OF-YEAR CEREMONY?
WHAT ARE YOU SAY—
DO YOU REALLY LIKE—
VMP

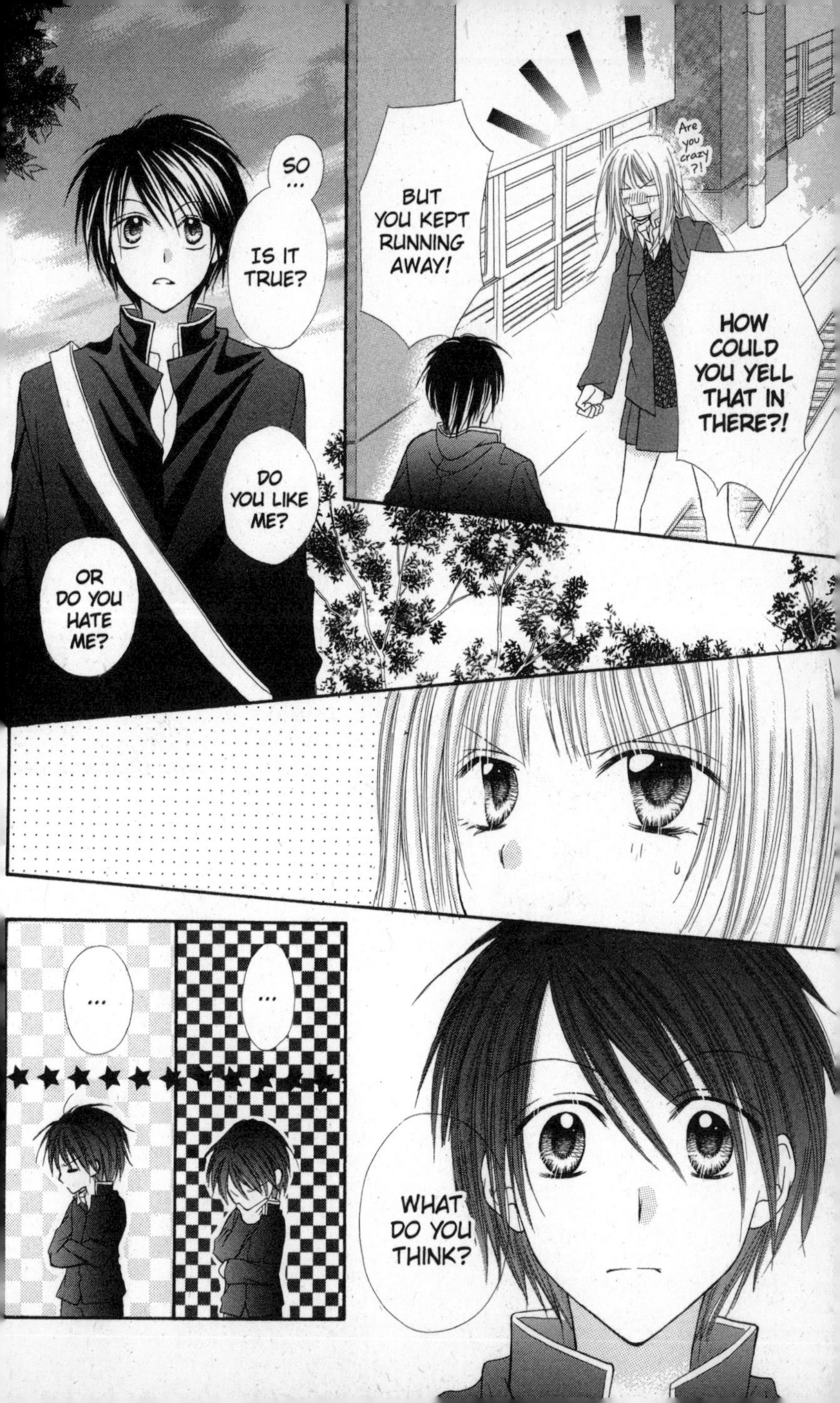

Are you crazy?!
HOW COULD YOU YELL THAT IN THERE?!
BUT YOU KEPT RUNNING AWAY!
SO...
IS IT TRUE?
DO YOU LIKE ME?
OR DO YOU HATE ME?
WHAT DO YOU THINK?
...
...

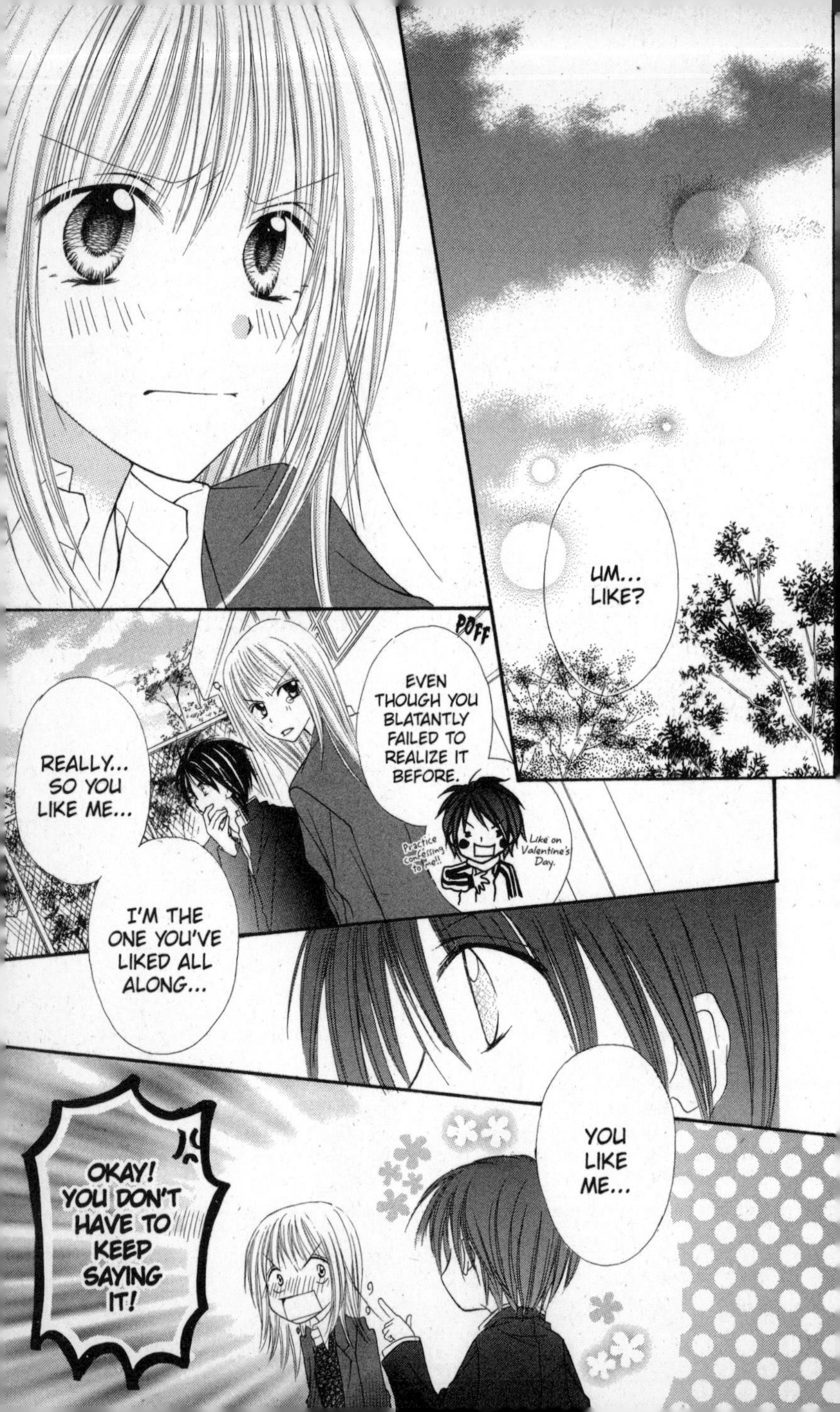
UM... LIKE?
POFF
EVEN THOUGH YOU BLATANTLY FAILED TO REALIZE IT BEFORE.
Like on Valentine's Day.
Practice confessing to me!!
REALLY... SO YOU LIKE ME...
I'M THE ONE YOU'VE LIKED ALL ALONG...
YOU LIKE ME...
OKAY! YOU DON'T HAVE TO KEEP SAYING IT!

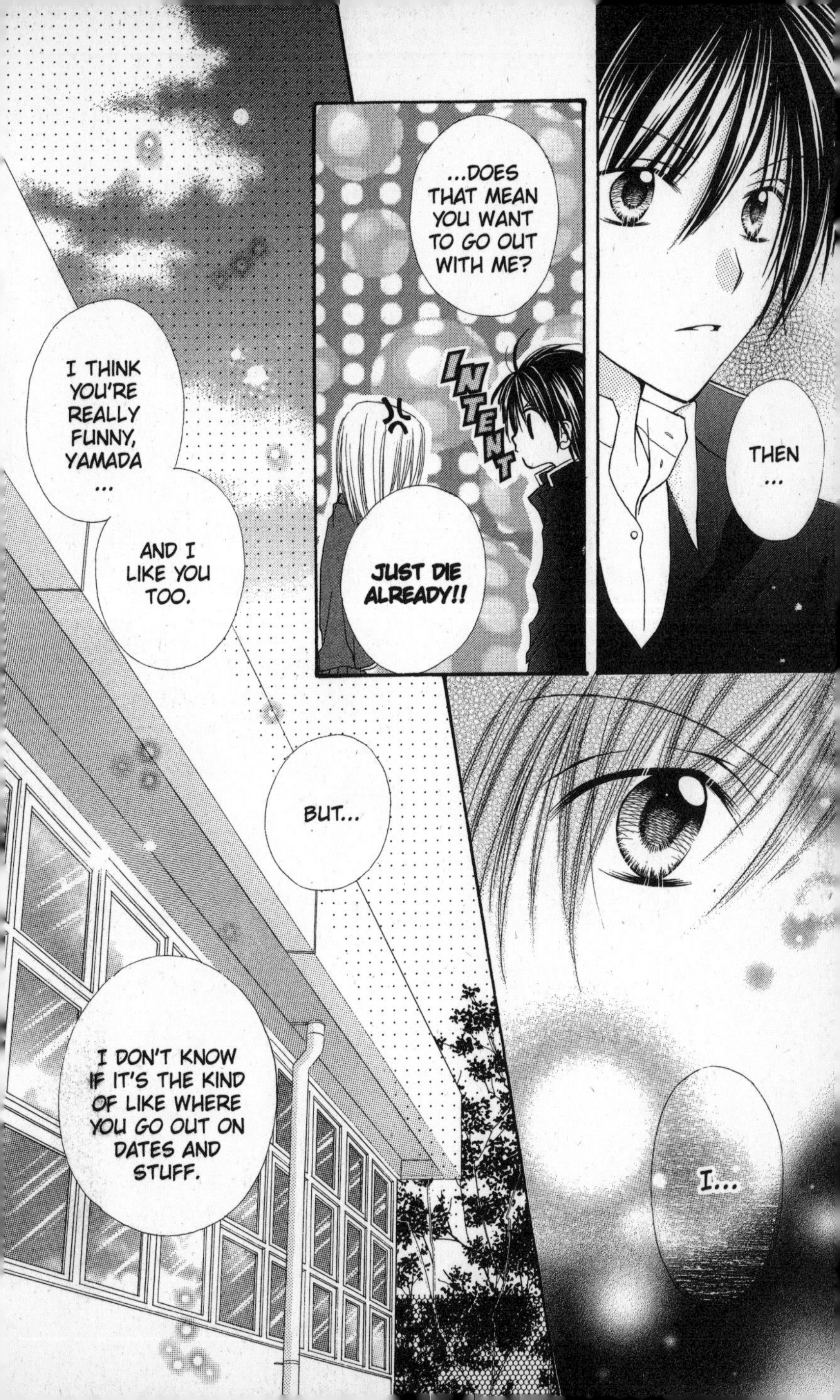
THEN ...
...DOES THAT MEAN YOU WANT TO GO OUT WITH ME?
INTENT
JUST DIE ALREADY!!
I...
I THINK YOU'RE REALLY FUNNY, YAMADA ...
AND I LIKE YOU TOO.
BUT...
I DON'T KNOW IF IT'S THE KIND OF LIKE WHERE YOU GO OUT ON DATES AND STUFF.

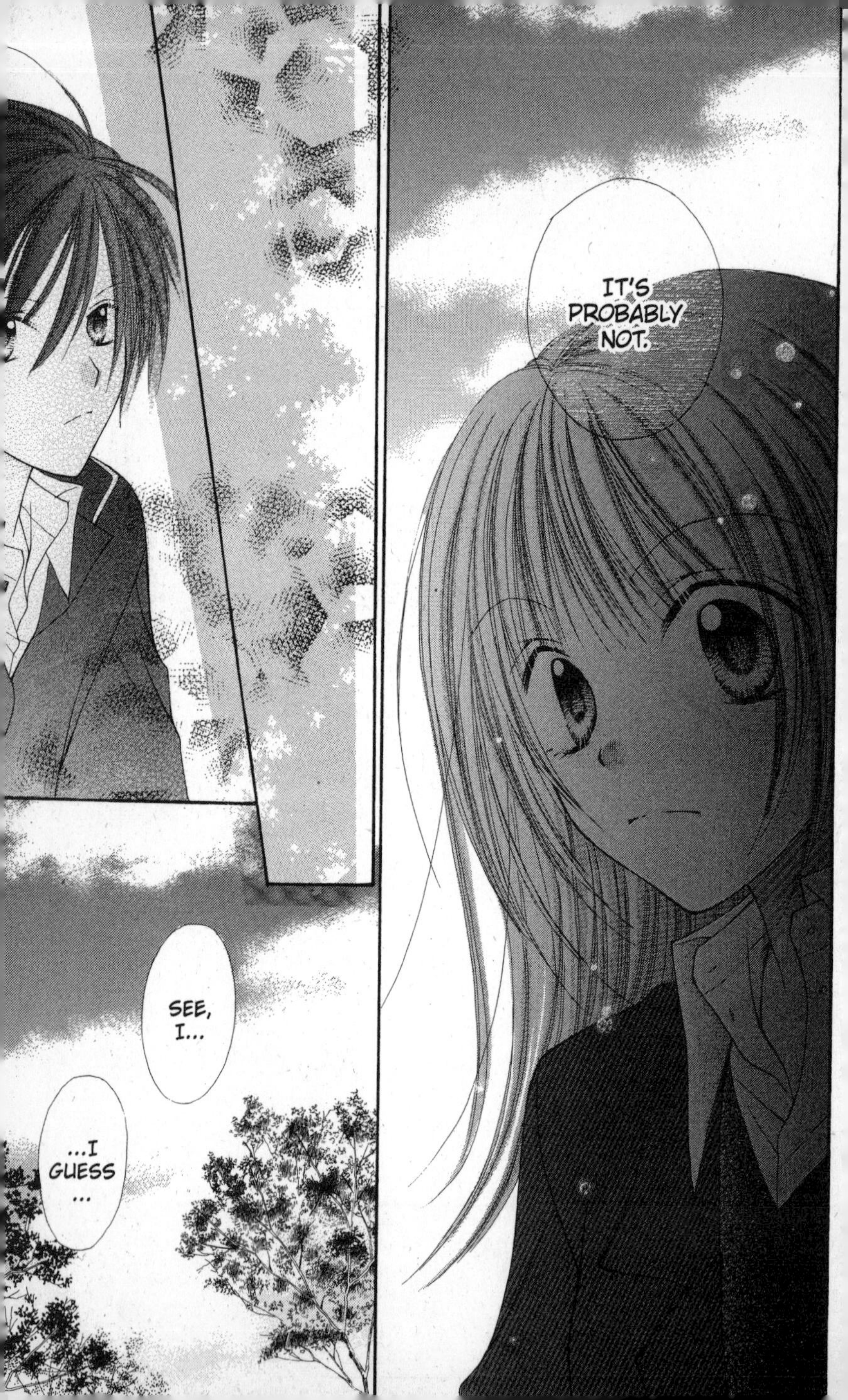
IT'S PROBABLY NOT.
SEE, I...
...I GUESS...

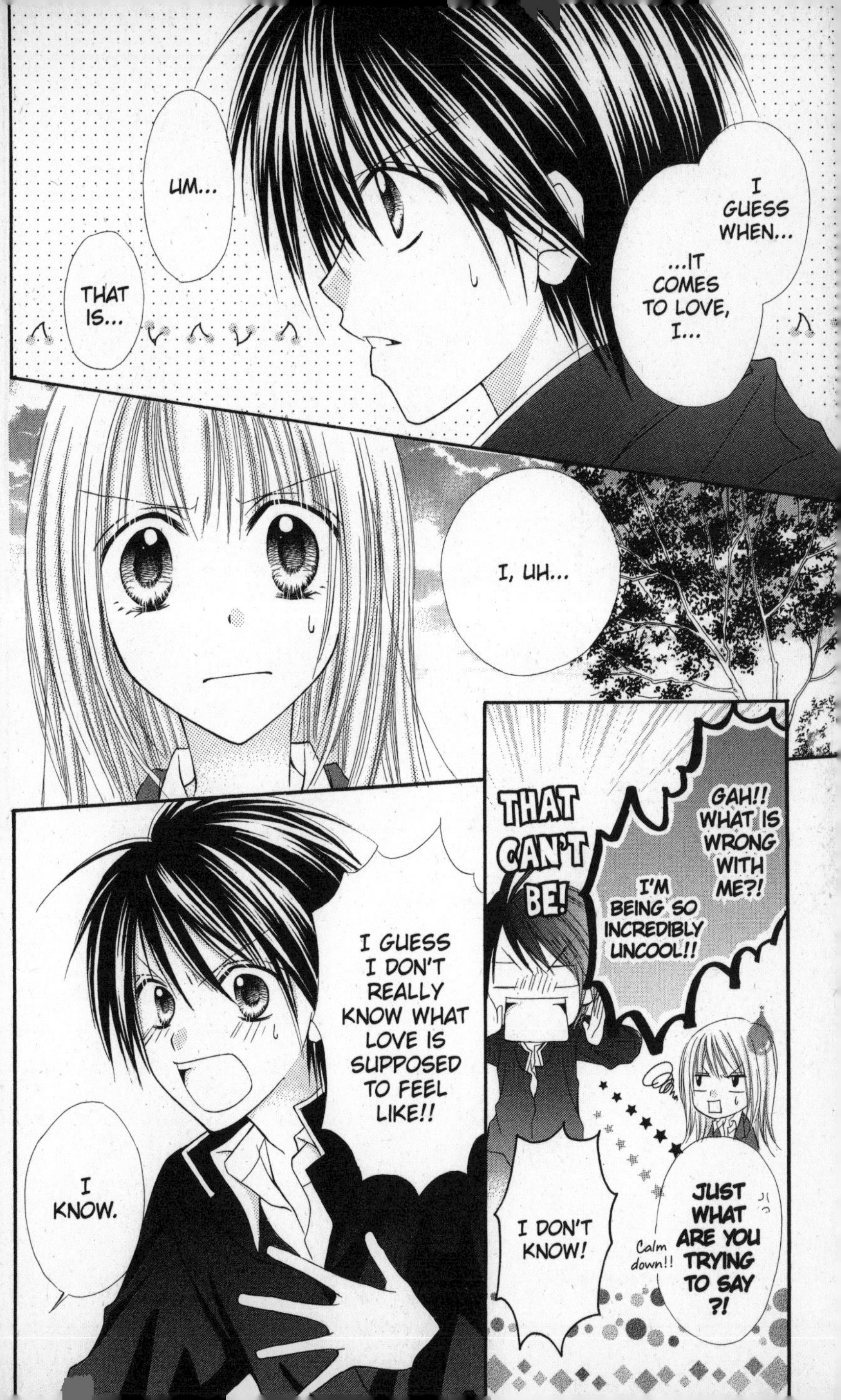
I GUESS WHEN...
...IT COMES TO LOVE, I...
UM...
THAT IS...
I, UH...
GAH!! WHAT IS WRONG WITH ME?!
I'M BEING SO INCREDIBLY UNCOOL!!
THAT CAN'T BE!
JUST WHAT ARE YOU TRYING TO SAY ?!
Calm down!!
I DON'T KNOW!
I GUESS I DON'T REALLY KNOW WHAT LOVE IS SUPPOSED TO FEEL LIKE!!
I KNOW.

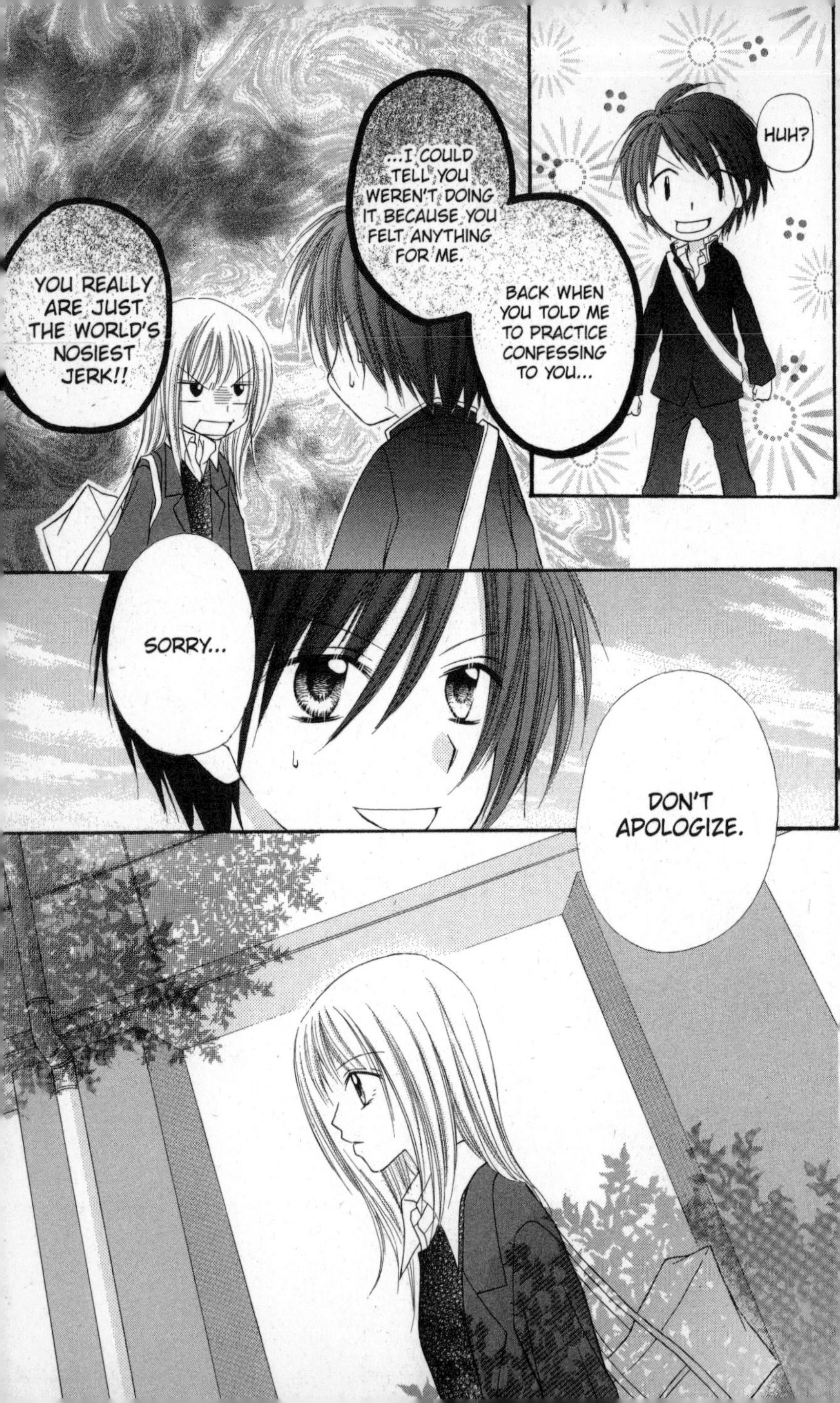
HUH?
BACK WHEN YOU TOLD ME TO PRACTICE CONFESSING TO YOU...
...I COULD TELL YOU WEREN'T DOING IT BECAUSE YOU FELT ANYTHING FOR ME.
YOU REALLY ARE JUST THE WORLD'S NOSIEST JERK!!
SORRY...
DON'T APOLOGIZE.

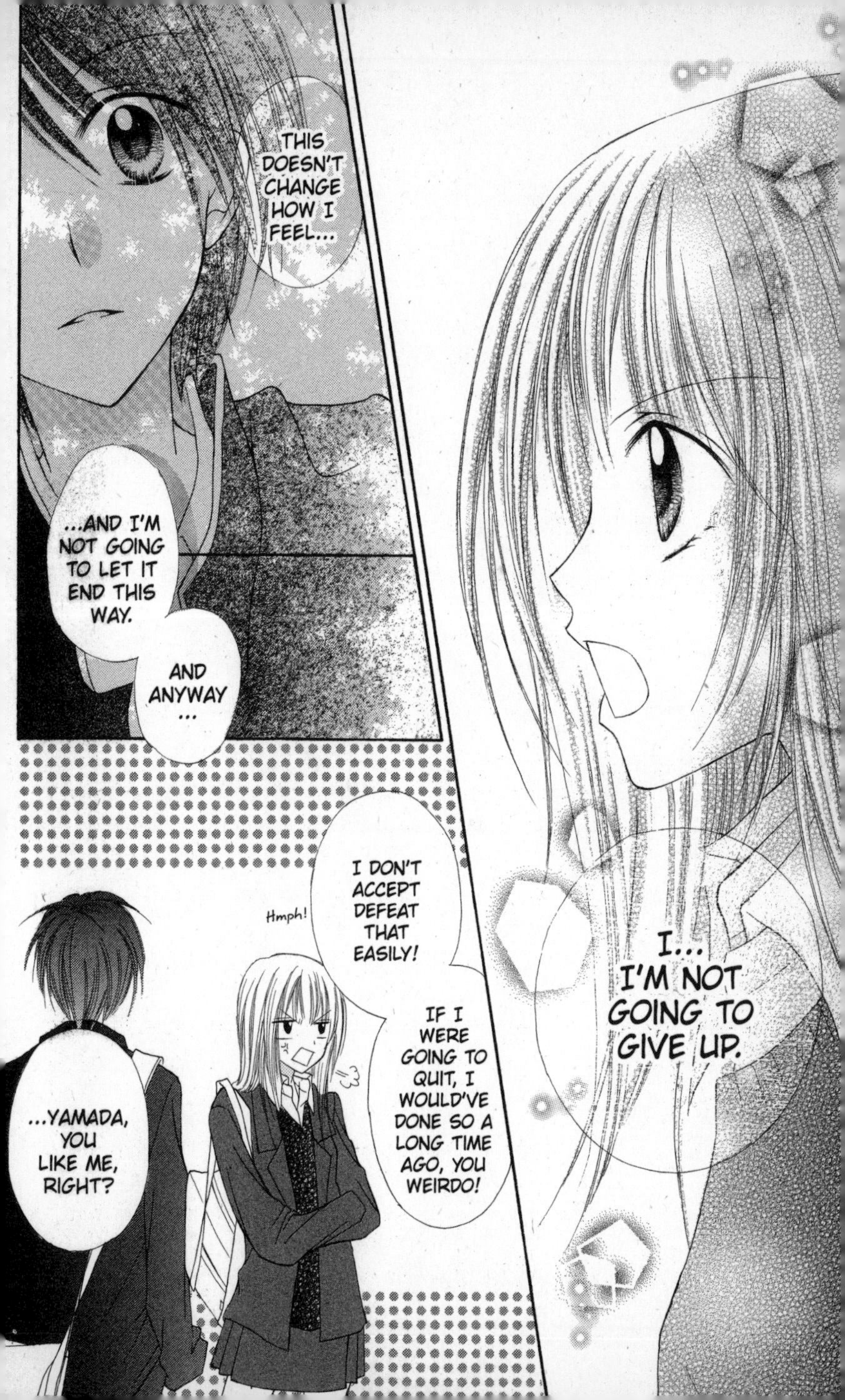
I... I'M NOT GOING TO GIVE UP.
THIS DOESN'T CHANGE HOW I FEEL...
...AND I'M NOT GOING TO LET IT END THIS WAY.
AND ANYWAY...
I DON'T ACCEPT DEFEAT THAT EASILY!
Hmph!
IF I WERE GOING TO QUIT, I WOULD'VE DONE SO A LONG TIME AGO, YOU WEIRDO!
...YAMADA, YOU LIKE ME, RIGHT?

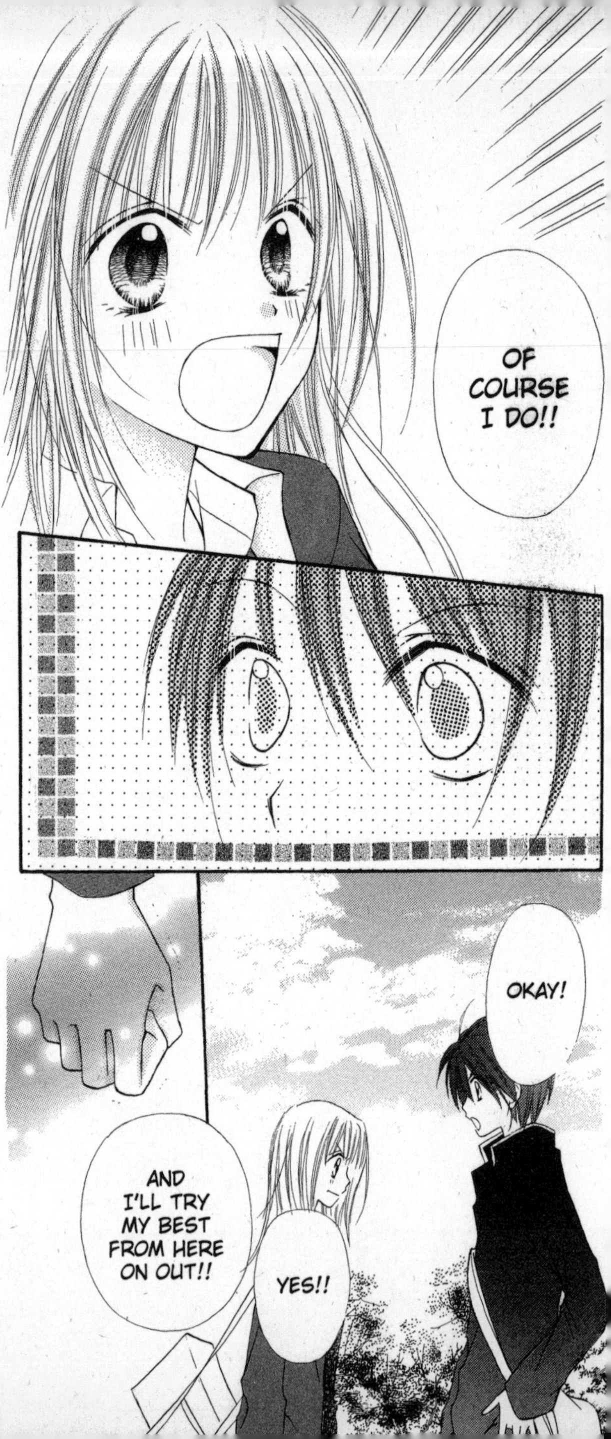
OF COURSE I DO!!
OKAY!
AND I'LL TRY MY BEST FROM HERE ON OUT!!
YES!!

13

LAST TWO SIDEBARS ......!!

RAAH!!

This bear up here. ↑ It seems to be pretty popular with my readers—no idea why. It's just a random sketch I drew in one quick go. (laugh) But a whole bunch of readers wrote in to ask, "What's the bear's name?" ...He doesn't have a name. Wah ha ha!!

There was a reader who said they'd kindly thought up a name for the bear. The name was something like "Haruo"... (laugh) Okay, then... Yo, Haruo! Or something.

Hey, hey!!

Is that really okay?!

Everyone, please welcome Haruo.

Wah! There's still some space left?! Oh, right! I've found a manga that I love so much I actually await its release dates with bated breath. Reading that manga has become my reason for living. (Okay, I'm going overboard now.) It's been a long time since I've been obsessed like this, and I'm kind of moved by that. This mangaka is really incredible. She must really think hard about the story. Oh, we're at the end of the page. Sorry!

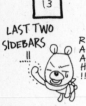

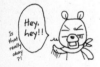

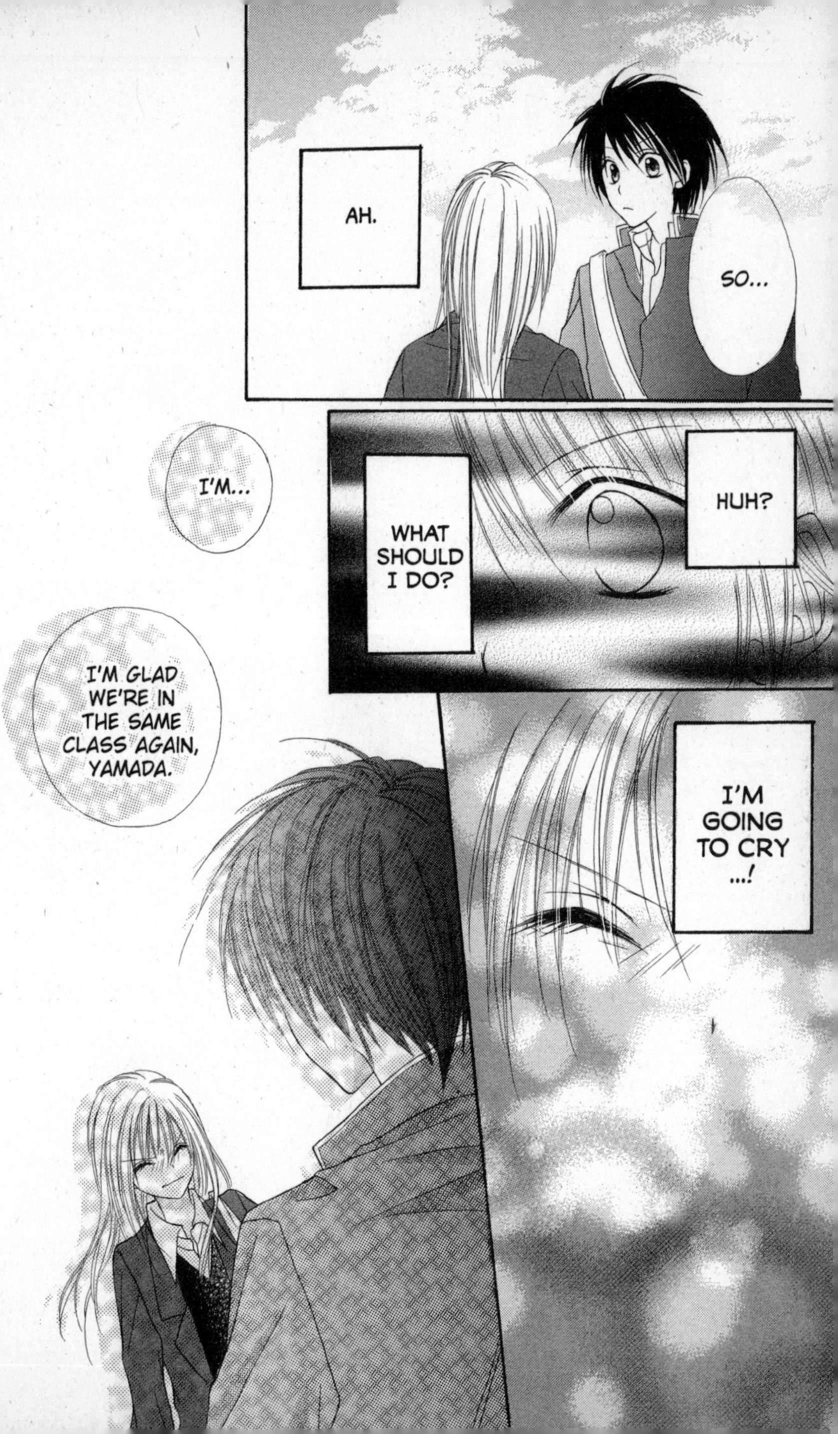
SO...
AH.
HUH?
WHAT SHOULD I DO?
I'M...
I'M GOING TO CRY ...!
I'M GLAD WE'RE IN THE SAME CLASS AGAIN, YAMADA.

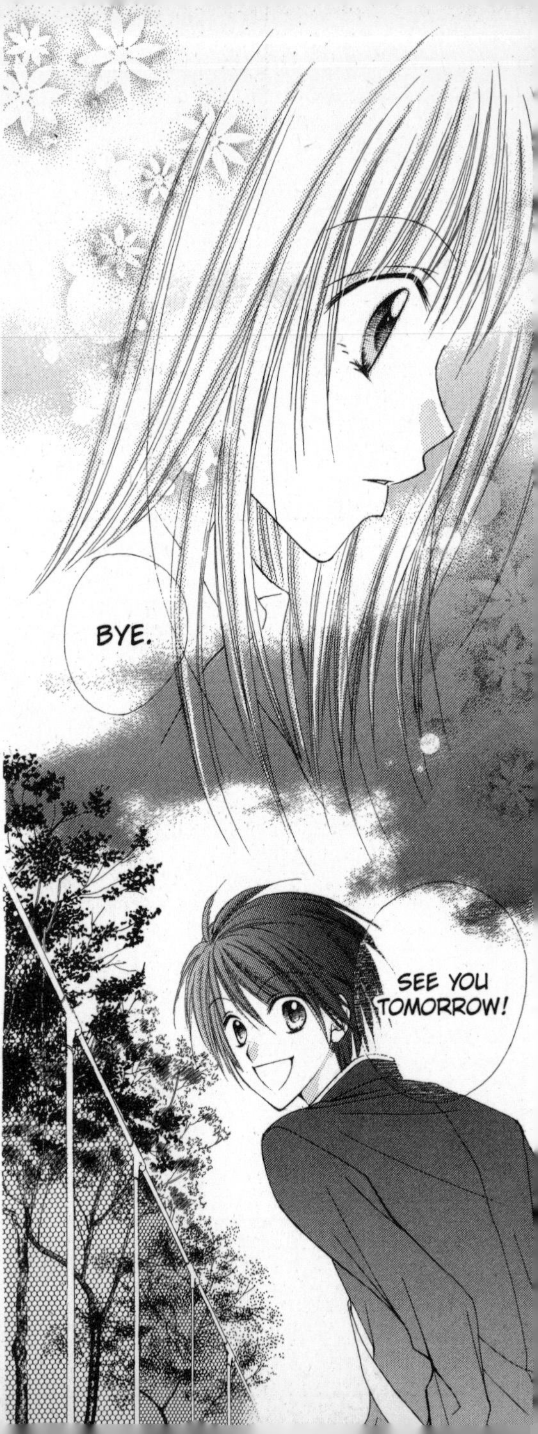

BYE.
SEE YOU TOMORROW!

14

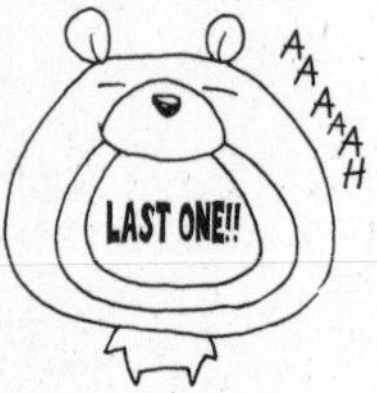

AAAAAH
LAST ONE!!

It's the last column! About my fan letters... Thank you so much for sending them every month! It takes me a while, but I do read all of them. Lately the pace of their arrivals has gotten faster, and I feel a little light-headed—light-headed with joy, that is!

I know I said in the bonus section of RMC's "Samurai Darling" that if people included a return envelope with their letters I'd definitely reply, but I just haven't been able to. Sorry about that!

Please send your letters here:

↓

Nancy Thistlethwaite, Editor
VIZ Media, LLC
P.O. Box 77010
San Francisco, CA 94107

I look forward to reading your thoughts on my work! See you again in the bonus section at the end!

← See you there!

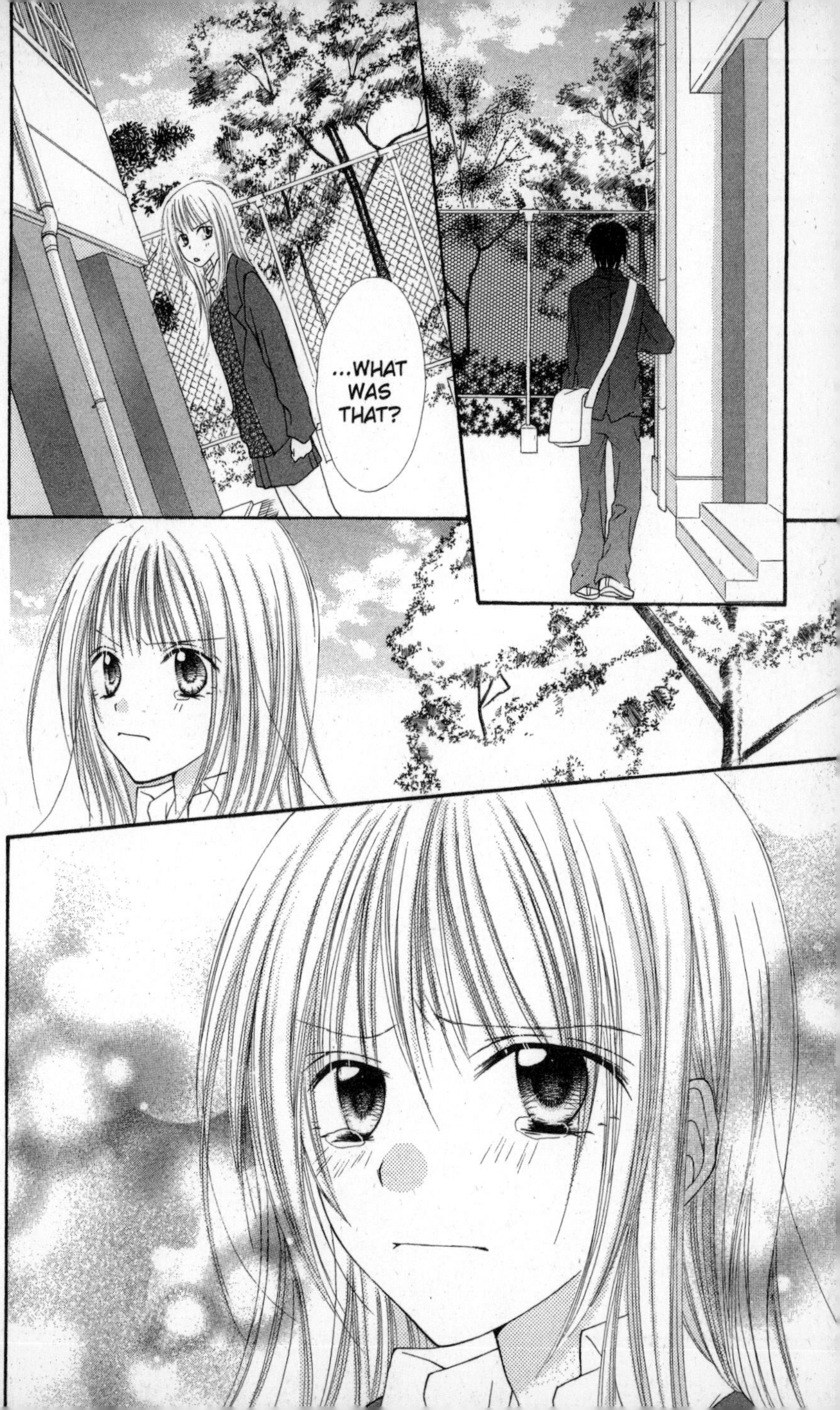
...WHAT WAS THAT?

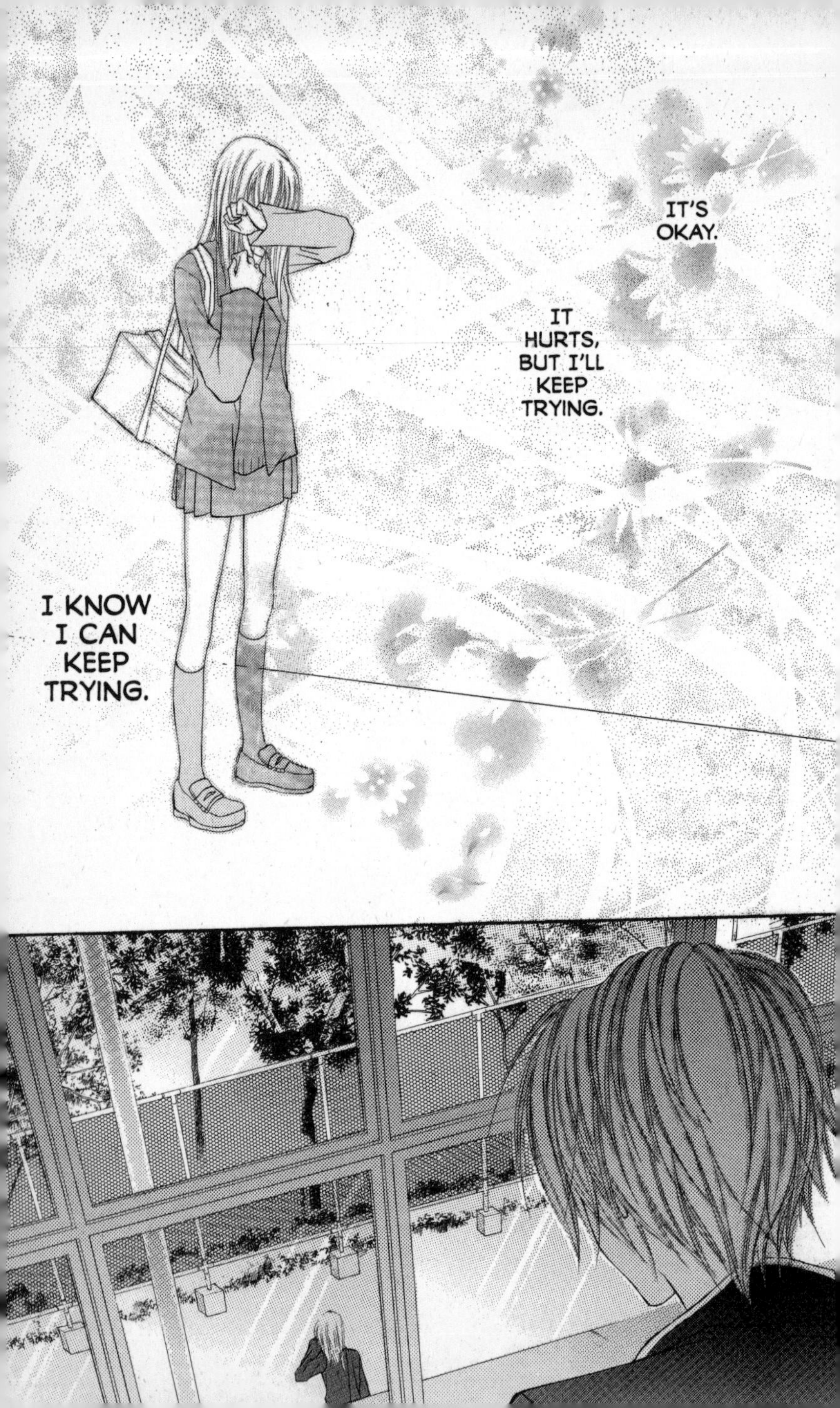
IT'S OKAY.
IT HURTS, BUT I'LL KEEP TRYING.
I KNOW I CAN KEEP TRYING.

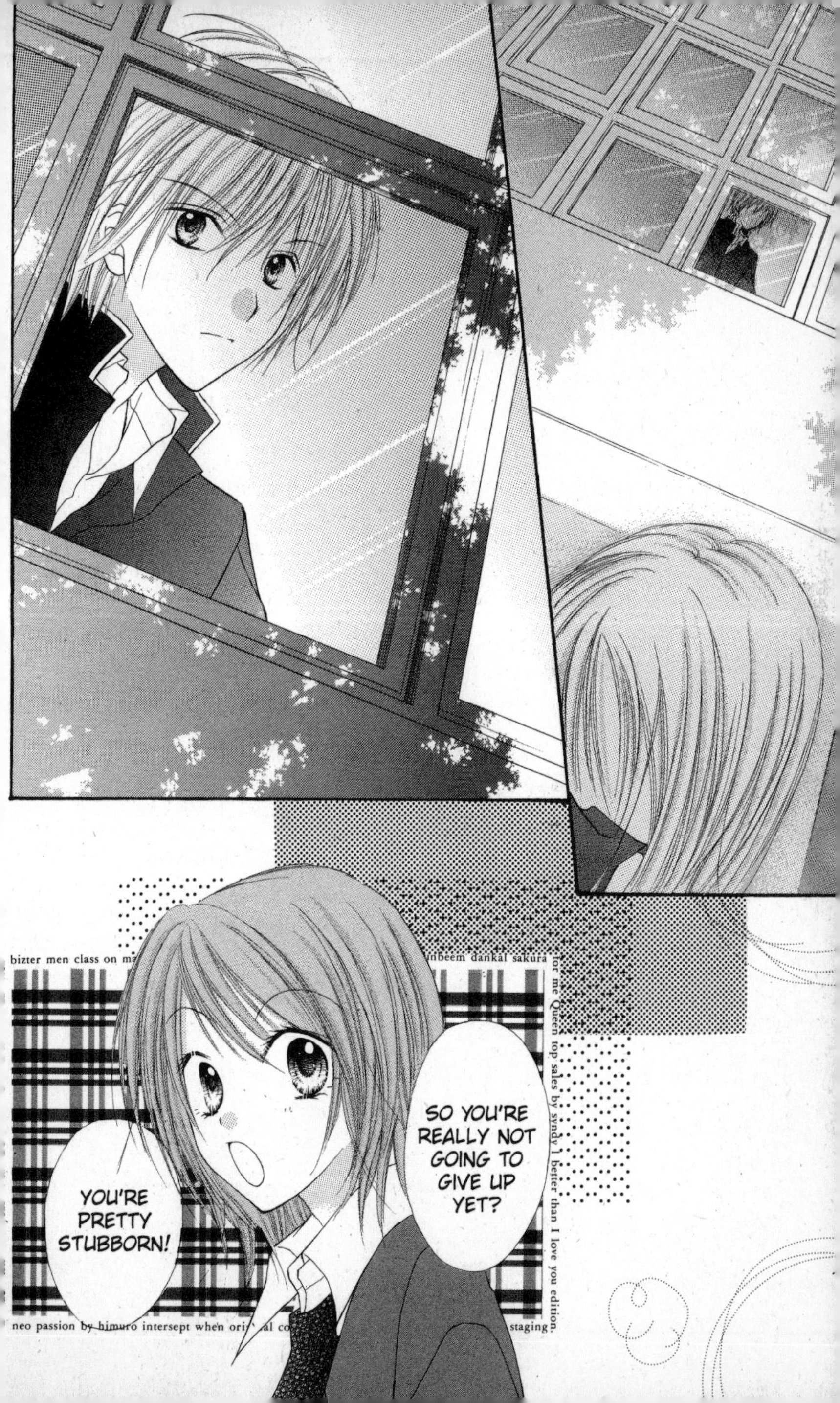
SO YOU'RE REALLY NOT GOING TO GIVE UP YET?
YOU'RE PRETTY STUBBORN!
bizter men class on ma
unbeem dankal sakura
for me Queen top sales by syndy 1 better than I love you edition.
neo passion by himuro intersept when ori al co staging.

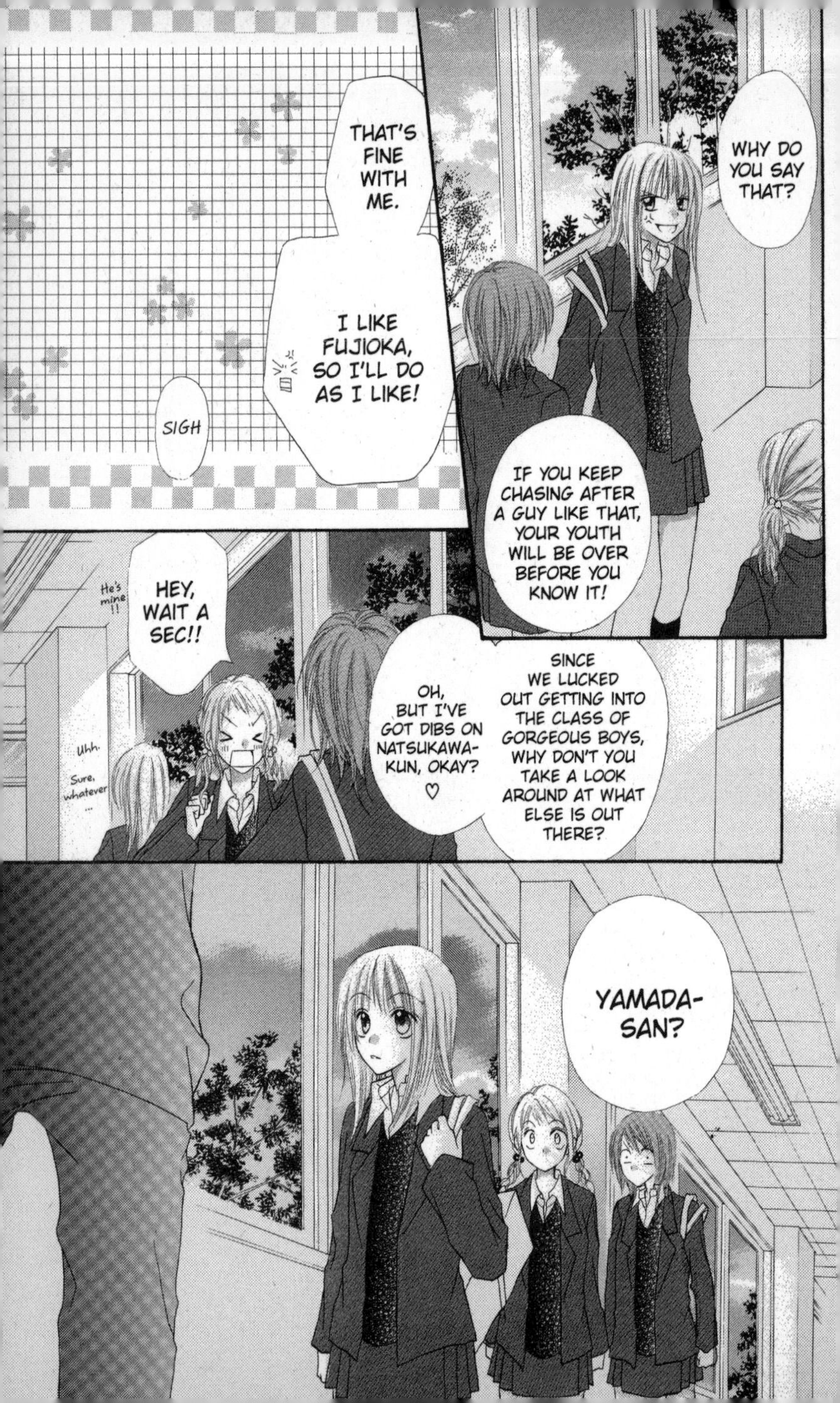
WHY DO YOU SAY THAT?
IF YOU KEEP CHASING AFTER A GUY LIKE THAT, YOUR YOUTH WILL BE OVER BEFORE YOU KNOW IT!
THAT'S FINE WITH ME.
I LIKE FUJIOKA, SO I'LL DO AS I LIKE!
SIGH
SINCE WE LUCKED OUT GETTING INTO THE CLASS OF GORGEOUS BOYS, WHY DON'T YOU TAKE A LOOK AROUND AT WHAT ELSE IS OUT THERE?
OH, BUT I'VE GOT DIBS ON NATSUKAWA-KUN, OKAY? ♡
HEY, WAIT A SEC!!
He's mine!!
Uhh.
Sure, whatever...
YAMADA-SAN?

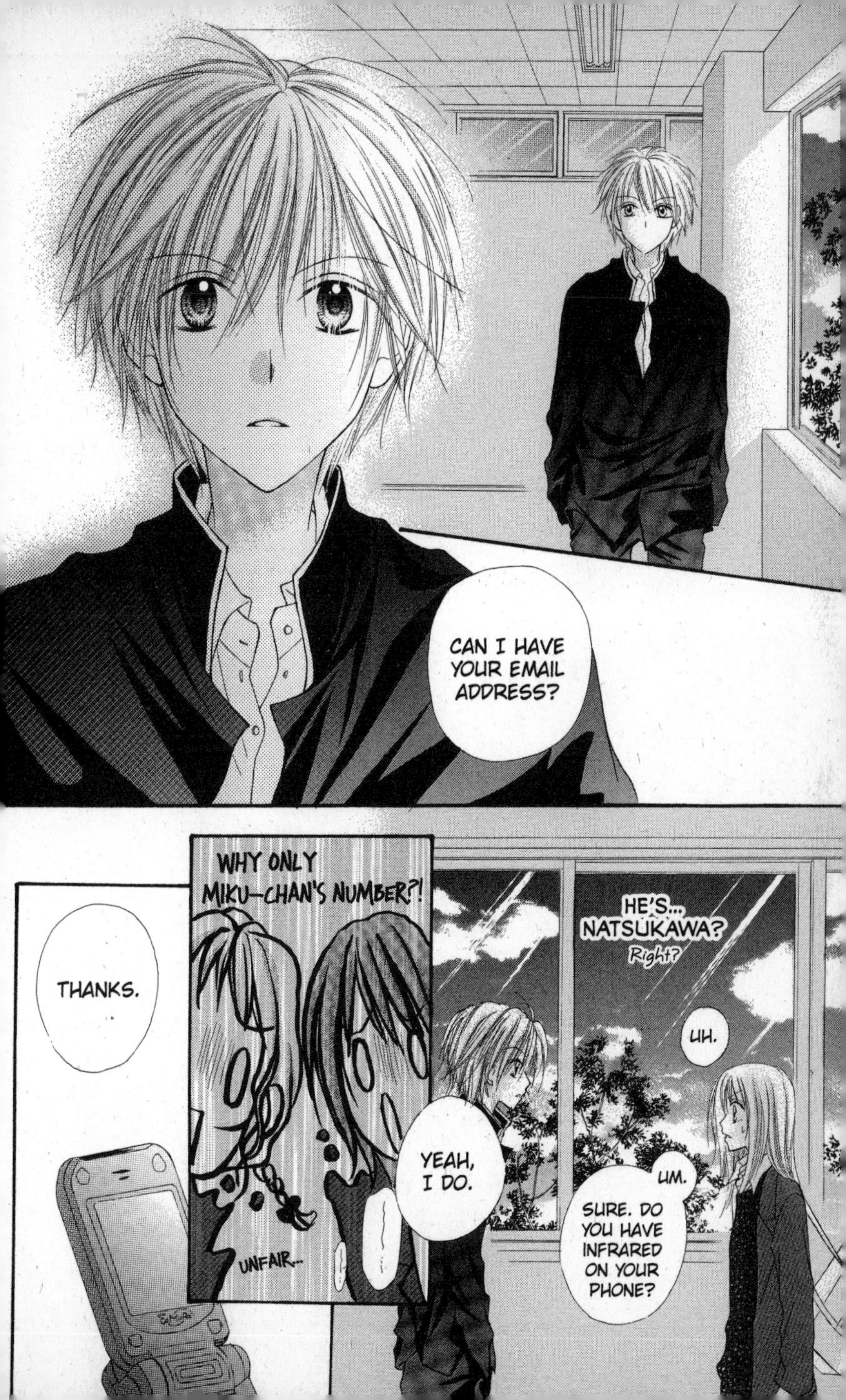
CAN I HAVE YOUR EMAIL ADDRESS?
HE'S... NATSUKAWA?
Right?
UH.
UM.
SURE. DO YOU HAVE INFRARED ON YOUR PHONE?
YEAH, I DO.
WHY ONLY MIKU-CHAN'S NUMBER?!
UNFAIR...
...
THANKS.

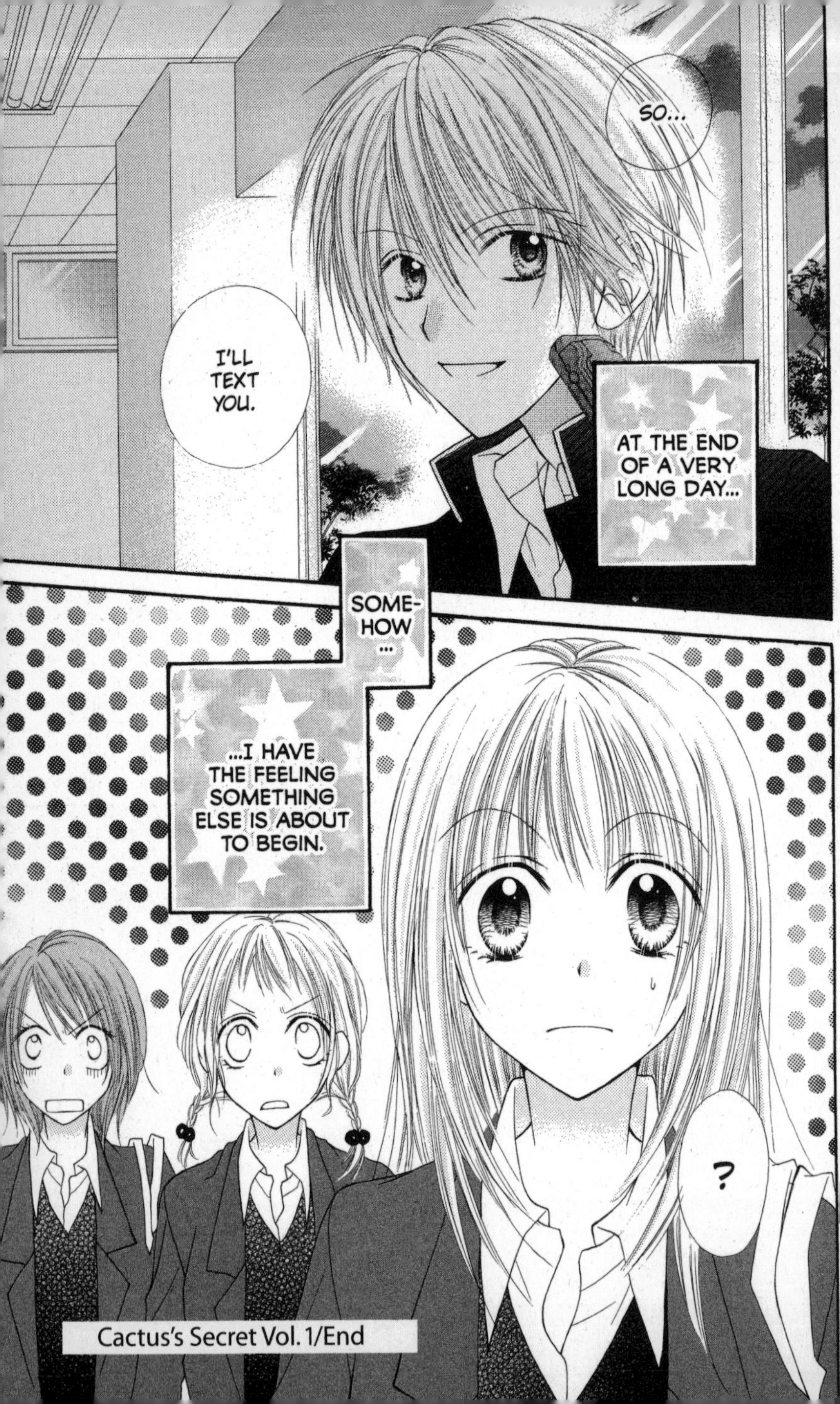
SO...
I'LL TEXT YOU.
AT THE END OF A VERY LONG DAY...
SOME-HOW ...
...I HAVE THE FEELING SOMETHING ELSE IS ABOUT TO BEGIN.
?
Cactus's Secret Vol. 1/End

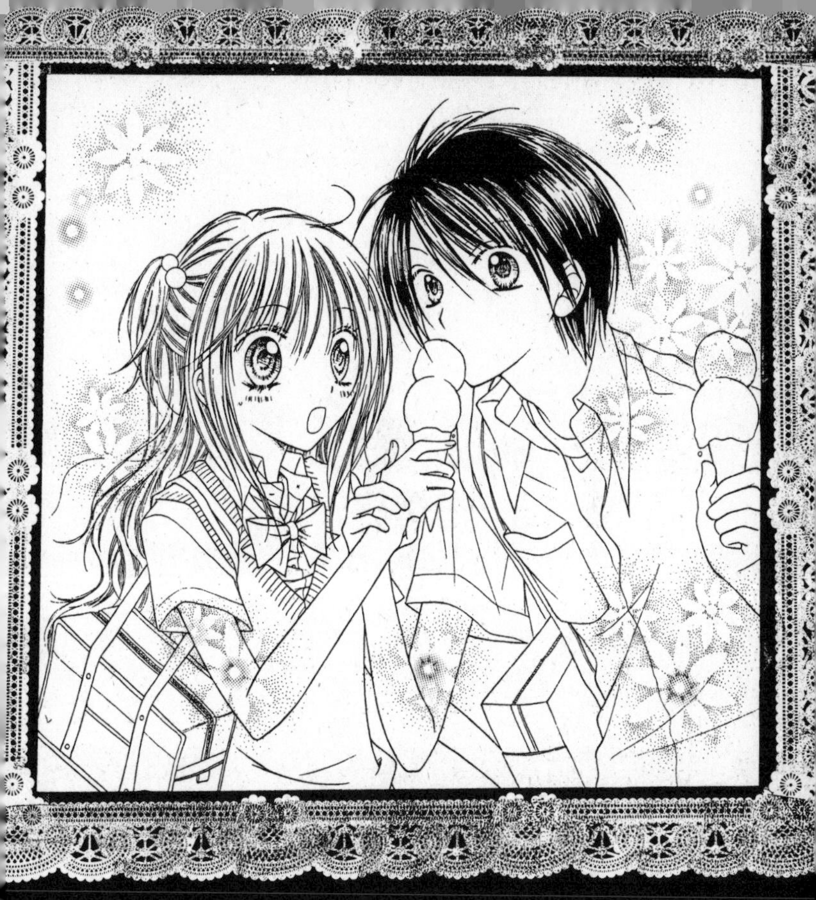

Wait! Haruta's Collaboration Manga with Mayu-pon Sakai!

Part 2...! (Part 1 is in volume 3 of *Nagata chou Strawberry*)

"What is up with this sloppy pic?! There is barely any screentone! And what's with the printing?!" I'm sure there are a lot of you who are thinking something like that... But I had to shrink the image... You might ask, why the crappy print quality? It's because it's on copier paper instead of manuscript paper. And why would I use copier paper, you ask?

I'M SORRY! I RAN OUT OF BLANK MANUSCRIPT PAPER!! FORGIVE ME!!! I'M SORRY!!! I HAVE NO EXCUSE!!!!

Oh, just give me the death penalty. Things have been so hectic for the last 3–4 months that I suddenly found myself out of manuscript paper without warning... To all of you who are Mayu-pon Sakai fans and only bought this volume for the collaboration manga (there are some of you like that out there, right?), I'm so sorry! To everyone else who was looking forward to this manga too, I'm so sorry! I tried to use more screentone, but it wouldn't work. Since the lines are printed with copier ink, they come off when I cut off the excess screentone, so I had to use it really sparingly. I'm really sorry!! I really apologize to Mayu-pon Sakai-sama too!!

I hate my own idiocy!

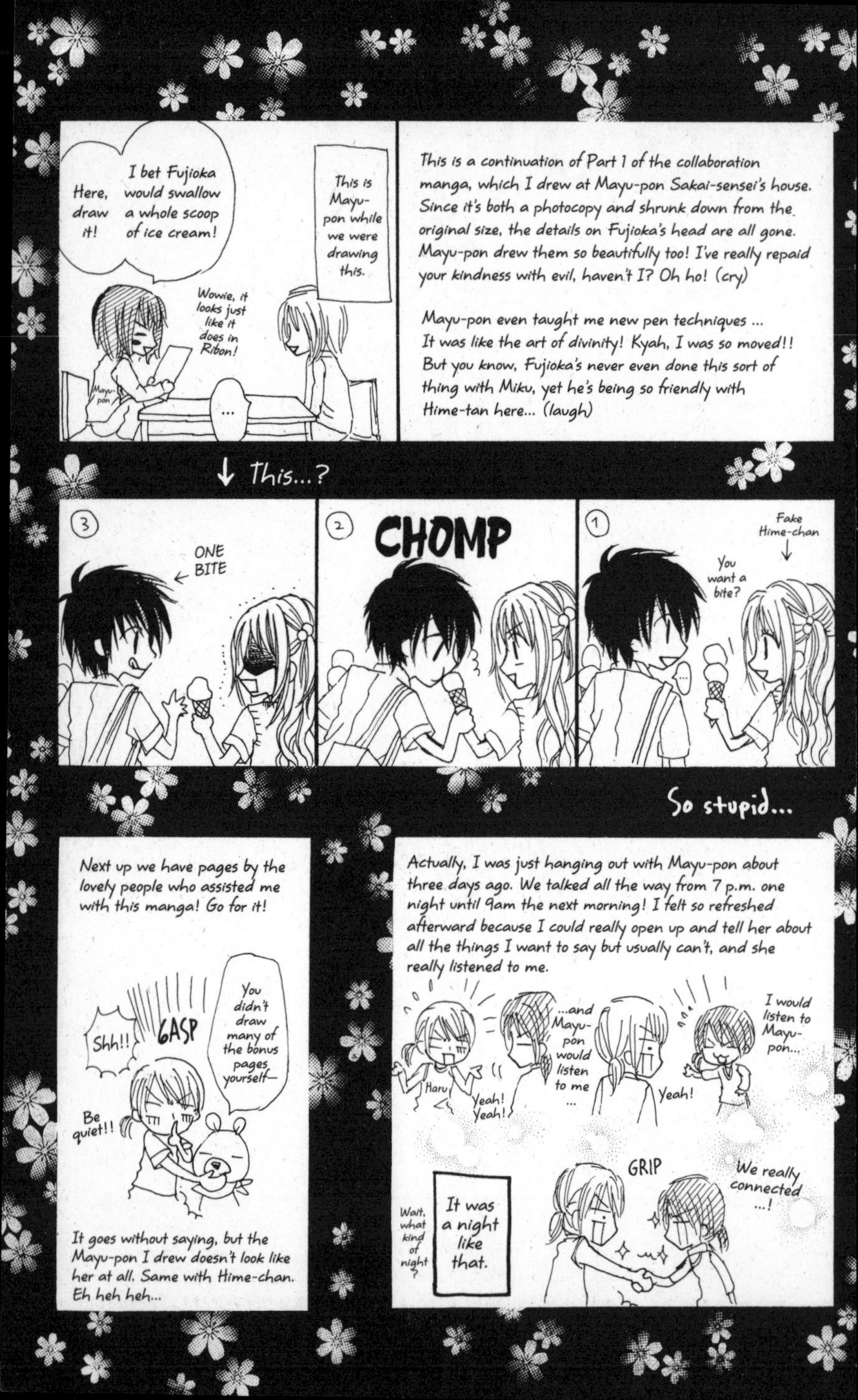
This is a continuation of Part 1 of the collaboration manga, which I drew at Mayu-pon Sakai-sensei's house. Since it's both a photocopy and shrunk down from the original size, the details on Fujioka's head are all gone. Mayu-pon drew them so beautifully too! I've really repaid your kindness with evil, haven't I? Oh ho! (cry)
Mayu-pon even taught me new pen techniques ... It was like the art of divinity! Kyah, I was so moved!! But you know, Fujioka's never even done this sort of thing with Miku, yet he's being so friendly with Hime-tan here... (laugh)
This is Mayu-pon while we were drawing this.
I bet Fujioka would swallow a whole scoop of ice cream! Here, draw it!
Wowie, it looks just like it does in Ribon!
Mayu-pon
...
↓ This...?
1
Fake Hime-chan
You want a bite?
...
2
CHOMP
3
ONE BITE
So stupid...
Actually, I was just hanging out with Mayu-pon about three days ago. We talked all the way from 7 p.m. one night until 9am the next morning! I felt so refreshed afterward because I could really open up and tell her about all the things I want to say but usually can't, and she really listened to me.
I would listen to Mayu-pon...
Yeah!
...and Mayu-pon would listen to me ...
Yeah! Yeah!
Haru
GRIP
We really connected ...!
It was a night like that.
Wait, what kind of night?
Next up we have pages by the lovely people who assisted me with this manga! Go for it!
You didn't draw many of the bonus pages yourself—
GASP
Shh!!
Be quiet!!
It goes without saying, but the Mayu-pon I drew doesn't look like her at all. Same with Hime-chan. Eh heh heh...

TO HARUNANA ☆

You really worked hard ☆ on Cactus!

Hi there, and sorry for butting in! I'm Nana's (I've never called her that before!!) assistant Yumeno Mizuki. ☆ I've been given the honor of doing a little bonus art for you this time—thank you so much!! Nana is a really interesting person. After hanging with her for a long time, you'll really see what I mean. (laugh) One time when the four of us were working on a manuscript, she stepped on a banana!! Why the heck was there a banana lying around on the floor of her room?!

I drew a picture of Miku and Fujioka below, but they don't really look like themselves, huh? I love characters like Fujioka! ♡ I'm really looking forward to seeing how Cactus is going to play out from here!!

See you! ☆

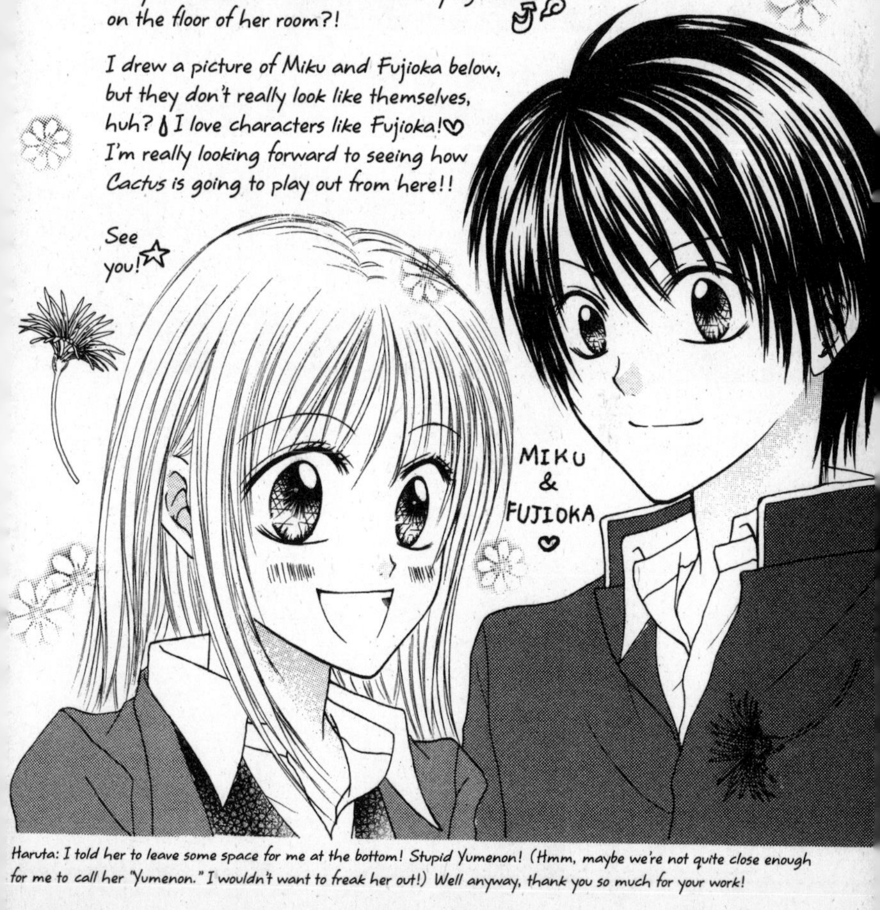
MIKU & FUJIOKA ♡

Haruta: I told her to leave some space for me at the bottom! Stupid Yumenon! (Hmm, maybe we're not quite close enough for me to call her "Yumenon." I wouldn't want to freak her out!) Well anyway, thank you so much for your work!

DEAR → Nana

Congratulations on your fourth volume of manga!!

Thanks to what seems like a fated meeting, here I am! I'm one of Nana's assistants, Marina Umezawa! I've also been published in *Ribon* magazine! ♪ Yay!! Congrats so much on the release of volume 1 of *Cactus*!! It's your first multi-volume series, huh, boss? Awesome!! I love the days when Assistant Mizuki helps too! And the time when we were all delirious from lack of sleep and started singing "Princess Mononoke" all together. That was a great memory! Nana, you'd better start participating in Assistant Mizuki's customary "impersonation showdowns"!! It's fun, even though I'm not sure how I feel about being told, "You really resemble the frog from *Spirited Away* and Meowth from **kēmon!" But I have so much fun. I love working here!! It's like we're a little club or something! (?) Lately I feel like I've been seeing the real you, Nana... And I think the real you is amazing! You're so much fun!! I love you!! (Confession!) Just kidding! ♥ Let's keep having lots of fun at our happy workplace from here on, okay? ♡

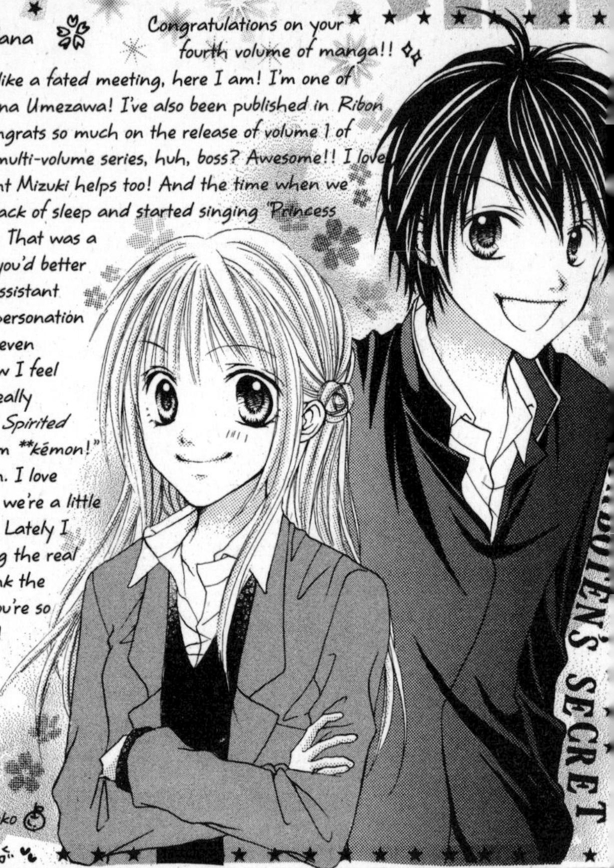

FROM Marinakko

P.S. Let's have tons of fun at the w-inds concert!!

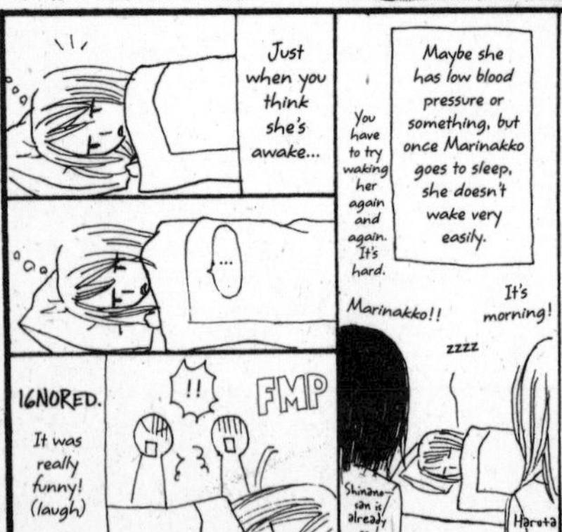

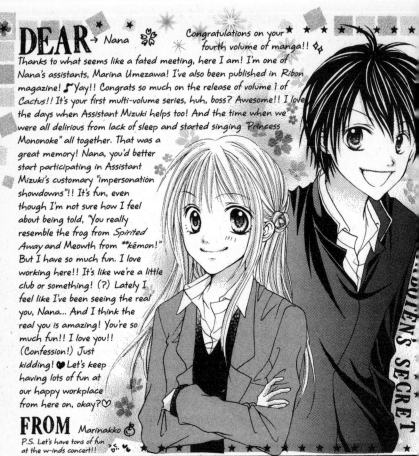

Maybe she has low blood pressure or something, but once Marinakko goes to sleep, she doesn't wake very easily.
You have to try waking her again and again. It's hard.
It's morning!
Marinakko!!
zzzz
Shinano-can is already up.
Haruta
Just when you think she's awake...
...
IGNORED.
It was really funny! (laugh)
!!
FMP

Yay!! I got a love confession! (laugh)

And that was **Marina Umezawa,** ladies and gentlemen!

It's only been about a year since I first met Marinakko, but our interests really match up, so we're having a lot of fun together! Everything she recommends to me totally resonates. Her real self resonates with me too! (laugh)

Her sense of how to design a manuscript is very close to mine, so she's helped me out a lot with the manga. When she does mob duty (drawing all the background people/crowd) for me, her work overflows with the essence of a fresh, young high school girl! It's a skill I completely can't imitate. ...Even though we're the same age... (laugh) Thank you for everything from here on out too!!

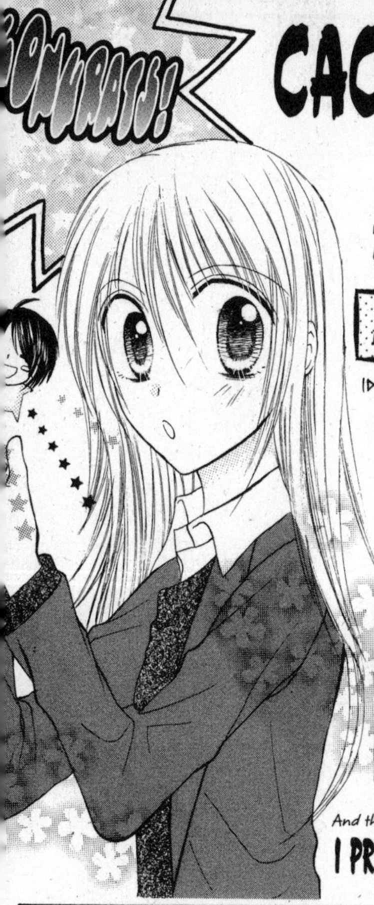
CONGRATS!

CACTUS VOL. 1 ☆

Haruta-sensei, congratulations on the release of your manga!! Wowie, I can't believe how fast time has flown by! (laugh)

Memories from During Production

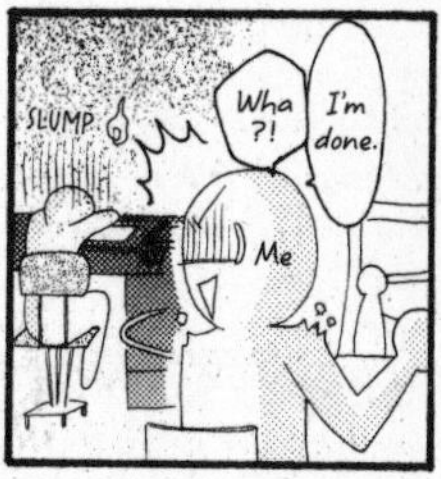
I'm done.
Wha ?!
SLUMP
Me

Whenever the deadline is near, I often see poor Haruta-san go from fighting extreme drowsiness to passing out at her desk. But it always happens without any warning, so it freaks me out every time! (She usually comes back to life in about five minutes.) Good work, Haruta-san!

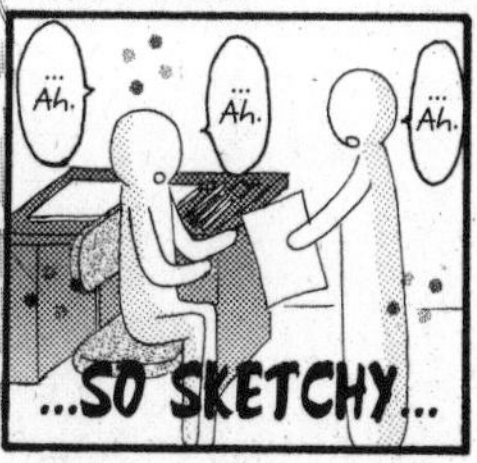
...Ah.
...Ah.
...Ah.
...SO SKETCHY...

Once while we were working, we had *Spirited Away* playing in the background, and we all started doing impressions of Kaonashi. Marina-chan did a dead-on impression of the frog too...!

My impression of the frog was incredibly lame.

And the thing I think every time I come to help out is

I PROMISE TO TRY HARDER NEXT TIME...!

By Mika Shinano

Both on my manga drawing and my impersonations! (laugh)

Ladies and gentlemen, **Mika Shinano!!**

Shinano-san is the type of person who can become good friends with anyone immediately, so she always brightens the mood in our studio. Thank you so much for that!!

Whenever she has one of her "Impersonation Showdowns" and loses to Marinakko, she's so cute and innocent that she actually seems to mope over her loss seriously. You're so funny! Of everyone I know, she's the No. 1 space case! Not that anyone else is in the running though. (laugh) Thank you for everything from here on out too!!

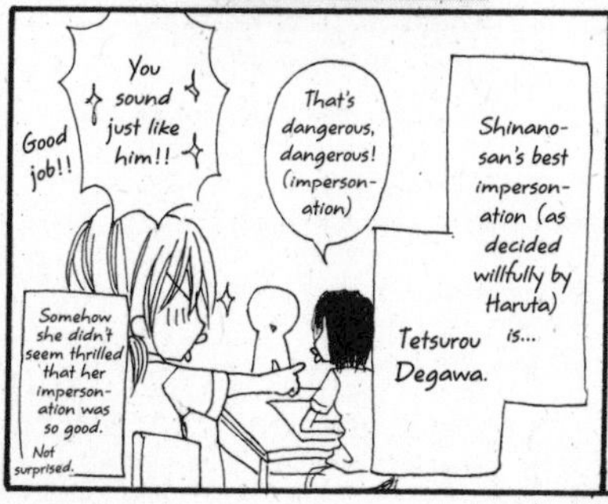
Shinano-san's best impersonation (as decided willfully by Haruta) is...
Tetsurou Degawa.
That's dangerous, dangerous! (impersonation)
You sound just like him!!
Good job!!
Somehow she didn't seem thrilled that her impersonation was so good.
Not surprised.

And this ends volume 1 of *Cactus's Secret*. See you again!

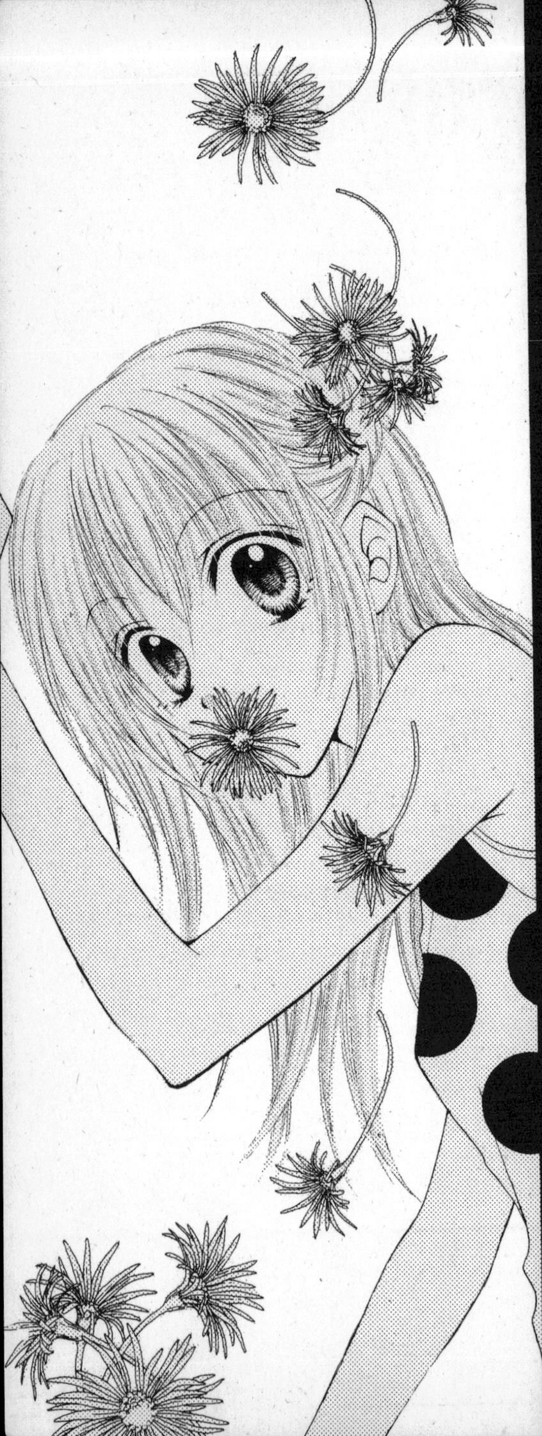

Special Thanks.

Y.Komura
Y.Miduki

M.Umezawa
M.Shinano
S.Nakano
A.Ryui

H.Kyono
H.Moriwake

and You!

Thank you
for reading.

2004.6
Nana.Haruta

Notes

Honorifics

In Japan, people are usually addressed by their name plus a suffix. The suffix shows familiarity or respect, depending on the relationship.

    MALE (familiar): first or last name + kun

    FEMALE (familiar): first or last name + chan

    ADULT (polite): last name + san

    UPPERCLASSMAN (polite): last name + senpai

    TEACHER or PROFESSIONAL: last name + sensei

    CLOSE FRIENDS or LOVERS: first name only, no suffix

Terms

Tenko Hikita, better known as "Princess Tenko," is one of the most famous magicians in Japan, known for her extravagant costumes and showmanship as well as daring magical feats. Though she's popular, her style and heavy makeup might be considered a little gaudy by the youth of Japan.

Ne-chan means "sister."

Ojarumaru is a popular manga and anime series for kids.

Zou means "elephant." *Ouji* means "prince."

"Hotaru no Hikari" (The Firefly's Glow) is a Japanese song which is often sung at closing ceremonies like graduations.

Cute "nickname" suffixes are sometimes added to show affection, like *–tsun, -pon, -pyon, -tan* and *-kko.*

Kaonashi (No-Face) is a mysterious spirit creature from the movie *Spirited Away* that floats around silently and communicates only with a vague "ah" sound.

Tetsurou Degawa is a Japanese actor-comedian known for his voice and signature phrase, "Yabai yo, yabai yo!" (That's dangerous, dangerous!)

So far in my works, I've never drawn a type like Fujioka before. He's very different from what typically appeals to me, but there are a lot of people who have told me that he's their favorite of all my characters. Which probably means my taste is pretty different from the mainstream. Though I kind of guessed that already.

-NANA HARUTA

Nana Haruta debuted in 2000 with *Ai no ♥ Ai no Shirushi* (Love's ♥, Love's Symbol) in *Ribon Original* magazine. She was born in Niigata Prefecture and likes reading manga and taking baths. Her other works include *Love Berrish!* and *Chocolate Cosmos*. Her current series, *Stardust ★ Wink*, is serialized in *Ribon* magazine.

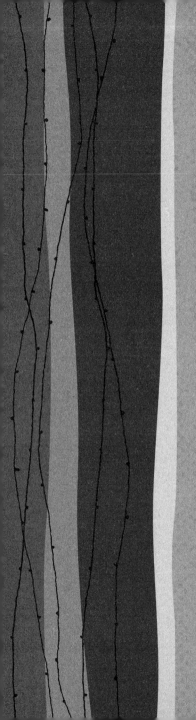

Cactus's Secret
VOL. 1
Shojo Beat Edition

Story and Art by
Nana Haruta

TRANSLATION & ADAPTATION Su Mon Han
TOUCH-UP ART & LETTERING Deron Bennett
DESIGN Courtney Utt
EDITOR Nancy Thistlethwaite

VP, PRODUCTION Alvin Lu
VP, SALES & PRODUCT MARKETING Gonzalo Ferreyra
VP, CREATIVE Linda Espinosa
PUBLISHER Hyoe Narita

SABOTEN NO HIMITSU © 2003 by Nana Haruta. All rights
reserved. First published in Japan in 2003 by SHUEISHA Inc.,
Tokyo. English translation rights arranged by SHUEISHA Inc.

The stories, characters and incidents mentioned
in this publication are entirely fictional.

Printed in the U.S.A.

Published by VIZ Media, LLC
P.O. Box 77010
San Francisco, CA 94107

10 9 8 7 6 5 4 3 2 1
First printing, March 2010

www.shojobeat.com   www.viz.com

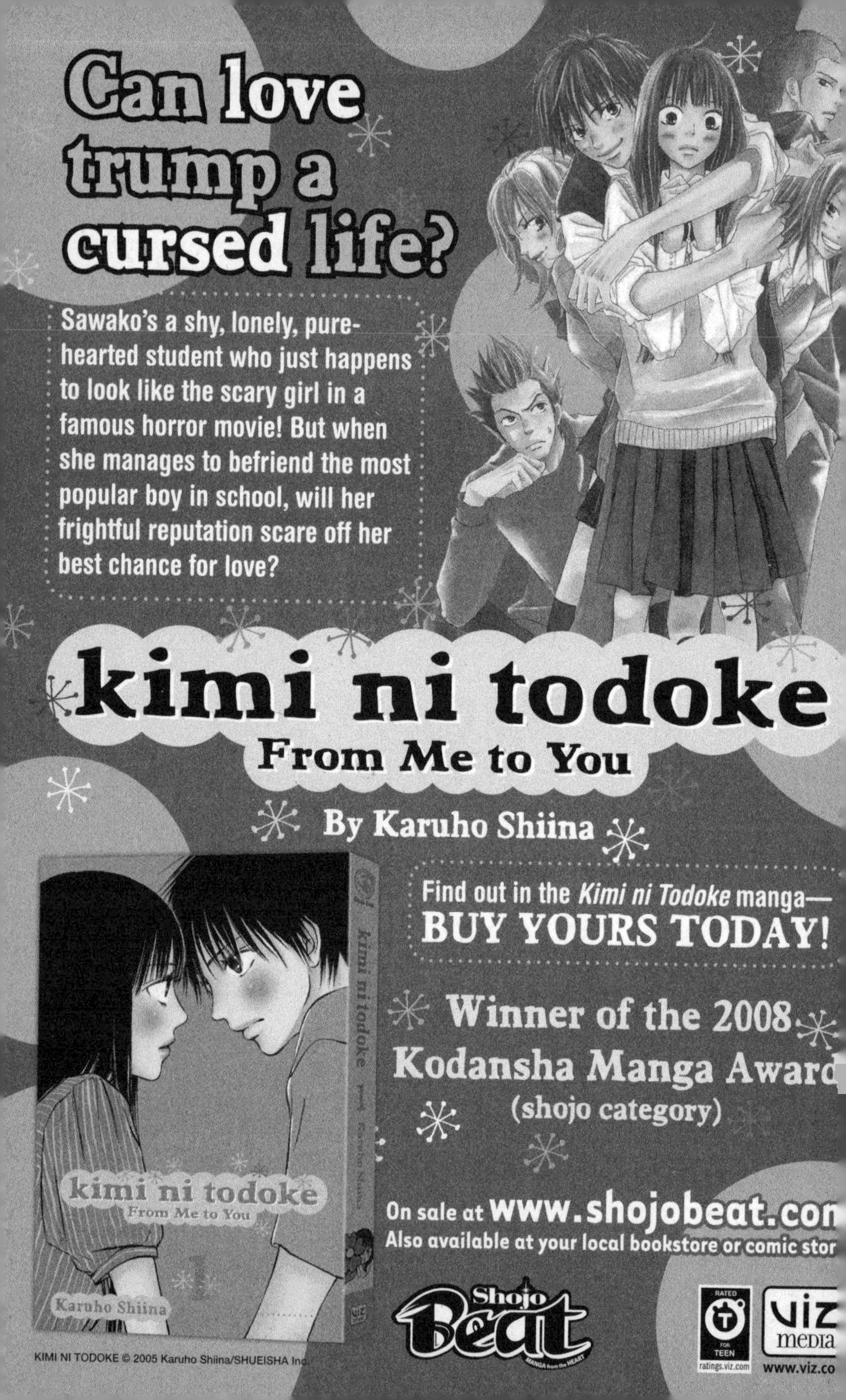
Can love trump a cursed life?
Sawako's a shy, lonely, pure-hearted student who just happens to look like the scary girl in a famous horror movie! But when she manages to befriend the most popular boy in school, will her frightful reputation scare off her best chance for love?
kimi ni todoke
From Me to You
By Karuho Shiina
kimi ni todoke
From Me to You
Karuho Shiina
Find out in the Kimi ni Todoke manga—
BUY YOURS TODAY!
Winner of the 2008 Kodansha Manga Award
(shojo category)
On sale at www.shojobeat.com
Also available at your local bookstore or comic store.
Shojo Beat
RATED T FOR TEEN
ratings.viz.com
VIZ media
www.viz.com
KIMI NI TODOKE © 2005 Karuho Shiina/SHUEISHA Inc.

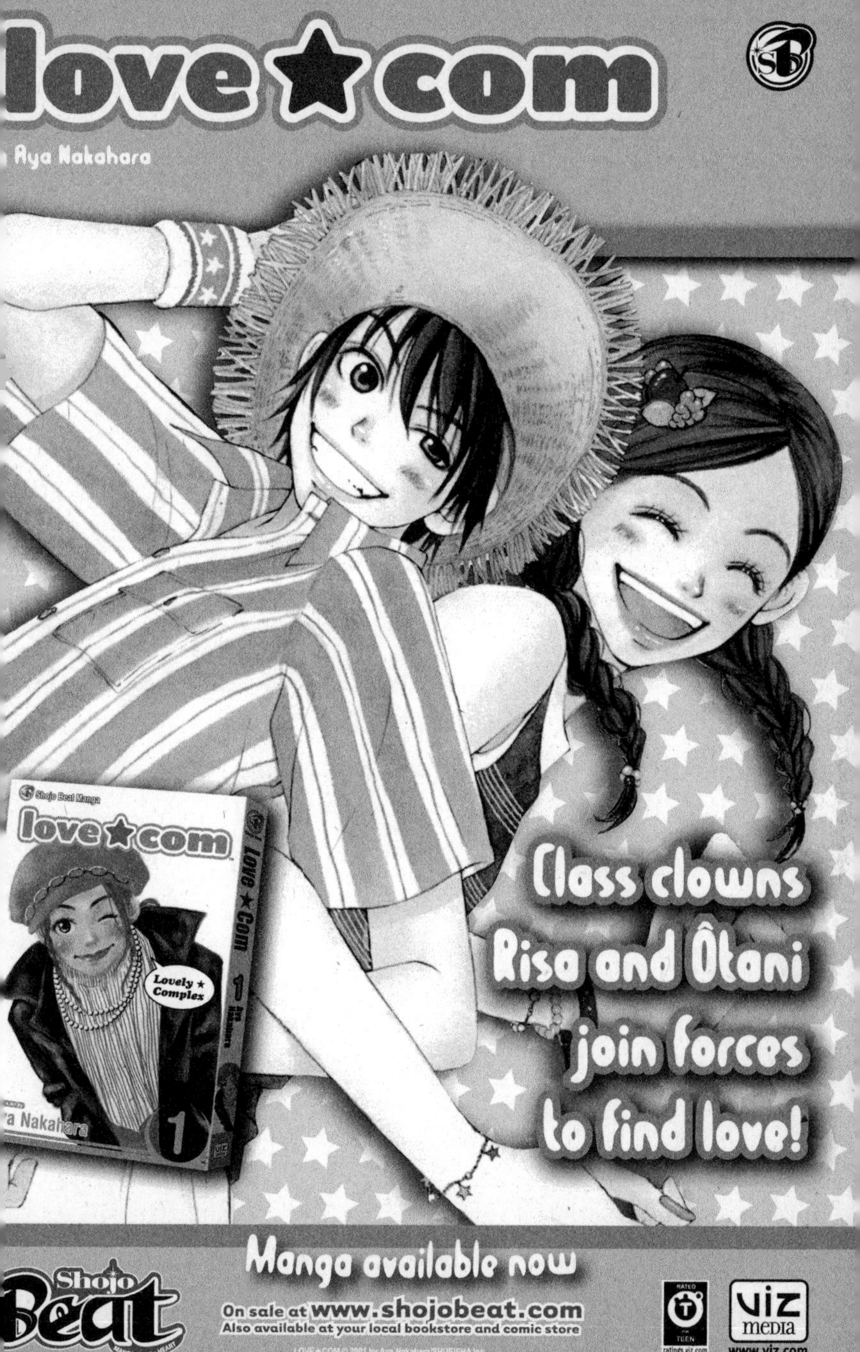
love★com
Aya Nakahara
Shojo Beat Manga
love★com
Lovely ★ Complex
Class clowns Risa and Ôtani join forces to find love!
Manga available now
Shojo Beat
On sale at www.shojobeat.com
Also available at your local bookstore and comic store
LOVE★COM © 2001 by Aya Nakahara/SHUEISHA Inc.
RATED T TEEN
ratings.viz.com
VIZ MEDIA
www.viz.com

Art book featuring 216 pages of beautiful color images personally selected by Tanemura

Read where Mitsuki's pop dreams began in the manga—all 7 volumes now available

Complete your collection with the anime, now on DVD

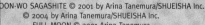

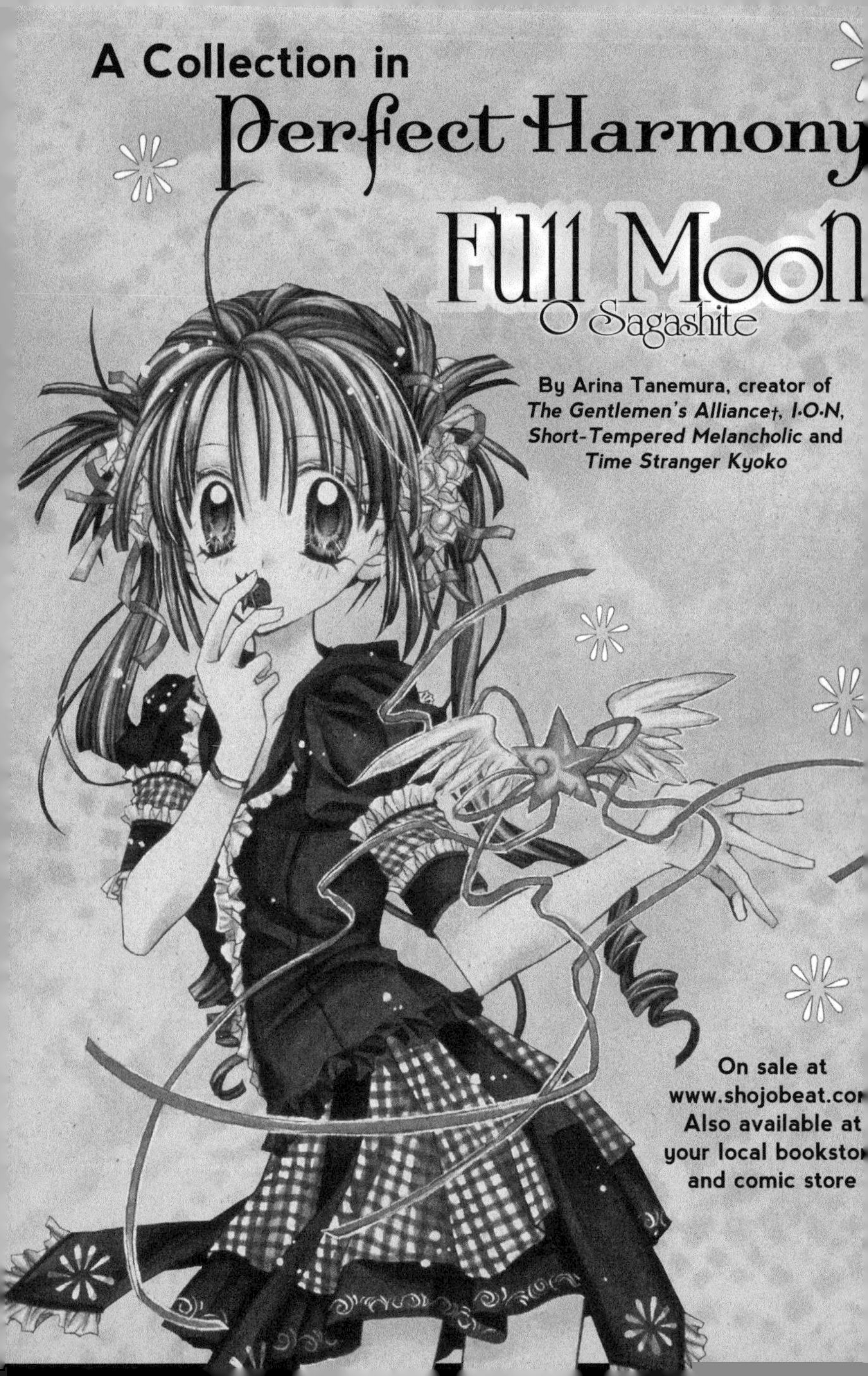
A Collection in
Perfect Harmony
Full Moon
O Sagashite
By Arina Tanemura, creator of
The Gentlemen's Alliance†, I·O·N, Short-Tempered Melancholic and Time Stranger Kyoko
On sale at
www.shojobeat.co
Also available at
your local booksto
and comic store